Music Of The Bible: Or, Explanatory Notes Upon Those Passages In The Sacred Scriptures Which Relate To Music, Including A Brief View Of Hebrew Poetry

Enoch Hutchinson

MUSIC

OF

THE BIBLE.

GRAND MUSICAL ENTERTAINMENT,

(Taken from an Engraving on the Ruins in Egypt).

VID. VILLOTEAU (1) ANTIQUITÉS, PLANCHES, TOM. V., PLANCHE: 17.

MUSIC OF THE BIBLE;

OR,

EXPLANATORY NOTES

UPON THOSE

PASSAGES IN THE SACRED SCRIPTURES WHICH
RELATE TO MUSIC,

INCLUDING A

Brief View of Hebrew Poetry.

BY

ENOCH HUTCHINSON.

BOSTON:
GOULD AND LINCOLN,
59 WASHINGTON STREET.
NEW YORK: SHELDON AND COMPANY.
CINCINNATI: GEORGE S. BLANCHARD.
1864.

PREFATORY REMARKS.

THE music of the ancient Hebrews is yet imperfectly understood, though the subject has been investigated by Calmet, Taylor, Pfeiffer, Saalchutz, Harenberg, Winer, Jahn, Reland, De Wette, Villoteau, and other distinguished scholars. Many of the terms, in the Sacred Scriptures, relating to the art, are obscure, chiefly, no doubt, from the fact that their antiquity is so great, that critical and authentic explanations of them have not reached our times, from a sufficiently early period to inspire confidence in their accuracy. It is perhaps impossible, in the present state of Oriental philology, to give, in every instance, a satisfactory translation of them; still, by a careful examination of their etymology, and of the probable resemblance between the instruments designated by them, and those found sculptured upon the ruins of ancient temples on the Nile and Euphrates, we can approximate, we think, nearly to their true signification.

In the following pages the writer has endeavored to present a *general* view of the subject, and yet one sufficiently critical, to secure, to some extent at least, the confidence of the learned.

As the *Poetry* of the ancient Hebrews has been, from its earliest existence, intimately connected with music, it was thought that it would not be inappropriate to give, in connection with an account of the latter, a brief general view of the former, and in so doing, it seemed best, on the whole, to present copious extracts from the most interesting poems of the sacred writers, rather than mere references to them, though the length of some quotations, which could not be divided without marring their beauty, has swelled the pages of this volume more than was originally intended.

That this slight contribution to biblical literature may aid, in some small degree, to elucidate the sacred text and advance the glory of our common Lord, is the earnest desire and prayer of

THE AUTHOR.

NEW YORK, *Nov.* 1863.

CONTENTS.

ILLUSTRATIONS.

MUSIC OF THE BIBLE.

INTRODUCTION.

In ancient times the signification of the term *music* was far more comprehensive than it is at present. It included dancing, gesture, poetry, and sometimes the aggregate of all the sciences. Hence philosophers were accustomed to speak of music human, divine, terrestrial, celestial, active, contemplative, enunciative, intellectual, and oratorical. Many passages of the early writers upon the subject, would be entirely unintelligible, did we not understand them as including, in the term, these ideas. Some also in *modern* times have similar conceptions. The *Chinese* speak of music as the science of the sciences —as the means of acquiring, and as lying at the foundation of every other species of knowledge. The union of Cadmus and Hermione in marriage, would seem to present all the sciences as having received their birth by the combined influence of music and letters.

Rosseau asserts that music is the art of combining tunable sounds in a manner agreeable to the ear. Aristides Quintilianus defines it to be the art of finding the beautiful and decorous in musical tones, and in their measure. Pfeiffer, a noted German writer, remarks that those seem to be about right, who think we shall never arrive at certainty in respect to ancient music in general, and especially in reference to that of the ancient Hebrews. The subject is indeed fraught with peculiar difficulties, still facts and considerations of an interesting nature may be presented which will throw some light upon it.

It is possible that music may be the oldest of all the fine arts. It is supposed by some to have been invented by the *Muses*, which opinion would indicate that it originated in the north of Greece. Kircher derives the term, indicating the art, from an Egyptian word, believing that music began to be cultivated first, after the deluge, upon the Nile. It is thought that vocal must have preceded instrumental music. In the earliest times, a difference in the tones of the human voice must have been discovered, as well as a variety of notes among the feathered tribe. Many of the ancients attributed the invention of the art to the Egyptian Mercury. Others have intimated that the Greeks received it from Cadmus, when he fled from the court of Phœnicia, carrying with him *Hermione* or *Harmony*. In Plutarch's dialogue on music, Lysias is made to say that it was invented by Amphion; in another place, Soterius informs us that Apollo invented it, and in a third passage, the honor seems to be given to Olympus. Following these supposed inventors were Chiron, Demodocus, Hermes, Lycurgus, Thales and Thamyris, who are said to have invented something in reference to it. Most of these musicians lived before the time of Homer.

Rosseau informs us that in none of the numerous works, which he had consulted on the subject, had the derivation of the term denoting music, or the inventor of the art, been settled to satisfaction. He supposed that the cries of nature must have suggested it before language was invented.

This is its probable origin, though we have no absolute proof of the fact; nor is it very material whether the cries of birds or of the human voice, or wind blowing through reeds, first suggested the idea. It certainly exists, and did exist in very early times, as it is mentioned in our most ancient records, and a knowledge of it has been handed down by tradition from an earlier period still. We know not who uttered the first note of regular music. We only have evidence from the sacred scriptures that musical instruments were used before the deluge, and believing that vocal preceded instrumental music, we infer that the former as well as the latter existed among the Antediluvians, but how long previously to the deluge, we cannot ascertain.

To learn the signification of the various musical terms employed by the sacred writers, it is important to inquire what was the music of the ancient Hebrews, and, in order to answer that question, we must allude to the history of countries lying adjacent to that of the Hebrews, as the latter must have been influenced more or less, in respect to the arts and sciences, by their immediate neighbors. These were the ancient Babylonians, Chaldæans, Assyrians and Egyptians. Some suppose that it is also necessary to inquire into the state of ancient and modern music in India, as it is thought that the Egyptians received many of their ideas of the arts and sciences from that country.

We cannot, within the limits of this introduction, enter

fully upon the investigation of these points; but shall only be able to give a general view of the subject.

It is very difficult to find well-authenticated facts in reference to the state of the arts and sciences in either of the ancient countries referred to above. There is much obscurity even in respect to the earlier music of Greece and Rome. But when we push our inquiries back still farther to the ancient Hebrews, Egyptians, and especially to the first inhabitants of the earth after the deluge, the rays of light which penetrate the darkness, are very faint and few. Let us, however, ascertain, if possible, what that light is.

In order to trace the first dawnings of the light of science and the arts, we must necessarily give a brief view of the early history of mankind.

A consideration of the primeval state of our race, from the creation to the deluge and immediately after that signal event, is fraught with peculiar interest though clouds of darkness seem to rest upon the subject. True, mythology, with its fragments of fabulous history, comes to our aid; but in many cases it increases the obscurity. Our only true guide is the sacred volume, and that is extremely brief. The following is probably the correct view.

We read in Gen. ix. 20, that Noah planted a vineyard soon after he came from the ark. It is probable that this was in the immediate vicinity of Mount Ararat,*

* Various opinions have been advanced in reference to the locality of this mountain. In almost every part of the East where there is a tradition of the deluge, the inhabitants locate it in their own country. The Afghans believe that it was identical with their *Sufued Koh*, or "*White Mountain.*" The inhab-

as nothing is said of removing to another land. It seems that the family first settled there, for Noah not only

itants of Ceylon maintain that it was their "*Adam's Peak.*" It is a remarkable circumstance that, in the Samaritan Pentateuch (Gen. viii. 4), it is called *Sarandib*, the Arabic name for Ceylon. The Sibylline verses assert that it was in Phrygia. Shuckford and Sir Walter Raleigh placed it farther east in the Caucasian range of mountains. But what say the inspired writers upon this subject? In Gen. viii. 4, the ark is said to have rested upon the mountains of *Ararat*. Here the term *Ararat* indicates a *country* on whose mountains the ark rested. In second Kings, xix. 37, (taken from Isa. xxxvii. 38), Armenia, which is supposed to be the country once called Ararat, is named as the land whither the sons of Sennacherib, King of Assyria, fled, after they had murdered their father. In Jer. li. 27, Ararat is mentioned as a kingdom in connection with Minni and Ashkenaz, and the three are called upon to arm themselves against her. In Isa. xiii. 2–4, there seems to be a reference to the same contest with Babylon, and those who marched against her are said to have issued from the mountains. Then if we consider that Minni was probably Minyas in Armenia, (vid. Joseph. Antiq. i. iii. 6), and that Ashkenaz was perhaps a country on the Euxine sea named after a son of Gomer (Gen. x. 2, 3), from whom the Cimmerians originated; we must conclude that Ararat was a mountainous country north of Assyria and very probably Armenia. The sons of Sennacherib seem to have fled to a place beyond the limits of Assyria. It may, however, have been near and was probably Armenia. There is a tradition that Sennacherib's sons were cordially received by king Paroyr, who assigned them lands bordering on Assyria. (vid. Avdall's Trans. of Chamich's Hist. of Armenia. Vol. i. pp. 33, 34). In Eze. xxxviii. 6, Togarmah, a part of Armenia, is mentioned in connection with Gomer. Moses of Chorene has preserved a tradition that the name of Ararat was derived from Arai, the eighth of the native princes who was killed in a battle with the Babylonians B. C. 1750. From these considerations it is very probable, as is generally believed, that Ararat was in Armenia. Still we cannot determine with certainty on what mountain of Armenia the ark rested. It is maintained by some eminent scholars that it did not rest upon planted a vineyard but drank of its wine, and his three sons are mentioned as living together after he drank.

the mountain itself; but was in a quiet state on the waters *over* the mountains of Ararat. This obviates some difficulties; still, the natural import of the sacred text seems to be that the ark rested *upon* the top of a mountain. The Hebrew preposition (עַל, *al*) translated *upon* (Gen. viii. 4), sometimes means *over*; but its native and usual signification is *upon*. During the deluge, the masses of ice, which generally render Mount Ararat almost inaccessible, were doubtless melted away, and the objection, that the animals leaving the ark, could not have passed down the sides of the mountain in safety, is obviated, at least, to a great extent. The earliest tradition indicates a peak of the chain which separates Armenia on the south from Mesopotamia, as the one on which the ark rested. As that chain incloses Kurdistan, it took the name of the Kardu or Carduchian range, corrupted into Gordiæan. Josephus informs us (Antiq. i. iii. 6) that Berosus advocated the same view. He calls the mountain range that of the Cordyæans, and remarks that some parts of the ark were said to have been found there. Reference is made to the same tradition by Abydenus (Euseb. Præp. Evang. ix. 4). The Chaldee paraphrasts as well as the Syriac translators and churches, adopted it. A monastery in honor of the ark was built upon the spot indicated by that tradition and destroyed by lightning A. D. 776. The Koran calls the mountain on which the ark rested Al-Judi, a corruption of Giordi or Gordiæan. The name was first given to the whole range and afterwards to a peak a little to the east of Jezirah ibu Omar (the ancient Bezabde) on the river Tigris. After the destruction of the monastery on Mount Judi, the Mohammedans still maintained that the ark rested on that mountain; but the Christians of the West gradually embraced the idea that a mountain in the north of Armenia was the one on which it rested, and finally it took the name of Ararat, though the Armenians called it Macis, and the Turks Aghur-dagh, meaning the *heavy* or *great mountain*. The mountain is mentioned by the early Persian writers, who call it *Kihi Nuch, Noah's Mountain*. It is mentioned by Josephus and Ptolemy under a name of similar import. It is impossible to determine beyond a doubt which mountain was

(Gen. ix. 21—23). Subseqnently, Noah's descendants became so numerous that it was necessary to extend their limits, and they began to explore other regions.

In Gen. xi. 2, we are informed that the posterity of Noah journeyed to the east, or from the east. The original will bear either rendering.* We are to understand that, before this time, they had doubtless wandered in different directions, but how far from Ararat we do not know. It seems that the great body of them were not separated far from each other, else how could such wandering hordes have been collected together on the plains of Shinar to build the tower of Babel?† They must have proceeded some distance from Ararat, for that is in a northerly direction from Babylon. If they had remained in the vicinity of that mountain it would have been said of them that they traveled *south* in going to Shinar, and not *east*, nor *from the east*. It is probable that they had traveled a considerable distance from Ararat, either south-east or south-west, and when they moved towards Shinar, they went either east or west—it is impossible to tell which, nor is it of much importance to decide that point. Still it should be considered that the preposition מִ (*mem*) more usually means *from*, and it is more natural to regard it here as having that signi-

indicated. But it is pretty evident that the spot was in some part of Armenia as we have shown, and as the mountain in the north of that country is much more elevated than any other peak it seems to accord more nearly with the scripture account to suppose that its summit, as is now generally believed, was the spot where the ark rested.

* The Hebrew word is מִקֶּדֶם.

† It is not probable that all of Shem's posterity returned to Shinar, though doubtless most of them did.

fication, than as signifying *to*. If it means *from* in this place, it is very probable that the posterity of Noah had wandered to the south-east of Ararat, before they set out for Babylon.

The erection of Babel was next commenced, whose object seems to have been to prevent being separated from each other. They wished to have some great central point around which they could permanently dwell (Gen.xi. 4); but their vain desire was not gratified. The lightnings of heaven demolished their lofty tower, their language was confounded and they were scattered abroad upon the face of all the earth (Gen. xi. 8). It is probable that from the commencement of the journeyings from Ararat they did not intend to be separated. They extended their limits when they found it necessary, still the largest portion of them probably continued together, and finally, before they had wandered a great distance from the place where the ark rested, they formed the plan of building a city of sufficient magnitude and splendor to furnish them a permanent residence, and central point of attraction.

The description of the deluge, and of the first settlement of mankind, was written by Moses more than 1450 years B. C., and the lawgiver must have either compiled the history of that and other events from records and monuments kept in the family of Noah; or from tradition, which must have been very correct in those early times, in reference to important events, as life was very long, and the circumstances of those occurrences would have to be handed down to Moses by few persons, and those relatives to each other; or finally, he must have received the facts which he presents, wholly from the immediate inspiration of God. In either case, it is very certain that he presented a true account, and the customs of his ancestors, to which he refers, are undoubtedly delineated with accuracy.

After the confusion of tongues the posterity of Noah dispersed in different directions, and in the tenth chapter of Genesis, we have an account of the lands which they occupied.

Japheth and his posterity were to inhabit the *Isles of the Gentiles* (Gen. x. 5). The Hebrew of this expression is אִיֵּי הַגּוֹיִם *iyyéy haggóyim*, and must refer, it would seem, to places where *Gentiles* or *Heathen* resided. But it may with propriety be asked, what islands, so soon after the deluge, had such inhabitants? Between the time of the occurrence of that event and that of the confusion of tongues, according to the usual computation, only 113, though according to Dr. Hales, 600 years intervened. During six centuries, and even during *one*, the descendants of Noah must have multiplied to a considerable extent, and may have extended their migrations to some of the islands of the Great Sea; but Moses is speaking (Gen. x) of these very descendants of Noah (i. e., Japheth's posterity) as going to occupy the *Isles* of the *Heathen*. This seems entirely to exclude the idea that Japheth's posterity may have *already* settled there and become *Heathen* or *Gentiles*. Farther, the terms *Heathen* and *Gentiles* are of later origin than that early period, and we think that the translators of the Scriptures might have employed less ambiguous terms. There may have been, in those early times, and probably *were*, persons who rejected the religion of Noah, their progenitor, and may have been called, in one sense, *Heathen;* but they could not properly have been designated, as in our English Bible, by the term *Gentiles*, for there were then neither *Jews* nor *Gentiles*. Nor can we believe that the sacred historian intended to indicate the *Antediluvians* by the term translated *Gentiles*—that Japheth's descendants were to inhabit the *Isles* occupied, before the deluge, by the *Heathen*. There were then, with a few individual exceptions, none but haters of God, who might properly enough be called heathen. There were, indeed, *Isles* of the *Heathen* at the time when Moses wrote this account; but is it not as reasonable to suppose that he intended to designate them as the residence of Japheth's posterity, as to suppose that his object was to give the appellation which those places, intended as the residence of Japheth's posterity, bore at the time that the division of the earth among the sons of Noah, was made?

The term translated *Isles* is often used in a general sense to denote islands, coasts, or maritime regions, especially of the Mediterranean, as in Ps. lxxii. 10. The Hebrew word translated *Gentiles* is the general term denoting *nations*, and especially such as did not belong to the jurisdiction of the Jews. May it not also denote not only Gentile *nations*, but *places*—any thing not Jewish? At the early period when the division of lands was made—when there were no such distinctions as Jews and Gentiles, the term, judging from its present signification, may have referred to places not in the possession of Noah's posterity—foreign regions, and both terms together may have been used as a general expression to indicate that Japheth was to occupy a region of sea-coast and islands which he did not then possess. Whether Noah and his posterity were near Mount Ararat, or in the vicinity of

Babylon, or in some other place, it is certain that the nearest maritime region, where there were many islands, was the Mediterranean, and it is natural to suppose the numerous islands of that sea to have been the region to which reference is made. Strong confirmatory evidence of the correctness of this supposition, is furnished by the name of one of Japheth's posterity. It is *Kittīm*, his grandson, after whom the place where he subsequently resided, was undoubtedly called. When the division of lands was made, perhaps different localities took the names of the individuals who were to occupy them. It has been a general custom in all ages to name places after distinguished individuals. Rosenmüller asserts that most of the proper names in the tenth chapter of Genesis, are names of places as well as of persons (Alterth. ii. p. 94; cf. Joseph. Ant. i. vi. 1). The Hebrew term for *Kittīm* or *Chittīm* is כִּתִּים or כִּתִּיִּים *kittīm* or *kittiyyīm*. It sometimes occurs in connection with אִיֵּי *iyyey*, translated *isles of Chittīm*, (Jer. ii. 10; Eze. xxvii. 6), sometimes in connection with אֶרֶץ *erets*, *earth*, and is translated *land of Chittīm*, (Isa. xxiii. 1,) and sometimes simply the term כִּתִּים *kittīm* is used and merely anglicized in our translation (Isa. xxiii. 12). Josephus, (Ant. i. vi. 1), Gesenius, (Heb. Lex. under כִּתִּים), and others, suppose the term to refer to the Island of *Cyprus*. The Hebrew word being in the plural, should be translated *Cyprians* or *Citienses*. As reference is made to more than one island, it would be natural to suppose that the islands in the vicinity were intended, i. e., the islands and coasts of Greece and of the Ægean sea. Indeed the term Kittīm, in its wider sense, comprehended the islands and coasts of the Mediterranean sea, especially the northern parts, and perhaps indicated the same region as Isles of the Gentiles, which we have considered above (vid. Gesen. Heb. Lex. under כִּתִּים *kittim*). According to this view, then, Japheth and his posterity inhabited the islands and coasts of Greece and of the Ægean sea. At length they extended their dominion to other northern and western parts of the Mediterranean.

Tarshish was another grandson of Japheth (Gen. x. 3, 4). Ancient Tarshish was doubtless named after him, and inhabited by his posterity (vid. Rosenm. Alterth. ii. p. 94). Winer, Gesenius and others suppose that Tarshish was the ancient Tartessus in the west of Spain. There was a large district, including modern Cadiz and other cities, called by that name.

It is probable that the nearest islands were first inhabited. Cyprus, being in the eastern part of the Mediterranean, would be likely to be first occupied, or at least *soon* after the confusion of languages, as it is not a great distance from the land of Shinar. It is about 76 miles west of Latagieh in Syria and 44 miles south of Cape Anamoor in Anatolia, Asia Minor. In ancient times, its distance from the main land was probably much less. Some think that it was once united to the continent. It is probable that means were found very early to pass to that island and make a settlement. The posterity of Japheth gradually formed colonies along the Mediterranean, until they reached the western extremity, and then moved towards the north of Europe. It is difficult now to ascertain how long a time elapsed before they reached the Great Sea, and the exact period when they settled in various parts of Europe. Their original knowledge of music and the arts and sciences in general, must have been considerable, and they doubtless gradually made advancement in that direction.

The Greeks and Romans were the most distinguished ancient descendants of Japheth. Greece was settled in very early times (For a farther description of Greece, vid. p. 46, *infra*). It is possible indeed that some of the descendants of Japheth proceeded into that country immediately after the dispersion, and there first commenced a settlement, or it may be that they first visited some of the islands bordering upon the country on the east, in the Ægean sea, and afterwards proceeded to the main land. Josephus informs us that some of the posterity of Noah passed over the sea in ships and inhabited the islands (Josephus, i. v. 1).

We learn from Gen. x. 6—20, that Ham's posterity founded and inhabited (for a short time at least) Babylonia and a part or all of what is now called Palestine, and other places more distant. Nimrod, the son of Cush, founded the Babylonian monarchy and its celebrated cities. It is difficult to define the precise limits of Babylon its splendid capital. It is supposed to have stood upon the Euphrates, a little above the union of that river with the Tigris. Its site was probably where the town of Hillah now stands, about sixty miles south of Bagdad.

According to Gen. x. 11, Nimrod went out into Assyria, or Ashur went out, and built Nineveh and other cities. The Hebrew will bear either rendering. The former is in accordance with the opinion of Gesenius, T. H. Horne, and others. Nineveh was the capital of Assyria, and probably stood upon the eastern bank of the

Tigris, opposite the present Mosul.* From Gen. x. 19, we perceive that the Canaanites occupied the region extending from "Sidon unto Gaza even unto Lashah." Sidon, now called Saida or Saide, is upon the coast of the Mediterranean, in the northern extremity of Palestine. Gaza is near the southern part of the same country. Lashah, according to Jerome (in Quæst.), was upon the north-eastern shore of the Dead Sea, where Callirhoe stands. Others suppose, with less reason we think, that Lashah is identical with Dan Laish, or Leshem, now called Tell-el-kady near Cæsarea Philippi towards the northern part of Palestine. Following the former view, which is adopted by Gesenius, these places bounded Palestine nearly on three sides.†

Mizraim was the grandson of Noah, and his posterity are supposed to have directed their course towards Egypt. That country was, no doubt, named after him, as the same Hebrew word is used for both. From the land of Shinar to the nearest part of Egypt was several hundred miles.

Two other countries were probably named after Cush, another grandson of Noah. Professor Stuart has proved conclusively, in the notes to his Hebrew Chrestomathy, that there was, anciently, a Cush Oriental as well as a

* Cf. Plin. H. N. 5, 6.

† The inhabitants of Babylonia and Assyria, in the most ancient times, seem from their languages, to have been of Shemitish origin, and though Babylon and Nineveh were founded by a descendant of Ham before the dispersion, probably Babylonia and Assyria after that event, were mostly inhabited by Shem's posterity.

Cush Southern. Cush Oriental extended east of the Tigris, and comprehended the country between the Caspian Sea and Persian Gulf. It is probable that the descendants of Cush first inhabited this country, and gradually extended their borders through Arabia to the Red Sea, then crossing over to Africa, occupied its eastern coast, and finally penetrated into the interior of Ethiopia. The term Cush seems to be equivalent to *Southern Country*. It must have been several years before the posterity of Ham wandered into the more central parts of Africa, as the distance from the land of Shinar is very great.

The posterity of Shem were to inhabit the region "from Mesha to Sephar (Gen. x. 30), a mount of the east." For the last clause, Gesenius translates: ("and beyond even unto) *the mountains of Arabia*." He supposes Mesha to have been what was subsequently called Mousa or Mouza, a city and harbor on the western coast of Arabia, not far from Mocha, where Maushid now stands. Thus Mesha would constitute the western border of Joktan's place of residence. J. Pye Smith remarks that Mesha is what is now called Maishon, or Mesene, at the northwest head of the Persian Gulf. Gesenius supposes Sephar to have been the chief city of the region called Shehr in Arabia, between the Provinces of Hadramaut and Oman. Smith thinks that it was upon the southwest coast of Arabia, on what is now called Mount Sabber. The mountains to which reference is made, beyond Sephar must have been the chain running across the middle of Arabia from the vicinity of Mecca and Medina to the Persian Gulf. According to this view, Joktan's posterity resided in the southern part of Arabia, the nearest point of which was not very far south of the land of Shinar.

The descendants of Aram doubtless resided in the region which received the name of their progenitor. It is impossible to determine with certainty, the exact extent of that region; but it probably comprehended Syria, and in its widest sense extended from Mount Taurus south as far as Damascus, and from the Mediterranean east beyond the Tigris into Assyria.

It is generally believed that the posterity of Shem occupied Western Asia. The Persians, Assyrians, Aramæans (at least in the restricted signification of the term), Hebrews and a part of the Arabians, are believed to have descended from him.

From this general view of the three sons of Noah, it seems that Japheth, after the confusion of tongues, proceeded towards the west, and settled the coasts of Asia Minor and Europe, and finally moved on to the extreme north and west; Ham went south, and finally reached the central regions of Africa; Shem turned his face eastward, and eventually his posterity reached India and the other eastern and northern countries of Asia.

It may be interesting now to inquire what countries were first settled, and whether any attention was bestowed by their inhabitants upon music.

Babylon was evidently the first city which was built after the confusion of tongues, having been commenced simultaneously with the tower of Babel. Pölitz supposes that Nimrod was the leader of an Arabian horde, that he rushed into Babylonia and conquered the country, and that after his time, it was called *Shinar*. The Hebrew term שִׁנְעָר (*Shinar*) is sometimes rendered *Shinar* and sometimes *Babylonia.* The origin of the word is unknown; but it is evident that Babylonia and Shinar refer to the same region of country surrounding Babylon.*

The displeasure of the Almighty, at the time of the confusion of languages, caused the building of Babylon to cease; but it was subsequently commenced again, though the exact time *when* and the person *by whom*, cannot with certainty be determined. We know that the Babylonian language was of Shemitish origin, though we are by no means to suppose that those who spoke languages thus derived, were all descended from Shem. Still this is evidence that most of the inhabitants were thus descended, especially as there is no proof that the ancient language of Babylonia was, from the remotest antiquity, changed in its essential features. The Hebrew is supposed by some to be the original of all the Shemitish stock, and is thought to bear strong marks of being the most ancient of all tongues, and to have been the general language spoken before the dispersion. Later critics, however, maintain with much reason, we think, that all of the Shemitish dialects are derived from the primitive tongue, and that fragments of the latter are found in each of those dialects.†

Moses informs us that "the whole earth was of one language." It is possible that Shem and his descendants continued to speak the original language used before the

* Pōlitz Welt Geschichte i. 19; cf. Gen. x. 10; xi. 2; xiv. 1; Isa. xi. 11; Dan i. 2.; Zech. v. 11.

† The Jewish Rabbis, Jonathan, author of the Chaldee Paraphrase, Solomon Jarchi and Aben Ezra, also Origen, Augustine and others, believe the Hebrew to have been the language spoken in Paradise.

dispersion, as they occupied lands in the immediate vicinity of Shinar, and even that country was probably, to a great extent, inhabited by them. Though at the destruction of Babel, there was a confusion of tongues, it is highly probable that it was of short duration, and that we must look to something else as the principal cause of the diversity of languages in various parts of the world. The Chinese, for instance, are probably the descendants of Shem; but their language and the Shemitish are radically different, and it would seem, could not have had the same origin. The most probable supposition is, that, as the people extended their borders and were more distant from the land of Shinar, various circumstances, such as climate, government, subjection to other nations, conquest and the physical power of enunciation, gradually changed their language so that it became, in some cases, entirely different from its original (vid. p. 48 *infra*). This, to us, is the most probable supposition, though it must be acknowledged that great obscurity rests upon the whole subject of the origin of languages.*

Dr. Jahn maintains that Nimrod's Babylon should not be regarded as the germ of that universal monarchy which took its rise in a later age and among a different people (Jahn's Heb. Commonwealth, Vol. I. p. 6). The tower of Belus mentioned by Herodotus is probably the tower of Babel repaired by Belus II, king of Babylon, who is frequently, by the ancient historians, confounded with Belus I, or Nimrod. In Gen. xiv. 1, Amraphel, king of Shinar is mentioned who must have ruled the

* Cf. Prof. Stuart's Notes to his Hebrew Chrestomathy, also Dr. Gr. Sharpe's Dissertations on the origin of languages, p. 22—.

same or nearly the same region of country as did Nimrod, for in both cases it was called by the same name. Amraphel was doubtless king of Babylonia,* in the time of Abram (Gen. xiv. 1, 9, 12). The battle to which reference is made in the passage to which we have just referred, and in which Amraphel took part, seems to have occurred between the seventy-fifth and eighty-sixth years of the life of Abram (Gen. xii. 4; xvi. 16). According to Usher, Abram was born B. C. 1996. Reckoning from that period, we shall have the years 1921 and 1910 B. C. between which the above named battle occurred, leaving a difference of eleven years. From Gen. xvi. 3, we learn that Abram had already been ten years in Canaan when he took Hagar for his wife, and, supposing it to be one year after that time when Ishmael was born, we have eleven years for the time of Abram's sojourn in Canaan at the birth of Ishmael. True, Abram visited Egypt, but subsequently to his first arrival in Canaan, and he could not have tarried long, as he had offended Pharaoh and was obliged hastily to leave (Gen. xii. 20). At first he proceeded immediately from Haran into Canaan according to Gen. xii. 5, 6. From Gen. xvi. 3, we are to understand that it had been ten years since he first came into Canaan. The battle abovementioned must have occurred between the years 428 and 439 after the deluge. We cannot decide the exact year, though it was probably not long after the year 428. Amraphel is called a *King* (Gen. xiv. 1). Whether his was the first kingdom formed after the dispersion, we

* Vid. Gesen. Heb. Lex. under אַמְרָפֶל *Amraphel*, where the same opinion is expressed.

are not able to decide with certainty. During more than 400 years there was certainly time for the formation and overthrow of several kingdoms upon the same spot. In those early times monarchies were of short duration. It is possible that Nimrod was still living in the time of Amraphel, as the cotemporaries of the former, Salah, Eber, Peleg and others lived to the age of about 400 years, and the above named battle must have occurred, according to the usual computation, 313 years after the dispersion. However that may have been, the country was not then under the rule of Nimrod. Much the most probable supposition is that the *Hunter's* monarchy was of short duration—that soon after the dispersion, a leader of some horde formed another monarchy. Perhaps several were thus formed and overthrown, and perhaps each had raised to the supreme command and dethroned more than one sovereign. Porphyry declares that Calisthenes brought an acquaintance with astronomical observations from Babylon to Greece more than nineteen hundred years before the time of Alexander the Great, pointing us back to a period only a few years after the dispersion of mankind. Little reliance, however, is to be placed upon this testimony as there is nothing extant in the Chaldæan astrology more ancient than the era of Nabonassar, which begins according to the usual computation, 747 B. C. From the occurrence of the abovenamed contest until the time when the later Babylonian empire flourished under Nabonassar, Nebuchadnezzar and other sovereigns, embracing a period of more than twelve centuries, we find very few historical facts in reference to Babylonia, upon which we can rely. In Micah v. 6, the land of Nimrod is mentioned; but the reference is merely to the later empire.

Assyria was an ancient country, having doubtless received its name from *Ashshur* a son of *Shem* (Gen. x. 22; 1 Chron. i. 17). The Hebrew term is אַשּׁוּר *Ashshur.* The feminine form of the word refers to the *country* of Assyria and the masculine form to the *empire.* Nineveh, its capital was built, according to the usual computation, at about the time of the dispersion. We know not with certainty its fate, when Nimrod's Babylonian monarchy was destroyed; but it is probable that its power as well as that of cities adjacent to it, was overthrown. Whether Assyria was at first, a separate monarchy or united with Babylonia and under the authority of Nimrod for a length of time, cannot now be determined with certainty. However that may have been, we find nothing authoritative in history concerning Assyria, until a considerable time after the dispersion. In Gen. x. 11, we read in our translation, "*out of that land went forth Asshur and builded Nineveh,*" מִן־הארץ ההוא יצא אשור ויבן את־נינוה. In the margin of the polyglot bible we read "*out of that land, he* (i. e. *Nimrod*), *went out into Assyria and builded Nineveh.* The most natural rendering of the passage is as it appears in the text of our bible. Still there are serious and perhaps fatal objections to that translation of it. Moses is speaking of the posterity of Ham, and does not mention that of Shem till in the twenty-first verse. It is not reasonable to suppose that the writer would thus introduce Shem's posterity in the eleventh verse before he was prepared fully to describe them. It is objected that if Moses intended to say that Nimrod went to Assyria, a preposition or ה *locale* would have been used; but it is often the case that verbs signifying *to go to a place* are construed with the noun in the accusative without the preposition. Also ה *locale* is sometimes omitted.* According to this view, which certainly seems the most probable and is supported by the Targums of Onkelos, Jerusalem, and of Jerome, also by Bochart, Hyde, Marsham, Wells, Faber, Hales and others, Nimrod, a powerful monarch, advanced northward, seized Babylonia and then rushed into Assyria, where the Ashshurites had already formed a colony, conquered them and built Nineveh and other cities. If this be correct Babylonia and Assyria were both under the authority of Nimrod. What is properly called the Assyrian empire, was of later origin, and, according to Gesenius (cf. Isa. x. 5, 9, 10; vii. 20,) comprehended Babylonia, and Mesopotamia. Assyria is mentioned in Gen. xxv. 18, in connection with the death of Ishmael. His death occurred at the age of 137 years, and Abram was 86 years of age when Ishmael was born (Gen. xvi. 16), and the latter was born according to our tables of chronology, 324 years after the dispersion of mankind. The death of Ishmael occurred 137 years afterwards, which, added to the preceding 324, make 461 years after the dispersion or 1773 B. C. when Assyria was mentioned by Moses as existing. This would be about 148 years after the battle occurred in which Amraphel was engaged (Gen. xiv. 1). The Assyrian monarchy, considering Nineveh as its capital, was first established not far from Babylon, though not in the land of Shinar (Gen. x. 10, 11).

* Cf. II Sam. x. 2, with I Chron. xiii. 13; xix. 2; (vid. Noldius' Concordance of Hebrew Particles, quoted by N. Morren, M. A. in his article on Assyria in Kitto's Cyclopædia of Bib. Lit.).

At different times its limits varied, still its centre of power probably continued to remain at Nineveh. Before the 148 years above mentioned and during that period, it is probable that different monarchies were formed in the land of Shinar and vicinity. Undoubtedly at different periods various adjacent regions were included under the name of Shinar or Babylonia. At the commencement of the 148 years Amraphel was monarch of the country, and during those years perhaps his kingdom continued to exist for a considerable length of time. Whether it was called the Assyrian, Babylonian, Babyloni-Assyrian monarchy or the kingdom of Shinar makes but little difference. That region of country was undoubtedly called by different names during the same period, and doubtless at times several kingdoms existed in the land of Shinar and vicinity at the same time. Subsequently to the 148 years alluded to above, the term Assyria seems to have been used to designate about the same region of country as was before indicated by Babylonia or Shinar.

Some other kings are mentioned in the fourteenth chapter of Genesis who ruled in countries adjacent to the land of Shinar. One is Arioch king of Ellasar, whose name Gesenius supposes to be of Assyro-Chaldaic origin, and thence infers that the land of Ellasar which he governed, was probably some province of Persia or Assyria (vid. Gesen. Heb. Lex. under אֶלָּסָר Ellasar). That monarch seems to have been an ally of Amraphel. Josephus considers these four kings (mentioned in Gen. xiv. 1) as merely commanders in the Assyrian army. As they were cotemporaries of Amraphel, it will not be necessary to consider their history farther.

In Gen. ii. 14, there is a reference to Assyria in describing the location of the Garden of Eden, showing that such an empire existed when Moses wrote the account. By ascertaining the antiquity of the writings we may learn that of the reference.

The Pentateuch was compiled in very ancient times. Daniel mentions it during his captivity in Babylon (Dan. ix. 11–13), and, from the first verse of the chapter, we perceive, that he uttered the prayer therein contained, during the first year of the reign of Darius, "of the seed of the Medes." This Darius was undoubtedly Cyaxares II, son and successor of Astyages and uncle of Cyrus. According to Gesenius, Darius governed in Media between the reigns of Astyages and Cyrus, 569–536 B. C. (vid. Ges. Heb. Lex. under דָּרְיָוֶשׁ), for Josephus asserts that Darius the Mede was the son of Astyages and called, among the Greeks, by another name (Joseph. Ant. x. xi. 4). The Pentateuch was existing in the time of Josiah (11 Chron. xxxiv. 15), in the time of Hoshea, King of Israel (11 Kings, xvii. 27; xviii. 1), and in the time of Jehoshaphat, King of Judah, (11 Chron. xvii. 1, 9). The above named Kings of Judah and Israel lived before the captivity. Farther, the whole temple service and worship were regulated by Solomon according to the law contained in the Pentateuch. The same was true of his father David. There are various references to the Pentateuch in the Psalms (Ps. i. 2; xix. 7–11; xl. 7, 8; cxix. etc.). It is evident that it was written even before the book of Joshua from numerous references to its pages there found (Josh. i. 7, 8; xxiii. 6; xxiv. 26; viii. 30-34), and it is quite certain that that book was originally composed by Joshua himself, soon after the death of Moses, though it was reduced to its present form in later times (Josh. xxiv. 25, 26; xviii. etc.). Moses died at the age of 120 years (Deut. xxxiv. 7). This was about forty years after he and Aaron, in accordance with the divine command, called upon Pharaoh and urged him to permit the children of Israel to leave Egypt. The same year the permission was given and they departed. Moses then was 80 years old (Ex. vii. 7), forty years, the difference between 120 and 80, being added to 2513, the year when the Hebrews left Egypt, we have A. M. 2553 or B. C. 1451, the year when Moses died. These forty years being after the institution of the Passover should be reckoned as solar years.*

About that time then there was a country called Assyria. It was about 322 years after the death of Ishmael, named in Gen. xxv. 18, in connection with the mention of that country. There is not that difference in the time when these passages (Gen. ii. 14. and xxv. 18) were written; but the fact that Assyria is mentioned in the latter passage in connection with the death of Ishmael, shows that the country existed at that early period. The Pentateuch was written a long time after most of the events there described occurred. So it was with the two passages named above. Moses, the author of the Pentateuch, was not born when Ishmael died (Gen. xxv. 18). In Gen. ii. 14, we have no historical circumstances to assist us, therefore the reference to Assyria in that passage simply furnishes evidence that such a country existed when the Pentateuch was written. About 320 years after this period, we have accounts of Assyria from profane histo-

* Before that feast was instituted, time was reckoned by lunar or luni-solar years, which are not as long as solar ones.

rians, which, though doubted by some, are thought to be reliable. Ninus is represented as the reigning sovereign at the time when Deborah and Barak judged Israel about 1535 B. C. Ninus was succeeded by his Queen Semiramis, who reigned 42 years. Fifty-two years after wards her son Ninyas ascended the throne. Ctesias supposes that the founder of the Assyrian monarchy and the builder of Nineveh were the same person, viz: Ninus, and that Nineveh derived its name from him. According to this view, Nimrod, signifying *rebel*, was not properly the name of the founder of the Assyrian capital, but a term of reproach given him by his enemies. Syncellus, and following him, Hales, think that Ninus succeeded Esarhaddon as sovereign of Assyria B. C. 667, and had as his successor, Nebuchodonosor B. C. 658. Herodotus and Ctesias are the leading profane authorities upon this subject, and their accounts are extremely contradictory, so that little reliance can be placed on them, and we are obliged to go back to the Scriptures for the fragmentary history of Assyria. It must be acknowledged, however, that with the Scriptures and all other accessible helps before us, there is great obscurity in reference to this subject.

The Scriptures are silent in respect to the history of that country for several centuries, until the time of the prophet Jonah, who flourished about 705 B. C. Then it is mentioned, but the name of its sovereign does not appear. About fifty years later Pul is named as King of the country (II Kings xv. 19; I Chron. v. 26). It is thought that he was the father of Sardanapalus, the last King. The kingdom was destroyed about 627 B. C. and from its ruins were formed the kingdoms of Nineveh, Babylon and Media.

Chaldæa, in the earliest times, was included between the Euphrates and Tigris. It is mentioned in Gen. xi. 28, 31, in connection with Terah and Abram. Terah, the father of Abram resided in Ur of the Chaldees. He was born about 223 years after the deluge, A. M. 1878, or B. C. 2126, and 108 years after the dispersion of mankind. Perhaps Ur had existed before Terah resided there. It is difficult to ascertain whether there was ever a Chaldæan empire distinct from the Babylonian. It is thought by many that Chaldæa in the earliest times, was another name for Babylonia. It is evident, however, that in remote antiquity there were Astrologers in Babylon called Chaldæans. It should be remarked that the terms Chaldæa and Chaldæans (כַּשְׂדִּים *kasdim*), seem to have been derived from *Kesedh*, a nephew of Abram (כֶּשֶׂד *kesedh*, vid. Gen. xxii. 22), or which is perhaps more probable, *Kesedh* was named after the country, as the term Chaldæans is mentioned at an earlier period in connection with Terah the father of Abram. It was customary in those early times to name countries from individuals and *vice versa;* but the former practice seems to have been more common, and it may have been so with *Kesedh*. His place of residence may have been designated by another name, though it was doubtless within the limits of Babylonia. Before he settled there the country may even have received no special designation excepting that it was a part of Babylonia. *Kesedh* doubtless was accompanied into the country by other persons, and became the leader of a tribe. It is very natural to suppose that the district which they occupied was named after their leader. Subsequently the term Chaldæans specially designated *astrologers*, probably from the fact that individuals of the original tribe were addicted to necromantic arts. Balaam is supposed to have been a Chaldæan priest and astrologer, who lived during the closing period of the life of Moses. The latter died about A. M. 2553, or B. C. 1451 (Num. xxii—xxvii. 13). All who were acquainted with the mysterious science of astrology were called Chaldæans. The same term has been applied by Asiatic and European nations to all of the astronomers and astrologers of Babylon. The Chaldæans mentioned by Daniel were of comparatively late origin (Dan. i. 1—7). The later Babylonian empire evidently included Chaldæa. It was established by Belesis, called by Isaiah, Baladan, (Isa. xxxix. 1), and by profane historians, Nabonassar. About 627 B. C. that Babylonian monarch conspired with Arbaces the Mede and destroyed the Assyrian empire, then governed by Sardanapalus, and thus the later Babylonian or Chaldæan empire was formed.

The three ancient monarchies which we have considered, viz: Babylonia, Assyria, and Chaldæa, were situated either between or very near the Euphrates and Tigris, and near each other, if not at times united into one empire. Those countries seem to have been first settled at about the same period. Their inhabitants were probably descendants of Shem, Ham and Japheth, as it was in the land of Shinar or Babylonia that the dispersion took place, and some of the posterity of each of the sons of Noah would be likely to remain in that region. From the languages there prevailing however, we infer that the original inhabitants were mostly descendants of Shem.

They were doubtless acquainted with those arts and sciences which Shem received from his father. Undoubtedly a knowledge of antediluvian music was transmitted through Noah to his posterity, and additions were gradually made to that information.

There is a reference to music in connection with a circumstance in the life of Jacob and Esau (Gen. xxxi. 27), which must have occurred according to the usual computation about 495 years after the dispersion (vid. Gen. xi. 18—26; xxi. 5; xxv. 26; xxvi. 34; xxxi. 27, 41), about A. M. 2250, or B. C. 1754. The Assyrian monarchy was then in a flourishing condition, and as it was situated near Syria, where Laban, to whom reference is made above, and who speaks of musical instruments, resided, it is highly probable that the Assyrians used the same kinds of instruments which are mentioned by him. Indeed parts of Assyria and Syria were, during some periods, at least, identical. The word *Syria* is supposed by some to be merely a contraction of *Assyria*, and that both terms indicated, in ancient times, the same district of country; but this opinion is evidently erroneous. Laban was the son of Bethuel, and the latter was the nephew of Abram, and Abram resided during the early part of his life in Ur, near the great capital of the Assyrian empire. It is very natural to suppose that Shem handed down the knowledge of music, which existed before the deluge, to his cotemporary Abram, and the latter to his nephew Bethuel, the Syrian, and Bethuel to his son Laban. The same kinds of musical instruments essentially, which were used before the deluge, and those used by Laban, doubtless continued to be used, with some improvements, by the posterity of Abraham, and of course by the Hebrews.

Both the Babylonian and Chaldæan music must have been received chiefly from Noah and his posterity, and consequently must have been essentially the same in both countries. The old Babylonian monarchy was commenced before the Assyrian and perhaps may have received a knowledge of music first, though the two capitals Nineveh and Babylon were built nearly at the same period, and the inhabitants of each had about the same opportunity to become acquainted with the music of the antediluvian world. It is probable that those cities continued to be inhabited until comparatively modern times by some of the posterity of Shem, who doubtless made improvements in music and handed down their knowledge of the art to future generations. The exact spot on which the proud city of Nineveh stood, has not, until recently been identified. Only four mounds were to be seen where, as was supposed, that city once reared its lofty turrets. One of these mounds was called Jonah, whose tomb it was supposed to contain, (vid. Buckingham's Travels in Mesopotamia, vol. ii. p. 49–50, 60). Numerous inscriptions were found but could not be deciphered. It remained for the nineteenth century to unfold the mysteries contained in Egyptian, Assyrian, and Babylonian inscriptions. The indefatigable Layard and Botta have done more than any other persons to give us a knowledge of the manners, customs, arts, and sciences of the ancient Assyrians by actually exhuming the palaces of the ancient capital. In describing a war scene, sculptured in bas-relief, on the walls of a chamber exhumed at Nimroud, Layard remarks : "two musicians are playing with a plectrum, on stringed instruments, or harps similar to those on slabs Nos. 19 and 20 of the same chamber" (vid. Layards Nineveh, P. i. c. x). He remarks again: "it is probable that the Assyrians, like the Egyptians, had various musical instruments; only one kind, however, is represented in the sculptures. It is in the shape of a triangle, is held between the left arm and the side, and appears to have been suspended from the neck. The strings, nine or ten in number, are stretched between a flat board and an upright bar through which they pass. Tassels are appended to the ends of the strings, and the bar itself is generally surmounted by a small hand, probably of metal or ivory. The instrument was struck with a plectrum held in the right hand; the left appears to have been used either to pull the strings, or to produce notes by pressure. Like the Egyptian harp, it had no crosspiece between the upright bar and the flat board or base; it is difficult, therefore, to understand how the strings could have been sufficiently tightened to produce notes" (vid. Layard's Nineveh, P. ii. c. vi). The writer then remarks in a note that this same instrument is represented in the bas-relief of the king standing over the crouching lion, also in many other places. He farther remarks that the god which Mr. Birch supposes to be Baal is represented at Talmis playing on a triangular lyre. The music and instruments there indicated must have been quite ancient, for Nineveh was destroyed about 606 B. C., still the *ten-stringed* harp is far from being the most ancient form of that instrument.

Immense ruins are found where ancient Babylon stood. Bricks are to be seen, which have been fire-baked and cemented together by zepht or bitumen. Between each layer are oziers. Some of the bricks are large, thick and imprinted with cuneiform characters. Their composition corresponds exactly with the account given by the sacred historian, of the bricks used in building the tower of Babel. Specimens of them are deposited in the British Museum, in the Museum of the East India Company, and in other repositories of antiquities. Some important facts have been made known in respect to the manners and customs of the Babylonians, from the inscriptions which have been deciphered; but it is doubtful whether any discoveries will be made in those ruins which will throw much light upon the arts and sciences among the antediluvians and especially during the time which elapsed between the deluge and dispersion of mankind.

Greece was inhabited in early times and was one of the first regions settled by the posterity of Japheth (vid. p. 27. *supra*). Josephus informs us that Gomer, one of sons of Japheth was founder of the Gomerites, called by the Greeks, in the time of Josephus, Galatians (Galls) (Josep. Ant. B. i. vi. 1). He mentions the seven sons of Japheth and the places in Asia Minor where most of them settled; but "from Javan," he remarks "Jonia (Ionia), and all of the Grecians are derived." It is probable that several places were occupied by the descendants of Japheth at about the same time; but we have more authentic information in reference to Greece than in respect to other places of their abode. In the Scriptures, Greece often signifies all of those countries inhabited by the posterity of Javan. In the Old Testament, Greece and the Greeks are indicated by the term Javan (יָוָן) (vid. Isa. lxvi. 19; Eze. xxvii. 13, 19; Dan. x. 20; xi. 2). It is supposed by some historians that Greece was first settled as early as 1800 years B. C. by the Pelasgi who seem to have emigrated from Egypt. Others place the settlement still earlier, while another class think that the credible history of the country does not extend so far into antiquity.

Little is known of the Pelasgi excepting that they lived in caves and were cannibals. They were much degraded, being almost entirely ignorant of the arts and sciences. History informs us that about 1514 B. C. (some say 200 years later), the Hellenes migrated into the country from Asia and either expelled or civilized the Pelasgi. The former were probably descendants of either Shem or Japheth. Subsequently Phœnician and Egyptian colonies settled in Greece and imparted some additional knowledge of the arts and sciences. It was about sixty years after the settlement of the Hellenes in the country when Cadmus, a Phœnician, introduced a knowledge of the Alphabet. The inhabitants of Argos and indeed of all Greece were distinguished for their love of music; but the art was cultivated on the plains of Shinar at a much earlier period. It is probable that the inhabitants of ancient Greece obtained their knowledge of the arts and sciences mostly from the Phœnicians, and perhaps, to some extent, from the Egyptians. Of course their music must have been formed after the Phœnician and Egyptian models, with the improvements which their own skill and taste may have suggested.

The Egyptian music, we shall consider hereafter. That of the *Phœnicians*, was probably about the same as that which the sons of Noah practised, as the earliest inhabitants of Phœnicia are believed to have been nomad tribes that wandered from the borders of the Arabian Sea and Persian Gulf. Hamaker, in his *Miscellanea Phœnicia*, asserts that the Phœnicians came from the borders of the

Arabian Sea. Their language is believed to have belonged to the Canaanitish branch of the Shemitish family, and is imperfectly understood, as no Phœnician writings are extant excepting a few fragments, found in Hebrew and ancient classical writers. During the time of Joshua, the Phœnician city of Tyre existed and was strongly fortified (Josh. xix. 29). That must have been as early as 1444 B. C. or about 790 years after the dispersion. Hengstenberg supposes that the Phœnicians commenced their colony immediately after that event (vid. De Rebus, Tyriorum, Berdini 1832. p. 93). They doubtless made improvements upon the music received through Noah and his posterity, though it is probable that they did not devote much attention to the subject, as we are informed by historians that they did not cultivate *poetry*, which in all ages, has been intimately connected with music. Notwithstanding this testimony of ancient history we cannot divest ourselves of the belief that effusions of poetry were frequent even among the Phœnicians, though it may not have been cultivated as an art.

China was inhabited in very early times. Pölitz informs us that several small kingdoms and States existed in that country 2000 years B. C.; but that its *credible* history began a little before the Christian era (Politz Welt Gesch. P. i. c. 11). About two hundred years B. C. the Emperor Xi Hoam Ti caused a general destruction of the ancient books. He ordered upon pain of death all monuments of antiquity to be destroyed, and executed many of the learned men of the empire. Since his time a few fragments only of ancient history can be found, so that we can learn little with certainty in respect to the antiquity of the country, before the reign of that tyrant.

Supposing, as was probably the fact, that the country was settled by some rude hordes 2000 years B. C. or about 234 years after the dispersion, we shall reach a period when the Assyrian empire was in a flourishing condition. It is very difficult if not impossible to ascertain the origin of the earliest inhabitants of China. Their features and skulls indicate that they originated from the Mongols. Sir William Jones, who investigated the subject, makes them of Indian descent (vid. Asiat. Resear. vol. II. mem. 24). This is, perhaps, the most probable supposition, though the Chinese language is entirely different from that of the Hindoos. Jones farther supposes that before they left India, they were of the military caste, and very much degraded, that they had probably lost a knowledge of the Indian tongue, and gradually, as they advanced in cultivation, formed a language which, by improvements, became what it now is, (vid. p. 32. *supra*). The origin of the Hindoos we shall consider hereafter, (vid. p. 50 *infra*). Assuming the Indian origin of the Chinese, their music must have been similar to that of India, unless they had entirely lost a knowledge of it, as they are supposed to have done of their language. Sir George Stanton, who accompanied the Earl of Macartney, in 1792 on an embassy to the Emperor of China, informs us that he witnessed the ceremonies of worshipping the Emperor at the palace of Zhe-hal in Tartary.— The principal officers of state were introduced into a vast hall and thence into a temple, furnished with great instruments of music, among which were cylindrical bells, suspended in a line from ornamented frames of wood, and gradually diminishing in size from one end to the other. There were also triangular pieces of metal arranged in the same order as the bells. To the sound of these instruments a slow and solemn hymn was sung by eunuchs. The performers, in gliding from one tone to another, were directed by the striking of a shrill and sonorous cymbal. The whole, says Stanton, had a grand effect. These instruments were of simple construction, of the percussion class, and probably the same, essentially, which had been used for centuries, as the Chinese are extremely slow to change any of their customs or habits, or to make improvements in their knowledge of the arts and sciences.

India was evidently settled in very early times, and some of the learned believe it to have been the most ancient country inhabited by man. The name India is derived from the Greeks, who seem to have borrowed it from the Persians as it is unknown to the natives. The term was used by the Greeks to denote an indefinite extent of country reaching beyond the Indus; the historian Pölitz intimates that, possibly, it was the most anciently inhabited country (Pölitz Welt Gesch. P. i. c. 6). Some modern historians are of the opinion that a portion of the sacred writings of the Hindoos is worthy of credit. Their most ancient epoch (called Caliyng) commences B. C. 3101, and there is a tradition among them indicating that they were not a colony from any other tribe. Their astronomical knowledge, existing before the period to which history extends, the antiquity ascribed to their alphabet, language and religious tradition, handed down by means of pictures and writings, are thought by many to point to a development of the human intellect from its first germ. The fact is well authenticated that a tender and imaginative poetry existed among them 1000 years

B. C., and the immense rock upon which their mythology is sculptured is a work, in comparison with which, the pyramids of Egypt appear young. A native tradition fixes the origin of the Vedas (being revelations from Brahma) at 4900 B. C. This, of course, is extravagant; but the Oupnek-hat (consisting of explanations of sacred mysteries), according to Darashaku, a distinguished prince in Cashmere, who translated the work into the Persian language, that the four Vedas must have been written at least 2000 years before Christ. When the Greeks traveled in India, they found their Bacchus and Hercules engaged in the same deeds as in their own country. They found a mythology similar to their own, hence they concluded that Pythagoras had traveled in that country, and there obtained much of the knowledge which he imparted to his own countrymen. It is thought that the deities of Greece were not originally of Greek nor Egyptian extraction; but that they had their origin in India, their names only being changed. Vishnu and Bhavani, Nared and Sereswatti gave place to Jupiter, Venus, Mercury and Ceres. The deities did not hold their court on Mount Meru, but on Mount Ida, at the head of the Scamander, and not on the Ganges. The same animals marked their shrines and gave occasion for the worship of brutes, plants and insects. The Greek historians regarded the traditions which they obtained from that country as remnants of its high antiquity. It seems clear that the Hindoos, in very early times, were engaged in commerce and acquainted with several of the arts and sciences, and probably with music. Some of their most ancient writings were in verse, and it is generally believed that, in ancient times, poetry and music were in constant coalescence. It is probable that the Indians had some kind of music to accompany the recital of their poems.

The country is mentioned in the sacred scriptures. In the book of Esther, i. 1, and viii. 9 (Heb. הֹדּוּ *hoddu* for הֹנְדּוּ *hondu*, Syr. ܗܢܕܘ *handu*). The writer remarks that Ahasuerus reigned from *India* to Æthiopia. The events described in that book occurred about 900 years B. C. and it was probably written soon after.

The exact time when a government was first established in India seems to be lost amid fragmentary, contradictory, imaginary, and foolish traditions and histories. The most probable supposition is that the country was settled by the descendants of Shem at a period not far from the dispersion of mankind. This opinion is corroborated from the fact to which we have already alluded, viz: that there is no authentic account that the first inhabitants were a colony from any other country; also from the fact that the posterity of Shem evidently moved eastward and must soon have reached India. It is worthy of remark that the principal language of that country which is the Sanscrit, seems to be of Shemitish origin.

It is possible that India was the first civilized country after the dispersion. There are strong reasons for believing that Babylonia, Æthiopia, and Egypt received their earliest knowledge of the arts and sciences from that country. Still there is so much obscurity and such a want of well authenticated facts upon the subject that it is now impossible to arrive at the truth.

Several countries were settled in very ancient times; but probably it is not possible now to determine with certainty which was first inhabited after Babylonia. It is pretty evident from the information now accessible that that was the first. It is also impossible to ascertain beyond a doubt which of the ancient countries, not excepting Babylonia, first cultivated the arts and sciences to any considerable extent. Pölitz asserts that Candahar, in the earliest times, was the most cultivated spot in India. It is now a city in Afghanistan a considerable distance east of ancient Babylon, where the dispersion occurred. It was not probably long after that event, as we have already intimated, when some of the nomad tribes of Shem's posterity reached the borders of India. The knowledge of music which the first inhabitants possessed, was probably derived chiefly from Shem and his immediate descendants. How rapidly they improved in the art we cannot now ascertain; but all of the facts which we have with regard to their cultivation of the arts and sciences, indicate a slow progress in improvements of every kind. It is probable that, in every country, modern vocal music and especially modern musical instruments bear much resemblance to ancient music and musical instruments in those countries. In the modern *instruments* at least we shall find the elements or outlines of the ancient ones, but much improved and adorned. It must be so especially in India, a country, the religious notions and peculiarities of whose inhabitants, forbid that they should make changes in their customs, and especially in those which pertain to religion. Their castes have no doubt handed down, century after century, nearly the same customs and the same music and musical instruments as were used in the earliest times. Musical instruments have not perhaps been materially changed for ages. The three grand classes exist at the present time in that country which were found among the ancient Hebrews and Egyptians, viz: Percussion, Stringed and Wind instruments. Rev. Dr. Malcom, in his book of travels in South Eastern Asia, gives drawings and descriptions of musical instruments which are now used in Burmah, a province of Farther India. We will present descriptions of two of them with drawings (vid. Malcom's Travels in S. E. Asia. Vol. i. pp. 204, 205).

"The *Tseing*, *S'hing* or Boundaw, is a collection of small drums," says Malcom, "suspended around the inside of a richly-carved frame of wood, about three feet high. They regularly diminish in size from that of a two-gallon measure to that of a pint. The player sits within the circle and with his hands produces a rude tune or accompaniment. Drumsticks are not often used. In the full band the Boundaw is never omitted."

FIG. II.

BOUNDAW OR BURMESE DRUMS.

Others of the percussion kind, Dr. Malcom informs us, are the *Moung* or *Gong*; *Pan-ma-gyee* or *Drum*; the *Kyay-wyng*, or sixteen Gongs in a square or circular form; the *Kyay-kouk*, similar to the last, and the *Patolah*, constructed by placing pieces of bamboo on strings which are struck by a stick.

The *Stringed Instruments* are the *Tey-au* or *Ta-yaw*, a *violin*, with two or three strings, played with a bow. The belly is sometimes carved out of a solid piece. The tone is far from being pleasant.

FIG. III.

TA-YAW OR BURMESE VIOLIN.

The *Soung* or *Harp*, the *Megoum* or *Me-kyoung*, a *Guitar*, are also stringed instruments. Their *Wind Instruments* are the *Pay-looay*, a kind of *hautboy;* and the *Hneh* or *clarionet* without keys.

Sir William Jones informs us that the musical scale of the Hindoos is divided into minute intervals, like that of the Arabs—twenty two quarters and thirds of a tone being unanimously reckoned in their octave. It would seem, however, that this enharmonic genus among them is rather scientific than practical, for Jones says that he had tried in vain to discover any difference in practice between the Indian and European musical scale. A thorough examination of the music, and especially the musical instruments of India, might throw light upon Egyptian music, if indeed, as some suppose, the Egyptians received their first cultivation from India.

Egypt was among the earliest inhabited countries. It is a fact pretty well established, that the Egyptian monarchy was formed by a colony from Æthiopia (the present Nubia and Abyssinia), in Upper Egypt, then inhabited by pastoral tribes. The languages and customs of the Egyptians and Æthiopians were very similar, and it is highly probable that the former received their first civilized inhabitants from the latter. There is a tradition, authenticated by an ancient astronomical observation, that, very early, the Babylonian Hermes (Thoth) went to Æthiopia and founded the state. This would indicate that the Egyptian monarchy was established after the Æthiopian, and the latter after the Babylonian. The monarchy of Egypt is supposed to have been founded by Menes, according to Usher's chronology, 2222 B. C., only about twelve years after the dispersion of mankind. Others have placed that event a few years later, and others many centuries later still. Hieroglyphics found upon ancient monuments have been deciphered and explained by Champollion, Young, Spohn, Akerblad, Zoega, Seyffarth, Kosegarten and others, still it is extremely doubtful whether it can be exactly ascertained when Menes commenced his reign. The statements of historians and chronologists are so various and contradictory that we are forced back to the inspired volume as the only reliable source of information in respect to the earliest history of that country. The Hebrew term (מִצְרַיִם *mitsráyim*) translated Egypt, is the name of a grandson of Noah, and refers us directly back to a period soon after the deluge (Gen. x. 1—6). We are informed in the twelfth chapter of Genesis, that Abraham, in consequence of a famine which was prevailing in the land of Canaan, went down into Egypt. This, according to our usual computation, was 1920 years B. C., or 314 after the dispersion. There the patriarch found a sovereign, a court, and princes. About 1720 B. C. Joseph was carried into Egypt, as described in Gen. xxxix.

Some suppose that the Egyptians were a colony from India, as the pyramids are very similar in their construction to the pagodas of that country, and contain sacred relics, and not the bones of kings, indicating that they may have been originally intended for Buddhist temples.

It has been said that India could not have received her religion from the Egyptians, Persians, Greeks or Romans, as that would have been in utter violation of her most sacred tenets. It is possible that Egypt, in very early times, received some knowledge of the arts and sciences and of religious customs from India; but there are so few well authenticated facts upon the subject it is difficult to decide.

The ancient Jews undoubtedly adopted many customs of the people among whom they dwelt. When in Egypt, they worshipped Egyptian deities, when in the wilderness, they did homage to the gods of the Canaanites, Egyptians, Ammonites and Moabites, and when in Judæa to those of the Phœnicians, Syrians and others. Jacob induced his family to adore the God of the Hebrews, but soon after his death, they forgot the instructions of a kind father and bowed down to Egyptian deities.

After the return of the Jews from captivity, however, they seem to have adhered more generally to the worship of Jehovah, as we do not find that they were rebuked for idolatry. With the exception of a few under Antiochus Epiphanes (Mac. i. 12, etc.) they preserved the worship of God in its purity. To imitate their heathen neighbors in religious matters was regarded as idolatry, and the severest denunciations were uttered against it.

It was different, however, in respect to music, which was innocent in itself and might be useful as well as pleasant for recreation, and very beneficial in religious worship. The Hebrews undoubtedly retained much of the knowledge of music and many of the forms of musical instruments with which they became acquainted while in Egypt. If they copied other things from the natives, it is reasonable to suppose that so attractive an art as music would be imitated.

Shall we then present a brief view of the art in ancient Egypt? There are strong reasons to believe that the Egyptians cultivated music nearly from the time of their existence as a nation, though within certain limits, as not all were permitted to practise it. So in the East at the present day, there are particular classes who may be musicians, such as the Almeh, Gasie, Tschingane, etc. Niebuhr informs us that "it is deemed improper for a respectable Turk or Arab to understand music. The people of rank, therefore, among the Orientals, being themselves, by no means, great connoisseurs of the art of music, and those who apply themselves to it being not so well paid as they are with us, it is not at all strange that this art has not advanced to such a degree in this part of the world as it has in Europe." It is probable that the Egyptians were acquainted with a rude kind of music, even in their nomadic state. The assertion of Diodorus Siculus, that they prohibited the cultivation of the art, is contradicted by Plato, who resided in Egypt, attending to literary pursuits, for thirteen years. Strabo informs us that the Egyptians taught their children letters, songs, and a certain species of music, which was established by government. *Instruments* of music must have been known by that people in very early times, as they are found sculptured on the ruins of their most ancient monuments. Distinguished travelers have visited the country at different periods, and abundantly proved the fact that the early inhabitants were acquainted with the three grand classes, viz: *percussion*, *stringed*, and *wind* instruments. It is possible, and perhaps probable, that the same kinds of instruments which were used before the deluge, were employed after that event, and perhaps in ancient Egypt. Indeed, Noah may have preserved some of them, and it is possible that antediluvian instruments or parts of them may have been found after that event. However this may have been, Noah, as we have before intimated (vid. pp. 43, 44, 52, *supra*), doubtless was acquainted with the antediluvian music, and transmitted that knowledge of the art to his posterity. It is evident that there were instruments after the deluge having the same names as those which were employed by Jubal.

Music is mentioned in the sacred Scriptures as existing about 600 years after the flood, or a little more than 1700 years B. C. About 1500 B. C. the lyrical effusions of Moses appear. From Gen. xxxi. 27, we perceive that both vocal and instrumental music was practised, and probably common at the time to which reference is made in that passage. The event there described occurred in Haran, where Laban resided, a little more than 600 years after the deluge. That town was on the way from Chaldæa to Canaan (Gen. xi. 31), and not a great distance from Egypt. But long before that time, as we have already intimated, music was cultivated on the Nile.

We find instruments of music sculptured on the most ancient monuments. Champollion informs us that the sculptures on the monument El Asaffif are ascertained to be more than 3500 years old, having been wrought about 1645 B. C., or, according to Usher, about 577 years after the monarchy of Egypt was established. The first coasting trade in Egypt is supposed to have commenced with

Phœnician smugglers, and with Inachus, who led an Egyptian colony to Greece in Phœnician vessels about 1836 B. C. The Scripture account of foreign states, names Shishak as the Pharaoh of Egypt and ally of Jeroboam about 975 B. C. (vid. 1 Kings xi. 40; xiv. 25; II Chron. xii. 2, 5, 7, 9). Psammeticus established a monarchy which continued from 636 to 525 B. C. The nation was then highly civilized, and music and the various arts and sciences were in a flourishing state. Egypt next became subject to Cambyses, and was incorporated into the Persian empire. Alexander conquered the country B. C. 332. After the division of the Macedonian empire, the reign of the Ptolemies began.

From very early times, improvements were doubtless made in music and the fine arts. The numerous sculptures and inscriptions on Egyptian monuments are full of interest, and richly repay the labor of investigation. Dr. Shaw traveled in several parts of Barbary and the Levant, and collected materials upon the subject for publication, between 1720 and 1733. He presents important information in reference to the music of those countries which he visited. In respect to ancient Egypt, he testifies, as many had done before him, that representations of musical instruments, and especially the sistrum, may be found sculptured on various ruins upon the Nile (vid. Vol. I., p. 202 sq.; Vol. II., p. 350 sq., ed. 1757). Dr. Alexander Russell, in his Natural History of Aleppo, published in 1754 and 1794, has given important information in respect to the present state of music and musical instruments in a part of the East; but he says very little about ancient music, and especially that of ancient Egypt (Vol. I., pp. 142, 145, 147, 150–156, with plate iv. and

Note xxxix. p. 386). In 1737 and 1738 Captain Norden and Dr. R. Pococke traveled in Egypt, and gave an interesting account of their discoveries; but said little concerning ancient music. Pococke brought a seal from that country upon which was engraved a kind of harp, but not of much authority. He also found a statue of Isis, upon which was sculptured a sistrum (Decr. of the East, Vol. I., p. 214, plate lxv). Sistra are described by Jablonski and Bernardo de Montfauçon, in their works on Egyptian antiquities. Dr. Pococke, on p. 186, describes the *Nakous*, a kind of castanet (plate lvii. fig. iv). Calmet informs us that Captain Norden found the guitar in use among the modern Egyptians. Pfeiffer investigated this subject in 1779; but there was then comparatively a small amount of information accessible to the scholar upon Egyptian antiquities, the only sources being occasional references to the subject contained in the sacred Scriptures, a little light from the Greeks, Romans, and Phœnicians, some sculptures from dilapidated ruins,* a small number of coins, and the Isiac Table. This last was discovered at Rome in 1525, but is now lost, though correct drawings of it are extant. It contained, among other sculptures, that of a harp and sistrum. Its origin is doubtful, some supposing it to be really Egyptian, while others believe it to have been made for the Egyptians at Rome.† Pfeiffer was only acquainted with these rather uncertain sources and what other information was

* Vid. Calmet, Vol. III., p. 259, No. 203, ed. Charlestown, 1813.

† Rees' Cyclop. Art. Isiac; Burney's Hist. Music, Vol. I., p. 205, 520; Montfauçon Antiq. Com. Red., p. 174, and Jablonskii Opuscula, Tres. Dis., Tom. XI., pp. 227–273.

then known in respect to music in the East. He, indeed, presents many interesting considerations; but since his day many important discoveries in respect to Egyptian antiquities have been made. The tomb of Ismonides or Osymandyas, particularly described by Diodorus Siculus (Lib. i., c. 47), is supposed to have been built 2000 years B. C. Pococke informs us that the walls of its rooms were adorned with sculptures consisting, among other things, of instruments of music. If Diodorus' testimony is to be credited, the tomb must have been built about 200 years after the monarchy of Egypt was founded, and about 350 years after the deluge, indicating the very early cultivation of music in that land. From a broken pillar of great antiquity in the Campus Martius at Rome, Dr. Burney obtained the drawing of an instrument—a kind of Dichord Guitar, corresponding, as nearly as can be ascertained from an imperfect sculpture, to the following cut, Fig. iv.

The globe or rounding part of the instrument, at the lower end, approaches nearer to a parallelogram with rounded corners, than the drawing would indicate. The pillar or obelisk from which this representation was taken, with another pillar, was brought to Rome by the command of Augustus after he had reduced Egypt to a Roman province. It is supposed to have been erected at Heliopolis by Sesostris, perhaps in commemoration of the invention of the Egyptian guitar nearly 400 years before the Trojan war. It was placed in the Campus Martius at Rome, and when the city was sacked and burned by the Duke of Bourbon, general to the Emperor Charles V. in 1727, this ancient obelisk was thrown down and broken.

Subsequently, Niebuhr traveled in Egypt and present-

FIG. IV.

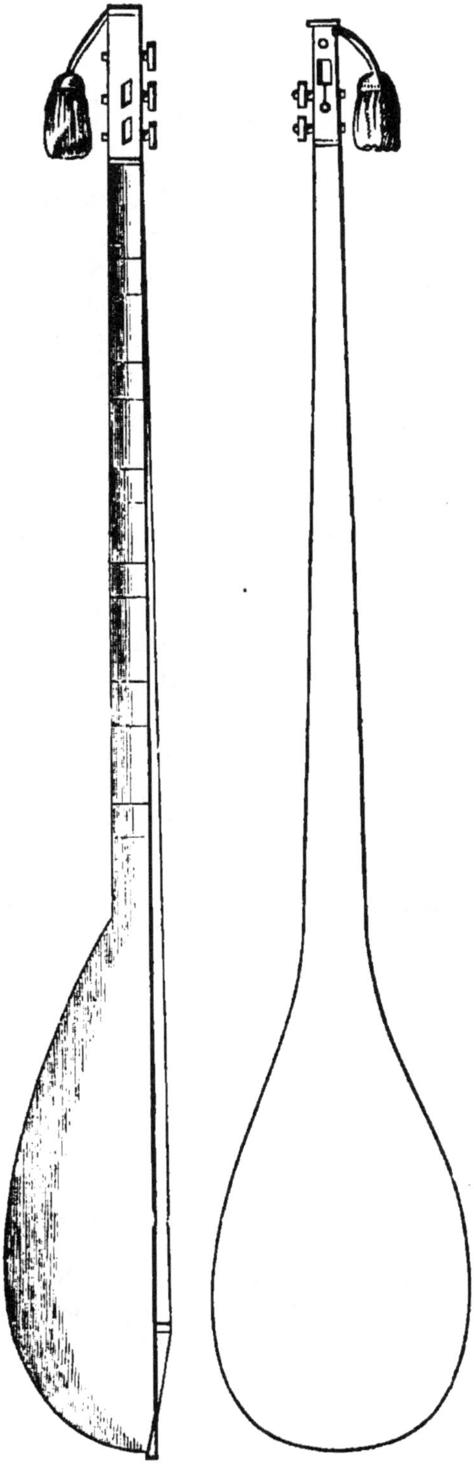

ANCIENT EGYPTIAN DICHORD GUITAR.

ed a more full and accurate account of modern music, and especially of musical instruments in that country than any one preceding him. Abbé de St. Non of Paris, a short time before his death in 1791, published his views in which are sketched from the walls of the Royal sepulchres west of Thebes and from the temple of Tentyra or Denderah, seven figures of musical instruments with their performers. There is found the ancient form of the harp with four strings. The information which he furnished was of much more importance than any thing which had previously been published. It was left for the Savans of Napoleon to lay open the true state of the arts and sciences in ancient Egypt. In some cases, they as well as other writers, have added in their drawings, modern drapery; for instance the priest described by Bruce as playing upon the harp, is clad in a deep black robe striped with white, instead of a white one spotted with red according to the Egyptian costume. The man, who is represented as sitting in a chair at a short distance listening to the music, appears in blue pantaloons and waistcoat and a cap resembling the cap of liberty, which are not Egyptian. The Savans have been criticised by Dr. Russell and others on that account; but they have given a far more reliable and full view than any of their predecessors.

The great work of the Savans, entitled "*Description de l'Egypte*"* is an important help upon this subject, as

* We would here present our acknowledgments to the librarians of Harvard University, and of the Astor Library in this city, in furnishing every requisite facility for the examination of this great work and others upon Egyptian antiquities. Several of our engravings of instruments were copied from the work of the Savans.

it treats extensively of modern as well as ancient Egyptian music. In respect to the latter, Villoteau, who had charge of the department relating to music, takes Jablonski chiefly, as his philological guide. He first made himself thoroughly acquainted with modern Egyptian music in all of its branches, then uniting his own observations with the learned investigations of Jablonski, he was enabled to present a very accurate and full view of the whole subject. In his plates we find elegant engravings of the three grand classes into which the musical instruments are usually divided, and under such circumstances as to fully authenticate their high antiquity. They were taken from ruins on the island of *Philæ*, at *Elethyia*, now called El Kab; *Tentyra* or *Denderah*; in the tombs of the Pyramids of *Memphis*; and the copious ruins of sepulchres and temples in and around *Thebes*. The exact antiquity of these splendid ruins cannot be ascertained. Of the island of Philæ, Belzoni remarks, "the prospect of the island and its ruins is truly magnificent, particularly at some distance, though it is extremely barren." * * * "The style of the hieroglyphics, proves that the edifice on it, which consists of two temples nearly united together, is of the last era of the Egyptian nation, in my opinion of the Ptolemies."

Elethyia (Ειληθυιας Ρολις, Latin, *Lucina*), is situated on the east side of the Nile between fifty and sixty miles north of Syene, and not as far south of Thebes. The ruins are quite extensive, lying in the modern village called El Kab, which is supposed to be near the place where the ancient city stood. These ruins have every appearance of being very ancient. Belzoni found the place surrounded by a high wall of unburned brick, also the ruins of three or four temples, and other ancient buildings. There are grottos, about a mile from the river, in the mountains, which are really sepulchres, and the sculptures and paintings on the walls are more important, in some respects, than those at Thebes, as the ornaments of the latter are principally confined to the higher ceremonies of religion, while those of the former refer to the pursuits and habits of the Egyptians in private life.* In the largest of the grottos is a wall upon which is represented a feast, enlivened by musicians and dancers. One female is playing on a harp, another on a double flute and three others are dancing in the same manner as do the Almeh at Cairo. Those who amuse the rich are a different class from those who exhibit to the multitude. The latter are probably the Gasie of whom Niebuhr speaks.

The temple of Tentyra now called Denderah is on the left bank of the Nile, eighteen miles north of Thebes. Belzoni supposes it to have been erected in the time of the first Ptolemy. There are strong reasons for believing that this temple and those of Philæ and Edfou were built by the Ptolemies, though some, as Dupuis and Jollois, maintain that they are much more ancient. The architects probably followed the ancient manner of building. Denon and Belzoni speak in the most enthusiastic terms of the elegance apparent in the temple of Denderah.

The pyramids of *Memphis*, as far as we can learn from

* Vid. Russell's View, p. 190, as quoted by O. A. Taylor, in an article on musical instruments of the ancient Egyptians, in the Biblical Repository, vol. ix, No. 26, from which we have derived much valuable information in the preparation of that part of this Introduction which relates to Egyptian music.

history and tradition, were very ancient, though their exact antiquity is not known. The Mausoleums or tombs near the pyramids also, are supposed to be of equal or even greater antiquity than the pyramids. Both are so ancient that we may safely regard their representations to a certain extent, as a true exhibition of the state of the arts and sciences in the earliest ages. The inscriptions on these tombs are numerous. Abdallotiph informs us that he saw as many as would fill ten thousand volumes, and others have used equally strong language. Some of the sculptures represent musical instruments. On the ruins of one of the tombs, there is a representation of a band of musicians, playing on the flute, harp, and a kind of clarionet, accompanied by dancing women, tinged with yellow.

The celebrated ruins of *Thebes* include those of Luxor and Carnac on the eastern bank of the Nile, Gornou, Biban el-Molauk, Medinet-Abu, and the Memnonium on the west, extending about nine miles in length along the Nile, and back to the mountains on the east and west, about eight miles in breadth. Dr. Pococke remarks concerning Thebes, that "the date of its *destruction* is older than the *foundation* of other cities. The Necropolis (city of the dead) called by the Savans, *Thebes* Hypogées (θῆβαι Ὑπογειαι, the subterranean Thebes), stands not far distant and contains splendid ruins which are probably as ancient as those of Thebes proper. From them many of the most important sketches of musical instruments have been taken. The three grand classes are painted and sculptured both on the ruins of Thebes and the Necropolis, under such circumstances as to induce scholars who have examined them to feel confident that they are of the highest antiquity, and that the *forms*, which the musical instruments of the Egyptians had during a space of several thousand years, have been in their essential characteristics handed down to the present time. They painted in fadeless colors and sculptured in solid granite or marble in and around their tombs in such a manner that it was impossible to erase the inscriptions. Thus the historical achievements, arts, sciences, habits and manners of the people were accurately handed down to modern times. This fact has doubtless, contributed much towards making oriental society so uniform and unchangeable as it is. If what we have said be correct, the forms of musical instruments painted and sculptured on the more modern temples of Egypt, may be safely considered as substantially the ancient ones. M. Villoteau presents numerous drawings of percussion and wind instruments, such as sistra, adufes or tambourines, and cymbals or castanets, trumpets and pipes. In carefully examining the numerous engravings of that Savan we did not discover the pipe of Pan. Mr. Taylor informs us that he did not find that ancient instrument. The adufe, cymbals or castanets and trumpets are the same in respect to variety and form as those which have always been used in the East. There are different sizes of the sistrum and it is variously ornamented. The flutes or pipes are single or double, straight or crooked. Villoteau represents some drawings in which all of the above mentioned and stringed instruments are found in concert. In his fictitious entertainments, the Egyptian guitar, and in most of the plates, the harp, may be seen. Stringed instruments are so numerous and varied in their construction, that passages in which there are references to them, are difficult to be explained.

Villoteau thinks it necessary to suppose that the many names of ancient instruments indicated those differing in their grand characteristics, and that very few of them were exactly alike. It is altogether probable that several names often denoted the same instrument, a little varied in the number of strings, in the form, or in some other way, from others of the same kind, like our different varieties of the flute, viol, etc. The same was doubtless true in respect to the Hebrews. Accordingly in some instances, several Hebrew words probably refer to the same general instrument a little varied in some peculiarity. They must be reduced to their respective classes, such as pipe, flute, viol, etc. The *forms* of a great variety of instruments are sculptured on Egyptian ruins; but we can learn very little concerning them from the ancient *language* of that country, as we have but a few fragments of it preserved.

From this brief general view of music among the ancient Egyptians, we think that they must have cultivated the art nearly 2000 years B. C. and perhaps earlier. The Hebrews, as we have already intimated, were doubtless much influenced, while in captivity, by the Egyptians, in respect to music as well as in reference to the arts and sciences generally.

We must next inquire whether the Hebrews were probably acquainted with music to any considerable extent before they were led into captivity in Egypt. That event occurred about 1921 B. C. Abram is considered as the father of the Israelites, being the son of Terah a resident of Ur in Chaldæa. From Gen. xi. 27—32, we learn that Abram, with his father and others set out to go into the land of Canaan; but they tarried at Haran in Mesopotamia. This must have been when Abram was quite young. He was born about 1996 B. C., or 353 after the deluge, and a few years afterwards, perhaps 25 or 30, he went to Haran. At the age of 75 (Gen. xii. 4) or 428 years after the deluge, he left Haran and entered the land of Canaan. We learn from Gen. xv. 18, that the land of Canaan which God gave to Abram and his posterity, extended from the river of Egypt to the Euphrates. Those possessions must have reached at least to the borders of Chaldæa and Babylonia. Thus the patriarch had an opportunity to become acquainted with music, and the other arts and sciences of those ancient monarchies. It is probable even that, through the descendants of Noah, he obtained some knowledge, as we have before intimated, of antediluvian music. After he had viewed the land of Canaan, he went down into Egypt, and there, doubtless, learned much more in respect to music, as the Egyptians had then probably cultivated the art for a long time. Subsequently Abram returned again to Canaan. About 1728 years B. C. or 621 after the deluge, Joseph was sold into Egypt. That must have been 300 or 400 years after the first monarchy was established in Egypt, and the Egyptians undoubtedly had cultivated the art of music during several centuries. Joseph was favored by Pharaoh, and finally the Israelites removed from Canaan and fixed their abode in Egypt; but they were soon reduced to bondage and remained in servitude 430 years (Ex. xii. 40). After wandering forty years in the wilderness, they returned again to Canaan about 1451 B. C.* They remained there about 864 years until 587 B. C. when they were carried

* It was in Egypt that the Hebrews, while in the midst of another people, first really grew up into a nation.

captive into Babylon by Nebuchadnezzar. They were there in bondage 70 years, at the end of which they returned again to the land of Canaan, which was then called Palestine.

From these considerations, it is reasonable to conclude that the Jews obtained much of their knowledge of music from the Egyptians, having resided so many years among them, though doubtless Abram had a knowledge of not only the antediluvian, but Babylonian and Chaldæan music before he visited Egypt. How far he adopted the views of the Egyptians in respect to music, before he imparted his knowledge to the Jewish nation, cannot now be ascertained; but it is reasonable to suppose that the knowledge which he obtained among that people, and that which those, who were in bondage, obtained, much influenced the Hebrews in respect to music and the various arts and sciences.

Concerning *Musical Notation* among the Egyptians and Hebrews we have no certain knowledge. Judging from their acquaintance with *instrumental* music, however, we think it highly probable that symbolic representations of musical sounds were known among them. The Greeks possess the most ancient system of musical notation which has reached our times, and our information even with regard to *that* is very limited and uncertain. The relics which have been preserved, show that that people must have been acquainted with a higher degree of cultivation in respect to practical and theoretical music than is generally supposed. Marpurg, Bottrigari, Galilei and others speak of hymns to Nemesis, Apollo and Calliope, and attempt an explanation of the notation of the music set to them; but there is so much contradiction and confusion in the account that it is hardly reliable. The same is true in respect to other writers who have endeavored to ascertain the musical notation of the ancient Greeks from the fragmentary historical remains upon the subject which have reached our times. All of their investigations are unsuccessful and unsatisfactory. When we go still farther back into antiquity to the Hebrews and Egyptians, an impenetrable darkness universally prevails. Some Jewish Rabbins have pretended that they have discovered the true system of musical notation among the ancient Hebrews; but they differ materially from each other in respect to its character. The Spanish, Roman, Prussian and Dutch Jews all have different systems of musical notation, and yet each, in the estimation of its advocates, is believed to be the true system of the ancient Hebrews, thus showing that no reliance can be placed upon *any* of them.

The Romans obtained their knowledge of musical notation from the Greeks, and we are informed by historians that they simplified the system of the latter by employing the Roman alphabet to indicate different sounds. We have authentic history informing us that Greek musical characters were used in the fourth century after Christ. In the fifth century they are mentioned by Bœthius and Martianus Capella (vid. fragments of their writings by Meibomius, vols. i and ii). Ambrose, one of the Fathers, in the latter part of the fourth century, improved the rhythm of church chants. In the sixth century Pope Gregory I. established a singing school at Rome, and essentially improved musical notation by substituting Roman instead of Greek letters. The Roman or Gregorian chant was introduced into England about A. D. 596 (vid. Introd. to the Art. Music in the Enciclo. Brittan. by G. F. Graham). Thus the present system of musical notation was gradually introduced.

We have remarked that the Egyptians had three classes of musical instruments, viz: *wind*, *stringed* and *percussion*. The Hebrews had the same, containing a considerable variety in each class, and especially in the first two; but these we shall examine in our remarks on particular passages of Scripture.

MUSIC OF THE BIBLE.

THE PENTATEUCH, OR FIVE BOOKS OF MOSES.

INTRODUCTORY REMARKS.

THE term in Hebrew for Pentateuch is חֲמִשָּׁה חוּמְשֵׁי תּוֹרָה, signifying, *the five fifths of the law;* but the more usual term is תּוֹרָה, *thora, the law.* Single books were called חוּמָּשׁ, *hhummash, a fifth part.* The Greek term is Πεντάτευχος, *Pentateuchos, Pentateuch,* from πέντε, *pente, five,* and τεῦχος, *teuchos,* an *implement.* After the Alexandrine period it signified *a book.* Many scholars, such as B. Spinoza, R. Simon, J. Clericus, J. G. Hase, F. C. Fulda, J. C. Nachtigal, J. S. Vater, G. M. L. De Wette, L. Bertholdt, C. F. Volney and Rosenmüller have maintained that the Pentateuch was not written by Moses. Within a few years the original documents from which it was taken have been critically examined, and the opinion advanced, that they were not composed nor arranged since the time of Moses (with the exception of what was done in Ezra's revision); but that they existed before his time, and were combined, arranged, and some of them perhaps translated by him and preserved in the families of Shem, Abraham and the Hebrew patriarchs. This view is, however, contested by a large number of the ablest biblical scholars, and the Mosaic origin of the Pentateuch strenuously advocated, which view is sustained by many irrefragable evidences, and is undoubtedly the correct one.

The object of Moses in writing the Pentateuch seems to have been the preservation of the Israelites from the contamination of surrounding idolatry. Indeed, throughout the *Old Testament Scriptures*, the two grand objects which the inspired writers seem to have kept continually in view, were *to turn men from idolatry* in all its forms of vice and error, and, by the gradual development of the scheme of prophecy to direct their attention to the future Messiah. When the Pentateuch was prepared, the world was absorbed in the grossest forms of Pagan superstition, originating principally in neglect, perversion or misapprehension of certain truths, once universally known. Hence, Moses commences his narrative by an allusion to those alarming considerations. Little is related which will enable us to judge of the manners and customs of the antediluvians. It is shown, however, that there were godly and wicked men, and that the latter so prevailed over the former that they were reduced to one family; and that the remainder of the human race were destroyed in order that holiness might not be entirely effaced from the earth.

There are but few allusions to music in the Pentateuch, still there are sufficient to show that the art was cultivated, to some extent, even before the deluge.

his cotemporaries, the number of the human family must have largely increased, and he may have instructed *many* to perform on the instruments which he had invented.

That Jubal was the inventor of those instruments is farther confirmed by the common opinion of the oriental nations. Chardin (Voyages en Perse T. v. p. 69) informs us that the Persians and Arabians call musicians and singers *Kayné, descendants of Cain.* Plato pretends that all traces of ancient music were lost by the deluge, and that, after that event, the art was again cultivated by the instrumentality of Marsyas, Olympus and Amphion (Lib. iii. de Legibus, p. 584); but he felt obliged to write thus in accordance with received traditions. In no other way could he do honor to the authors just named.

It is probable that many of the antediluvian ideas in respect to music were partially lost, so that the people of each nation, after the deluge, were obliged to search anew for the origin of music. Thus the various inventions and improvements which may have existed before the deluge would have to be made the second time. Even searching out what really existed in the most ancient times, would, among the first nations after the deluge, have the honor, in many cases, of being new discoveries. Sulzer asserts, that every nation may lay claim to have discovered its own kind of music (Theorie, B. ii. p. 791).

The *place* where the art was first cultivated was probably not far from the Garden of Eden, and that sacred place is generally supposed to have been near where Bassora now stands—a little below the junction of the river Tigris with the Euphrates in Turkey in Asia, and very near Arabia. Cain resided in the land of Nod east of Eden (Gen. iv. 16). Jubal was his sixth descendant, and probably lived in the same place, or not far distant, though Moses does not mention the fact. In the time of Jubal, probably, the human race had not extended very far around Eden.

It is quite evident, from ancient inscriptions upon monuments, that music was cultivated in Egypt, as we have intimated in the introduction, about 350 years after the deluge, making, between the time of Jubal's and the first Egyptian music, about 1850 years. The places (Egypt and that part of Turkey in Asia where stood the Garden of Eden) have Arabia between them. Or, if music was cultivated in India and Babylonia about fifty years after the deluge, as is quite probable, there would intervene, between Jubal's and the first Indian and Babylonian music, about 1600 years, and Babylonia included the Garden of Eden. A part of India, considered in its widest extent, was not far distant. Between the time of Jubal's music and that of Haran (Gen. xxxi. 27) there is an interval of about 2150 years, and the places were not distant from each other.

Jubal is said to be "the father of all such as *handle* the harp and organ." The Hebrew word for *handle* is תֹּפֵשׂ, *tophes*, a participle of the verb תָּפַשׂ, *taphas*, *to lay hold of*, *to handle*. The signification of the participle is *handling* or *playing upon*. The Septuagint uses καταδείξας, *katadeixas*, *showing*, *teaching*. This seems to indicate that the LXX regarded Jubal as the father of all who *taught* to play on the harp and organ, as well as the father of those who performed upon those instruments. We have shown that it could not have been, in all probability, more than about 160 years after Adam's creation when Jubal practised music. If, then, there was *teaching* of music, as the LXX seem to have thought, Jubal must have become acquainted with the art when very young, as he must have been the teacher of those instructors.

This idea suggested by the Septuagint would only have a tendency to carry the origin of the art back a little farther into antiquity.

Harp.—The Hebrew word is כִּנּוֹר, *kinnor*, which evidently represents a stringed instrument; but before considering that term, it will be necessary to present a brief general view of the whole class to which the instrument here indicated belongs.

The general term in Hebrew denoting stringed instruments is נְגִינוֹת, *N'gînôth*. It is found in the superscription to several of the Psalms, and signifies ***a stringed instrument of music, music on a stringed instrument***, or ***a song for a stringed instrument.***

It is derived from נָגַן *nagan, to play on a stringed instrument.* The Hebrews had, according to Dr. Jahn, four kinds, viz.: the *cithara*, *nebhel*, *sambuke*, and *psaltery*. There were some variations from these, but none sufficient, in his view, to constitute a distinct instrument.

Villoteau informs us, as we have already intimated, that upon the ruins of Egypt are to be found sculptured three principal kinds of stringed instruments, viz.: *harps*, *lyres*, and *guitars*. There are many other kinds, but they appear to be improvements upon, or modifications of these three. The general name for stringed instruments, among the Egyptians, was *tebouni* (*τε βουνι*). Jablonski, who is Villoteau's authority, remarks that the term denotes a musical instrument of the ancient Egyptians, which was mentioned by one Joseppus or Josephus, a writer of uncertain age, by some supposed to be of the fifth century, but by others of a much later date. Josephus quotes from Porphyry, and has, for the term, *το βυνι, to buni* (Por. Lib. v. c. 144). Thomas Gale found the same orthography in a Cambridge manuscript; but he maintains that it should be written *τε βουνι, tĕ bouni*. Fabricius, who first brought Josephus' works to light, has for this term in the Greek text *το βονι, to boni;* but in the Latin *buni*. Jablonski remarks that the term should form but one word, thus: Τεβουνι, *tebouni*. He thinks it probable, from Josephus' quotation, that the term is of Egyptian origin, and should be referred to the Coptic dialect. There it is written thus: ϯⲃⲟⲩⲓⲛⲓ. In Gen. xxxi. 27, the Septuagint has *κιθαρας*, *kitharas*, and the Coptic translator ⲃⲟⲩⲓⲛⲓ, and, in Rev. xiv. 2, a harper is called ⲣⲉϥⲉⲣ ⲃⲟⲩⲓⲛⲓ. From the fact that the Greek letters *υ*, *u*, and *ου*, *ou*, are often interchanged with *β*, *b*, as in the word Remoboth, perhaps the writer was authorized to employ the Greek term *τε βουνι* for ϯⲃⲟⲩⲓⲛⲓ. Remoboth was used by Jerome to express Egyptian monks, which in Coptic is ⲣⲉⲙⲃⲟⲩⲁⲓⲧ. Jablonski had conversation at Paris with Montfauçon, who agreed with him in respect to the orthography of the word. La Croze, in a letter to Jablonski, also approves of this view. The latter says of the former, "who informed me by letter in the year 1735, that he very much approved of my observation respecting ⲦⲈⲂⲞⲨⲚⲒ, and considered it one to which nothing could be opposed." The musical instrument denoted by that term is similarly described by Jablonski and Villoteau, excepting what the former says of the plectrum. Jablonski ranks the instrument with the *σαμβύκη*, *sambuke* of Suidas, the *τρίγωνον*, *trigonon*, described by Hesychius, and the *πανδούρα*, *pandoura*, mentioned by Martianus Capella, in his work Denuptiis Philolog. et Mercur. ed. Grot. p. 313, where Harmonia is made to say: "Panduram Ægyptios attentare permisi."

All these terms seem to indicate instruments of the same general form and somewhat triangular. Most instruments of the harp kind described by Villoteau, in his Antiquities of Egypt, are of a similar form. From these considerations, *Τεβουνί*, *tĕbouni* is considered as a general term to indicate Egyptian stringed instruments of the harp kind, and particularly those of the triangular form. It is probable that the term had as extensive a signification as the Greek cithara, or perhaps as the Hebrew kinnor. The plectrum, indicating the particular manner of playing on the instrument, does not affect the question. We find in the drawings upon the ruins of Egypt by the savans of Napoleon and others, as we have already intimated, *tebouni* of three kinds or species, in accordance with what Villoteau remarks upon the subject, though it is possible that he may have given a meaning to the term rather too extensive, and we might expect to find other general terms for instruments of music in the ancient Egyptian language.

I. Stringed instruments of the harp kind are far the most numerous in the drawings of the savans, exhibiting a great variety of *forms*, though evidently derived originally from the same pattern. In its most simple form, the harp was a plain unornamented section of a circle, varying more or less in curvature.

Finally it took nearly the form of a triangle, like the modern harp, with the front-piece wanting. It is probable that this was the grand *original* of all stringed instruments, the lyre and guitar, with all their varieties, having originated from it, though some suppose the lyre and others the guitar to have been the most ancient. The strings of the harp number from two or three to more than thirty, which appear to be fastened near the top by pegs in the sides. Sometimes the instrument was so large as to be higher than the head of the performer, and sometimes not more than half or two-thirds as high as an adult. In the drawings of the savans it usually stands nearly in front of the performer, or against the right or left shoulder, and is played with the fingers. A plectrum, according to Villoteau, is nowhere to be found in the ruins of Egypt. In the Antiquities, Planc. Tom. i. pl. 70, No. 2, El Kab, or Elethyia, there is a representation of a musical entertainment in connection with a double flute.

Fig. V.

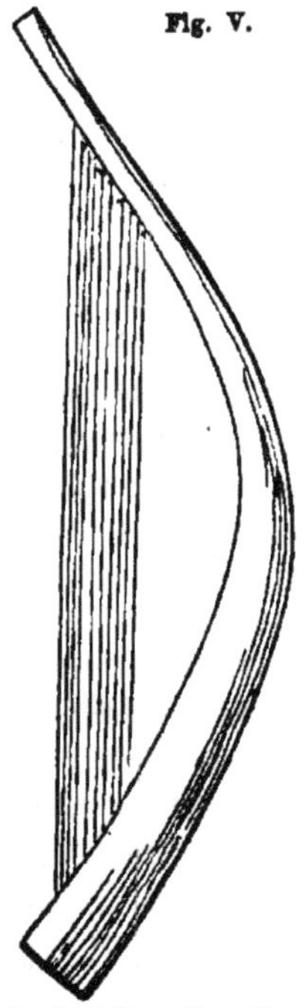

Ancient Egyptian Harp.

Here is a harp, taken from Villoteau, of an oblong, circular form, leaving an elliptical bend in the centre, gradually swelling from the top to the bottom, has ten strings, and no ornaments. It is pretty accurately represented in the accompanying cut (Fig. V), and is played on by a female standing erect, having the harp nearly opposite her

Fig. VI.

Ancient Egyptian Harps.

left shoulder and extending from the ground to some distance above her head. No. 1, of the group Fig. VI. on p. 83 is a similar one.

The following (Fig. VII.) is another, which is somewhat similar, taken from the Anti. Planc. Tom. ii. pl. 44, No. 6, Thebes Hypogées. It is, however, much more highly finished, and represents an instrument of later origin. It is carved, is much larger towards the lower part, and rests on a foot ornamented with a hawk's head. The instrument resembles that usually put into the hands of David excepting that the front piece is wanting. It has twenty-one strings. Some of the instruments are nearly composed of the two sides of a triangle, and sometimes the segment of an ellipse. In both cases the back part is gradually swelled and curved as it descends to form the belly or chest, and the base. It is rather triangular than circular and the performer kneels. Harps resembling the above are found in (1) Ant. Planc. Tom. V. pl. 17, etc. Number 1 contains something like a musical concert. The harp, in that case, is a segment of a circle, all the way of a size, and has six strings. It was taken from the tomb east of the second of the Pyramids of Memphis. The female who is playing kneels. The harp stands on the ground, and leans against her shoulder.

Fig. VII.

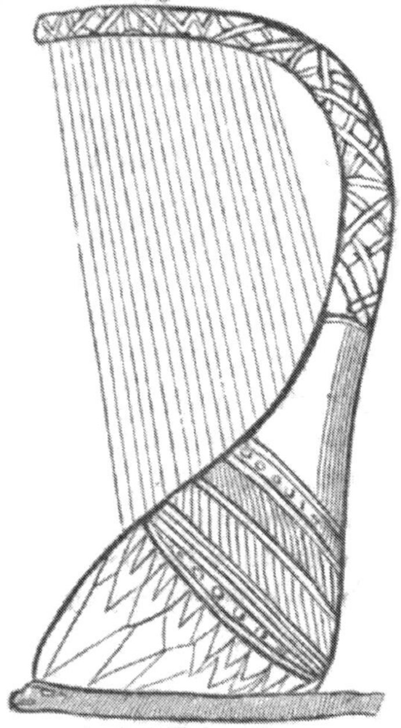

Ancient Theban Harp.

No's 1, 2, 3 and 4 of the group Fig. VI, are similar instruments.

In the fictitious musical concert named above there are three harps. Each is formed of an arc of a circle, has four strings, and is carried with the end in the left hand, supported against the shoulder, and played with the right hand.

The following, (Fig. VIII) is fancifully ornamented, being composed of a serpent with his head at the top, while his tail rests upon a hare with his long ears turned back. The top is ornamented by a human head. A drawing of it is found in Rees' Cyclopedia, also in the Comprehensive Com. under Gen. iv. 21, as well as in Villoteau. It was first taken, with other instruments, by M. St. Non.

Fig. VIII.

Ancient Ornamented Egyptian Harp.

The following (Fig. IX) is found in Villoteau, also in Rees, pl. 3. Fig. 10.

It is semi-circular, stands on a pedestal is played by a female standing erect. It is plain, and has but eight strings. The female's head is ornamented with stocks and flowers of the lotus.

Fig. IX.

Ancient Harp and the manner of performing upon it.

In Fig. X. are represented three similar ones.

Fig. X.

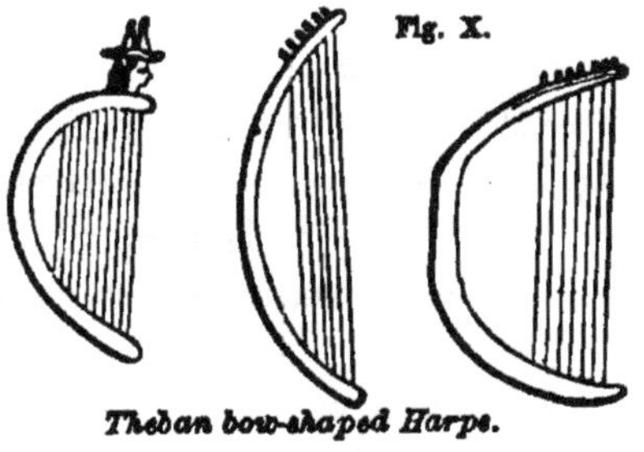

Theban bow-shaped Harps.

There are many other harps presented by Villoteau of essentially the same form, their number of strings varying from three to more than thirty. Some of the most simple are extremely ancient, and probably the most ancient of all stringed instruments. Such are those with three strings, a drawing of one of which (Fig. XI) we will now present from Dr. Jahn's Archæology. It is taken from *Analibus Syriæ*, sports pictured on two coins of the Makkabees. Tab. xviii. Nor. XIX, and of Jahn's V. Kupfertafel Nro. VI.

Fig. XI.

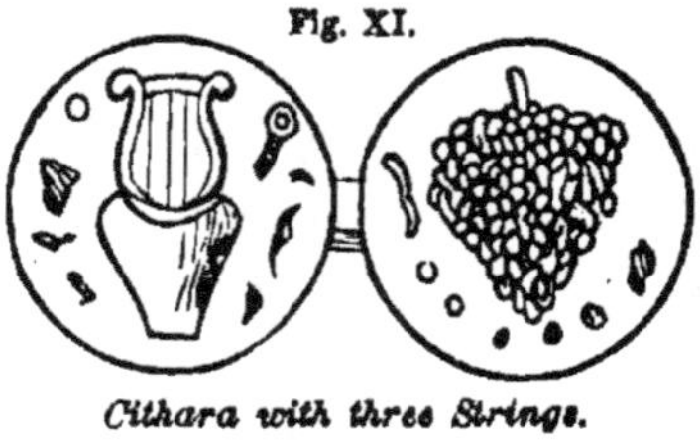

Cithara with three Strings.

The strings are tightened upon a sounding board, which is perhaps oval, as is now the case, with most instruments of this class in the East (Niebuhr Reisel. i. s. 177).

The following (Fig. XII), is another from the same source with eight strings.

Fig. XII.

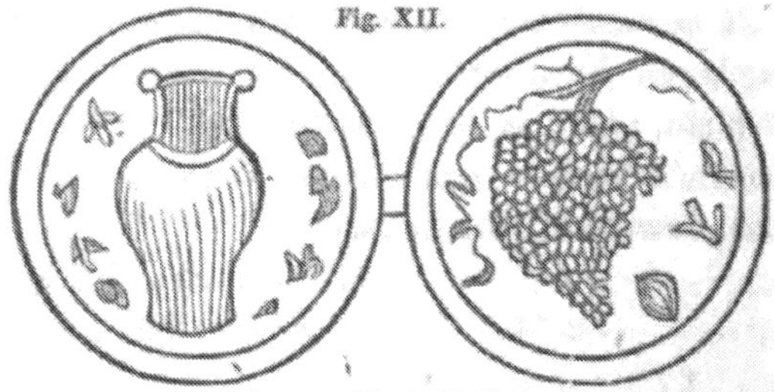

Cithara with eight Strings.

Jahn would have each of these represent the Hebrew *kinnor*, and Greek *cithara*. Figs. XI and XII seem to be quite similar in form to the lyre, and some suppose them to belong to that class of instruments.

Fig. XIII

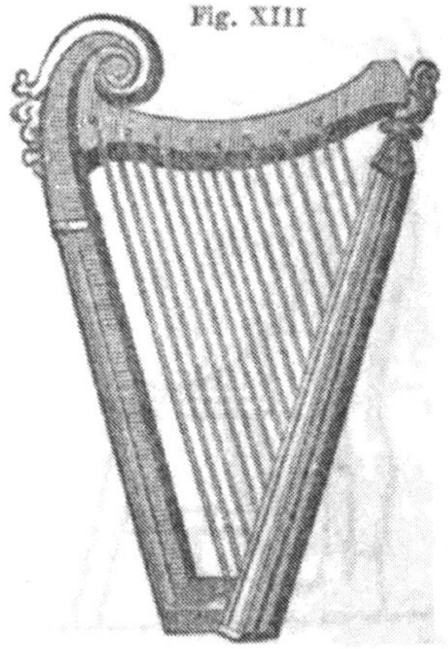

Ancient Harp from the ruins of Herculaneum.

Fig. XIII is a harp with sixteen strings found at Herculaneum, which has laid buried beneath the ruins since A. D. 79.

We will close our illustrations of this class of stringed instruments by presenting the two following grand Egyptian Harps (Fig. XIV) highly ornamented. One has ten and the other twenty-one strings.

II. The *Tebouni*, or stringed instruments of the second class, according to Villoteau, are in the form of the *lyre*. Says he, "we have discovered instruments of this kind in but two places in the temple of Denderah." The first, he informs us, had four strings and the second three, and that they resembled the con-

Fig. XIV.

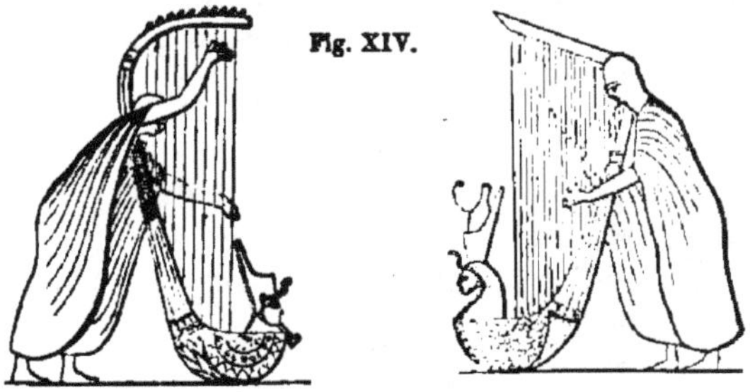

Grand Egyptian Harps.

stellation of the same name. He remarks that it is the instrument which Diodorus Siculus described in his Universal History, and Homer in his hymn to Mercury, and that it is now common in Africa and called *Kussir*.

Diodorus Siculus makes Hermes (one of the councillors of Osiris in Egypt), the inventor of the Lyre, furnishing it with three strings which produce three sounds, the grave, mean and acute, representing the seasons. The grave sound indicated winter, the mean, spring, and the acute, summer. It is a well authenticated fact, that not only the Egyptians, but the ancient Greeks divided their year into no more than three seasons, spring, summer, and winter, which, according to Hesiod, were called *ὥραι*, *horai*, *hours*.

The same instrument is found pictured on maps and globes of the heavens. It has been found copiously sculptured on the monuments of Greece. Passow informs us that it had a deeper sounding board or chest than the cithara, and that, according to Lucian, horns proceeded out of it as out of a goat's skull.

What Villoteau says upon the subject is correct, though not new. Many have testified to the same facts before him. Numerous traditions preserved in fable, indicate that this was one of the earliest instruments of Egypt, though not so much used as in Greece. It is undoubtedly very ancient, and perhaps was invented in Babylon or possibly in India. A very ancient painting at Beni Hassan in Egypt represents the arrival of some foreigners in that country who are supposed to have been Joseph's brethren. The following engraving (Fig. XV) exhibits the variety of costume of the individuals indicated. No. 1 represents a person holding in his hands a lyre with four strings. From the supposed ancient character of the person holding the lyre, some suppose that instrument to have been more ancient than the *harp;* but it is not certain that these individuals *were* Joseph's brethren, nor that they were persons as ancient as they. Again, future discoveries may reveal the fact that the *harp* was as anciently used, and until we have more substantial evidence to the contrary, we incline to the opinion that the harp *was* the most ancient stringed instrument, and that it represents the Hebrew *kinnor*. The five following forms of the lyre are taken from the ruins in Egypt, viz.: No's 1, 2 and 3 of Fig. XVI, and No's 1 and 2 of Fig. XVII.

Fig. XV.

Joseph's Brethren.

III. The third class of *Tebouni* had the form of the *Guitar*. This instrument resembled the Turkish *Tambura*. Niebuhr asserts that it was called by the Greeks at Kahi-

Fig. XVI.

Ancient Egyptian Lyres.

ra (Cairo), *Beglama* and *Tambura*. The first is probably the Grecian, and the last the Arabian general term indicating Grecian stringed instruments.

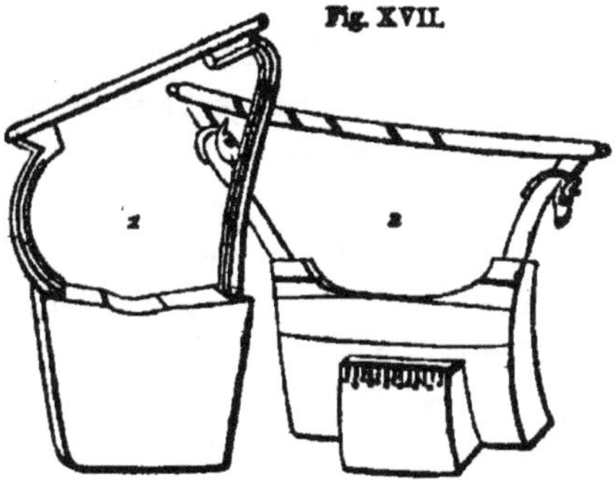

Fig. XVII.

Egyptian Lyres of the Leyden Collection.

Villoteau writes the word *tambour* or *tanbour*, and informs us that it was much more rare and less important than those mentioned above. "We have seen none of them" he remarks, "except in one place." This must have been a very ancient instrument. Burney found it sculptured on a broken pillar. Villoteau gives a specimen of it (Ant. Planc. Tom. ii. pl. 44, Thebes Hypogées No. 6), and describes it as a kind of *mandoline* or *tanbour*, as the instrument is now called in Turkey. It has been frequently seen by travelers sculptured or painted in grottos and other places in Egypt. Belzoni saw it in a mummy-pit which he opened at Gornou. The guitar is now common in Europe and this country, but is evidently of Spanish origin, it being a national instrument in that country, originally derived from the Moors, and through them from the Eastern nations. The Spaniards believe it to be as ancient as the harp or lyre.

Judging from the similarity between the *kussir* or *tambura** and the *harp* and *guitar*, Mr. Taylor supposes the latter to be an improvement upon the lyre in the Egyptian shape, or hand form. Villoteau found hand shaped harps.

The guitar is seldom found sculptured on the monuments of Greece and Rome. It would seem that it has been common there from its close resemblance to the modern *tambura*. The fact that it was not considered as a dignified instrument, may account for its not appearing on the ruins of those proud

*The *tambura* is thought by Niebuhr and Pfeiffer to be the ancient *Nebel*.

cities. The circumstance that the instrument was small and had but few strings, would indicate that it was not much used, as the Grecians and Romans did not appreciate the means it furnished of diminishing the number of strings. It was, undoubtedly, one of the most ancient musical instruments of Egypt.

We here present in No. 1, of Fig. XVIII, a specimen of an Egyptian guitar; in No. 2, an ancient lute, and in No. 3, an Arabian *tanbur*. Numbers 1, 2 and 3 of Fig. XIX, represent Egyptian instruments of the lute class. Numbers 1, 2 and 3 of Fig. XX, represent Egyptian stringed instruments of the guitar class with necks.*

Fig. XVIII.

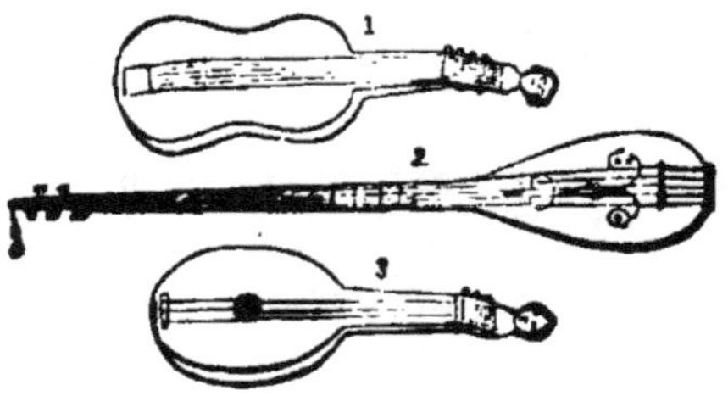

Ancient Guitar, Lute and Arabian Tanbur.

The three classes of stringed instruments which we have briefly considered, were certainly very ancient. In the earliest ages of Egypt, instruments having the same general form as the harp, lyre and guitar of modern times, were common, as the discoveries by various travelers in that country have clearly proved. The ancients had many other stringed instruments, but these three classes were the principal and contain the grand characteristics of the several classes at the head of which they stand. Having

Fig. XIX.

Egyptian Lutes with Necks.

* It will be noticed that, in the groups of musical instruments which we have presented, we have, in several cases, followed the arrangement of Dr. Kitto, in his Cyclopædia of Biblical Literature.

made these general remarks, we will now return to the particular consideration of the Hebrew term כִּנּוֹר *kinnor* (vid. p. 68, *supra*). The usual Greek word for this instrument is *κινυρα*, *kinura*, or *κιννυρα*, *kinnura*. In the Septuagint *ψαλτήριον*, *psalterion*, *psaltery*, is used and in Gen. xxxi. 27, the LXX have employed *κιθάρας*, *kitharas*, *cithara* for the same Hebrew term, indicating that they did not understand accurately what the Hebrew *kinnor* was, although it is very probable that they were native Egyptians who understood the Hebrew and Greek languages (vid. Horne's Introd. P. i. c. iii. Sect. iii. § 2. 2—vol. i. p. 265). Possibly they did not know what kind of an instrument it was, but believed it to be one with strings and accordingly represented it sometimes by a term signifying one kind of a Greek stringed instrument and sometimes by another. What is more probable is, that, in ancient times, and even at the time when the Septuagint translation was made, there was not much difference in this class of instruments. They resembled each other in their general characteristics, and the LXX perhaps thought that *ψαλτηριον*, *psalterion*, *psaltery*, and *κιθάρα*, *kithara*, *cithara* would both very well represent the general characteristics of the Hebrew *kinnor*. Dr. Jahn supposes that the term is properly represented by the Greek *cithara* (vid. p. 86, *supra*, where cuts of two citharas are given), and that the Hebrew *kinnor* and Chaldee קִיתָרוֹס *qaythros* have nearly the same signification. From *qaythros* was probably derived the Greek *κιθάρα*, *kithara*, *cithara*. This last word, or *κινυρα*, *kinura*, would best represent *kinnor*, although there was a difference between those two Greek

Fig. XX.

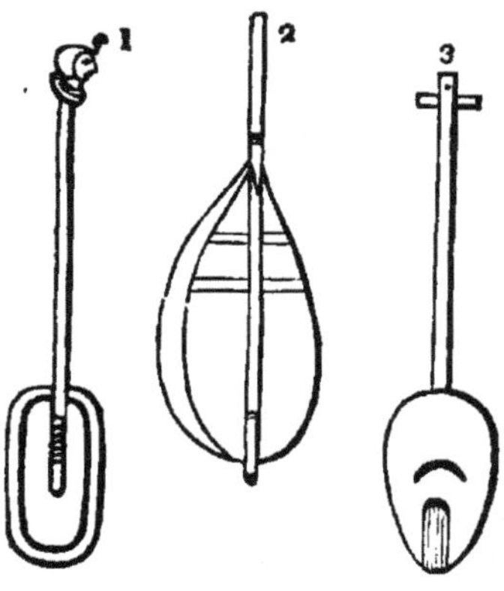

Ancient Egyptian Guitars.

instruments. Strabo (p. 471) affirms that *cithara* is an Asiatic term, and differs from *kinura*. The former was undoubtedly derived from the Chaldee language, and *kinura* from the Hebrew *kinnor*. The *cithara*, or harp with three strings, may be considered as near an approximation to the Hebrew *kinnor* as we can attain with our present knowledge. It is a species of *harp*. Horne considers it as a harp, somewhat similar to the modern instrument by that name.

We are not to suppose that every Hebrew or Greek name of a musical instrument indicated one essentially different from others of the same class, but often, merely the same instrument a little varied. There were classes and then individuals under them, differing very little from each other. With us the *flute* is at the head of a class of instruments differing in a small degree from each other, as the German, English, octave flute, flageolette, etc. Of the *viol* kind, we have the violin, violoncello, viola da gamba, guitar, etc. So we suppose *kinnor* in Hebrew to have been a general term, and that many instruments differing a little from each other were probably included under it. The Grecian *cithara*, in like manner had an extensive signification. The harp, answering to the Hebrew *kinnor* was doubtless the instrument on which David performed so skilfully.

In the passage (Gen. iv. 21) under consideration, we find the term translated *Organ* (Heb. עוּגָב *ugabh*). It is derived from the verb עָגַב *ugabh*, *to blow*, clearly indicating that it represented a wind instrument. The simplest form of this class of instruments was, doubtless, a reed, forming a rude fife or flute. Subsequently it was made of other materials.

Flutes and pipes are found among all nations, even the most uncivilized. The New Zealanders and inhabitants of other South Sea Islands had them when first discovered.

The pipe of Pan, or Hebrew *ugabh*, here presented, perhaps, originally consisted of one and subsequently several pipes joined together as in the accompanying engraving (Fig XXI).

The Alexandrine translators represent the term *ugabh* by *κιθάραν*, *kitharan*, *cithara*, as though it were a stringed instrument; but they must have been mistaken, as the origin of the word shows. Jerome rendered it by *organon*, *organ*, a double or manifold pipe, an instrument consisting of many pipes. Horne affirms that it cannot have been like our modern organ. He supposes it to have been a kind of flute, at first composed of one or two and afterwards of about seven pipes, made of reeds of unequal length and thickness, which were joined together.

Fig. XXI.

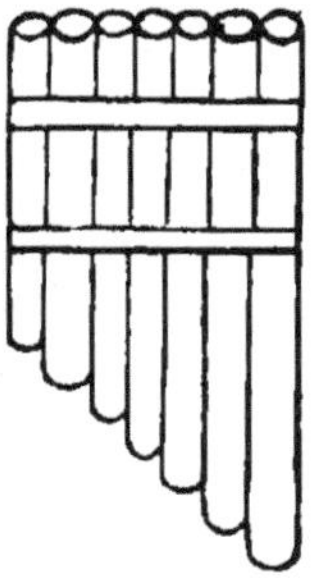

Pipe of Pan, or Hebrew Ugabh.

It most nearly corresponds, he thinks, with the *σύριγξ*, *syrinx*, or pipe of Pan among the Greeks. Dr. Jahn also supposes that it was this instrument which the ancients represent as of very high antiquity. Niebuhr saw it in the hands of a Boor at Cairo (Reiseb. i. 181). Kampfer found it in common use among the shepherds in Persia. It is still a pastoral instrument in Syria (vid. Alex. Russell's Nat. Hist. of Alleppo). It is so ancient that the early writers knew not the inventor of it. Virgil (Ecl. ii) ascribed it to Pan; Pindar (Od. xii. de Pallade) to Mercury; Athenæus (iv. 182) to Marsyas and Silenus. It must be considered as among the most ancient Oriental instruments. Russell in his Nat. Hist. of Alleppo (i. 155, 156) informs us that "the higher notes are clear and pleasing, but that the longer reeds are apt, like the dervise flute, to make a hissing sound, though blown by a good player. The number of reeds in the *syrinx* varies in different instruments from five to twenty-three.

The following, No's 1 and 2, Fig. XXII, are two other forms of this instrument approaching to the shape of the organ. In No. 1, the pipes are of different size, usually fixed in a box, open at the top and closed at the bottom by wood covered with skin. Wind is conveyed into the box from the lips of the performer, through a tube fitted into it. The pipes vary in length, and by stopping or unstopping them at the top, the melody is varied

Fig. XXII.

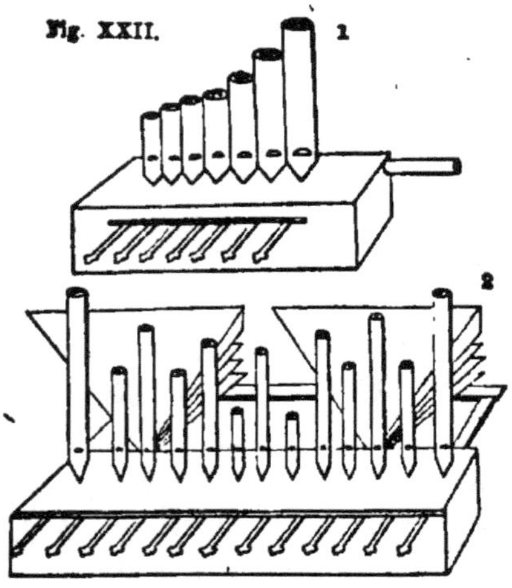

Ancient Organ.

as desired. No. 2 is a modification of No. 1. These forms bear a high antiquity though it is not absolutely certain that they were known to the ancient Hebrews.

We are then to regard Jubal as the inventor of stringed and wind instruments. All stringed instruments, probably, originated from the *kinnor, harp*, and all wind instruments from the *ugabh, organ*, which Jubal invented.

Genesis, xxix. 34.

And she conceived again, and bare a son; and said, Now this time will my husband be joined unto me, because I have borne him three sons: therefore was his name called Levi.

We have inserted this passage in order to make some remarks upon the term *Levi*, which refers to a class of persons who were engaged in the music of the temple service.

לֵוִי *Levi, Levi*, is derived from the verb לָוָה *lava to join*, which has no reference to music. Levi was the third son of Jacob by Leah (Gen. xxix. 34; xxxiv. 25; xxxv. 23), and stood at the head of the tribe bearing his name. The Levites were solemnly set apart to conduct the services of the temple at Jerusalem. Some were employed as singers and accustomed to stand in the courts of the temple, rendering thanksgiving and praise to God every morning and evening (1 Chron. xxiii. 30). In the time of David four thousand were engaged in this service and some performed upon instruments of music (1 Chron. xxiii. 5). Asaph, Heman and Jeduthun were the grand-masters of song in the tabernacle under David, and in the temple under Solomon. Asaph had four sons, Jeduthun six and Heman fourteen, making in all twenty-four. These were at the head of twenty-four bands of musicians, who served in the temple by turns. The number of performers on all occasions was large and especially at the chief solemnities. Their position was around the altar of burnt sacrifice, the family of Gershon standing on the right, that of Merari on the left and that of Kohath between the other two. The whole business of their lives was to learn and practice music and they were required to be good vocal or instrumental performers. Asaph was the chief master of music under David. During the performance of religious exercises in the temple, *female*, as well as male singers, were allowed to aid in the music. It will not be necessary to insert the numerous passages in which there are references to the Levites, unless some circumstance, worthy of remark, is named in connection with them.

Genesis, xxxi. 27.

Wherefore didst thou flee away secretly, and steal away from me; and didst not tell me, that I might have sent thee away with mirth, and with songs, with tabret, and with harp?

These are the words of Laban, the Syrian, who pursued Jacob as he fled from him with his wives, who were Laban's daughters. It appears that the Syrian had improperly detained Jacob in his service and the latter, feeling, under the circumstances, that his determination was justifiable, left his employer with his wives and property. Laban was highly displeased and pursued the fugitives in a rage. But being warned of God in a dream, not to lay his hand upon them, he merely reproved Jacob and expressed his regret that he did not know the time of his departure, that he might have escorted him and his companions with a band of musicians. As it was the custom for the bridegroom, attended by the nuptial guests, to conduct the bride to his house at night, accompanied by her virgin train of attendants with torches and music, so Laban wished to have it understood that he desired to make such a demonstration at Jacob's departure.

Mirth. Heb. שִׂמְחָה *simhhah*, from the verb שָׂמַח *samahh*, *to rejoice*. This term here means simply, *joy*, *rejoicing*. The Hebrews used it to express *joy*, especially on important occasions (vid. Neh. xii. 43; II Chron. xxiii. 18). The term employed by the Alexandrine translators is *εὐφροσύνης*, *euphrosunes*, and was used particularly by the Greeks to indicate *joy on public occasions*.

Songs. Heb. שִׁירִים *shïrïm*. This is a general term, signifying *music* or *song*. It is expressed in the Septuagint by the general terms *μουσικῶν mousikōn*.

Tabret. תֹּף *toph*. This is one of the third class or *percussion* kind of *instruments*. These, according to T. H. Horne, were three, viz.: the *Tabret*, *Cymbal* and *Sistrum*. Dr. Jahn supposes that there were four kinds, viz.: the Tabret, Castanet, Sistrum and an instrument in the form of a triangle, which he could not accurately describe, found in the Hebrew term שָׁלִישִׁים *shalïshïm*. Villoteau found sistra, tambourines and cymbals. The Hebrews often employed *toph* to indicate *all kinds* of drums and percussion instruments. It was also frequently used to designate one particular instrument of the percussion kind. Gesenius informs us, that it consisted of a thin wooden rim covered with membrane and hung around with brass bells or rattles. It was, probably, held in the left hand and beaten to notes of music with the right, accompanied, generally, with dancing. It is common at the present day in the East and in Spain, where it is called *adduff.* Jahn asserts that it is not our kettle-drum, as the word is generally rendered, but a wooden or metal ring, a little wider than a hand-ring, with a hide drawn over it and usually having thin, round metallic plates, rings or bells hung on the edges. *Now*, as in ancient times, the performers upon this instrument are females, who dance and keep time with the music. Kampfer remarks that the tabret when set with rings, is called, in Persia, *Daireb.* This is, probably, the same instrument which is called in Barbary, *Carr* (vid. Amoen. Exot. p. 740. sq). It has been found engraved upon ancient monuments and on precious stones, in the hands of Bachanals and the Cybils and their priests. It was not used in war, but at festivals and public rejoicings. The LXX represented this instrument by *τυμπάνων, tumpanōn, tympanum.* The terms, tabret, tabor, timbrel and tambourine indicate the same, or nearly the same instrument. The Mœnades, a rude tribe, inhabiting the Thracian mountains, in their bachanalian songs, make use of kettle drums and tambourines. The Arabians call this instrument *deff*, and it was, probably, carried into Spain by the Moors. During the middle ages it was in use and called *tambour* or *cloquette.* It appeared in almost every concert throughout the East. The larger tambourine is called *tambour de basque*, from the fact that it is used in Biscay, to accompany all of the national songs and dances. It appears from Gen. xxxi. 27, that the Hebrews were acquainted with the tabret before they left Syria, and it is the first instrument mentioned after their exode from Egypt (Ex. xv. 20). It seems to have been a favorite instrument both on sacred and joyful occasions. There were three kinds, varying in form and, probably, in sound. One kind was round, another square or oblong and the third consisted of two squares with a bar separating them.

The following are some of the pulsatile instruments of the ancient Egyptians, undoubtedly representing those of the Hebrews.

Fig. XXIII.

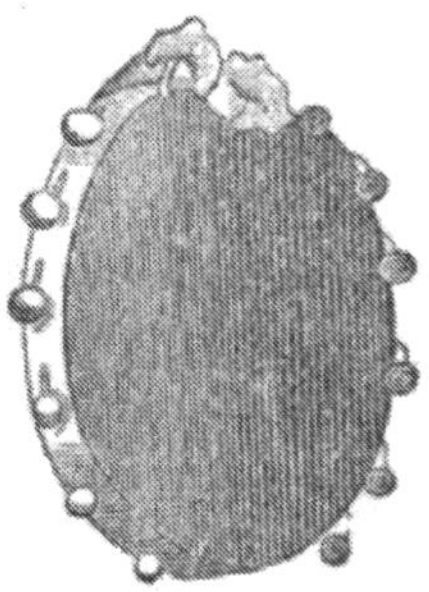

Ancient Toph or Tabret from the ruins of Herculaneum.

This is an imperfect specimen taken from the ruins of Herculaneum. It was carried in the hand aud beaten with the fingers. The bells are an appendage and perhaps, constituted a *tabret* or *timbrel.*

The following (Fig. XXIV) represents two ancient Egyptian tambourines. No. 1, is of an angular form, and No. 2, of a circular form.

We present on p. 99, five forms of ancient Egyptian Sistra (Fig. XXV). They are found in Kitto's Encyclopædia of Biblical Literature, vol. ii. p. 380, and other works.

The four in Fig. XXVI, are other forms of Egyptian Sistra.

In Fig. XXVII, we have different forms of pulsatile instruments. No. 1 represents castanets, or smaller Egyptian cymbals, placed upon the fingers of each hand and struck together. No. 2 represents a tabret-drum struck by balls suspended from it. No. 3 a kettle drum, and No. 4 two forms of drums upon a supposed ancient Hebrew coin.

Fig. XXIV.

Two Ancient Egyptian Tambourines.

In Fig. XXVIII, there are three forms of ancient Egyptian drums.

In Fig. XXIX, there are three modern Oriental drums and one from the ruins of ancient Egypt. No. 5 represents the sticks for No. 3.

Some other forms of percussion instruments will be given, as we proceed in the examination of Hebrew musical terms.

Fig. XXV.

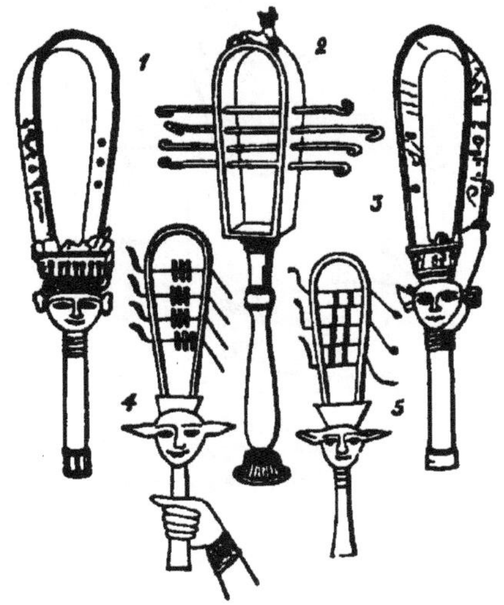

Ancient Sistra of various forms.

Fig. XXVI.

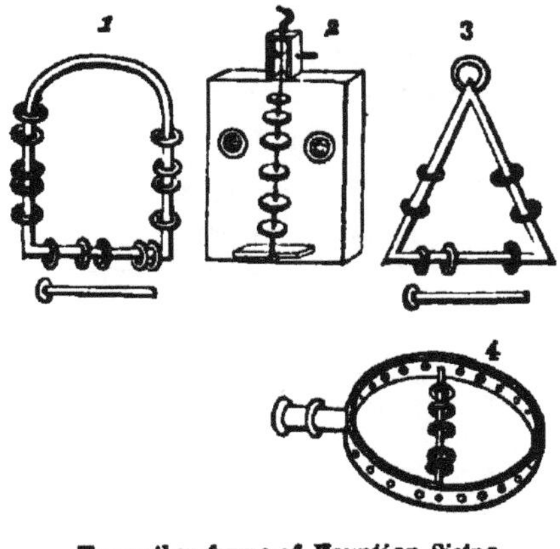

Four other forms of Egyptian Sistra.

Fig. XXVII.

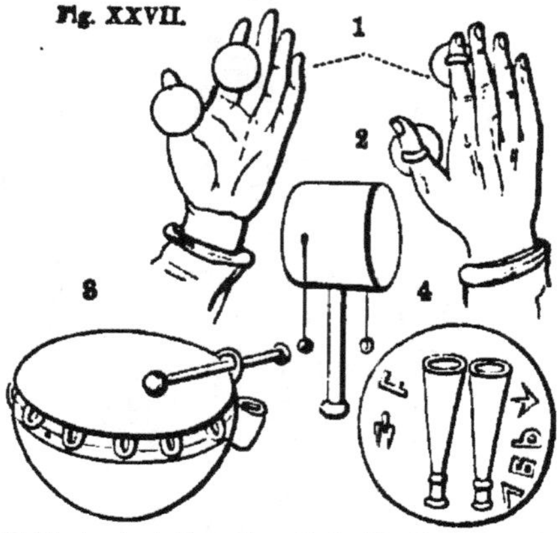

Eight Ancient Egyptian Pulsatile Instruments.

Fig. XXVIII.

Three forms of Ancient Egyptian Drums.

Fig. XXIX.

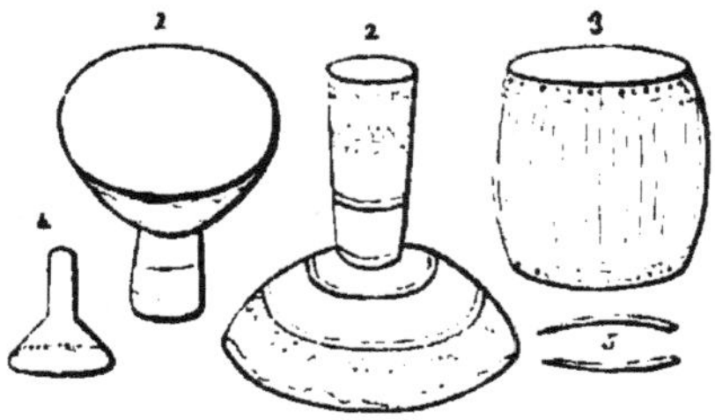

One Ancient Egyptian and three Modern Oriental Drums.

EXODUS, OR THE SECOND BOOK OF MOSES.

INTRODUCTORY REMARKS.

THE name of this book, adopted from the Septuagint, indicates the principal transaction recorded in its pages, viz.: the departure of the Israelites from their captivity in Egypt. Exodus contains a history of the events which occurred during the space of 145 years from 1635 to 1490 B. C., or from the death of Joseph to the erection of the Tabernacle. It was undoubtedly composed by Moses, and probably soon after he wrote the book of Genesis. It must have been after the giving of the law on Sinai and the erection of the Tabernacle as they are described in its pages. It was probably designed not only to chronicle the departure of the Israelites from Egyptian bondage, but the wonderful preservation of the Church of God from destruction, though passing through the deepest afflictions and persecutions. The book records the intense sufferings of the Jews in Egypt, under Pharaoh Rameses II—the birth, exposure and preservation of Moses—his subsequent flight into Midian, his call and admission to Pharaoh Amenophis II—the miracles performed by him and Aaron—the ten plagues inflicted upon the Egyptians by the divine displeasure—the institution of the Passover—the miraculous passage of the Israelites through the Red Sea, and the destruction of their enemies—their journeyings in the wilderness—their idolatry and murmurings against God—the promulgation of the law on Sinai and the erection of the tabernacle.

There are several allusions to music in this book, which we shall proceed to consider.

Exodus, xv. 1–18.

Then sang Moses and the children of Israel this song unto the Lord, and spake, saying,

I will sing unto the Lord, for he hath triumphed gloriously:
The horse and his rider hath he thrown into the sea.
2 The Lord is my strength and song,
And he is become my salvation:
He is my God, and I will prepare him an habitation;
My father's God, and I will exalt him.
3 The Lord is a man of war:
The Lord is his name.
4 Pharaoh's chariots and his host hath he cast into the sea:
His chosen captains also are drowned in the Red Sea.
5 The depths have covered them:
They sank into the bottom as a stone.
6 Thy right hand, O Lord, is become glorious in power:
Thy right hand, O Lord, hath dashed in pieces the enemy.
7 And in the greatness of thine excellency
Thou hast overthrown them that rose up against thee:
Thou sentest forth thy wrath,
Which consumed them as stubble.
8 And with the blast of thy nostrils
The waters were gathered together,
The floods stood upright as an heap,
And the depths were congealed in the heart of the sea.
9 The enemy said, I will pursue, I will overtake,
I will divide the spoil;
My lust shall be satisfied upon them;
I will draw my sword,
My hand shall destroy them.

10 Thou didst blow with thy wind,
The sea covered them:
They sank as lead in the mighty waters.
11 Who is like unto thee, O Lord, among the gods?
Who is like thee, glorious in holiness,
Fearful in praises, doing wonders?
12 Thou stretchedst out thy right hand,
The earth swallowed them.
13 Thou in thy mercy hast led forth the people
Which thou hast redeemed:
Thou hast guided them in thy strength
Unto thy holy habitation.
14 The people shall hear, and be afraid:
Sorrow shall take hold on the inhabitants of Palestina.
15 Then the dukes of Edom shall be amazed;
The mighty men of Moab, trembling shall take hold upon them;
All the inhabitants of Canaan shall melt away.
16 Fear and dread shall fall upon them;
By the greatness of thine arm they shall be as still as a stone;
Till thy people pass over, O Lord, till the people pass over, which thou hast purchased.
17 Thou shalt bring them in,
And plant them in the mountain of thine inheritance,
In the place, O Lord, which thou hast made for thee to dwell in,
In the Sanctuary, O Lord, which thy hands have established.
18 The Lord shall reign for ever and ever!

This is a song of Moses and the Israelites in view of their miraculous passage through the Red Sea, and deliverance from their enemies, while the latter were overwhelmed by the returning waters. Bishop Lowth informs us that the Hebrews were accustomed to sing or chant their sacred hymns, accompanied by instrumental music, while answering choirs alternately uttered their songs of praise. Sometimes one choir performed the hymn while the other sung a particular distich, regularly interposed at stated intervals. The responsive method was undoubtedly employed on this joyful occasion (Exod. xv. 20, 21). Moses and the male Israelites sung one part while Miriam and the other female performers uttered the answering strains of this lyric poem. (For a description of Heb. poetry vid. p. 232 *infra.*)

Verse 1.—*Sang.* In the Hebrew the general term is used signifying *to sing* (vid. Remarks on Gen. xxxi. 27. *supra*).

Song.—The noun is here used having the same derivation as *sang*, above. The verb of the same signification is employed in the original of the expression "*I will sing*," in the same verse.

V. 2.—*Song.* The original term זִמְרָת *zimrath* signifies *song*, though that is not the most usual expression. It is derived from זָמַר *zamar*, *to prune.* In the Peal conjugation it signifies *to cut off discourse at regular periods, to utter in rhythmical numbers, to sing.* In the Syriac and Arabic it has the same signification. The LXX translate it by σκεπαστης, *skepastes*, meaning *protector.* This signification, of course, has no allusion to music, and we cannot perceive how it could be derived from the Hebrew term.

Exodus, xv. 20.

And Miriam the prophetess, the sister of Aaron, took a timbrel in her hand; and all the women went out after her with timbrels and dances.

Timbrel.—Heb. תֹּף *toph.* This is the same term as that used in Gen. xxxi. 27, and probably indicates the same *instrument*, viz.: the *timbrel, tabret or tambourine.* The LXX also employ the same word, as they do in Gen. xxxi. 27. This was about 250 years after the time when Jacob left Laban, and it is probable that the tabret was, essentially, the same at both periods (for a description of this instrument, vid. Rem. on Gen. xxvi. 27. *supra*).

Timbrels.—The plural form of *toph* is here used in the original. There may have been several kinds of *tophs.* At least the term seems often to have been used in a very general sense. It is supposed by some as we have already intimated, that *toph* included all of the percussion instruments of the Hebrews.

Dances.—The disposition to make use of rhythm or measured language and motion, is deeply implanted in human nature. As far back into antiquity as history extends, it reveals to us the fact that even the rudest nations have expressed their feelings, when elevated, by measured movements or the dance. This exercise was practised, in early times, as a religious ceremony, and as we pass, we shall take notice of allusions to it by the sacred writers. As the people advanced in civilization and refinement, and restrained the full expression of their emotions, dancing was cultivated as an elegant amusement, though often leading the unwary into scenes of vice. The mild, calm and chastened character of the Christian religion soon excluded this exercise from its sacred services. Among the Jews, dancing was generally an accompaniment to music. It was common at their feasts, public triumphs and during all seasons of mirth and rejoicing. At the present day, in the East, girls exhibit voluptuous performances in dancing.* In our own country among a sect, called *Shakers,* this exercise constitutes a part of their religious services.

In the passage under consideration, the dancing mentioned, was, undoubtedly, considered by the Hebrews as an important part of the celebration of their victory and as a fit accompaniment of their triumphant song of praise to God.

The Hebrew word for *dancing* is מְחֹלֹת *m^ehhōlōth,* derived from חוּל *hhul* or חִיל *hhïl,* signifying literally *to turn, to*

*Vid. Carnes' Letters from the East p. 165. Pareau; Antiq. Heb. p. 481.

twist, to turn around. The Arabic word is حَالَ *hhala to be turned.* The Septuagint designates it by χορῶν, *chŏrōn*, often signifying *a dance accompanied by singing.*

It is probable that the Hebrews were not very precise or accomplished in their movements. They had a higher object than celerity and gracefulness in the exercise and especially after their victory over the Egyptians at the Red Sea, for their vocal and instrumental music and dancing on that occasion were all employed as an expression of their gratitude to God in view of their miraculous deliverance from their enemies.

Exodus, xv. 21.

And Miriam answered them:

Sing ye to the Lord for he hath triumphed gloriously;
The horse and his rider hath he thrown into the sea.

Miriam answered them. It seems from this that a part of the performers had been singing, but had now ceased, and Miriam with the female Israelites uttered the answering strains in beautiful lyric poetry (vid. Remarks on Ex. xv. 1. 18, *supra*).

Sing.—The general term is here used in the original (vid. Remarks on Gen. xxxi. 27).

Exodus, xix. 13.

There shall not an hand touch it, but he shall surely be stoned, or shot through; whether *it be* beast or man, it shall not live: when the trumpet soundeth long, they shall come up to the mount.

The inspired writer is here narrating the circumstances of

an august scene, viz.: the giving of the law on Mount Sinai. Jehovah, through his servant Moses, commanded the Israelites to sanctify themselves and be prepared for the great event which was to transpire at the end of three days, when the Divine power and goodness would be manifested. Moses was directed to set bounds, beyond which none could pass, and to inform his people that whoever should touch the Mount, would be instantly destroyed. When all things should be ready, a *long* blast of the trumpet was to be the signal for the people to approach the Mount and hear the message of Jehovah.

Trumpet.—Here is an instrument not before mentioned by the inspired writers. Its use in this instance was about 250 years after that of the timbrel mentioned in Gen. xxxi. 27, and about 2353 years after the use of the harp and organ mentioned in Gen. iv. 21. From the Scriptures we learn that the harp and organ were played about 1495 years before the deluge, the timbrel about 610, and the horn 851 years *after* that catastrophe.

The Hebrew word here translated *trumpet*, is יֹבֵל *yōbhe̱l*, generally יוֹבֵל *yōbhe̱l*, signifying a *joyful shout*, the *clangor of trumpets*, *trumpet-signal*, *alarm*. The Chaldee paraphrasts and rabbins supposed that it signified *a ram*, and that קֶרֶן הַיּוֹבֵל, *qérĕn hayyobhe̱l* signified *a ram's-horn;* but this is a mere conjecture. Rabbi Levi and Akiba assert that it has the same meaning in Arabic; but this must be a mistake, as such a definition does not appear in Arabic lexicons (vid. Bocharti Hieroz. p. i. lib. ii. c. 43). קֶרֶן *qe̱rĕn*, *horn*, generally precedes, יוֹבֵל *yōbhe̱l* or הַיֹּבֵל, *hayyobhe̱l*, though here it does not. When used together, the two words signify *horn of jubilee*, *horn of alarm*, i. e., a horn with which a signal or alarm is sounded. Sometimes it is written, as, probably in this case, elliptically, קֶרֶן, *qérĕn*, *horn*, being implied. *Yōbhe̱l*, then, signifies here, *jubilee* or *jubel horn*. Jahn supposes that קֶרֶן, *qe̱rĕn* was one of the most ancient instruments of music and was originally nothing more than the horn of an ox with an opening made in the top. Subsequently, a ram's horn was made hollow and used for a wind instrument, and finally, the *qe̱ren* was made of brass.* The same learned author thinks it not unlikely that Jubal invented this instrument. He may have first used the horn; but it is probable that the jubilee horn received its name from the fact that it was used to proclaim the commencement of the jubilee among the Jews (vid. Lev. xxxv. 9, 10). It was also employed to announce the beginning of the civil and sabbatical year (Lev. xxiii. 24; Num. xxix. 1); but as the jubilee was the most important event, it doubtless gave its name to the instrument. Being subsequently improved, it was probably called by different names. Josephus informs us that the tube or pipe of the trumpet was of the thickness of the common flute. The mouth was barely wide enough to admit the breath of the performer, and the end bell-shaped like that of the modern trumpet (Joseph. Ant. iii. xii. 6). The instrument had then become much improved. At first, the Israelites had but two in the camp, though subsequently they had more. In Joshua's time, there were at least seven (vid. Josh. vi. 4), and at the dedication of Solomon's temple 120 priests sounded with trumpets (II Chron. v. 12). The Hebrew generals also used them in war. Originally, they were horns or crooked trumpets, and subsequently, straight tubes like those described by Josephus, to which reference is made above. Of this latter kind, probably, were those mentioned in Num. x. 8, 10; I Chron. xv. 24; II Chron. vii. 6 and xxix. 26. In time of peace when the rulers or people were to be called together, these trumpets were blown softly; but when the camps were to move forward, or the people to rush to battle, they were sounded with a deeper tone. Moses caused two silver trumpets to be made for the priests; but in the time of David, these and other musical instruments were much more numerous, ornamented and varied in form. T. H. Horne maintains that the horn and trumpet were two distinct instruments. When made of a cow's or ram's horn, he calls it *horn* or *crooked trumpet*, and when straight, and perhaps made of

* Cf. Varro de lingua Lat. IV. p. 85, where he says, "Cornua, quod ea, quæ nunc sunt exære, tunc fiebant ex bubulo cornu."

other materials, he calls it ***trumpet*** or ***straight trumpet.*** This distinction is perhaps proper, as the ***horn*** or ***crooked trumpet*** is much more ancient than the ***straight*** one. That mentioned in Ex. xix. 13, was doubtless a *crooked* one, made, perhaps, of the horn of an ox.

Fig. XXX.

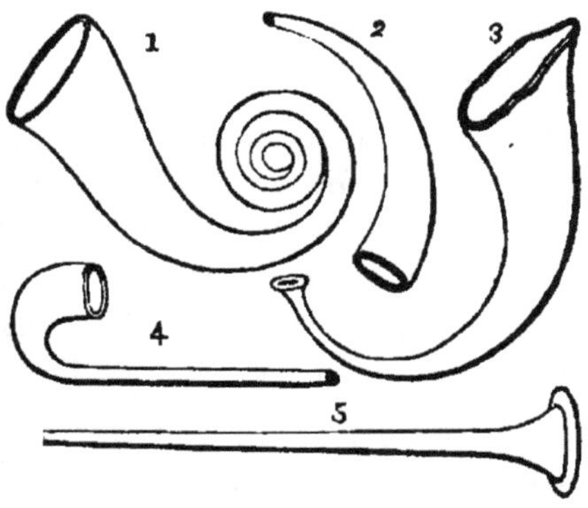

Four forms of the ancient Hebrew Shophar or crooked Trumpet, and one straight Trumpet.

We here present some specimens of the ancient trumpet. The following (Fig. XXX) represents four (Nos. 1, 2, 3 and 4) crooked trumpets, and one straight one. *Soundeth long* (Ex. xix. 13). The occasion was a very solemn one, and the trumpet was sounded longer and louder than usual in time of peace. The LXX employ the term σαλπιγγες, *salpinges, trumpets.* The word מְשֹׁךְ, *m^eshŏk, soundeth* is from מָשַׁךְ, *mashák, to seize, to draw* (Arabic مسك *masaka*), *to draw the trumpet,* i. e. *to sound it.*

Exodus, xix. 16.

And it came to pass on the third day in the morning, that there were thunders and lightnings, and a thick cloud upon the mount, and the voice of the trumpet exceeding loud; so that all the people that was in the camp trembled.

This is a striking instance of the effect which the sound of the trumpet sometimes produced on the minds of the Israelites. At this time, the effect was much greater than usual in consequence of the solemn circumstances under which the blast was made; but the sound of the trumpet always produced a thrilling effect upon the mind of an Israelite, as it was a sacred instrument and only blown on important occasions. They *trembled* in their camps.

Trumpet. שֹׁפָר, *shōphar*, usually שׁוֹפָר, *shōphar*, *a trumpet*, *a horn*. Jerome remarks on Hos. v. 8; "Buccina pastoralis est et cornu recurso efficitur, unde et proprie Hebraice *sophar* Græce *κερατίνη* appellatur." "The pastoral trumpet is made of a crooked horn, hence it is properly called in Hebrew *shophar* and in Greek *κερατίνη*, *keratinē*," signifying *made of horn*. The *shophar* was, doubtless, the same instrument as the יוֹבֵל, *yobhel*, the *jubilee horn* or *crooked trumpet*. Gesenius remarks, that there seems to have been no difference between קֶרֶן הַיֹּבֵל, *qerĕn hayyobhel* and שׁוֹפַר הַיֹּבֵל, *shophar hayyobhel*, both designating the *horn* or *crooked trumpet*. It is evident that the instrument was made of horn or in the shape of a horn, as it is frequently interchanged with קֶרֶן, *qerĕn*, *horn* (vid. Josh. vi. 5; cf. verses 4, 6, 8 and 13 of same chap.; also, Job, xxxix. 25). The Septuagint has *σάλπιγγος*, *salpingos*, *trumpet*, the same word which is used for יֹבֵל, *yobhel* (vid. Remarks on Ex. xix. 13 *supra*). Dr. Jahn thinks that the *shophar* was very similar, if not the same instrument as the *qerĕn*, since both words are often exchanged with each other, and both instruments were used in war. It is now customary in crusades to blow horns. The ancient Thracians used these instruments to give necessary signals in war, and the Persian armies blew upon the same as a signal to march (vid. Exped. Cyr. viii. 4. 15; Cyr. v. 3; xix. 19). Aquila, Symmachus and the Alexandrine translators often render the word by *κερατινη*, *keratinē* (from *κερας*, *keras*, *a horn*). Josephus asserts that the instruments blown by Gideon's warriors were *shophars*. In course of time, they were made of metal. The horn is now retained among the Persians. Those used by the Hebrews must have been more like the crooked *lituus* (employed in war) than the straight *tuba* of the Romans. The Greek *σαλπιγξ*, *salpinx*, by which the Alexandrine translators often represent the *shophar* and *hatsotsera* (vid. Rem. on Num. x. 2, *infra*), had six different forms, and it would, perhaps, have been better if they had expressed the former by *salpinx*, meaning the Egyptian *salpinx*, which the Greeks usually call *χνουη*, *chnouē*. The Egyptians, and, subsequently, the Hebrews, were called together by this instrument (which was evidently the crooked trumpet), for sacrifices and other purposes. The LXX translate *qeren* by *salpinx* (vid. Josh. vi. 4, verse 5 in our translation). The former, however, and the *shophar*, were not only used in war, but also on joyful occasions (vid. II Sam. vi. 15; I Sam. xiii. 3; Judges, iii. 27; Isa. xviii. 3; Jer. iv. 5; Ez. xxx. 6). The sound of the trumpet, and especially of the horn, was, at least, in the minds of the people, solemn and awful, like heavy thunder (vid. Matt. xxiv. 31; I Cor. xv. 52; Heb. xii. 19; cf. Ex. xix. 16, 19; xx. 18; Ps. xlvii. 5; Isa. xxvii. 13; Zech. ix. 14; Rev. i. 10; iv. 1; viii. 2, 6, 13; ix. 14).

Exodus, xix. 19.

And when the voice of the trumpet sounded long, and waxed louder and louder, Moses spake, and God answered him by a voice.

Reference is here made to the same event as in Ex. xix. 16, and the same words are used in the Hebrew and Septuagint for *trumpet* as in that passage.

Exodus, xx. 18.

And all the people saw the thunderings, and the

lightnings, and the noise of the trumpet, and the mountain smoking: and when the people saw it, they removed, and stood afar off.

The scene here described was exceedingly thrilling and terrific. The thunders were roaring, the lightnings flashing, the trumpet sounding, the mountain smoking, and the Almighty speaking to Moses on the Mount. It is not strange that the people feared and trembled, and withdrew from those terrors. The original words here are the same as in Ex. xix. 19.

Exodus, xxxii. 17.

And when Joshua heard the noise of the people as they shouted, he said unto Moses, There is a noise of war in the camp.

It seems that the children of Israel had waited for Moses to return from the Mount, until their impatience had induced them to forsake the God of their fathers. They constructed a golden calf, and had already commenced to worship it. As Moses came down, he saw the people with astonishment, sporting and shouting in the midst of their idolatrous services.

Shouted.—בְּרֵעֹה *reō*, from רוּעַ *rüah* or רִיעַ, *rïah*, *to cry aloud.* This word is sometimes used in *warlike shouts*, as in Josh. vi. 16, and in 1 Sam. xvii. 20; sometimes as a shout of joy, in triumph, as in Judges, xv. 14, and sometimes it signifies *to sound a trumpet*, Num. x. 9. Here it indicates *a shout of joy.* The LXX have κραζόντων *kradzǫntōn*, *to croak, to cry out with a great clamor.* The Israelites were evidently making an unusual disturbance, and the outcry may have been really a *war shout* as Joshua supposed. Some were for God, and some for the golden calf. The idolaters may have been about to make an attack upon their brethren who opposed them.

EXODUS, xxxii. 18.

And he said, It is not the voice of them that shout for mastery, neither is it the voice of them that cry for being overcome: but the noise of them that sing do I hear.

The cause of the shouting among the Israelites to which reference is made in Ex. xxxii. 17, is here explained. It was "the noise of them that sing."

Shout.—A word different from that in verse 17, translated "*shouted*," is here used. It is עֲנוֹת, *ᵃnōth*, from עָנָה, *ana*, *to sing, to chant, to sing of any one, to celebrate by song, to cry aloud like soldiers in battle, to shout in triumph.* The last is probably the true definition here. The worshippers of the golden calf were probably triumphing over the Levites who seem to have adhered to the worship of the true God. It was probably a shout of exultation over Jehovah and all of his true worshippers. It may also have been a kind of war shout or signal of attack upon the friends of God, as in the preceding verse.

Cry.—The original of this both in the Heb. and Septuagint is the same as that of *shout*, above; but signifies here a cry of fear when one is overcome by an enemy.

Sing.—The same original words are used here as in the two cases above, though translated differently. "The *noise* of them that sing." This was probably a noisy shout of triumph, connected with vociferous singing. It was customary among the Israelites as well as among other nations in the times of which we are speaking, to *shout* before making an attack upon an enemy (vid. I Sam. xvii. 20, 52; II Chron. xiii. 15; Jer. i. 42). The same custom prevails at this day among the Cossacks, Tartars, Turks, and our own Indians. Sometimes the Hebrews advanced to battle singing hymns (II Chron. xx. 21, 22), and the priests gave the signal by sounding their silver trumpets.

Exodus, xxxii. 19.

And it came to pass, as soon as he came nigh unto the camp, that he saw the calf, and the dancing: and Moses' anger waxed hot, and he cast the tables out of his hands, and brake them beneath the mount.

Dancing.—It appears that there was not only shouting and singing on the occasion to which reference is here made, but *dancing*. This was usually an accompaniment of triumphant shouting and singing (vid. Rem. on Ex. xv. 20, *supra*). The same words are used in the original as in Ex. xv. 20.

LEVITICUS, OR THE THIRD BOOK OF MOSES.

INTRODUCTORY REMARKS.

THIS book is called by the LXX Λευιτικον *Leuitikon, Leviticus*, because it presents a description of the religious ceremonies, laws, and especially the sacrifices of the Hebrews, the superintendence of which was committed to Aaron the Levite and his sons, who alone held the priestly office in the tribe of Levi. The Babylonish Talmud, followed by the Arabic and Syriac versions of the Scriptures, calls this book the *Law of the Priests*.

Leviticus was evidently written by Moses, and contains the history of one month, from the erection of the tabernacle to the numbering of the people, who were fit for war, or from the beginning of the second year after Israel's departure from Egypt to the commencement of the second month of the same year, B. C. 1490 (cf. Ex. xl. 17, with Num. i. 1). We cannot ascertain when the laws not relating to sacrifices were promulgated, as the Hebrews have no chronological works.

The object of the book is to direct the minds of the Israelites to the Messiah, by describing the Levitical laws, sacrifices, and ordinances as "shadows of good things to come."

LEVITICUS, ix. 24.

And there came a fire out from before the Lord, and consumed upon the altar the burnt-offering and the fat: which when all the people saw, they shouted, and fell on their faces.

It appears that Aaron and those Israelites who were not destroyed on account of their idolatry in worshipping the golden calf, offered burnt-offerings to appease the Divine displeasure. Moses and Aaron went into the tabernacle of the congregation, and returning, blessed the people. A fire issued from before the Lord and consumed the burnt-offering upon the altar. When the people saw this wonderful display of the power and glory of God, they shouted and fell upon their faces in astonishment.

Shouted.—וַיָּרֹנּוּ *vayyárnu*, from רָנַן, *ranán*, *to give forth a tremulous sound, to shake or trill the voice*, hence, *to utter inarticulate cries of joy, to shout.* In this instance, the Israelites probably shouted for joy, because the Lord had again appeared merciful to them—ready to forgive their iniquities.

Leviticus, xxiii. 24.

Speak unto the children of Israel, saying, in the seventh month, in the first day of the month, shall ye have a sabbath, a memorial of blowing of trumpets, an holy convocation.

This passage refers to one of the annual festivals of the Jews. There were three, viz.: the *Passover*, the feast of *Pentecost*, and that of the *Tabernacles.* To these Moses added two others which were celebrated with great solemnity, though all of the Israelites were not required to be present. The first of those added by Moses, was the *Feast of Trumpets*, and the second, that of *Expiation* or *Atonement.*

In the passage before us, reference is made to the *Feast of Trumpets*, which was celebrated on the first and second days of the month Tisri (a part of our September and October), which was the commencement of the civil year of the Jews. Trumpets were blown in the temple with more than usual solemnity, and from this circumstance the feast took its name (Num. xxix. 1). On this occasion, the people abstained from all labor (Lev. xxiii. 25), and offered special sacrifices to God, as described in Num. xxix. 1–6.

Blowing of trumpets.—The original word here, is תְּרוּעָה *t'rúah*, from רוּעַ *rúah*, the same as that from which the word translated "shouted," in Ex. xxxii. 17, is derived. It means *to cry aloud*, and sometimes, to *sound a trumpet*, as in this place. Its literal signification is *blowing* (trumpets being implied). In Num. x. 9, the word for trumpets is *expressed* (vid. Rem. on Ex. xxxii. 17, *supra*). It is probable that the trumpets were blown much of the time during this feast as it received its name from that circumstance, and as may be inferred from Num. xxix. 1. Reference is, doubtless, here made to the *straight trumpet*. The silver ones constructed by the command of Moses, were, undoubtedly of the same kind, and made between the fourteenth day of the first month and the twentieth day of the second month (Num. ix. 1, 5; x. 11), in the second year after the Israelites left the land of Egypt, or about 1489 B. C. Before the twentieth day of the second month Moses was commanded to make the two silver trumpets and the probability is that he immediately commenced the work, so as to have them ready before the Israelites should proceed on their journey from the wilderness of Sinai (Num. x. 1–12).

The passage under consideration (Lev. xxiii. 24.), refers to a feast which was to be celebrated the seventh month of the same year. The trumpets were undoubtedly ready before that time, so that the reference must have been to the *straight trumpets*.

Leviticus, xxv. 9.

Then shalt thou cause the trumpet of the jubilee to sound, on the tenth day of the seventh month, in the day of atonement shall ye make the trumpet sound throughout all your land.

This passage refers to a *special* festival of the Jews. Besides their *annual* feasts they had two extraordinary ones, viz: the *Sabbatical year* and the *year of jubilee.* Every seventh year was considered as a sabbatical one and was carefully observed as such. Every seventh *sabbatical year* was the *year of jubilee.* This was kept as a Sabbath and considered more solemn and important than the *sabbatical year.* It is the *year of jubilee* to which reference is made in the passage before us. At the commencement of the year the jubilee trumpet was sounded throughout the land.

Trumpet.—שׁוֹפָר *shōphár*, the same word which is used in Ex. xix. 16, and evidently referring to the *crooked trumpet*, made of the horn of an ox or ram. It was first made of the former and afterwards of the latter (vid. Rem. on. Ex. xix. 16). In the latter part of the verse reference is made to the same instrument.

NUMBERS, OR THE FOURTH BOOK OF MOSES.

INTRODUCTORY REMARKS.

THE Alexandrine translators call this book ΑΡΙΘΜΟΙ *arithmoi*, *numbers*, and the Latin translators, *Numeri*, *numbers*. This term is adopted in our English version. It was probably written by Moses on the plains of Moab (xxxvi. 13), just before his death, about 1451 B. C. The last event narrated in the book occurred during the time which elapsed between 1452 and 1451 B. C., and it must, of course, have been after the occurrence of the events described that their history was written. But the death of Moses is supposed to have occurred near the close of the year 1451 B. C. Therefore it is very probable that the lawgiver composed this book some time during that year. It contains a history of the Israelites from the beginning of the second month of the second year after the departure from Egypt to the commencement of the eleventh month of the fortieth year of their journeyings, which was a period of thirty eight years and nine or ten months (cf. Num. i., and xxxvi. 13 with Deut. i. 3). Most of the events recorded, occurred in the second and thirty-eighth years of that peroid. The dates of the events described in the middle of the book, cannot with certainty, be determined.

NUMBERS, x. 2.

Make thee two trumpets of silver; of a whole piece shalt thou make them; that thou mayest use them for the calling of the assembly, and for the journeying of the camps.

Trumpets.—There seems to have been a great improvement in the trumpets here mentioned. God commanded that two should be made of silver. They are designated by a Hebrew term different from any which we have previously considered. It is חֲצֹוצְרֹת *hh^{a}tsōts^{e}rōth*, a verbal noun from חָצַר *hhạtsár*, the same as the Arabic حضر *hh$^{\delta}$tsúr, to be present.* In the Hebrew Pael conjugation, it signifies, *to call together*, which was done by a *trumpet.* Hence, it was subsequently used to signify the *instrument* itself. The sound of the word in pronunciation was doubtless intended to imitate the sound of the instrument, like the Latin *taratantara* and the German *trarara.* It appears that this instrument was used particularly for calling together an assembly, and as a signal for the moving of the camps of Israel, as in the case before us.

The silver trumpet was to be blown only by the priests (Num. x. 8; 1 Chron. xv. 24). T. H. Horne believes this to be the *straight trumpet.* Jahn remarks that it was decidedly different from the *shophạr* and was made of metal. Josephus asserts that it was straight, about an ell (*cubitus*) in length and a little thicker than a flute. In this form are four *hatsotseras* in the sports (Annal. Syr. Table xviii) engraved on two coins. The following cut (Fig. XXXI) is a representation of two of them (vid. p. 109, *supra*). The opening at the top is sufficiently large for blowing conveniently with the mouth; but at the bottom it is larger and bell shaped like our trumpet.

Fig. XXXI.

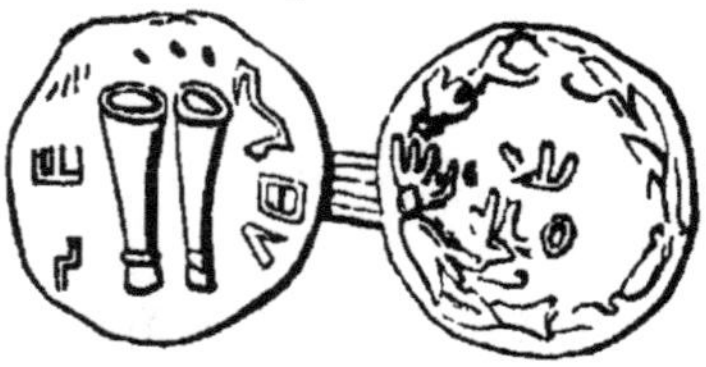

Two Hebrew Hatsotseras, or Straight Trumpets engraved on an ancient coin.

The following cut (Fig. XXXII) represents another ancient coin, just mentioned, taken from the "sports," containing two more trumpets similar to those given above.

Jahn does not doubt that the silver trumpets of Moses were of this kind. Josephus informs us that Solomon increased the number of these instruments to 200,000 (Ant. viii. iii. 8). They seem to have been constructed of one piece of silver, and without holes for the fingers as in modern trumpets.

Fig. XXXII.

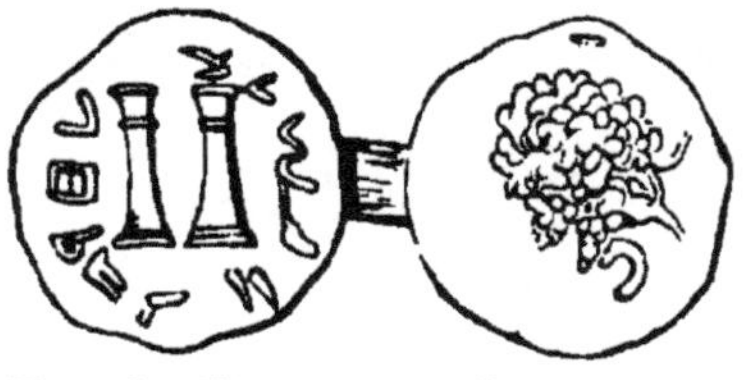

Two other Hatsotseras, or Straight Trumpets engraved on another ancient coin.

Numbers, x. 3.

And when they shall blow with them, all the assembly shall assemble themselves to thee at the door of the tabernacle of the congregation.

Blow.—תִּקְעוּ *taq^{e}u*, from תָּקַע *taqá, to strike, to strike the trumpet*, i. e., *to give a blast.* A different word in the original was used when an *alarm* was to be sounded. Gesenius thinks that there was but one blast when the people were to be called together, as in this place.

Numbers, x. 4.

And if they blow but with one trumpet, then the princes, which are heads of the thousands of Israel, shall gather themselves unto thee.

Blow.—The same original word is here used as in the preceding verse, indicating according to Gerenius, that there was but one blast. *Trumpet* is supplied in the translation and does not appear in the Hebrew. Reference is made to the same species of trumpet as in the previous verse. It appears that the

Israelites gave various signals with these instruments. One blast of the *trumpets* called the assembly together as we have intimated—one blast of *one trumpet* called together the princes of thousands, and other signals indicated the time for marching and for alarms.

Numbers, x. 5.

When ye blow an alarm, then the camps that lie on the east parts shall go forward.

Here was another signal given by the trumpet for a *part of* the people to move forward.

Blow an alarm.—The original of "*blow*," is derived from the same Hebrew word as that of "*blow*," in the two preceding verses. The original of the word "*alarm*" is תְּרוּעָה *t^eruah*, which in Ex. xxxii. 17, means a *shout of joy* (vid. Rem. on xxxii. 17), and in Lev. xxiii. 24, *the blowing or sounding of trumpets* (vid. Rem. on that passage). Here it seems to mean a *sounding of trumpets* in a peculiar manner, perhaps louder and more suddenly than usual, something like a war-sound, so as to raise an alarm. The Septuagint has *σημασιαν seemasian*, *signal*, *alarm*.

Numbers, x. 6.

When ye blow an alarm the second time, then the camps that lie on the south side shall take their journey: they shall blow an alarm for their journeys.

Blow an alarm.—The same original words are used here as in the preceding verse, and it is reasonable to conclude that the same kind of signal was given; but it was distinguished from the other, in that it was the *second blast of alarm.* A similar expression occurs in the last part of the verse, the original word being the same excepting that the person is changed.

" *They shall blow an alarm.*"—The Alexandrine translators supplied what they supposed to be the ellipsis, and instead of saying, "They shall blow an alarm for their journeys;" rendered the phrase as follows: "Ye shall blow an alarm the third time, then the camps that lie on the west side shall take their journey, and ye shall blow an alarm the fourth time, then the camps that lie on the north side shall take their journey: they shall blow an alarm for their journey." It is probable that there was a special sound of alarm for each division that moved forward. While the Israelites were in the wilderness the form of their camp according to Num. ii., seems to have been quadrangular, having three tribes on each side, under one general standard, but so arranged as to inclose the tabernacle, which stood in the centre. The priests and Levites pitched four smaller camps between the four principal ones and the tabernacle. Moses, Aaron, and his sons, who were the ministering priests and had charge of the sanctuary, pitched their camp on the east side of the tabernacle, near its entrance. Every family and household had their particular ensigns, under which they marched or encamped. The Rabbins inform us that the standard of Judah was a lion, that of Reuben the figure of a man, of Ephraim an ox, and of Dan an eagle with a serpent in his talons, but this is mere conjecture. It is far more probable that they had standards with the names of their respective tribes embroidered in large letters upon them. The Jewish encampment was arranged in excellent order. The following diagram from Dr. A. Clarke gives a tolerably correct view of it. It will be observed that the Tabernacle is in the centre; Moses, Aaron, and the Priests are encamped immediately east of the sacred enclosure; the Merarites on the north, the Gershonites on the west, and the Kohathites on the south. A little farther distant on the east stand the hosts of Judah, on the north Dan, on the west Ephraim, and on the south Reuben. Farthest from the Tabernacle, in the same order, stand the Grand Divisions.

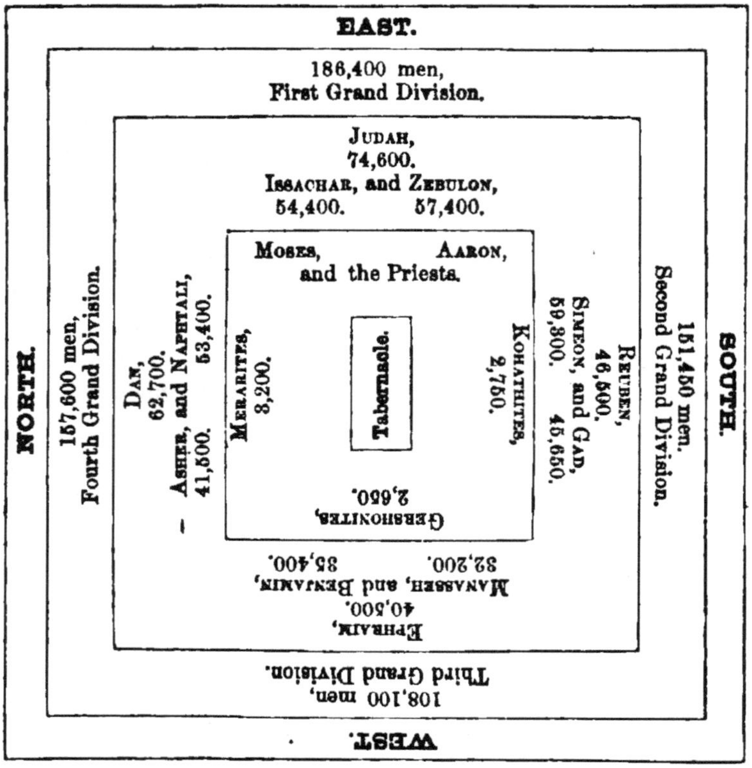

The order of march was somewhat similar to that of caravans or assemblages of oriental travelers at the present day. It was arrranged as follows (vid. Num. x.): when they were to remove (the rising of the cloud from the tabernacle being the miraculous signal) the trumpets were sounded by the sons of Aaron, and at the first alarm, the standard of Judah was raised and its three tribes moved forward. Then the Levites took down the tabernacle, the Gershonites and Merarites (two families of the Levites) attending the wagons with the boards, staves, and other implements. After all of these had commenced their march a second alarm was sounded by the trumpets and the standard of Reuben advanced with the three tribes under it. Then the Kohathites (the third family of the Levites) bearing the Sanctuary or Holy of Holies and its utensils, moved on. This sacred treasure, being regarded as more holy than other parts of the tabernacle, was not placed in wagons, but carried upon the shoulders of persons designated for the service. Next, the standard of Ephraim was raised and the accompanying tribes advanced. Finally, the three tribes of Dan formed the rear of the imposing procession. Moses and Aaron superintended the whole and were careful that every thing was arranged in accordance with the Divine command. Before the silver trumpets were made, probably the *crooked* ones were sounded, and as but two silver ones were at first constructed, perhaps others of the more ancient kind were used at the same time, until the number of the straight trumpets was sufficiently augmented. There must have been something peculiarly grand and terrific in the march of the Israelites as they moved off, the cloud passing before them by day and a pillar of fire by night. As the cloud arose from the tabernacle when they were departing, as the trumpets sounded the alarm and as that vast army of more than three millions marched onward with their banners floating in the breeze, their appearance must have impressed the beholder with feelings of awe and admiration.

NUMBERS, X. 7.

But when the congregation is to be gathered together, ye shall blow, but ye shall not sound an alarm.

This is similar to the third verse of this chapter, intimating that when the congregation was to be assembled, the trumpets were to be blown, but no *alarm* sounded.

NUMBERS, x. 8.

And the sons of Aaron, the priests, shall blow with the trumpets; and they shall be to you for an ordinance for ever throughout your generations.

Here is evidence of the fact that the sons of Aaron were the individuals designated to blow the trumpets. The same original word is used as in verse second, referring to the *straight* instrument.

NUMBERS, x. 9.

And if ye go to war in your land against the enemy that oppresseth you, then ye shall blow an alarm with the trumpets; and ye shall be remembered before the Lord your God, and ye shall be saved from your enemies.

It seems that in all cases of calamity and danger from their enemies the Israelites were to blow the trumpets—blow an alarm—and Jehovah promised assistance. This was a positive command, from the observance of which there could not be the slightest departure without incurring the Divine displeasure.

In the preceding verse it is said that the blowing of the trumpets should be for an ordinance for ever throughout their generations, thus intimating that future generations were to observe the same directions, *i. e.*, that they were to blow the trumpets as a signal for God to interpose in their behalf.

NUMBERS, x. 10.

Also in the day of your gladness, and in your

solemn days, and in the beginnings of your months, ye shall blow with the trumpets over your burnt-offerings, and over the sacrifices of your peace-offerings; that they may be to you for a memorial before your God: I am the Lord your God.

There seems to be a reference here to the festivals of the Jews. The trumpets were to be blown "as a memorial" or to remind the Israelites that God had promised to bless them provided they were careful to observe his commandments.

Numbers, xxi. 17, 18.

Then Israel sang this song,

Spring up, O well; sing ye unto it:
The princes digged the well,
The nobles of the people digged it,
By the direction of the Lawgiver, with their staves.

This lyric poetry was sung by the Israelites, when, during their journeyings in the wilderness, they had reached *Beer* or the *Well.* It seems to have been a song of joy, in view of the fact that water had been found. On their way to the promised land they passed through several dry and sandy deserts where travelers often suffer exceedingly from thirst. When the Israelites were in the desert of Zin (Num. xx) they experienced great distress from thirst and Moses smote the rock and waters gushed forth. The desert of Arabia extends from the Red Sea, an arm of which the children of Israel crossed, to the land of Canaan, whither they were bound. Moses calls it a "waste, howling wilderness" (Deut. xxxii. 11. 10). Also, "that great and terrible wilderness, wherein were fiery serpents, and scorpions, and drought, where there was no water" (Deut. viii. 15). Jeremiah calls it "a land of deserts and of pits, a land of drought, and of the shadow of death, a land that no man passed through, and where no man dwelt" (Jer. ii. 6). The distinguished traveler, M. Belzoni, after having passed through a desert in Upper Egypt, on the western side of the Red Sea, remarks: "Generally speaking, in a desert there are few springs of water, some of them at the distance of four, six and eight days' journey from one another and not all of sweet water; on the contrary, it is generally salt or bitter; so that, if the weary traveler drinks of it, his thirst is augmented, and he suffers more than before. But, when the calamity happens, that the next well, which is so anxiously sought for is found dry, the misery of such a situation cannot be well described. The camels, which afford the only means of escape, are so thirsty, that they cannot proceed to another well, and if the travelers kill them to extract the little liquid which remains in their stomachs, they themselves cannot advance any farther. The situation must be dreadful and admits of no resource. Many *perish victims of the most horrible thirst.*"*

The Israelites were in the great Arabian desert when they arrived at Beer, having suffered many times from thirst and other causes. Just before they reached this place they had probably been distressed for want of water, but at last they came to the favored spot where they could quench their parching thirst. Of course, the occasion must have been a joyful one, and worthy to be celebrated with songs of joy. The subject of their rejoicing seems to have been the discovery of a well, indicating that their approach to water was the grand cause of their joy.

Numbers, xxiii. 21.

He hath not beheld iniquity in Jacob, neither hath he seen perverseness in Israel: the Lord his

* Belzoni's Narrative of his Operations and Researches in Egypt, etc., pp. 341–3.

God is with him, and the shout of a king is among them.

These are the words of Balaam while uttering to Balak what the Lord had revealed to him concerning Israel. Although Balak desired Balaam to curse Israel, the latter informed him that he could not comply with his wishes without Divine permission. On the contrary, he spoke in the highest terms of the Israelites, declaring that the Lord was with them and that the *shout* of a king was among them.

Shout.—The original word here has the same derivation as that in Ex. xxxii. 17, translated *shouted.* It probably means here a *warlike-shout*, as in Josh. vi. 16 and I Sam. xvii. 20.

NUMBERS, xxix. 1.

And in the seventh month, on the first day of the month, ye shall have an holy convocation; ye shall do no servile work: it is a day of blowing the trumpets unto you.

This refers to an annual festival of the Jews, called the *Feast of the Trumpets.*

Blowing the trumpets.—The Hebrew term is תְּרוּעָה *terua*, *blowing*, the word for trumpets being implied, as in Lev. xxiii. 24 (vid. Rem. on that passage).

NUMBERS, xxxi. 6.

And Moses sent them to the war, a thousand of every tribe, them and Phinehas the son of Eleazar the priest, to the war, with the holy instruments, and the trumpets to blow in his hand.

It appears that God directed Moses to take a thousand men from each tribe of the Israelites and march against the hosts of Midian. He did accordingly, and sent Phinehas the son of Eleazar the priest, with the holy instruments to accompany them.

The *trumpets* mentioned are doubtless the same as those named in the tenth chapter of Numbers, as the same original word is used in both places. They were undoubtedly the *straight trumpets.*

DEUTERONOMY, OR THE FIFTH BOOK OF MOSES.

INTRODUCTORY REMARKS.

THE term Deuteronomy is taken from the Greek ΔΕΥΤΕΡΟΝΟΜΙΟΝ, *deuteronomion*, signifying the *second law*. It was thus called because it contains a second statement of the laws which Moses had formerly promulgated to the Israelites. By comparing Deut. i. 1, 5, with Deut. xxxiv. 1, 5, it appears that the Lawgiver wrote the book just before his death, while on the plains of Moab. From the fact that his death is recorded in the last chapter and that some explanatory words are inserted in other parts of the book, it has been maintained by some that Moses could not have composed it, as he could not have recorded his own death. But it should be observed that his narration evidently concludes with the thirty-third chapter, and the thirty-fourth was undoubtedly added to complete the history. The first eight verses of it were probably written by his successor, Joshua, immediately after Moses' death, and the last four by some later historian, probably Samuel, Ezra, or some prophet who succeeded Samuel. It should also be noticed that, what is now the last chapter of Deuteronomy, was formerly the first chapter of Joshua. It was placed at the end of the former as a kind of supplement to the book.

Deuteronomy comprises the transactions in reference to the Israelites during five lunar weeks, or, according to some chronologists, two months, from the first day of the eleventh month of the fortieth year after their departure from Egypt, to the eleventh day of the twelfth month of the same year, or B. C. 1451.

The object of the book seems to have been to repeat to the Israelites, before their great Lawgiver should leave them, the principal enactments which God had commanded them to observe. Moses, with great solicitude, speaks to his brethren, and endeavors to furnish them with such instructions as would best prepare them for the promised land to which they were journeying.

DEUTERONOMY, xxxi. 19.

Now therefore write ye this song for you, and teach it the children of Israel: put it in their mouths, that this song may be a witness for me against the children of Israel.

In this book there are no references to musical *instruments* and few allusions to music.

Song.—The original word is שִׁירָה *shïra*, *song*, the same as that used in Num. xxi. 17 and translated *song*. Here it refers to Moses' directions to the Israelites just before his death, in respect to the regulations of their lives. These instructions were probably sung and their recital accompanied by instrumental music. We learn from history, that in the early ages of Greece, poetry and music always accompanied each other. Prophecies and even speculative dogmas were sung.* It was so to some extent among the ancient Hebrews. David's poetry contains many moral precepts and laws for the direction of the Israelites. The same was true in respect to Moses. *Song*, in the latter part of the verse as in the first part, refers to Moses' farewell address.

* Athenæus, a distinguished Greek historian, informs us that anciently all laws Divine and human, exhortations to virtue, a knowledge of what concerned the gods and heroes, the lives and actions of illustrious men, were written in verse, and sung publicly in chorus to the sound of instruments.

DEUTERONOMY, xxxi. 21, 22, 30.

And it shall come to pass, when many evils and troubles are befallen them, that this song shall testify against them as a witness; for it shall not be forgotten out of the mouths of their seed: for I know their imagination which they go about, even now, before I have brought them into the land which I sware.

Moses therefore wrote this song the same day, and taught it the children of Israel.

And Moses spake in the ears of all the congregation of Israel the words of this song, until they were ended.

The term *song*, found in each of these verses, refers to Moses' last song and address, and needs no farther explanation.

DEUTERONOMY, xxxii. 44.

And Moses came and spake all the words of this song in the ears of the people, he, and Hoshea the son of Nun.

This again refers to the Lawgiver's farewell address, which immediately precedes. That discourse or prophetic ode (contained in Deut. xxxii. 1–43), as we have already intimated, is evidently lyric poetry and was probably accompanied in its delivery by instrumental music.

Deuteronomy is the closing book of the Pentateuch, and contains a history of the grand events which occurred upon the earth during the first 2500 years of its existence. We have also, in these writings, an imperfect and fragmentary history of music and musical instruments during the period which elapsed between 2844 B. C. and the latter part of the year 1451 or beginning of 1450 B. C. We find that during this time, various musical instruments were used by the Hebrews. They seem to have been familiar with the *harp*, *organ* or pipe of Pan (vid. Ex. xv. 20), *tabret* or *tambourine*, *horn* or *crooked trumpet* made of cows' or rams' horns, and the *straight trumpet*—five instruments, contained in the three grand classes, viz: *stringed*, *wind*, and *percussion* instruments. It is probable that there were varieties under these general classes, which are not mentioned in the sacred text. When Miriam the prophetess and all the females among the Israelites went out with timbrels in their hands (Ex. xv. 20), it is probable that they had varieties of that instrument differing more or less from each other. They had at least two kinds of trumpets, viz., crooked, including two varieties (cows' and rams' horns), and straight trumpets.

There are also in the Pentateuch various allusions to vocal music showing that the children of Israel were familiar with that as well as with instrumental music. There are, in those remarkable writings about thirty passages which relate to vocal or instrumental or both vocal and instrmental music. There are also a few references to religious *dances*.

HISTORICAL BOOKS OF THE OLD TESTAMENT.

INTRODUCTORY REMARKS.

THE twelve historical books, including Joshua, Judges, Ruth, First and Second Samuel, First and Second Kings, First and Second Chronicles, Ezra, Nehemiah, and Esther, immediately follow the Pentateuch, and contain a record of the events which occurred during about one thousand years, from the death of Moses, in the latter part of the year B. C. 1451, to the time of the great national reform effected by Nehemiah after the Jews had returned from captivity, about 420 years B. C.

These books are important to aid in understanding other parts of the sacred volume. Many references in the prophecies and psalms are here explained. There are also various incidental notices in these histories, in reference to the state of surrounding nations, which is a matter of great importance, from the fact that, before the time of Ezra and Nehemiah (the latest Jewish historians), little, if any dependence can be placed upon the narratives of heathen writers. The two earliest profane histories extant are those of Herodotus and Thucydides, whose authors were contemporary with Ezra and Nehemiah, and could not with any certainty describe events which occurred long before their time. The historical books of the Old Testament should not be considered merely as containing an account of the Jews, but also as clearly illustrating the dealings of God with the whole human family. They furnish a melancholy but impartial view of the depravity of the human heart, as well as of the faithfulness of God in fulfilling his promises to his people, and his willingness to extend mercy to the returning penitent. They exemplify the excellence of the Christian religion, and its tendency to promote the happiness of those who confide in it, both in this life and that which is to come.

They have occasional references to music, both vocal and instrumental. Several new instruments are mentioned showing that the art of music continued to be cultivated, and that improvements were gradually made in it.

THE BOOK OF JOSHUA.

INTRODUCTORY REMARKS.

THIS book takes its name from Joshua, the son of Nun, whose achievements it narrates. That Israelitish chieftain had been the prime minister of Moses, and succeeded him in the command of the Hebrews. Gerhard, Diodati, Huet, Aller, Bishops Patrick, Tomline, and Gray, and Dr. A. Clarke, suppose that the book of Joshua is very ancient, and was originally composed by him whose name it bears.

Dr. Lightfoot ascribes it to Phineas, Calvin to the high priest Eleazar, Henry to Jeremiah, and Moldenhawer and Van Till, to Samuel. It is somewhat uncertain who was its author; still it appears to have been written before the seventh year of David's reign (B. C., 1212; cf. Josh. xv. 63, with ii. Sam. v. 5–8), showing that Ezra could not have been its author, as some suppose, for he lived long after that time.

It comprises the history of about seventeen, or, as some

think, twenty-seven or thirty years. It should always be connected with the Pentateuch, as it seems to be a continuation and completion of those writings. The latter presents a history of the acts of the great Hebrew legislator and the laws upon which the commonwealth was established. The book under consideration contains the history of Israel under the command and government of Joshua; the conquest of Canaan, and its division subsequently among the Israelites, and the provision made for the settlement and establishing of the Jewish congregation in Canaan.

The design of the writer seems to have been to exhibit the faithfulness of God in the fulfilment of his promise to the patriarchs, that the children of Israel should possess the land of Canaan; also, to show forth the divine power and mercy as displayed in cherishing, protecting, and defending his people amid all of the afflictions which they were called to endure. There are several references to music in the book, which we shall consider in their proper places. Most of the events here recorded occurred after Moses' death; but some of them probably transpired during the year 1450 B. C.

JOSHUA vi. 4.

And seven priests shall bear before the ark seven trumpets of rams' horns: and the seventh day ye shall compass the city seven times, and the priests shall blow with the trumpets.

Trumpets of rams' horns.—The Heb. is שׁוֹפְרוֹת הַיּוֹבְלִים *shōphᵉrōth hăyyōbhᵉlīm, trumpets of rams' horns, jubel horns, or trumpets*; i. e., the same kind of trumpets as those used at the jubilee. Sometimes שׁוֹפָר *shōphar* alone means *crooked trumpet* (Ex. xix. 16). Also some form of הַיּוֹבְלִים *hăyyobhᵉlīm*, is used to denote the *crooked trumpet*, without the help of any other word (Ex. xix. 13), but usually קֶרֶן *qéren, horn*, precedes it. Here both words are employed and may properly be rendered *trumpets of rams' horns*, as above. The expression שׁוֹפְרוֹת הַיּוֹבְלִים *shōphᵉroth hăyyobhᵉlīm*, is evidently used in the same sense as קֶרֶן הַיּוֹבְלִים, *qéren hayyobhᵉlīm*;* i. e., *horn of the Jubilee*, or *Jubilee trumpet*. The manner in which the Israelites marched around Jericho, preceded by seven priests bearing seven trumpets before the ark, must have been peculiarly solemn and imposing. They were to pass around the city once a day for seven days in succession, and on the seventh to encircle it seven times, and the priests were to blow with their trumpets. The Hebrew word, translated trumpets in the latter part of the verse, is *shophᵉroth*, evidently referring to the same instruments as those mentioned in the first part of the verse.

JOSHUA vi. 5, 6, 8, 9, 10, 13, 16, 20.

5 And it shall come to pass, that when they make a long *blast* with the ram's horn, *and* when ye hear the sound of the trumpet, all the people shall shout with a great shout; and the wall of the city shall fall down flat, and the people shall ascend up every man straight before him.

6 And Joshua, the son of Nun, called the priests, and said unto them, Take up the ark of the covenant, and let seven priests bear seven trumpets of rams' horns before the ark of the Lord.

* Comp. the original of Joshua vi. 5 with this passage. Vid. also Gesenius' opinion, p. 110 *supra*.

8 And it came to pass, when Joshua had spoken
unto the people, that the seven priests bearing the
seven trumpets of rams' horns passed on before
the Lord, and blew with the trumpets: and the
ark of the covenant of the Lord followed them.
9 And the armed men went before the priests that
blew with the trumpets, and the rere-ward came
after the ark, *the priests* going on, and blowing
with the trumpets. 10 And Joshua had commanded
the people, saying, Ye shall not shout, nor make
any noise with your voice, neither shall *any* word
proceed out of your mouth, until the day I bid
you shout; then shall ye shout.

13 And seven priests bearing seven trumpets of
rams' horns before the ark of the Lord went on
continually, and blew with the trumpets: and the
armed men went before them; but the rere-ward
came after the ark of the Lord, *the priests* going
on, and blowing with the trumpets.

16 And it came to pass at the seventh time, when
the priests blew with the trumpets, Joshua said
unto the people, Shout; for the Lord hath given
you the city.

20 So the people shouted when *the priests* blew
with the trumpets: and it came to pass, when the
people heard the sound of the trumpet, and the peo-
ple shouted with a great shout, that the wall fell
down flat, so that the people went up into the city,
every man straight before him, and they took the
city.

These verses refer to the same event which is mentioned in Joshua vi. 4.

This is a remarkable instance in which the power of God was manifested by the instrumentality of feeble means. The Israelites marched around Jericho thirteen times, blowing their rams' horns, and finally shouted, when the walls of the city immediately fell to the ground, thus strikingly exhibiting to the enemies of Jehovah his irresistible power and willingness to bless his people Israel.

Verse 5. *Long blast.*—This is similar to the expression "*soundeth long*," in Ex. xix. 13. The occasions upon which both were uttered were very solemn. In the former, Jehovah was about to descend upon Mount Sinai and deliver, through his servant Moses, to the children of Israel, his holy law. When the *trumpet sounded long*, the people were to draw near to the Mount. The sounding of the trumpet in a peculiar manner was a signal, indicating that the Lord was about to perform some memorable achievement. In the case before us, after all other preliminary arrangements had been made, the seven priests were to sound a *long blast* with their trumpets, as a signal for the people to *shout*, for the walls to fall, and for the city to surrender—a signal indicating that Jehovah was about to make some striking manifestation of his power.

Yobhẹl is here used (verse 5), and a little further on, in the same verse, *shophạr* for the same instrument, showing that they were often interchanged with each other.

Shout with a great shout.—This evidently refers to a *war shout.* When the trumpets should sound a long blast, the people were to utter the war shout and rush on to victory. Probably the trumpets continued sounding after the Israelites shouted, as it was customary in those early times for armies, when they were about to attack their enemies, to make as much noise as possible by shouting and sounding instruments of music (vid. Rem. on Ex. xxxii. 17). *Shout* has the same signification in verses 10, 16, and 20. The term translated trumpets, occurring in verses 6, 8, 9, 13, 16, and 20, is either *yobhẹl* or *shophar*, and the connection shows that they were the same instruments as those mentioned in verse 4, viz., the *crooked trumpets.* There are no more references to music in the book of Joshua. All of the allusions to it are to the crooked trumpet, although silver straight ones had been made before that time. The latter, however, were considered as sacred, and were used in the temple and on religious occasions, while the former were employed principally in war.

THE BOOK OF JUDGES.

INTRODUCTORY REMARKS.

THIS book contains the history of the Israelites from the death of Joshua, 1443 B. C., to the time of Eli, about 1146 B. C., comprising a history of nearly 300 years (some make it a few years longer) under the administration of thirteen judges, whom God raised up on special occasions to deliver his people from their enemies, and to direct their civil and ecclesiastical polity. The Judges frequently acted by divine suggestions, and were endowed with preternatural strength and fortitude (cf. Judg. ii. 18; vi. 14, 34; xi. 29; xiv. 6, 19), though they sometimes abused those endowments. The preternatural gifts of God we believe are as liable to abuse as those which he bestows in the ordinary course of nature. There is some difference of opinion in reference to the time when this book was written; but it was evidently composed before David captured Jerusalem (cf. II Sam. v. 6, with Judges i. 21).

The prophet Samuel, the last of the judges, was probably the author. There are in the book several allusions to music, though no new instruments are mentioned.

JUDGES iii. 27.

And it came to pass when he was come, that he blew a trumpet in the mountain of Ephraim, and the children of Israel went down with him from the mount, and he before them.

It appears that Ehud, of the tribe of Benjamin, had delivered the Israelites from the tyranny of Eglon, king of the Moabites, by taking the life of that haughty monarch. Ehud then fled to Seirath, and blew a trumpet in the mountain of Ephraim. It seems that the blowing of that instrument was a signal for the Israelites to revolt. They immediately assembled, and determined to follow their leader. They did so, and conquered the Moabites. The trumpet which that revolutionary chieftain blew was doubtless the *crooked*, war-trumpet.

JUDGES V. 1–31.

1 Then sang Deborah, and Barak, the son of Abinoam, on that day saying,
2 Praise ye the Lord for the avenging of Israel,
When the people willingly offered themselves.
3 Hear, O ye kings;
Give ear, O ye princes:
I, *even* I, will sing unto the Lord;
I will sing *praise* to the Lord God of Israel.
4 Lord, when thou wentest out of Seir,
When thou marchedst out of the field of Edom,
The earth trembled, and the heavens dropped,
The clouds also dropped water.
5 The mountains melted from before the Lord,
Even that Sinai from before the Lord God of Israel.
6 In the days of Shamgar, the son of Anath,
In the days of Jael,
The highways were unoccupied,
And the travelers walked through by-ways.
7 *The inhabitants of* the villages ceased,

They ceased in Israel,
Until that I, Deborah, arose,
That I arose a mother in Israel,
8 They chose new gods;
Then *was* war in the gates:
Was there a shield or spear seen among forty thousand in Israel?
9 My heart *is* toward the governors of Israel,
That offered themselves willingly among the people.
Bless ye the Lord.
10 Speak, ye that ride on white asses,
Ye that sit in judgment, and walk by the way.
11 *They that are delivered* from the noise of archers
In the places of drawing water,
There shall they rehearse the righteous acts of the Lord.
Even the righteous acts *toward the inhabitants* of his villages in Israel:
Then shall the people of the Lord go down to the gates.
12 Awake, awake, Deborah:
Awake, awake, utter a song:
Arise, Barak, and lead thy captivity captive,
Thou son of Abinoam.
13 Then he made him that remaineth have dominion over the nobles among the people:
The Lord made me have dominion over the mighty.

14 Out of Ephraim *was there* a root of them against
Amalek;
After thee, Benjamin, among thy people;
Out of Machir came down governors,
And out of Zebulun they that handle the pen
of the writer.
15 And the princes of Issachar *were* with Deborah;
Even Issachar, and also Barak:
He was sent on foot into the valley.
For the divisions of Reuben *there were* great
thoughts of heart.
16 Why abodest thou among the sheep-folds,
To hear the bleatings of the flocks?
For the divisions of Reuben *there were* great
searchings of heart.
17 Gilead abode beyond Jordan:
And why did Dan remain in ships?
Asher continued on the sea-shore,
And abode in his breaches.
18 Zebulun and Naphtali *were* a people *that* jeoparded their lives unto the death
In the high places of the field.
19 The kings came *and* fought,
Then fought the kings of Canaan in Taamach
by the waters of Megiddo;
They took no gain of money.
20 They fought from heaven;
The stars in their courses fought against Sisera.
21 The river of Kishon swept them away,
That ancient river, the river Kishon.

O my soul, thou hast trodden down strength.
22 Then were the horse-hoofs broken by the means of the prancings,
The prancings of their mighty ones.
Curse ye Meroz, said the angel of the Lord,
23 Curse ye bitterly the inhabitants thereof;
Because they came not to the help of the Lord,
To the help of the Lord against the mighty.
24 Blessed above women shall Jael the wife of Heber the Kenite be,
Blessed shall she be above women in the tent.
25 He asked water, *and* she gave *him* milk:
She brought forth butter in a lordly dish.
26 She put her hand to the nail,
And her right hand to the workman's hammer;
And with the hammer she smote Sisera,
She smote off his head,
When she had pierced and stricken through his temples.
27 At her feet he bowed, he fell, he lay down:
At her feet he bowed, he fell:
Where he bowed, there he fell down dead.
28 The mother of Sisera looked out at a window,
And cried through the lattice,
Why is his chariot *so* long in coming?
Why tarry the wheels of his chariots?
29 Her wise ladies answered her,
Yea, she returned answer to herself,
30 Have they not sped?
Have they *not* divided the prey;

To every man a damsel *or* two;
To Sisera a prey of divers colors,
A prey of divers colors of needle-work,
Of divers colors of needle-work on both sides,
Meet for the necks of *them that take* the spoil?
31 So let all thine enemies perish, O Lord:
But *let* them that love him *be* as the sun
When he goeth forth in his might.

This is a song of triumph by Deborah, a judge of Israel (the only female who was ever elevated to that office), and Barak, her general, who had delivered her people from the Canaanites (Judges iv. 5). The children of Israel had been oppressed twenty years by Jabin, king of Canaan, whose captain was the notorious Sisera. Being thus remarkably delivered from their enemies, it was a suitable occasion on which to triumph and celebrate their victory by song. Deborah was a prophetess, and doubtless received intimations from Jehovah that she must march against Jabin (Judges iv. 6). She seems to have been divinely inspired in the utterance of this triumphal ode. Bishop Lowth considers it as an admirable specimen of the sublime. The remarkable display of the divine majesty which had been witnessed by the Israelites on Mount Sinai, is described in verses fourth and fifth, in beautifully poetic language, and is impressively contrasted with the divine interposition in behalf of Israel. All nature had been convulsed by the presence of the Most High. The thunders roared, the lightnings flashed, the torrents rushed from the clouds, the mountain quaked and melted from before the Lord.

This ode is a specimen of lyric poetry. It was *sung*, accompanied, probably, by musical instruments.

In the first, third and twelfth verses the Hebrew word usually translated to *sing* is employed. In the third verse the expression "*I will sing*" occurs twice and is expressed by different Hebrew words. First, the common Hebrew term denoting *song* (אָשִׁירָה *ashiru*), is employed, but in the other case אֲזַמֵּר *ązammer*. This is from זָמַר *zamăr* whose secondary signification is *to sing*. Sometimes it refers to instrumental music (vid. Ps. xxxiii. 2; lxxi. 22; Dan. iii. 5, 7, 10, 15); but it is not certain that it does here (cf. Rem. on Ex. xv. 2 *supra*), though the Alexandrine translators express the term by *ψαλῶ psalo*, from *ψαλλῶ psallo*, *to touch*, *to cause to move* (the strings of a musical instrument). It is possible that the word here refers to playing on the harp or some other stringed instrument. Such, undoubtedly, were employed at that time, and must have accompanied this song, whatever may be the meaning of *zamar*.

JUDGES, vi. 34.

But the spirit of the Lord came upon Gideon, and he blew a trumpet; and Abiezer was gathered after him.

It appears that Gideon was directed by Jehovah to deliver the children of Israel from the Midianites, by whom they had been oppressed during seven years. Accordingly, he called together his army for the purpose, by the sound of the *trumpet*. This was the *war-trumpet*, or *shophar*.

JUDGES, vii. 8, 16, 18, 19, 20, 22.

8 So the people took victuals in their hand, and their trumpets: and he sent all *the rest of* Israel every man unto his tent, and retained those three hundred men: and the host of Midian was beneath him in the valley.

16 And he divided the three hundred men *into*
three companies, and he put a trumpet in every
man's hand, with empty pitchers, and lamps within
the pitchers.

18 When I blow with a trumpet, I and all that
are with me, then blow ye the trumpets also on
every side of all the camp, and say, *The sword* of
the Lord, and of Gideon. 19 So Gideon, and the
hundred men that *were* with him, came unto the
outside of the camp in the beginning of the middle
watch; and they had but newly set the watch:
and they blew the trumpets, and brake the pitch-
ers that *were* in their hands. 20 And the three
companies blew the trumpets, and brake the pitch-
ers, and held the lamps in their left hands, and the
trumpets in their right hands to blow *withal;*
and they cried, The sword of the Lord, and of
Gideon.

22 And the three hundred blew the trumpets;
and the Lord set every man's sword against his fel-
low, even throughout all the host: and the host
fled to Beth-shittah in Zererath, *and* to the bor-
der of Abel-meholah, unto Tabbath.

This is a striking instance of divine interposition in behalf of the children of Israel. Gideon's army consisted of only three hundred men who were to contend with the multitudes of Midian (vid. Judges, vi. 5).

Gideon's host were directed each to take a trumpet, and a pitcher containing a lamp, in his hands. They moved towards the camp of the enemy at the middle watch of the night, and as they approached, blew their trumpets, brake their pitchers, rushed upon the Midianites, and speedily subdued them. The usual war-shout was uttered. They cried, "*The sword of the Lord and of Gideon.*" In each of the verses quoted above, there is reference to the same instrument of music, viz., the *shophar*, or *crooked trumpet.*

JUDGES, xi. 34.

And Jephthah came to Mizpeh unto his house, and, behold, his daughter came out to meet him with timbrels and with dances: and she *was his* only child; beside her he had neither son nor daughter.

Jephthah had led a victorious army against the Ammonites, and was returning in triumph to Mizpeh, the place of his residence, *when his only daughter* came out with timbrels and dances, to welcome him home. The *toph* is the instrument here mentioned. Probably there was a company of musicians with Jephthah's daughter, as there were *timbrels* and *dances*, the plural number being employed. This music seems to have been similar to that mentioned in Ex. xv. 20 (vid. Rem. on this passage *supra*). Miriam and the female Israelites celebrated their victory over Pharaoh at the Red Sea with *timbrels* and *dances*. The same original words are used for those instruments as in the case before us. Females generally performed upon timbrels, dancing as they played. In Gen. xxxi. 27, the tabret is mentioned in connection with the harp. Laban reproved Jacob because he went away privately and did not give him an opportunity to escort him with songs and instrumental music. The same original word for tabret appears in Gen. xxxi. 27 as in Judg. xi. 34 and Ex. xv. 20, excepting that in Genesis the singular number is used. It is very possible that those who accompanied Jephthah's daughter had different kinds of instruments, as was usual on such occasions. For further remarks on timbrels and dances, vid. notes on Gen. xxxi. 27 and Ex. xv. 20.

JUDGES, xxi. 21, 23.

21 And see, and behold, if the daughters of Shiloh
come out to dance in dances, then come ye out of
the vineyards, and catch you every man his wife
of the daughters of Shiloh, and go to the land of
Benjamin.
23 And the children of Benjamin did so, and took
them wives, according to their number, of them
that danced, whom they caught: and they went
and returned unto their inheritance, and repaired
the cities, and dwelt in them.

Reference is here made to the custom of dancing at the Jewish festivals. The one to which there is special reference here, was an *annual* feast, about to be celebrated at Shiloh (v. 19). It was usual at those festivals to have dancing, vocal and instrumental music. On this occasion, probably, the female dancers *sung* and played on *timbrels* and *harps* and perhaps other instruments.

THE BOOK OF RUTH.

INTRODUCTORY REMARKS.

THIS book is generally considered as an appendix to that of Judges, and an introduction to those of Samuel. In the ancient Jewish canon Ruth and Judges formed but one book. The events which are here described probably occurred about 1241 B. C. It is evident from the genealogy in Ruth iv. 17–22, that the narrative could not have been reduced to its present form until the time of Samuel; and the most probable supposition is, that it was composed by that prophet.

Its object is partly to give the descent of David through the line of Ruth, a heathen proselyte to the Jewish religion, and wife of Boaz, whose adoption into the line of Christ has generally been considered as a preintimation of the admission of the Gentiles into the Christian church. The further design of the book is to exhibit the care of Jehovah over those who fear and sincerely love him, by elevating pious Ruth from a state of great adversity to that of the highest prosperity.

There are no allusions here to music vocal or instrumental; but as the history is in reality an appendix to the book of Judges, this brief notice of it is not perhaps inappropriate.

THE TWO BOOKS OF SAMUEL.

INTRODUCTORY REMARKS.

In the Jewish canon the two books of Samuel are both in one. In the Septuagint they are called the first and second book of Kings, or of the kingdoms, being two of the four narratives in which is written the history of the kings of Israel and Judah. They seem to have been composed by more than one person. The most probable opinion is, that the first twenty-four chapters of the first book of Samuel were written by the prophet whose name they bear, and that the remainder of the first and all of the second book were prepared by the prophets Gad and Nathan. It is probable that the latter wrote all of the second book after the fifth chapter. The prophets were accustomed to write memoirs of the transactions of their respective times. Reference is made to such documents in 1 Chron. xxix. 29, as separate books; but it would be natural to suppose that Ezra, who completed the canon of Jewish scripture, would throw all the contents of those memoirs into the two books of Samuel.

The first book contains the history and polity of the Jewish church from the birth of Samuel 1135 B. C., or, according to Archbishop Usher, 1271 B. C., to the death of Saul, 1055 B. C., or, according to Usher, 1219 B. C., a period of about 80 or 52 years. This book is a continuation of the history of the Israelites under Eli and Samuel, the last two judges, and Saul their first monarch, and gives the reason why their form of government was changed from an aristocracy to a monarchy. It also exhibits the preservation of God's people amid all of their trials and dangers, and cites remarkable instances of mercy towards those who have trusted in Jehovah.

1 Samuel, iv. 5, 6.

5 And when the ark of the covenant of the Lord came into the camp, all Israel shouted with a great shout, so that the earth rang again.

6 And when the Philistines heard the noise of the shout, they said, What *meaneth* the noise of this great shout in the camp of the Hebrews? And they understood that the ark of the Lord was come into the camp.

It seems that the Israelites had sinned against God and consequently did not receive divine assistance as they led on their armies against the Philistines. The latter were victorious, and succeeded in seizing the ark of the covenant and conveying it to their own camp. They, however, found it to be a troublesome and dangerous treasure, and hastened to return it to the Israelites, for the curse of God rested upon them in consequence of their sacrilege. Many of those who laid their hands upon it were miserably destroyed.

The children of Israel had been mourning the loss of many of their number, and especially of the ark of the covenant; but when they saw the sacred treasure again returning into the camp, they were exceedingly rejoiced at this evident token of the divine favor, and *shouted with a great shout.* It is probable that they not only *shouted* for joy, but accompanied their songs of praise by *instrumental music*, in accordance with the custom on such occasions. In both verses the term *shout* is expressed by the same original word.

1 Samuel, x. 5.

After that thou shalt come to the hill of God, where *is* the garrison of the Philistines: and it shall come to pass, when thou art come thither to the city, that thou shalt meet a company of prophets coming down from the high place, with a psaltery, and a tabret, and a pipe, and a harp, before them; and they shall prophesy.

Reference is here made to Saul whom Samuel had anointed king. After that ceremony had been completed, Saul was directed by the prophet to go to Zelzah and Tabor, and then to the hill of God, where the garrison of the Philistines was encamped. He was further informed that when he should approach the city, he would meet a company of prophets coming down from the high place, with various instruments of music. When he met them, in accordance with the prediction, he caught the flame of inspiration and began to prophesy.

This company of seers, probably, came from the *schools* of the *prophets*. Such institutions seem to have been established by Samuel while he was a judge and prophet in Israel. At least they are not mentioned before that time. Under the ministry of Eli, the degeneracy of the priesthood was alarming, and the spirit of prophesy had become almost entirely extinct.

These, it is thought, were the leading causes which resulted in the first establishment of those seminaries, in which there was ample provision made for the education of those who were to enter the prophetic office.

These schools were first established in the cities of the Levites, being dispersed through the several tribes of Israel for the more convenient instruction of the people (vid. 1 Sam. x.

5, 10; xix. 20; 1 Kings ii. 5; xxii. 14). Suitable edifices were erected for the residences of the prophets, and their disciples, who were called *sons of the prophets.* Some venerable and divinely inspired prophet presided over them, who was called their father (2 Kings ii. 12). It is probable that Samuel was the first of those fathers (1 Sam. xix. 20), Elijah another (2 Kings ii. 12), and Elisha the next (2 Kings vi. 1). The sons of the prophets lived together in a community or society (2 Kings iv. 38), and were instructed in the principles of the Hebrew religion, in the knowledge of the law, and in the sacred art of psalmody. This last is called prophesying with psalteries, harps, and cymbals (1 Sam. x. 5; 1 Chron. xxv. 1, 7). Calmet supposes that these schools continued until the Babylonish captivity. It is probable that God selected from them those who were suitable to exercise the prophetic office and make known to the people his will. The students or young prophets were frequently dispatched by their instructors to carry prophetic messages (2 Kings ix. 1). It is a fact which should be more frequently remembered, that in ancient times the greatest and best men acquired a knowledge of music, both vocal and instrumental. It seems that it was an indispensable requisite for the prophets, who were the holiest and generally the most learned men of their age, to be thoroughly trained in this sacred art. It was so important that even their prophecies must be uttered in poetry, and attended by instrumental if not vocal music. It is probable that they made great proficiency in the art, as they spent much time in its study and practice. David's great masters of music, Asaph, Heman, and Jeduthun, and his four thousand Levitical performers of vocal and instrumental music, were doubtless instructed in these colleges, and must have been very skillful performers, as they devoted a great part of their lives to the study of the art. Music and poetry reached a higher state of cultivation under the reign of David than ever before, and he commenced his reign soon after the occurrence mentioned in the passage under consideration.

When those seers prophesied, they probably uttered their poetic effusions in a chant accompanied by some musical instruments. Hence it is said that they prophesied with "psalteries, cymbals, and harps" (1 Chron. xxv. 1). Probably some performed on musical instruments while a prophecy was being uttered. A *pipe* was one of the instruments mentioned in the passage before us, and the one who performed on it could not have uttered poetry, as the pipe is a wind instrument blown with the mouth.

Psaltery.—This is an instrument which does not occur in any previous passage. The Hebrew term is נֵבֶל *nebhel*, originally signifying *a bottle*, *i. e.*, a leathern bag. It had the form of a pyramid or cone. A secondary meaning of the word is *a musical instrument*, and, like a bottle, its shape is supposed to have been that of an inverted cone or delta (▽). Its form, it is believed, suggested its name. The Greek term is *νάβλα nabla* or *ναύλα naula*, and the Latin, *nablium*. *Νάβλα nabla*, appears in the Septuagint. Gesenius supposes that it was a *species* of *harp* or *lyre*. Josephus (Ant. vii. xii. 3) describes it as a species of harp or lyre, having twelve strings, and played with the fingers and not with a key. נֵבֶל עָשׂוֹר *nebhel asŏr*, *a ten* (*stringed*) *nebhel*, in Ps. xxxiii. 2; cxliv. 9, would seem to indicate that it was an instrument with ten strings. Jerome informs us that its figure was triangular, resembling an inverted delta, which also was the form of the harp or *sambuca* (Vitruv. vi. 1). Dr. Jahn asserts that the Greeks acknowledged the name of this instrument (*nabla*) to have been derived from the Phœnicians. The same learned author remarks, that in the time of Josephus it had twelve strings. At an earlier period, however, according to Ps. xxxiii. 2; cxliv. 9, it had only ten. This view is probably the correct one, for the *nebhel*, like other stringed instruments, at first had a small number of strings, and subsequently their number was increased. From the derivation of the name one might suppose that the sounding-board was in the form of a leathern bag or bottle; but *nebhel* very early signified a vessel of any kind, like *dolium* of the Romans, and the sounding-board was probably a round wooden dish. Niebuhr saw, in Egypt, an instrument of this kind in the Nubias (Reis. 1. Th. S. 179). Jahn has given an engraved profile of it (Kupfertaffel Nro. 1), which we here present.

Fig. XXXIII.

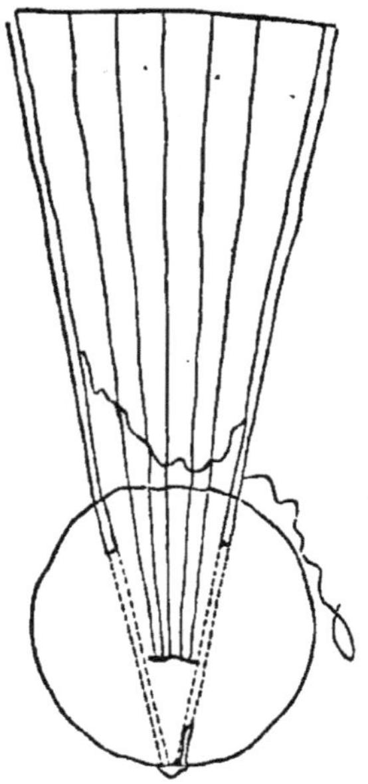

Ancient Guitar (נֵבֶל *nebhel*) *of the Hebrews.*

The belly of this instrument projects from a round wooden dish, having a small aperture beneath. A hide is drawn over the top of the dish, or, according to Wansleb. in P. Samml. iii. 36, "a piece of red leather is drawn tightly over, which is higher in the middle than where the strings are tied." Through this skin or red leather two sticks pass in such a manner that, with a third, which is fastened above to the end of the two in an oblique direction, they form an inverted delta. The strings pass across the hide on a narrow bridge, and are made fast to the cross-stick above. This specimen has but five strings. Perhaps at first this was the usual number. Afterwards they were increased to ten and twelve. The Hebrews made this instrument not only of the fir-tree, but sometimes of costly red sandal-wood, or the almug (2 Sam. vi. 5; 1 Kings x. 12). Josephus and Gesenius, as we have intimated, called the *nebhel* a species of *harp* or *lyre*. Pfeiffer considers it as properly represented by the modern *guitar*. It is difficult to decide precisely what it was and what modern instrument it most nearly resembled; but as the three great classes, viz., harps, lyres, and guitars, have been discovered among the ruins of Egypt, and as they must, in all probability, have been, in their general characteristics, the representatives of Hebrew musical instruments, and as both generally correspond with the three similar classes of modern stringed instruments, it must follow that those instruments sculptured on the Egyptian ruins may properly bear the names of the modern instruments which they most nearly resemble.

Then let us compare the specimen presented from Jahn, above, with the three classes of modern stringed instruments, and ascertain if possible what it should be called. In our English translation it is termed *psaltery*. Modern instruments of this kind are flat, in the form of a trapezium or triangle truncated at the top. They are strung with thirteen wire cords, tuned in unisons or octaves, mounted on two bridges, and played with a plectrum. The guitar is a stringed instrument, the body of which is of an oval-like form, and the neck similar to that of a violin. The strings are distended in parallel lines from the head to the lower end, passing over the sounding-hole and bridge. The modern harp consists of a triangular frame, with cords running parallel from the top to one of the sides. It stands erect at the feet of the performer, and is played with the thumb and fingers. This instrument had only three strings at first, but their number was afterwards increased to more than thirty. The lyre is considerably like the harp; but anciently, according to Passow, it had a deeper sounding-board or chest.

From these descriptions it is probable that the *ne̱bhel* more nearly resembled the ancient and modern guitar than any other instrument. The harp has no bridge, the psaltery has two, and the lyre has none; but the ancient and modern guitar has a bridge, and but one. It is probable that the ancient guitar and psaltery, and even the lyre, were improvements upon the harp, and might be called, without much impropriety, in the language of Josephus and Gesenius, "a species of harp or lyre." As Jahn's drawing is like the guitar, he must have considered the *ne̱bhel* as best represented by that instrument. It had various forms, more or less resembling the inverted Greek delta.

The following, Fig. xxxiv, are four taken from the ruins of Egypt.

Fig. XXXIV.

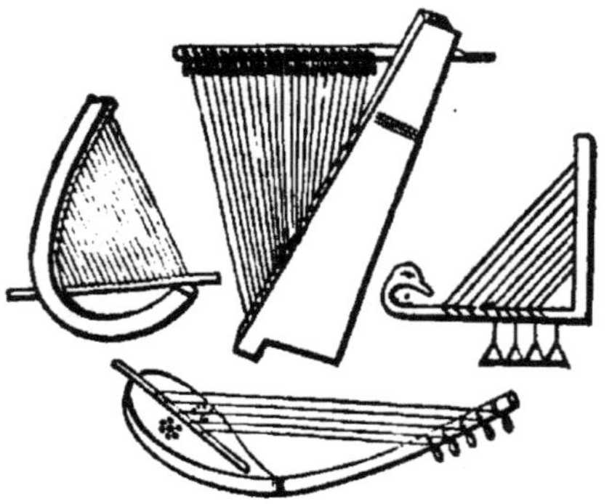

Four Ancient Guitars (nebhels) taken from the Ruins of Egypt.

Tabret.—This is probably the timbrel, and the same instrument which is mentioned in Judges xi. 34. It is in the singular number as in Gen. xxxi. 27, where it evidently indicates more than one instrument. In the case before us it is probable that there was more than one timbrel or tabret, as was usually the case in concerts, though it is possible that there was but one instrument of each kind (for a description of the tabret vid. Rem. on Gen. xxxi. 27 *supra*).

Pipe.—The Hebrew of this term is חָלִיל *hhalil*, a verbal from חָלַל *hhulál*, *to pierce*, *to bore through* (Arabic خَلَّ), hence, a *pierced* or *bored instrument*, a *flute*, a *pipe*. The Septuagint has *αυλος aulos*, *a flute*. It was evidently a wind instrument. Dr. Jahn supposes that it was made out of reed, horn, bone, or wood, and was used on joyous as well as mournful occasions. It is probable that the Hebrews, as well as the ancient Greeks, Romans, and modern Arabians, had several kinds of this instrument. Niebuhr (vid. Reis. I Ch. S. 180. tab. 26) found in Arabia not only single but double flutes, both tubes of which were blown at once, one giving the bass. Jahn, in table v. and Nr. 11 of his Archæology, has copied

Fig. xxxv.

Double Arabian Flute.

from Niebuhr three specimens of the Arabian flute, the first of which has a mouth-piece; but the second has only an opening above, which, according to the testimony of Niebuhr, is difficult to blow. Perhaps this last was the נֶקֶב *néqebh*, found in Eze. xxviii. 13, and the others the חָלִיל *halil*. The plural נְחִילוֹת (Ps. v. Tit.) *n^ehîlôth*, he thinks was used to indicate the double flute, which was known to the Romans (Adam's Roman Ant. ii. 633 f.). The following, Fig. xxxv, is a specimen taken from Niebuhr.

The *halil* was probably different from the *ugabh* (עוּגָב) though some suppose them to have been identical. Villoteau found various kinds of pipes and flutes sculptured on the ruins of Egypt. The flute as well as the pipe of Pan was undoubtedly used by the ancient Hebrews. The following, Fig. xxxvi, are specimens taken from Egyptian ruins.

Fig. xxxvi.

Two Ancient Egyptian Reed Pipes.

These forms of the instrument were, no doubt, of later origin than that of the *ugabh*. The event described in the passage under consideration probably occurred about 1095 B. C., or 2749 years after the *ug bh* was employed as mentioned in Gen. iv. 21.

The following, Fig. xxxvii, represents several Egyptian flutes, with the performers:

Fig. XXXVII.

Four Egyptian Pipes or Flutes.

Harp.—This is the *kinnōr*, (כִּנּוֹר) rightly translated *harp.* The event here described probably occurred about 644 years after the mention of the same instrument in Gen. xxxi.27. During so long a period there was ample time for the harp to reach a high degree of improvement, and it was doubtless far superior to that mentioned in Genesis iv. 21, or even to the one named in Gen. xxxi. 27.

1 Samuel xiii. 3.

And Jonathan smote the garrison of the Philistines that *was* in Geba, and the Philistines heard *of it.* And Saul blew the trumpet throughout all the land, saying, Let the Hebrews hear.

Saul had reigned over Israel two years when he commenced a war with the Philistines. He summoned the Hebrews to the battle by blowing the *crooked* or *war trumpet.* It is said that Saul blew the trumpet all over the land; probably indicating not only that he sounded this instrument himself, but commissioned others to blow and summon the people generally to war.

1 Samuel xvi. 16, 18, 23.

16 Let our lord now command thy servants, *which are* before thee, to seek out a man *who is* a cunning player on an harp: and it shall come to pass, when the evil spirit from God is upon thee, that he shall play with his hand, and thou shalt be well.

18 Then answered one of the servants, and said, Behold, I have seen a son of Jesse the Bethlehemite, *that is* cunning in playing, and a mighty valiant

man, and a man of war, and prudent in matters, and a comely person, and the Lord *is* with him.

23 And it came to pass, when the *evil* spirit from God was upon Saul, that David took an harp, and played with his hand: so Saul was refreshed, and was well, and the evil spirit departed from him.

Here is a remarkable instance of the singular effect of music upon one possessed of an evil spirit. It appears that Saul, after he had reigned over Israel about thirty-eight years, was deserted by the Lord and hurled from his throne because he interfered with the priestly office, did not obey the command of Jehovah in reference to the destruction of the Amalekites, and patronized necromancy. David was anointed king, and became Saul's successor. The prophet informs us (1 Sam. xvi. 14) that the spirit of the Lord departed from Saul, and that an evil spirit from the Lord troubled him. This seems to indicate that whatever Saul's disease may have been the Lord sent it upon him on account of his sins. Horne thinks that it was insanity of the melancholic or atrabilarious kind, as it was termed by the ancient physicians. The fits of madness returned at uncertain periods, as is frequently the case in this kind of malady (vid. Horne's Intro. P. iv. Ch. ix. Sec. 1, 4, Vol. ii. p. 196, Phil. ed.). In the judgment of experienced physicians, the remedy which was applied, viz., playing upon the harp, was a good one. The character of the oriental music was expressive rather than scientific. The unstudied and artless strains of David certainly calmed the perturbed imagination of Saul. On one occasion, when messengers, who were sent by the latter to capture David, heard the sound of musical instruments in the hands of the prophets, they were influenced by a divine enthusiasm and began to prophesy. Saul dispatched persons the second and third time, and they were similarly affected by the music. Finally the king himself went, and when he approached the seers, and heard them prophesying, and, doubtless, performing on instruments of music, he also joined, and began to prophesy (1 Sam. xix. 20–24). The prophet Elisha, once being agitated, caused a minstrel to play, in order to calm his mind and prepare it for the reception of the divine influence (2 Kings iii. 15).

These remarkable effects of music would seem to imply great skill in the performers. The natural effect of sweet and harmonious sounds is to calm the spirits and elevate the soul. The pious feelings of the Christian are aroused by music, and he rejoices to unite in singing spiritual songs. David seems to have been very skillful in performing upon the harp, being able to excite the most varied emotions by his joyous and plaintive strains. Some musicians of modern times, by devoting their lives to performing upon a single instrument, have been able to produce astonishing effects. The celebrated Nicolo Paganini, of Genoa, who is supposed to have been the most skillful performer upon the violin who ever lived, inspired wonder and admiration in all who heard him. He visited Berlin, Paris, London, and many other great cities in Europe, and all who witnessed his performances agree in declaring that the violin in his hands became an instrument entirely different from what they had ever supposed it could be, and most who heard him agreed in considering his performances as perfection itself. The music of David's harp, and that of other musical instruments in his time, seemed wonderfully to calm the mind and prepare it for the reception of the divine afflatus, and for prophesying (vid. Rem. on 1 Sam. x. 5, *supra*).

Player on a harp.—Literally, *one playing on a harp.* It appears that Saul sent for David because he was said to be skilled in performing upon that instrument. This was before his anger had been kindled against David. When the son of Jesse came and played (v. 23) Saul's disease entirely left him. The harp to which reference is here made was the *kinnōr* (vid. Rem. on Gen. iv. 21, *supra*). Josephus (Ant. B. vii. Ch. xii. Sec. 3) informs us that it had ten strings, and was struck with a plectrum or key; but this must be a mistake, as in I Sam. xvi. 23; xviii. 10, and xix. 9, David is said to have played with his hand.

I Samuel xviii. 6, 7, 10.

6 And it came to pass as they came, when David
was returned from the slaughter of the Philistine,
that the women came out of all the cities of Israel,
singing and dancing, to meet king Saul, with tab-
rets, with joy, and with instruments of music.
7 And the women answered *one another* as they
played, and said, Saul hath slain his thousands, and
David his ten thousands.

10 And it came to pass on the morrow, that the evil spirit from God came upon Saul, and he prophesied in the midst of the house: and David played with his hand, as at other times: and *there was* a javelin in Saul's hand.

It seems by verses 6 and 7 that an allusion is here made to the combat between David and Goliath. The latter was the champion of the Philistines, whom David slew, and was thus instrumental in discomfiting the enemies of Israel. When David and Saul returned from their victory, females came out to meet them, from various cities, singing and dancing, and performing upon various instruments of music. It was customary among the Hebrews to give their victorious chieftains a public triumph. On such occasions, females, with instruments of music, preceded the males. They played, sung, danced, and made every possible demonstration of joy. Thus Jephthah was hailed by his daughter and other female musicians on his return, after having conquered the Ammonites (vid. Jud. xi. 34). The victorious army of Jehoshaphat triumphantly entered Jerusalem, being led on by the king in person, accompanied by musicians, with psalteries, harps, and trumpets (vid. II Chron. xx. 27, 28). The same custom now prevails in India and Turkey. In the instance under consideration, the females preceded the males, and repeated with each other answering strains of music.

Tabrets.—These were *tophs* (תֻּפִּים *tuppim*). On such occasions of joy as this, it is probable that not only the *toph*, but other pulsatile as well as wind and stringed instruments were employed (vid. Rem. on Gen. xxxi. 27, and the accompanying engraving).

Instruments of music.—The term in Hebrew for this expression is שָׁלִשִׁים *shalishim*, from שָׁלִישׁ *shalish*, or שָׁלִשׁ *shalish*. It signifies *a third*, i. e., a measure for grain. In the plural, as in this case, it signifies, according to Gesenius, *a triangle*, i. e., a triangular instrument of music, struck in concert with drums, as in modern military music. When it refers to a measure, it indicates one which is hollow, and consequently some have supposed that the musical instrument sometimes indicated by it, was similar in form. Others believe that, as it means *third*, it refers to a stringed instrument of three strings. Dr. Jahn thinks it probable that it was a triangle, from the signification of the word, which Athenæus (Deipnos op. iv. 23) proves to be of Syriac origin. Horne maintains that there is no ground to consider it, with some ancient translators, as the castanet. The LXX express it by κυμβαλοις *kumbalois*, which may be rendered *cymbals* or *castanets*. Jerome translated the word by *sistris*. The sistrum consisted of a rod of iron bent into an oval or oblong shape, or square at two corners and curved at the others. Upon the rod were a number of movable rings. They were shaken or struck by another rod of iron. Engravings of sistra may be seen on pages 98–100 above. Villoteau found this instrument sculptured on the most ancient ruins of Egypt. He discovered different sizes of it, and variously ornamented. It is not certain that the *shalishim* were *sistra*;

but as their original signification seems to refer to a three-sided or triangular instrument, and as the term occurs in connection with tabrets, it is probable that it was a pulsatile instrument, and had one of the many forms of the sistrum. As *shalishim* is in the plural, probably several *sistra* were used, perhaps of different forms.

In verse 10 it appears that David performed again on his harp before Saul, but with less effect than before, for Saul was enraged at him, and, regardless of the sweet and pious strains of the minstrel, thrust his javelin at him, though he did not succeed in his murderous attempt.

I Samuel xix. 9.

And the evil spirit from the Lord was upon Saul, as he sat in his house with his javelin in his hand: and David played with *his* hand.

David, by the intercession of Jonathan, had been restored to the favor of Saul; but no sooner did the former contend with the Philistines and deliver Israel from their hands, than the king was again incensed against him, and made an attempt upon his life with a javelin while he was playing sweetly upon his harp. It would seem that a *part* of Saul's disease, at least, was malicious envy, from the fact that he always seemed to be enraged at David when he performed some achievement which caused the people to think more of the minstrel than of himself.

I Samuel xix. 20, 21, 23, 24.

20 And Saul sent messengers to take David: and when they saw the company of the prophets prophesying, and Samuel standing *as* appointed over them, the Spirit of God was upon the mes-

sengers of Saul, and they also prophesied. 21
And when it was told Saul, he sent other messen-
gers, and they prophesied likewise. And Saul
sent messengers again the third time, and they
prophesied also.

23 And he went thither to Naioth in Ramah:
and the Spirit of God was upon him also, and he
went on, and prophesied, until he came to Naioth
in Ramah. 24 And he stripped off his clothes
also, and prophesied before Samuel in like manner,
and lay down naked all that day and all that
night. Wherefore they say, *Is* Saul also among
the prophets?

Here is a reference to the school of the prophets (vid. Rem. on I Sam. x. 5, *supra*) over which Samuel presided. It appears that David was with them, and Saul sent messengers at three different times, to capture him, and finally made the attempt himself; but when they saw the company of prophets, with Samuel at their head, prophesying in a solemn manner, while various instruments of music were pouring forth their sweet and soothing strains, a divine influence seemed to overwhelm Saul and his messengers, and they joined the seers and began to prophesy with them (vid. Rem. on I Sam. xvi. 16, 18, 23; I Chron. xxv. 1, 3, 5, 6, 7).

I SAMUEL xxi. 11.

And the servants of Achish said unto him, Is not this David the king of the land? did they not sing one to another of him in dances, saying, Saul hath slain his thousands, and David his ten thousands?

David had fled from the fury of Saul, to the king of Gath, whose servants suspected the character of their guest, and uttered the language quoted above.

Sing one to another of him in dances.—Here is a reference to I Sam. xviii. 6, 7, where it is said that women came out of the cities of Israel to meet Saul and David after the latter had conquered the Philistines. They approached with singing, dancing, tabrets, and instruments of music, proclaiming that David had slain his tens of thousands, while Saul had only slain his thousands.

I Samuel xxix. 5.

Is not this David, of whom they sang one to another in dances, saying, Saul slew his thousands, and David his ten thousands?

This refers to the same occurrence, and, of course, to the same kinds of music as the passage last considered.

I Samuel xxx. 16.

And when he had brought him down, behold, *they were* spread abroad upon all the earth, eating and drinking and dancing, because of all the great spoil that they had taken out of the land of the Philistines, and out of the land of Judah.

These words were spoken in reference to the Amalekites, who had, in David's absence, captured Ziklag, burned the city, and led her inhabitants into captivity. When the king returned and saw what was done, he took the four hundred men, who were with him, and pursued the enemy. Finding them spread abroad upon the earth, feasting upon the spoils which they had taken in other places, he fell upon them and slew them.

Dancing.—The Amalekites were evidently engaged in rejoicings and festivities on account of their victories. One of their sports was *dancing*, and they probably, in accordance with oriental custom, had various musical accompaniments. That people lived in Arabia Petræa, inhabiting hamlets, caves, or dens, like the present Arabs. They were doubtless familiar with various kinds of musical instruments, as it is certain that the Arabs were, long before that period. The Amalekites, no doubt, used instruments similar to those of other tribes around them, and probably the same, essentially, as those of the Israelites.

The Hebrew term translated *dancing is* חֹגְגִים *hhogᵉgim*, from חָגַג *hhagăg*, *to move around in a circle*, hence, *to dance.*

THE SECOND BOOK OF SAMUEL.

INTRODUCTORY REMARKS.

THIS book contains the history of David, the second king of Israel, during a period of nearly forty years, from about 1055 to 1015 B. C. It records an account of the transferring of the kingdom of Israel from the tribe of Benjamin to that of Judah. There is a description of the victories of David, the wise administration of his government, his exertions to promote true religion, his sins and repentance, and the grievous judgments which fell upon him and his subjects. This narrative evidently bears an intimate relation to the first book of Samuel and the first book of Kings, forming a connected history. The two books of Samuel are important from the fact that they illustrate, and indeed constitute the key, to an explanation of the Psalms.

II SAMUEL ii. 28.

So Joab blew a trumpet, and all the people stood still, and pursued after Israel no more, neither fought they any more.

It appears that Joab led on the army of David against the forces of Saul under the direction of Abner. Joab gained the victory, pursued his foes, and slew large numbers, until Abner, having been pursued without mercy, inquired if the "sword should devour forever" (v. 26). Then Joab blew the *trumpet.* This was the *shophar* or *crooked trumpet*, blown on this occasion to indicate a truce. It was probably sounded in a soft tone, as when the people were called together in time of peace.

II Samuel vi. 5.

And David and all the house of Israel played before the Lord on all manner of *instruments made of* fir-wood, even on harps, and on psalteries, and on timbrels, and on cornets, and on cymbals.

There is an allusion in this passage to a grand concert of the minstrels of Israel, called together to celebrate an important event. David, the king of Israel, had assembled thirty thousand of his people, and led them in solemn procession to the house of Abinadab, a Levite of Kirjath-jearim, whither the ark of the covenant had been carried by persons sent from that place to receive it from the Philistines at Beth-shemesh, where it had been deposited by the latter.

After the Israelites had received the holy treasure and turned their faces toward the city of David, the king and the multitudes who were with him *played* on all kinds of *instruments of music*. This was considered by the children of Israel as an important event, from the fact that the blessing of God generally followed the ark unless it was seized contrary to the divine command. The Philistines had thus carried it away and incurred the displeasure of Jehovah, as we have already intimated. David, undoubtedly, selected persons of the greatest influence in the kingdom—chosen men of Israel, and the most skillful performers upon instruments of music—to take part in this grand procession.

David and all the house of Israel played.—This general expression might seem to include *all* of the Israelites—those who accompanied David and those who did not; but it is more natural to suppose that there is reference only to the former, for it is not probable that there were instruments of music enough to supply all the thousands of Israel, and it is said that "all played." Perhaps even all of those who accompanied David were not supplied with instruments. *All*, in the scriptures, is frequently used for a part. It is possible, however, in this case, as the occasion was so important, that every one of the thirty thousand had an instrument of music and played. The king, undoubtedly, could have easily supplied such a number. However this may have been, there can be no doubt that there was a great number of musicians. Perhaps all of the four thousand Levite singers employed in the tabernacle, and afterwards in the temple, were there. It is probable that the variety of instruments was considerable. Perhaps a large proportion, if not *all* of the kinds, known to the Hebrews, were used on the occasion. This opinion seems to be confirmed by the expression, "*on all manner of Instruments made of fir-wood*," which is qualified by the following: "*even on harps, and on psalteries, and on timbrels, and on cornets*," apparently intimating that these were the instruments indicated by "*all manner of instruments*." The writer, however, may have been speaking in general terms, and may have intended to name the principal kinds of instruments, to show that those which were used on the most solemn and important occasions were employed here. The king, undoubtedly, formed as complete a band as was possible in those early times. The sacred writer mentions five instruments; but perhaps varieties of each kind were intended, as the plural number is used in each case. The LXX supposed that more instruments were employed than are mentioned. They render the passage thus:

ἐν ὀργάνοις ἡρμοσμένοις ἐν ἰσχύι, καὶ ἐν ᾠδαῖς, καὶ ἐν κινύραις, καὶ ἐν νάβλαις καὶ ἐν τυμπάνοις, καὶ ἐν κυμβάλοις, καὶ ἐν αὐλοῖς. *With powerful organs, and with songs, and with harps, and with guitars, and with tabrets, and with cymbals, and with flutes.*

They supposed that there was vocal as well as instrumental music, which was the fact, as it appears from I Chron. xiii. 8.

On all manner of instruments made of fir-wood.—The Hebrew of this expression is בְּכָל עֲצֵי בְרוֹשִׁים *b[e]kol [a]tse b[e]roshim*, literally, *on all wood of cypress-trees.* We are to understand by this phrase that the Israelites played on all kinds of instruments made of cypress-wood. The term בְרוֹשִׁים *b[e]roshim*, *cypress-trees*, may have included other trees of the pine genus, though that is uncertain (vid. Gesen. Thesaurus p. 246). We have no means of ascertaining how many kinds of musical instruments were made of cypress-wood. Of course we must except those which were constructed of metal, horn, and perhaps others.

Harps.—These are the *Kinnors*, so often referred to above.

Psalteries.—The Hebrew term is the same as the one which occurs in 1 Sam. x. 5, and translated psalteries, excepting that in this passage the plural form is used, viz., נְבָלִים *n[e]bhalim*, clearly indicating that there were more instruments than one of this kind used on the occasion. These were probably *guitars* (vid. Rem. on 1 Sam. x. 5, *supra*).

Timbrels.—The same original word is used as in Judges xi. 34.*

Cornets.—Here we find an instrument which is not mentioned before. The Hebrew term is מְנַעַנְעִים *m[e]năănim*, a participle, in the Peal conjugation used as a noun in the masculine plural, from נוּעַ *nuăh*, *to move to and fro, to waver.* The Greek term is *νεύω neuō*, Latin *nuo*, German *nicken*, all of which mean *to nod backwards and forwards.* From the origin of the word we have reason to believe that the instrument intended was one which was shaken. The Vulgate renders it *sistra.* It was evidently some kind of timbrel which was shaken when played. Consequently, the English translation must be incorrect, as Cornets are wind instruments. It is difficult to ascertain exactly the form of this instrument. Jahn supposes that it must have been of the pulsatile kind. The Septuagint translators

* For a description of this instrument, vid. Rem. on Gen. xxxi. 27; cf Rem. on Judg. xi. 34, and Ex. xv. 20.

have rendered it by *αυλας aulas, flutes;* but they were certainly mistaken in supposing that it was a wind instrument. Jahn thinks that it probably consisted of an iron rod with two square corners and rounded at the top, or that it was similar to an arc in form, with rings hung loosely upon it, making a tinkling sound when the instrument was struck or shaken. This explanation is probably correct, as the sistrum, according to Jablonski and others, was common in Egypt (Opusc. i. p. 306–309). Horne maintains the same opinion (Intro. P. iv. c. vii. Sec. ii). This is the only place in the scriptures in which this instrument is mentioned. The engraving, Fig. xxvi. No. 2, on page 99, is supposed to represent the ancient Hebrew *menaanim*.

Cymbals.—This is also an instrument which is not mentioned before. The Hebrew term is צֶלְצְלִים *tsĕltsĕlim*, a plural noun derived from the verb צָלַל *tsalăl*, in the Arabic صَلَّ and in Syriac ܨܠ. In all, it means *to tingle, to tinkle.* The noun signifies *a tinkling, tingling, clinking, ringing, clanging.* It may signify a *clanging instrument of music.* Gesenius (vid. his Heb. Lex. under this word) thinks that the word here signifies *cymbals,* similar to those now used in martial music. Jahn is sanguine in the belief that the term should be translated *castanets,* and remarks, that they are used at the present day in the East. There were anciently, as in modern times, two kinds, the smaller and larger cymbals. The smaller ones were metallic plates or shells, the size of a large button. Females, when dancing, had two fastened to each hand, one on the thumb and the other on the middle finger, and beat them against each other, thus keeping time. Josephus* describes the larger kind as broad, large, and made of brass. The musician held one in each hand and struck them together, keeping time as is customary with us; but the dishes of ours are more shallow than those in the East. The following are specimens of the larger kind taken from the ruins of Egypt (vid. Fig. xxxviii).

* Ant. vii., xii. 3. His words are κυμβαλα πλατεια καὶ μεγαλα χαλκεα.

Fig. xxxviii.

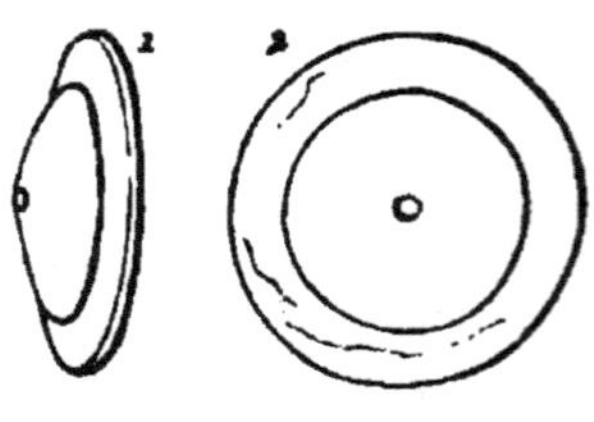

Two larger Ancient Egyptian Cymbals.

Specimens of the small kind may be found in Fig. xxvii, No. 1, on p. 100, *supra*.

Judging from the etymology of the word indicating them, they must have been pulsatile instruments, and probably those which were struck against each other.* In Zech. xiv. 20, the term is translated *bells*, referring to the ancient custom of attaching them to horses. Camels and horses sometimes wear bells in the East at the present day. Probably the Hebrews attached small pieces of brass to the necks of their horses, which would make a tinkling noise when they moved. The Romans attached to their war-horses pieces of metal called *phalarea*, to produce terror in their enemies. These might with some propriety be called a species of cymbal.

II Samuel vi. 14.

And David danced before the Lord with all *his* might; and David *was* girded with a linen ephod.

Danced.—מְכַרְכֵּר *mekărker*, part. Palpel from כָּרַר *karăr*, *to dance, to move in a circle.* The corresponding Greek word is σκαίρω *skairō*, *to leap, to exult.* The LXX assert that David *played* on *instruments* of *music.* This was probably the fact, while the ark was moving towards Jerusalem. He and his attendants doubtless *played* as well as *danced*, though the Hebrew term only refers to the latter exercise.

II Samuel vi. 15, 16.

15 So David and all the house of Israel brought

* Cf. Sonnerat's Travels in the East Indies and China, p. 3; Käupfer Amoen. Exot. Fasc.; Niebuhr Reis. 1. Th. S. 184. Tab. xxviii.; Jahn's Bib. Arch. § 96; Horne's Intro. P. iv. ch. vii. Sec. ii. (vol. ii. p. 183. Philadelphia ed. 1836).

up the ark of the Lord with shouting, and with the sound of the trumpet. 16 And as the ark of the Lord came into the city of David, Michal, Saul's daughter, looked through a window, and saw king David leaping and dancing before the Lord; and she despised him in her heart.

Shouting—Sound of the trumpet.—Every demonstration of joy seems to have been made, when the procession with the ark of the covenant solemnly moved towards the city of David. There was *shouting*, *singing*, *dancing*, and *playing* upon various instruments of music. It appears that the ***crooked trumpet*** or ***shophar*** was one of the instruments used on that august occasion. From the sixteenth verse, we learn that Saul's daughter despised David when she saw him dancing, rejoicing, and praising God. She seemed to entertain towards him some of the enmity of her father.

II Samuel vi. 21.

And David said unto Michal, *It was* before the Lord, which chose me before thy father, and before all his house, to appoint me ruler over the people of the Lord, over Israel: therefore will I play before the Lord.

I will play (שִׂחַקְתִּי *sihhăqtīy*)—According to Gesenius, this term here signifies *to dance, accompanied with song and instrumental music* (vid. Gesen. Heb. Lex. under שָׂחַק).

II Samuel xv. 10.

But Absalom sent spies throughout all the tribes

of Israel, saying, As soon as ye hear the sound of the trumpet, then ye shall say, Absalom reigneth in Hebron.

Absalom had wickedly conspired against his father David, and was making preparations to take possession of the kingdom. His plan was, to retire to Hebron apparently for the purpose of paying a vow, and there, by the sound of the trumpet, to proclaim himself king. The instrument which he used was the *shophar* or *war trumpet.*

II Samuel xviii. 16.

And Joab blew the trumpet, and the people returned from pursuing after Israel: for Joab held back the people.

It appears that Absalom failed in his insurrection, to which reference is made above, and came to a miserable end. David's forces subdued the rebels, and finally the *war trumpet* or *shophar* was sounded as a signal for the army to cease the pursuit.

II Samuel xix. 35.

I *am* this day fourscore years old: *and* can I discern between good and evil? can thy servant taste what I eat or what I drink? can I hear any more the voice of singing men and singing women? wherefore then should thy servant be yet a burden unto my lord the king?

These are the words of Barzillai the Gileadite, in answer to David, who desired the former to accompany him to Jerusalem and there reside.

Singing men and singing women.—Literally *male singers and female singers.* Females (generally the daughters of Levites) as well as males, were admitted into the tabernacle and subsequently temple service. Heman had fourteen sons and three daughters, skilled in music. When Ezra enumerated those who returned with him from the Babylonish captivity, he reckoned two hundred singing men and singing women. In the tabernacle and temple, the Levites, both male and female, were the legal musicians. It is uncertain whether Barzillai referred to the temple service or to private music, or both, and it is immaterial which. He evidently intended to intimate that, on account of his age, he had ceased to enjoy the pleasures connected with David's splendid court, and that he was only an obstacle to the happiness of his friends.

II Samuel xx. 1, 22.

1 And there happened to be there a man of Belial, whose name *was* Sheba, the son of Bichri, a Benjaminite: and he blew a trumpet, and said, We have no part in David, neither have we inheritance in the son of Jesse: every man to his tents, O Israel.

22 Then the woman went unto all the people in her wisdom. And they cut off the head of Sheba, the son of Bichri, and cast *it* out to Joab. And he blew a trumpet, and they retired from the city, every man to his tent. And Joab returned to Jerusalem unto the king.

Sheba, a Benjaminite, had raised a rebellion against David, and had blown the *war trumpet* or *shophar* as a signal of revolt. From the twenty-second verse, we perceive that he was taken and slain by the king's army, and his head thrown over the wall to Joab, the commander of David's forces. Then the *shophar* or *crooked trumpet* was blown, as a signal for Joab to raise the siege and retire from the city of Abel.

II Samuel xxii. 1–51.

1 And David spake unto the Lord the words of
this song, in the day that the Lord had delivered
him out of the hand of all his enemies, and out of
the hand of Saul.

2 The Lord is my rock, and my fortress, and my deliverer.
3 The God of my rock; in him will I trust:
He is my shield, and the horn of my salvation,
My high tower, and my refuge, my Saviour;
Thou savest me from violence.
4 I will call on the Lord *who is* worthy to be praised:
So shall I be saved from mine enemies.
5 When the waves of death compassed me,
The floods of ungodly men made me afraid;
6 The sorrows of hell compassed me about;
The snares of death prevented me;
7 In my distress I called upon the Lord,
And cried to my God;
And he did hear my voice out of his temple,
And my cry *did enter* into his ears.
8 Then the earth shook and trembled;
The foundations of heaven moved
And shook, because he was wroth.
9 There went up a smoke out of his nostrils,
And fire out of his mouth devoured:
Coals were kindled by it.
10 He bowed the heavens also, and came down;
And darkness *was* under his feet.

11 And he rode upon a cherub, and did fly:
And he was seen upon the wings of the wind.
12 And he made darkness pavilions round about him,
Dark waters, *and* thick clouds of the skies.
13 Through the brightness before him
Were coals of fire kindled.
14 The Lord thundered from heaven,
And the Most High uttered his voice.
15 And he sent out arrows, and scattered them;
Lightning, and discomfited them.
16 And the channels of the sea appeared,
The foundations of the world were discovered,
At the rebuking of the Lord,
At the blast of the breath of his nostrils.
17 He sent from above, he took me;
He drew me out of many waters;
18 He delivered me from my strong enemy,
And from them that hated me.
For they were too strong for me.
19 They prevented me in the day of my calamity:
But the Lord was my stay.
20 He brought me forth also into a large place:
He delivered me, because he delighted in me.
21 The Lord rewarded me according to my righteousness:
According to the cleanness of my hands hath he recompensed me.
22 For I have kept the ways of the Lord,
And have not wickedly departed from my God.
23 For all his judgments *were* before me:
And *as for* his statutes, I did not depart from them.
24 I was also upright before him,
And have kept myself from mine iniquity.
25 Therefore the Lord hath recompensed me according to my righteousness;

According to my cleanness in his eye-sight.
26 With the merciful thou wilt show thyself merciful,
And with the upright man thou wilt show thyself upright.
27 With the pure thou wilt show thyself pure;
And with the froward thou wilt show thyself unsavory.
28 And the afflicted people thou wilt save:
And thine eyes *are* upon the haughty,
That thou mayest bring *them* down.
29 For thou *art* my lamp, O Lord:
And the Lord will lighten my darkness.
30 For by thee I have run through a troop:
By my God have I leaped over a wall.
31 *As for* God, his way *is* perfect;
The word of the Lord *is* tried:
He *is* a buckler to all them that trust in him.
32 For who *is* God, save the Lord?
And who *is* a rock, save our God?
33 God *is* my strength *and* power:
And he maketh my way perfect.
34 He maketh my feet like hinds' *feet:*
And setteth me upon my high places.
35 He teacheth my hands to war:
So that a bow of steel is broken by mine arms.
36 Thou hast also given me the shield of thy salvation:
And thy gentleness hath made me great.
37 Thou hast enlarged my steps under me;
So that my feet did not slip.
38 I have pursued mine enemies, and destroyed them;
And turned not again until I had consumed them.
39 And I have consumed them,
And wounded them, that they could not arise:
Yea, they are fallen under my feet.

40 For thou hast girded me with strength to battle:
Them that rose up against me hast thou subdued under me.
41 Thou hast also given me the necks of mine enemies,
That I might destroy them that hate me.
42 They looked, but *there was* none to save;
Even unto the Lord, but he answered them not.
43 Then did I beat them as small as the dust of the earth.
I did stamp them as the mire of the street,
And did spread them abroad.
44 Thou also hast delivered me from the strivings of my people.
Thou hast kept me *to be* head of the heathen:
A people *which* I knew not shall serve me.
45 Strangers shall submit themselves unto me:
As soon as they hear, they shall be obedient unto me
46 Strangers shall fade away,
And they shall be afraid out of their close places.
47 The Lord liveth: and blessed *be* my rock;
And exalted be the God of the rock of my salvation.
48 It *is* God that avengeth me,
And that bringeth down the people under me,
49 And that bringeth me forth from mine enemies:
Thou also hast lifted me up on high above them that rose up against me:
Thou hast delivered me from the violent man.
50 Therefore I will give thanks unto thee, O Lord, among the heathen,
And I will sing praises unto thy name.
51 *He is* the tower of salvation for his king:
And showeth mercy to his anointed,
Unto David, and to his seed for evermore.

The above is a psalm of praise containing a general review of God's mercies to the king of Israel through life, and the many wonderful deliverances which he had experienced. This ode, with a few variations, is found in the book of Psalms (Ps. xviii). We have it here as originally composed by David for his own private devotions. In Psalms we have it as amended and delivered to the chief musician for the services of the temple. The hymn extends through the chapter, and contains some of the finest specimens of oriental imagery extant. The last words of David, and a kind of supplement to this hymn, are found in the twenty-third chapter, verses 1–7, as follows:

1 Now these *be* the last words of David. David, the son of Jesse, said, and the man *who was* raised up on high, the anointed of the God of Jacob and the sweet Psalmist of Israel, said:

2 The spirit of the Lord spake by me,
And his word *was* in my tongue.
3 The God of Israel said,
The rock of Israel spake to me,
He that ruleth over men *must be* just,
Ruling in the fear of God.
4 And *he shall be* as the light of the morning,
When the sun riseth, *even* a morning without clouds;
As the tender grass *springing* out of the earth,
By clear shining after rain.
5 Although my house *be* not so with God,
Yet he hath made with me an everlasting covenant,
Ordered in *all things* and sure;
For *this is* all my salvation and all *my* desire,
Although he make *it* not to grow.
6 But *the sons* of Belial *shall be* all of them as thorns thrust away,
Because they cannot be taken with hands:

7 But the man *that* shall touch them
Must be fenced with iron and the staff of a spear;
And they shall be utterly burned with fire in the *same* place.

The two books of Samuel throw much light upon the Psalms, and may be considered as a key to their explanation. Psalm iii. is elucidated by II Samuel xv. 14 and onward; Ps. iv. by I Sam. xxii., xxiii., and xxvi; Ps. vii. by II Sam. xvi. 2, 11; Ps. xxiv. by II Sam. vi. 12 and onward; Ps. xxx. by I Sam. v. 11; Ps. xxxii, and li. by II Sam. xii; Ps. xxxiv. by II Sam. xxi. 10–15; Ps. xxxv. by II Sam. xv.–xvii.; Ps. xlii, and xliii. by II Sam. xvii. 22–24; Ps. lii. by I Sam. xxii. 9; Ps. liv. by I Sam. xxiii. 19, and xxvi. I; Ps. lv. by II Sam. xvii. 21, 22; Ps. lvi. by I Sam. xxi. 11–15; Ps. lvii. by I Sam. xxii. 1, and xxiv. 3; Ps. lix. by I Sam. xix. 11; Ps. lx. by II Sam viii. 3–13, and x. 15–19; Ps. lxiii. by I Sam. xxii. 5, and xxiii. 14–16; Ps. lxviii. by II Sam. vi. 3–12; Ps. lxxxix by II Sam. vii. 12; Ps. cxlii. by I Sam. xxii. 1, and xxiv. 1 and onward.

THE TWO BOOKS OF KINGS.

INTRODUCTORY REMARKS.

THERE is a close connection between the books of Samuel and those of Kings. In the former the origin and gradual increase of the united kingdom of Israel under Saul and David are described; and in the latter an account is given of that kingdom in its higher state of prosperity under Solomon, its division under his son and successor Rehoboam, the causes of that division, and the consequent decline of the two kingdoms of Israel and Judah, until their subversion after Shalmaneser had carried the ten tribes captive into Assyria, and Nebuchadnezzar had carried Judah and Benjamin captive into Babylon.

In the most ancient and correct editions of the Hebrew Bible, the two books of Kings constitute but one. They have been divided, at some unknown period, into two parts for the convenience of the reader.

There is a great diversity of opinion in regard to the author or authors of these books; but the most probable supposition is, that they were arranged in their present order by Ezra from memoirs written by different persons, who described the events soon after their occurrence.

FIRST BOOK OF KINGS.

This book embraces a period of one hundred and twenty-six years from the anointing of Solomon and his admission as a partner in the throne with David B. C.

1015, to the death of Jehoshaphat B. C. 889. The latter part of David's life is described, and, in general, the history of the undivided kingdom of Israel under Solomon is given, and a history of the *divided* kingdom under Rehoboam, Jeroboam, and their successors.

I Kings i. 34, 39.

And let Zadok the priest and Nathan the prophet anoint him there king over Israel: and blow ye with the trumpet, and say, God save king Solomon.

And Zadok the priest took an horn of oil out of the tabernacle, and anointed Solomon. And they blew the trumpet; and all the people said, God save king Solomon.

The occasion to which reference is made in these verses, was an important one, viz., the inauguration of Solomon as king of Israel. The *crooked trumpet* or *shophar* was used.

I Kings i. 40.

And all the people came up after him, and the people piped with pipes, and rejoiced with great joy, so that the earth rent with the sound of them.

After Solomon had been anointed king, every possible demonstration of joy was exhibited by the people.

Piped with pipes.—The Hebrew is מְחַלְּלִים בַּחֲלִלִים *m^{e}hhall^{e}lîm bahh^{a}lilîm*, literally, *piping with pipes*, or *fluting with flutes.* These were undoubtedly the Hebrew flutes (*hhallelim*), which, according to Dr. Jahn, were used on joyful as well as on mournful occasions, and were appropriate instruments to be employed at the coronation (vid. description of this instrument in the remarks on 1 Sam. x. 5, *supra*).

It is said that the *people piped*, indicating that many of these instruments were used. Perhaps some had the double flute, and so performed the bass as well as the air.

Rejoiced with great joy.—The original of this denotes a *loud expression of joy*, as *songs*, or *shouts*. There must have been loud bursts of mirth, for it is said that "the earth rent with the sound of them."

I Kings i. 41.

And Adonijah and all the guests that *were* with him heard *it* as they had made an end of eating. And when Joab heard the sound of the trumpet, he said, Wherefore *is this* noise of the city being in an uproar?

Adonijah, it seems, had usurped the throne, and was much surprised when he heard the loud rejoicing and sound of the *shophar* or crooked trumpet, announcing the fact that Solomon was made king instead of himself.

I Kings iv. 32.

And he spake three thousand proverbs: and his songs were a thousand and five.

Solomon was distinguished for his wisdom, excelling all of his contemporaries in the East and even in renowned Egypt (vid. I Kings, iv. 30). Like his father David, he was acquainted with music, and composed more than a thousand songs to be accompanied in their recital by instrumental music. It seemed to be an essential part of one's education in those early times, to be thoroughly instructed in music.

I Kings x. 12.

And the king made of the almug trees pillars for the house of the Lord, and for the king's house, harps also, and psalteries for singers: there came no such almug trees, nor were seen unto this day.

Solomon constructed of the almug tree not only pillars, but instruments of music for the temple and for his palace.

Harps.—These were the *kinnors* (כִּנֹּרוֹת *kinnoroth*), the instruments in which Solomon's father, David, so much delighted (vid. Rem. on Gen. iv. 21, *supra*).

Psalteries.—These were the *nebhels or guitars* (נְבָלִים *n^ebhalim*, vid. Rem. on I Sam. x. 5, *supra*). They were made of the almug tree. It is supposed by modern interpreters that this was the red sandal-wood, which now grows in China and in the Indian Archipelago. It is used in India and Persia, at the present day, for costly instruments and utensils (vid. Gesen. Heb. Lex. under אַלְמֻגִּים *almuggîm*).

Harps and psalteries for singers.—It seems by this expression that those instruments were made *for singers*, implying that they not only *played on instruments*, but *sung*. It is probable that they sung at the same time that they performed on instruments, as is frequently the case at the present day.

SECOND BOOK OF KINGS.

INTRODUCTORY REMARKS.

THIS book contains the history of the two kingdoms of Israel and Judah from the death of Jehoshaphat, B. C. 889, to the destruction of Jerusalem and the temple by Nebuchadnezzar, B. C. 588, a period of about 300 years. This history may be divided into two parts. 1st. That of the two monarchies of Israel and Judah, until the end of the former. 2d. The history of Judah until its subversion.

II KINGS iii. 15.

But now bring me a minstrel. And it came to pass, when the minstrel played, that the hand of the Lord came upon him.

Here is a confirmation of the fact, that the ancient seers considered music as peculiarly adapted to prepare their minds for prophetic vision. The kings of Israel, Judah, and Edom asked the prophet Elisha to inquire of the Lord for them, as they were destitute of water in their expedition against the Moabites. The seer called for a minstrel to play before him, and when he heard the enchanting sound of music, the hand of the Lord came upon him—a divine enthusiasm seemed to take possession of his mind, and he began to prophesy. It appears by the fourteenth verse, that the prophet exercised a pious indignation against the king of Israel, and, in order to calm his feelings, it seemed to be necessary for him to listen to the sweet, soothing strains of oriental music.

Minstrel.—(מְנַגֵּן *m^enaggen*) literally, *one playing on an instrument of music—a player on an instrument.*

The minstrel played.—Literally, *the player played.* The term *minstrel* is a word introduced into England by the Normans, and included singers, performers on musical instruments, also jugglers, dancers, and other similar persons whose profession was to amuse kings, or others who could pay them for their services. In some periods of history they are represented as the friends and favorites of princes, and at other periods they are classed with beggars and vagabonds, and forbidden to practise their arts. Among the Hebrews, as we think from the etymology of the word, they were performers on musical instruments, and perhaps sung an accompaniment at the same time.

II Kings ix. 13.

Then they hasted, and took every man his garment, and put *it* under him on the top of the stairs, and blew with trumpets, saying, Jehu is king.

Elisha directed one of the sons of the prophets to go to Ramoth Gilead and anoint Jehu king over Israel. He did so, and Jehu's attendants blew the *shophar* or crooked trumpet, and proclaimed him king. In the original the singular number is used, though reference is made to more than one trumpet.

II Kings xi. 14.

And when she looked, behold, the king stood by a pillar, as the manner *was*, and the princes and the trumpeters by the king, and all the people of the land rejoiced, and blew with trumpets: and

Athaliah rent her clothes, and cried, Treason, treason!

Athaliah had usurped the throne of Israel, and to secure her authority had slain all the seed royal of David that she could find. It happened, however, that Joash, the son of Ahaziah, who had been concealed, was proclaimed king, and it is not strange that Athaliah cried *treason*. The occasion was an important one, and *trumpeters* were present.

Blew with trumpets, i. e., with straight trumpets (*hatsotserôth*, vid. Rem. on Num. x, 2, *supra*).

II Kings xii. 13.

Howbeit, there were not made for the house of the Lord bowls of silver, snuffers, basins, trumpets, any vessels of gold or vessels of silver of the money that was brought into the house of the Lord.

Trumpets—(*hatsotseroth*) *straight trumpets.*—In repairing the temple, it seems that the trumpets and other implements, here named, were not made of the money which was brought into the house of the Lord, as that was designed to pay the workmen laboring upon the temple itself. Perhaps some of these implements had been previously made, or were constructed out of other materials.

THE BOOKS OF CHRONICLES.

INTRODUCTORY REMARKS.

The Jews called these books דִּבְרֵי הַיָּמִים *dibhrey hăyyamim*, i. e., *the words of the days or annals*, probably because they were compiled from diaries or annals. The LXX designate them by ΠΑΡΑΛΕΙΠΟΜΕΝΑ *Paraleipomena*, *the things left or omitted*, supposing them to be a supplement either to Samuel and the book of Kings, or to the whole Bible. Jerome gave them the name of Chronicles, because they contain an abstract of sacred history up to the time in which they were written.

They were undoubtedly compiled from other records, prepared at different times before and after the Babylonish captivity, as it is evident that they are not the original and more copious chronicles to which there are so frequent references in the books of Kings.

It is uncertain who wrote the Chronicles. It is evident, however, that they were compiled by some person who lived after the captivity, and that he obtained his materials from the memoirs of writers contemporary with the events recorded, and who flourished long before his time.

The object of the books of Chronicles is to present accurately the genealogies, dignity, powers, and order of the priests and Levites, that they might be prepared after the captivity to assume again their proper rank, and reënter the sacred office. The author wished further to show how the lands had been distributed among the families before the captivity, so that the tribes could, upon their return, obtain the original inheritance of their fathers. Ancient records are quoted, and four rolls or numberings of the people are recited.

The Chronicles are an abridgment of sacred history, but especially during that period which elapsed between the first establishment of the Jewish nation and their return from the first captivity.

The *first book* describes the rise and propagation of the people of Israel, and subsequently gives a particular account of the reign and transactions of David. In the *second book* the narrative is continued. The progress and dissolution of the kingdom of Judah, up to the year of the return of the Jews from the Babylonish captivity, are described. The period embraced in Chronicles is about 3468 years.

I Chronicles vi. 31–33.

31 And these *are they* whom David set over the
service of song in the house of the Lord, after that
the ark had rest. 32 And they ministered before
the dwelling-place of the tabernacle of the congregation with singing, until Solomon had built the
house of the Lord in Jerusalem: and *then* they
waited on their office according to their order.
33 And these *are* they that waited, with their
children. Of the sons of the Kohathites; Heman
a singer, the son of Joel, the son of Shemuel.

These verses refer to the arrangements in the tabernacle, and first temple built by Solomon. After the ark was removed from the house of Obed-edom (II Sam. vi. 7), and deposited in the tabernacle erected by David (I Chron. xvi. 1), the king appointed suitable persons to sing and play upon musical instruments before that sacred treasure.

With singing (v. 32).—The Septuagint renders this ἐν ὀργάνοις *ĕn organois, on organs*, thus indicating that musical instruments were used. The Hebrew term is properly translated in the English version, though it is doubtless true that those who ministered before the ark not only sung, but performed upon instruments of music. David appointed four thousand of the Levites to be singers before the ark in the tabernacle, and the arrangement was subsequently confirmed by Solomon, after the temple was completed (II Chron. viii. 14).

I Chronicles ix. 33.

And these *are* the singers, chief of the fathers of the Levites, *who remaining* in the chambers *were* free: for they were employed in *that* work day and night.

It appears that there were services in the tabernacle at night as well as during the day. We read in I Chron. xxiii. 30, of the Levites standing every morning and evening in the tabernacle to thank and praise the Lord. The lamps of the golden candlesticks were lighted at evening, and kept burning during the night. There were morning and evening sacrifices, and the Levites were in constant attendance, in the temple, day and night, and ready to perform by turns any *required* service. The singers seem to have been persons of influence, as they are called "chief of the fathers of the Levites."

I Chronicles xiii. 8.

And David and all Israel played before God with all *their* might, and with singing, and with harps, and with psalteries, and with timbrels, and with cymbals, and with trumpets.

This refers to the solemn ceremony of carrying the ark from Kirjath-jearim to the city of David. Reference is made to the same circumstance in II Sam. vi. 5, where the musicians are said to have played upon all manner of instruments made of fir-wood, even on harps, psalteries, timbrels, cornets, and cymbals. The same instruments are mentioned in both places with two exceptions. In Samuel בִּמְנַעַנְעִים *bimnăahnīm*, translated *cornets*, occurs, which is not found in the parallel passage in I Chronicles. These were undoubtedly a species of timbrels, and not wind instruments as the erroneous English translation of "cornets" implies (vid. Rem. on II Sam. vi. 5). The passage in I Chronicles has *trumpets*, not mentioned in II Samuel. The Hebrew word is בַּחֲצֹצְרוֹת *băhhᵃtsōtsᵉrōth*, the straight trumpets so frequently mentioned in previous passages.

I Chronicles xv. 16, 19, 20, 21, 22, 24, 27, 28, 29.

16 And David spake to the chief of the Levites,
to appoint their brethren *to be* the singers with
instruments of music, psalteries, and harps, and
cymbals, sounding, by lifting up the voice with
joy.
19 So the singers, Heman, Asaph, and Ethan,
were appointed to sound with cymbals of brass;
20 And Zechariah, and Aziel, and Shemiramoth,
and Jehiel, and Unni, and Eliab, and Maaseiah, and
Benaiah, with psalteries on Alamoth; 21 And
Mattathiah, and Elipheleh, and Mikneiah, and
Obed-edom, and Jeiel, and Azaziah, with harps
on the Sheminith to excel. 22 And Chenaniah,
chief of the Levites, *was* for song: he instructed
about the song, because he *was* skillful.

24 And Shebaniah, and Jehoshaphat, and Nethaneel, and Amasai, and Zechariah, and Benaiah, and Eliezer, the priests, did blow with the trumpets before the ark of God: and Obed-edom and Jehiah *were* door-keepers for the ark.

27 And David *was* clothed with a robe of fine linen, and all the Levites that bare the ark, and the singers, and Chenaniah the master of the song with the singers: David also *had* upon him an
ephod of linen. 28 Thus all Israel brought up
the ark of the covenant of the Lord with shouting, and with sound of the cornet, and with trumpets, and with cymbals, making a noise with psalteries
and harps. 29 And it came to pass, *as* the ark of
the covenant of the Lord came to the city of David, that Michal, the daughter of Saul, looking out at a window, saw king David dancing and playing; and she despised him in her heart.

These passages refer to the grand procession which accompanied the ark to Jerusalem. Three months before, David, with a large number of his people, took this sacred treasure from Kirjath-jearim, as related in II Sam. vi. 2–11, and I Chron. xiii. 3–14. While they were moving towards Jerusalem, Uzza put forth his hand to steady the ark, and was immediately struck dead by its side. David was offended at this severity from the hand of the Lord, and feared to receive the ark into Jerusalem. It was therefore deposited in the house of Obed-edom, the Gitite. At the end of three months, the king was desirous to remove it to the Holy City, and proceeded with singers, musicians, and the high officers of his court, to perform the ceremony. The passages above cited refer to that occasion (vid. II Sam. vi. 12–17; I Chron. xv. 25–29). The procession was doubtless similar to the one that conveyed the ark from Kirjath-jearim to the house of Obed-edom three months before. Probably the instruments of music used on both occasions were the same, though more are named as used on the former than on the latter occasion. Those mentioned in II Sam. vi. 5, and used when the ark was conveyed from Kirjath-jearim to the house of Obed-edom, are *kinnors*, *nebhels*, *tophs*, *menaanim*, and *tseltselim*, translated *harps*, *psalteries*, *timbrels*, *cornets*, and *cymbals*, and in I Chron. xiii. 8, *kinnors*, *nebhels*, *tophs*, *metsiltayim*, and *hatsotseras*, translated *harps*, *psalteries*, *timbrels*, *cymbals*, and *trumpets*. In I Chron. xv. 28, the instruments named, and employed when the ark was removed from the house of Obed-edom to the city of David, are *shophars*, *hatsotseras*, *metsiltayim*, *nebhels* and *kinnors*, translated *the cornet*, *trumpets*, *cymbals*, *psalteries*, and *harps*. It will be perceived that *tophs*, *menaanim*, and *tseltselim*, mentioned in II Sam. vi. 5, and I Chron. xiii. 8, are not found in I Chron. xv. 28, and *shophar*, in the latter passage, is not found in the former verses. It is probable, however, that on both occasions, the instruments of music did not materially vary in kind or number. The writer may not have thought it necessary, in enumerating them, to be so explicit and full in respect to the latter, as in reference to the former procession.

In our English translation, cornets are named as being used in both processions; but different Hebrew words are employed, indicating different instruments in those cases. In II Sam. vi. 5, בִּמְנַעַנְעִים *bimnaanim* is translated *on cornets;* but it was evidently a kind of *timbrel*—an instrument which was *shaken* (vid. Rem. on II Sam. vi. 5, *supra*), and not a *wind* instrument. In I Chron. xv. 28, the word translated *cornet* is שׁוֹפָר *shophar*, the *crooked trumpet.* The cornet is now but little known, as more than a century ago it gave place to the hautboy. There were three kinds of these instruments, designed for the treble, tenor, and bass. The treble and tenor instruments were simple curvilineal tubes, about three feet in length, gradually increasing in diameter from the mouth-piece towards the lower end. The bass cornet was a tube of a serpentine form, four or five feet in length, and increasing in diameter in like manner.

The shophar might be considered as a kind of *bass cornet*, and consequently designated by that name; but it is more correctly called a *crooked trumpet*. The real *cornet* was of much later origin. The expression, "*instruments of music*" (v. 16), signifies, literally, instruments of song (בִּכְלֵי־שִׁיר *bikley shir*). כְּלֵי *k^eley* is a noun in the construct state and derived from the verb כָּלָה *kala*, *to be completed, ready*. The noun signifies an *implement* or *instrument*, and sometimes an *instrument of music*, especially when connected with שִׁיר *shir*.

Singers with instruments of music.—The expression indicates that, in this case, *vocal* was accompanied by instrumental music.

Sounding.—There is probably a reference here to the music of the whole choir, both vocal and instrumental.

Verse 19. *Cymbals of brass.*—This is indicated in the original by one word, signifying *cymbals*. It is the same word which is used in verse 28, and translated *cymbals*. These instruments were made of brass: hence that is added in the translation of verse 19.

Verse 20. *With psalteries on alamoth.*

עֲלָמוֹת *alamoth* denotes *virgins*.—Gesenius supposes that the expression *al alamoth* which occurs here, means, *after the manner of virgins*, i. e., with the female voice, referring to the part usually sung by females, which is our *treble*. Hengstenberg, Tholuck, and others, take a similar view. Calmet supposes that it means a chorus of *female voices*. The etymology of the word evidently refers to *females*, and it very probably indicates that part of a tune called *treble*, and may have indicated, in some cases, a full *choir* on that part (vid. Remarks on Ps. ix, and xlvi, *infra*). It occurs in connection with the *nebhel* or *psaltery* (similar to our *guitar*), which is an appropriate instrument for females.

In the passage under consideration (v. 20), Zechariah, Aziel, Shemiramoth, Jehiel, Unni, Eliab, Maaseiah, and Benaiah, were appointed to perform with psalteries on *Alamoth*, i. e., the *treble*, according to the above explanation.

With harps on the Sh^{e}mīnīth (שְׁמִינִית).—This is an ordinal adjective from שְׁמֹנֶה Sh^{e}mōnęh, *the eighth*. The word here used is in the feminine gender, and signifies *octave* in music. It denoted among the Hebrews the lowest and gravest notes of the scale, sung by males. It is similar to the modern bass, and is opposed to the term עֲלָמוֹת ^{a}lāmōth. The former refers to the *descending*, and the latter to the *ascending* scale; the former to the octave below, and the latter to the octave above. There is no philological reason to suppose that either of these terms referred to an instrument of music as some have maintained (vid. Rem. on Ps. vi. *infra*).

I Chronicles xvi. 5–36, 42, 43.

5 Asaph the chief, and next to him Zechariah,
Jeiel, and Shemiramoth, and Jehiel, and Matti-
thiah, and Eliab, and Benaiah, and Obed-edom:
and Jeiel with psalteries and with harps; but Asaph
made a sound with cymbals: 6 Benaiah also and
Jahaziel the priests with trumpets continually be-
fore the ark of the covenant of God. 7 Then on
that day David delivered first *this psalm* to thank
the Lord into the hand of Asaph and his brethren.

8 Give thanks unto the Lord,
Call upon his name,
Make known his deeds among the people.

9 Sing unto him,
Sing psalms unto him,
Talk ye of all his wondrous works.

10 Glory ye in his holy name:
Let the heart of them rejoice that seek the Lord.
11 Seek the Lord and his strength,
Seek his face continually.
12 Remember his marvellous works that he hath done,
His wonders, and the judgments of his mouth;
13 O ye seed of Israel his servant,
Ye children of Jacob, his chosen ones.
14 He *is* the Lord our God;
His judgments *are* in all the earth.
15 Be ye mindful always of his covenant;
The word *which* he commanded to a thousand generations;
16 *Even of the covenant*, which he made with Abraham,
And of his oath unto Isaac;
17 And hath confirmed the same to Jacob for a law,
And to Israel *for* an everlasting covenant,
18 Saying, Unto thee will I give the land of Canaan,
The lot of your inheritance;
19 When ye were but few,
Even a few, and strangers in it.
20 And *when* they went from nation to nation,
And from *one* kingdom to another people;
21 He suffered no man to do them wrong:
Yea, he reproved kings for their sakes.
22 *Saying*, Touch not mine anointed,
And do my prophets no harm.
23 Sing unto the Lord, all the earth;
Show forth from day to day his salvation.
24 Declare his glory among the heathen;
His marvellous works among all nations.
25 For great *is* the Lord and greatly to be praised;
He also *is* to be feared above all gods.
26 For all the gods of the people *are* idols:

But the Lord made the heavens.
27 Glory and honor *are* in his presence;
Strength and gladness *are* in his place.
28 Give unto the Lord, ye kindreds of the people,
Give unto the Lord glory and strength.
29 Give unto the Lord the glory *due* unto his name:
Bring an offering, and come before him:
Worship the Lord in the beauty of holiness.
30 Fear before him, all the earth;
The world also shall be stable, that it be not moved.
31 Let the heavens be glad, and let the earth rejoice:
And let *men* say among the nations, The Lord reigneth.
32 Let the sea roar, and the fulness thereof:
Let the fields rejoice, and all that *is* therein.
33 Then shall the trees of the wood sing out at the presence of the Lord,
Because he cometh to judge the earth.
34 O give thanks unto the Lord, for *he is* good;
For his mercy *endureth* for ever.
35 And say ye, Save us, O God of our salvation,
And gather us together, and deliver us from the heathen,
That we may give thanks to thy holy name, *and* glory in thy praise.
36 Blessed *be* the Lord God of Israel for ever and ever.
And all the people said, Amen, and praised the Lord.

42 And with them Heman and Jeduthun, with
trumpets and cymbals for those that should make
a sound, and with musical instruments of God.
And the sons of Jeduthun were porters. 43 And
all the people departed every man to his house,
and David returned to bless his house.

These passages refer to the solemn ceremonies observed at Jerusalem, in view of the arrival of the ark from the house of Obed-edom the Gitite. The sacred treasure was placed in the midst of the tent which David had prepared for the purpose. Burnt and peace offerings were then made to Jehovah. The king blessed the people, and appointed Levites to minister before the ark and celebrate the praises of the Lord. The arrangements seem to have been made on a grand scale. It was a solemn yet joyful occasion, and the priests in their sacerdotal robes, with David at their head, worshipped before God. The sacred singers were also called upon to sound forth their highest songs of praise. Asaph, Heman, and Jeduthun, chiefs of the choir, led off the anthems upon cymbals and trumpets.

Psalteries and Harps (v. 5).—These were the same kinds of instruments as those mentioned in I Sam. x. 5, and Gen. iv. 21. In the Septuagint *οργανον, organ*, is mentioned in addition to the other instruments; but we do not perceive by what authority, as it is not found in the Hebrew text.

Cymbals (verses 5, 42).—The Hebrew word is מְצִלְתַּיִם *m*[e]*tsiltáyim*, in the dual number from מְצֶלֶת *m*[e]*tséleth*, a different word from that used for cymbals in some other passages, though it has the same derivation, viz., from צָלַל *tsalál, to tinkle* (vid. II Sam. vi. 5, *supra*, and Rem. on II Chron. xxix. 25, *infra*).

Trumpets (verses 6, 42).—These were the *hatsotseras*, or *straight silver trumpets*, the same as those mentioned in Num. x. 2. It appears that David presented this psalm to Asaph and his brethren. It contains several references to music, but nearly similar to those which we have already considered. The expression "*then shall the trees of the wood sing out*" (v. 33), varies a little. The Hebrew term יְרַנְּנוּ *y*[e]*rann*[e]*nu*, *shall sing*, is from רָנַן *ranan, to give forth a tremulous sound.* The Psalmist probably refers to the musical voice of nature in the forests as the gentle zephyrs breathe upon the trees.

Musical instruments of God (v. 42).—כְּלֵי־שִׁיר *k*[e]*ley shir*, literally *instruments of song.* כְּלֵי *k^e ley* is a general term and may refer to any kinds of musical instruments. *Of God.* This indicates that the reference is to *sacred* instruments—those used in the services of the temple. The LXX. have *οργανα ῳδων organa ōdōn*, *instruments of song.*

I Chronicles xxiii. 5.

Moreover four thousand *were* porters: and four thousand praised the Lord with the instruments which I made, *said David*, to praise *therewith.*

The music for the temple was arranged upon a grand scale. Such an immense number of performers, and all probably well trained, must have produced tremendous choruses in the house of the Lord. The reverberations through the spacious domes of that sacred edifice must have been solemn and majestic.

Instruments.—There seems to be a reference here, as in 1 Chron. xvi. 42, to all of the sacred instruments used by the Levites.

Which I made.—We are not to suppose that David constructed these instruments with his own hands; but that they were manufactured by his direction and under his supervision.

I Chronicles xxv. 1–7.

1 Moreover David and the captains of the host separated to the service of the sons of Asaph, and of Heman, and of Jeduthun, who should prophesy with harps, with psalteries, and with cymbals: and the number of the workmen according to their
service was: 2 Of the sons of Asaph; Zaccur, and Joseph, and Nethaniah, and Asarelah, the sons of Asaph under the hands of Asaph, which prophe-

sied according to the order of the king. 3 Of Jedu-
thun: the sons of Jeduthun; Gedaliah, and Zeri,
and Jeshaiah, Hashabiah, and Mattithiah, six, under
the hands of their father Jeduthun, who prophe-
sied with a harp, to give thanks and to praise the
Lord. 4 Of Heman: the sons of Heman; Buk-
kiah, Mattaniah, Uzziel, Shebuel, and Jerimoth,
Hananiah, Hanani, Eliathah, Giddalti, and Ro-
mamti-ezer, Joshbekashah, Mallothi, Hothir, *and*
Mahazioth: 5 All these *were* the sons of Heman the
king's seer in the words of God, to lift up the horn.
And God gave to Heman fourteen sons and three
daughters. 6 All these *were* under the hands of their
father for song *in* the house of the Lord, with
cymbals, psalteries, and harps, for the service of the
house of God, according to the king's order to
Asaph, Jeduthun, and Heman. 7 So the number of
them, with their brethren that were instructed in
the songs of the Lord, *even* all that were cun-
ning, *was* two hundred fourscore and eight.

These verses refer to the arrangements made in respect to the temple service: *Harps, psalteries, cymbals, the horn, and song,* are mentioned as before; but we are informed also that the performers were to *prophesy* with these instruments.

The term in the original is נְבִיאִים *nibb'im,* from נָבָא *nabha, to boil up, to pour out words with emotion, to prophesy.* A secondary meaning of it is, *to chant, to sing sacred songs, to praise God* while under divine influence. The will of God was made known to the prophets in various ways, but especially by direct *inspiration,* which Maimonides, one of the most learned of the Jewish doctors, explains to be *a divine impulse, enabling* and urging the subject of it to utter psalms, hymns, important moral precepts or matters, civil, sacred, and divine. This occurred while the seer was awake. The inspiration or sacred impulse was of a calm and gentle nature, and not violent and furious as among the heathen. Such was the inspiration of Zacharias and Elizabeth (Luke i. 41, 42, 67–79), who are said to have "*been filled with the Holy Ghost*," and to have made some sublime predictions. The hymns uttered by inspired persons and preserved in our sacred volume, may be classed under various kinds of verse, one of which is *lyric poetry*, or that which is designed to be accompanied with music, vocal or instrumental, or both. Such, for instance, is the ode of Moses, uttered after the children of Israel had miraculously passed through the waters of the Red Sea (Ex. xv), and a prophetic ode of the same writer recorded in Deut. xxxii, which we have already considered (vid. Rem. on Ex. xv. 1, and Deut. xxxii. 44, *supra*). The prophets, and especially David, often uttered divine songs and played upon instruments of music while under the influence of inspiration. In the passage before us, we are informed that the king *appointed* persons for the temple service, *to prophesy with instruments of music*, indicating, it would seem, that it was common for those who prophesied to have musical accompaniments, or even to perform sometimes themselves on harps and other musical instruments.

Instructed in the songs of the Lord (v. 7).—It appears that great attention was paid to *instruction* in sacred songs, as vocal and instrumental music constituted an important part of religious worship. In I Chron. xxv. 7, we are informed that two hundred and eighty-eight who had thus been instructed were employed in the temple service.

II Chronicles v. 12, 13.

12 Also the Levites *which were* the singers, all
of them of Asaph, of Heman, of Jeduthun, with

their sons and their brethren, *being* arrayed in white linen, having cymbals and psalteries and harps, stood at the east end of the altar, and with them an hundred and twenty priests sounding with
trumpets: 13 It came even to pass, as the trum-
peters and singers *were* as one, to make one sound to be heard in praising and thanking the Lord; and when they lifted up *their* voice with the trumpets and cymbals and instruments of music, and praised the Lord, *saying*, For *he is* good; for his mercy *endureth* for ever; that *then* the house was filled with a cloud, *even* the house of the Lord.

These passages refer to the august ceremony of moving the ark of the covenant from the place where it had been deposited in the "city of David" to the temple of Solomon. Three months before, it had been carried from the house of Obed-edom to Jerusalem, and placed in the tabernacle erected by David for that purpose. Then, as the temple had been completed by Solomon, and the sacred utensils and furniture, prepared by his father, David, had been arranged in their proper places, the king assembled the elders of Israel, and all the heads of the tribes and chief men of the nation to bring up the ark and deposit it within the inner veil in the Holy of Holies. The Levites, bearing this treasure, moved forward amid the smoking sacrifices of sheep and oxen "which could not be told or numbered for multitude." After it had been deposited in the most holy place, and the priests had come out probably into the sanctuary where the altar of incense stood, the Levites, being arrayed in white linen, and standing at the east end of the altar with various instruments of music, mingled their harmonious notes with the blast of a hundred and twenty trumpets in the hands of priests. As their songs of joy and praise reverberated with solemnity and grandeur through the sacred edifice, and as the *vocal* choir raised their exalted strains in adoration of the great Creator, exclaiming: "*For he is good; for his mercy endureth forever,*" the glory of God came down and a cloud filled the temple, so that the priests could not stand to minister. It is probable that the priests then came out of the sanctuary into the inner court of the temple, called the court of the priests, which encircled the altar of burnt offering. In this court we suppose Solomon stood, upon the brazen scaffold which he had erected, to offer his prayer in dedicating the temple. He was where he could see all of the people, and yet near the altar. He blessed them, and, kneeling down before all the congregation, spread out his hands towards heaven and uttered fervent supplications to God. As soon as he had ceased, fire from heaven descended and consumed the sacrificial victims upon the altar of burnt offering. The glory of God so filled the house that the priests could not again enter. When the multitudes, standing in the court of the Israelites, beheld the divine glory, they bowed with their faces to the ground and worshipped God, saying, "*For he is good; for his mercy endureth forever.*" Then the king and the people offered an immense number of sacrifices to the Lord, continuing the ceremonies seven days in succession.

II Chronicles vii. 6.

And the priests waited on their offices: the Levites also with instruments of music of the Lord, which David the king had made to praise the Lord, because his mercy *endureth* for ever, when David praised by their ministry; and the priests sounded trumpets before them, and all Israel stood.

This passage refers to the closing ceremonies at the dedication of Solomon's temple. The performances of the Levites on instruments of music, constituted an important part of those imposing ceremonies.

Instruments.—The general term (כְּלֵי-שִׁיר *k'ley shir*) for musical instruments, is here employed (vid. Rem. on I Chron. xvi. 5–36 *supra*). As complete a choir as could be raised, with a full band of instruments, undoubtedly performed on that occasion.

Trumpets.—These were the *hh'tsots'rim* (חֲצֹצְרִים) or *silver trumpets*, used by the priests only on important occasions (vid. Rem. on Num. x. 2, *supra*).

And all Israel stood.—None excepting the kings of the house of David were allowed, however weary they might be, to sit down in either the priests' or Israelites' court. During the solemn ceremonies of the dedication, the people stood in the courts and joined in the hymns of adoration which ascended as a sweet savor before the Lord.

II Chronicles ix. 11.

And the king made *of* the algum-trees terraces to the house of the Lord, and to the king's palace, and harps and psalteries for singers: and there were none such seen before in the land of Judah.

Harps and Psalteries.—These were the *kinnōrs* (כִּנּוֹר) and *nebhels* (נֵבֶל). The Septuagint uses *cithara*, to denote the former (vid. Rem. on Gen. iv. 21; II Sam. x. 5).

For singers.—It seems that the instruments were made *for singers*, indicating that those who sung, at the same time often performed on instruments. That practice was common from the earliest times. Poets sung their own productions, and sometimes also played an accompaniment at the same time, on some instrument of music.

And there were none such seen before in the land of Judah.—This expression indicates an improvement in the construction of musical instruments. The king had now made them superior to any which had been seen in the land. The improvements probably related more to ornaments than to the tone and capacity of the instruments.

II Chronicles xiii. 12–15.

12 And, behold, God himself *is* with us for *our*
captain, and his priests with sounding trumpets to
cry alarm against you. O children of Israel, fight
ye not against the Lord God of your fathers; for
ye shall not prosper. 13 But Jeroboam caused an
ambushment to come about behind them: so they
were before Judah, and the ambushment *was* be-
hind them. 14 And when Judah looked back, be-
hold, the battle *was* before and behind: and they
cried unto the Lord, and the priests sounded with
the trumpets. 15 Then the men of Judah gave a
shout: and as the men of Judah shouted, it came
to pass, that God smote Jeroboam and all Israel
before Abijah and Judah.

There is reference in these passages to a battle which occurred between Abijah, king of Judah, and Jeroboam, king of Israel. The latter had been rebellious, made images and worshipped them, forsaking the God of his fathers. He had raised an army of 800,000 men, and marched against one of 400,000 under Abijah, who warned Jeroboam not to contend against the Lord, as he would not prosper in so doing. He informed Jeroboam that God was with Judah, and had directed her captain and the priests of the Lord, to sound, with trumpets, the alarm against him. The contest commenced; but ended in the overthrow of Jeroboam and the slaughter of 500,000 of the Israelites.

Trumpets (vs. 12, 14).—These were the *h^a tsots^e roth* (חֲצֹצְרוֹת) or straight trumpets. Here is a remarkable instance in which the sound of the war-trumpet and the shout of Judah struck the hosts of rebellious Israel with dismay, causing them to flee before the armies of the Lord.

II Chronicles xv. 14.

And they sware unto the Lord with a loud voice, and with shouting, and with trumpets, and with cornets.

The music, to which reference is here made, was in confirmation of an oath made by the children of Judah and Benjamin, that whosoever would not seek the Lord God of Israel, should be put to death. They had, as a people, departed from the worship of God, but, when exhorted by the prophet Azariah, they decided to cast their dumb idols away, and return to the worship of the God of Israel. Taking this oath of fealty to Jehovah was of the highest importance, and the people proclaimed the event with a *loud voice, a shout,* with *hh^a tsots^e roth* (חֲצֹצְרוֹת) or *straight trumpets* (vid. Num. x. 2, and Rem. on the same, *supra*), and *shophars* (שׁוֹפָרוֹת) or *crooked trumpets,* though our English translation has *cornets.* The *cornet* was a wind instrument; but differed from the *shophar.* In II Sam. vi. 5, a pulsatile instrument is translated *cornets.* The LXX *have κερατιναις keratinais, trumpets, bugles, cornets.*

II Chronicles xx. 19–22, 28.

19 And the Levites, of the children of the Kohathites, and the children of the Korhites, stood

up to praise the Lord God of Israel with a loud
voice on high. 20 And they rose early in the
morning, and went forth into the wilderness of
Tekoa: and as they went forth, Jehoshaphat stood
and said, Hear me, O Judah, and ye inhabitants of
Jerusalem; Believe in the Lord your God, so shall
ye be established; believe his prophets, so shall ye
prosper. 21 And when he had consulted with the
people, he appointed singers unto the Lord, and
that should praise the beauty of holiness, as they
went out before the army, and to say, Praise the
Lord; for his mercy *endureth* for ever. 22 And
when they began to sing and to praise, the Lord
set ambushments against the children of Ammon,
Moab, and Mount Seir, which were come against
Judah; and they were smitten..

28 And they came to Jerusalem, with psalteries
and harps and trumpets, unto the house of the
Lord.

These verses refer to the overthrow of the enemies of Judah, by the special interposition of Providence. The Moabites, Ammonites, and other hostile tribes came up in battle array against Jehoshaphat, king of Judah. The latter proclaimed a fast, and called upon his people to invoke divine assistance. While they were assembled and engaged in earnest prayer, the spirit of the Lord came upon Jahaziel, and he declared to the oppressed children of Judah that they need not fear the armies, as the Lord would deliver them into their hands. Then Jehoshaphat and the assembly bowed down again in adoration before their Heavenly Father. The Levites stood up *to praise the Lord God of Israel with a loud voice on high.* There may have been *singing* as well as other forms of worship performed by the Levites on that occasion.

Singers.—Persons were appointed to sing as the children of Judah should go out to meet their enemies. The Hebrew word is מְשֹׁרְרִים *m'shor'rim* a Participle, Pilpel conjugation from שִׁיר *shir, to sing.* Accordingly, as they moved on, they sung praises to God with a *loud* voice, and no sooner had they begun, than Ammon and Moab found that the inhabitants of Mount Seir had laid in ambush for them, and thus the foes of Judah were put to flight without the necessity of striking a blow.

Psalteries, Harps, and *Trumpets.*—These were *nebhels, kinnors* and *hatsotseras* or *straight trumpets* (vid. Rem. on I Sam. x. 5; Gen. iv. 21; Num. x. 2, *supra*).

II Chronicles xxiii. 13, 18.

13 And she looked, and behold, the king stood at his pillar at the entering in, and the princes and the trumpets by the king: and all the people of the land rejoiced, and sounded with trumpets, also the singers with instruments of music, and such as taught to sing praise. Then Athaliah rent her clothes, and said, Treason! treason!

18 Also Jehoiada appointed the officers of the house of the Lord by the hand of the priests the Levites, whom David had distributed in the house of the Lord, to offer the burnt-offerings of the Lord, as *it is* written in the law of Moses, with rejoicing and with singing, *as it was ordained* by David.

After the death of Azariah, king of Judah, Athaliah his mother ruled in his stead. She was a monster of cruelty, and made an attempt to put to death all the seed royal, so that she might continue, unmolested, to occupy the throne; but Jehoash, a son of Ahaziah, was concealed, and escaped the violence of that desperate woman. He was finally escorted to a public place and anointed king. After the coronation, Athaliah heard the sound of rejoicing, and cried, *Treason!* But it was too late. Her fate was sealed, and she was soon led out of the temple to the place of execution.

On that important occasion, probably all of the usual instruments of music were employed. At such times, the ceremonies were performed with great pomp. First, the candidate was anointed with holy oil (vid. Ps. lxxxix. 20). If, however, one of the same family had preceded him in the regal office, as it was hereditary in the kingdom of Judah, the ceremony of anointing was dispensed with, excepting when the right to the throne was disputed. The candidate was next proclaimed king by the sound of the trumpet (vid. I Kings, i. 34, 39). A crown was placed upon his head, and a sceptre in his right hand. The newly elected king then promised to govern according to the law of Moses. Some other ceremonies were observed, and then loud acclamations arose from the people, accompanied by music, and the king entered the holy city. In the case before us, there were similar observances.

Trumpets—Sounded with trumpets.—Hatsotseras or *straight trumpets* were here employed in both cases.

Singers with instruments of music.—The general term כְּלֵי־שִׁיר *k*^{e}*ley shir* for musical instruments is used. It seems that those who *sung*, performed also upon instruments, probably of the stringed or pulsatile kind.

II Chronicles xxix. 25–30.

25 And he set the Levites in the house of the
Lord, with cymbals, with psalteries, and with harps,
according to the commandment of David, and of

Gad the king's seer, and Nathan the prophet: for
so was the commandment of the Lord by his proph-
ets. 26 And the Levites stood with the instru-
ments of David, and the priests with the trumpets.
27 And Hezekiah commanded to offer the burnt-
offering upon the altar. And when the burnt-of-
fering began, the song of the Lord began *also* with
the trumpets, and with the instruments *ordained*
by David king of Israel. 28 And all the congre-
gation worshipped, and the singers sang, and the
trumpeters sounded: *and* all *this continued* until
the burnt-offering was finished. 29 And when
they had made an end of offering, the king and all
that were present with him bowed themselves and
worshipped. 30 Moreover Hezekiah the king and
princes commanded the Levites to sing praise unto
the Lord with the words of David, and of Asaph
the seer. And they sang praises with gladness,
and they bowed their heads and worshipped.

Ahaz, king of Judah, had abandoned the worship of Jehovah, destroyed the sacred utensils of the temple, and desecrated and shut up that holy edifice. When Hezekiah, his son, ascended the throne, he overthrew the idols of gold and silver which Ahaz had made, repaired the temple of Solomon, and dedicated it anew to the service of God. The verses under consideration refer to the ceremonies of that occasion.

Cymbals, *psalteries*, and *harps* (v. 25).—The original words are derivatives of *m'tsiltàyim* (מְצִלְתַּיִם), *nebhel* and *kinnor*. The first, which is translated *cymbals*, is supposed by Jahn and others, not to refer to *instruments of music*, nor to *bells*, as the word is translated in Zech. xiv. 20, but to *concave plates of brass*, sometimes attached to horses for the sake of ornament (vid. Jahn's Biblic. Archæology, § 96. II). They were doubtless designed to make a tinkling sound, as well as for show. Those intended for horses were probably of smaller size than those used as accompaniments to music. In the passage above mentioned, the word cannot mean any part of the trappings of a horse, as nothing is said of that animal in the connection. The reference is evidently to a pulsatile instrument similar to that mentioned in I Chron. xvi. 5, 42, and may have been of the same form as that of *steed* ornaments (vid. Rem. on I Chron. xvi. 5, 42, *supra*).

Instruments of David (v. 26).—*K'ley* (כְּלֵי), the general term for *instruments of music* (vid. Rem on I Chron. xvi. 42), probably referring to the various kinds prepared by David and used by Solomon in the temple service.

Trumpets, (v. 26).—*Hatsotseras*, or *straight, silver trumpets.*

Song of the Lord, (v. 27).—When the burnt-offering began to smoke upon the altar, the song of praise to God commenced. It seems that the priests first sounded with their silver trumpets, and then followed the whole choir of instrumental music "*ordained by David.*"

Singers sang.—Not only was there instrumental, but vocal music. Probably the full choir of Levites now either sung, or performed on instruments of music. It is probable also that the Israelites in their court joined in the song. This oriental music continued till the victim of the burnt-offering was consumed.

With the words of David and of Asaph the seer (v. 30).—Asaph, as well as David, composed hymns, and those prepared by both were sung on this occasion.

II Chronicles xxx. 21.

And the children of Israel *that were* present at Jerusalem kept the feast of unleavened bread seven days with great gladness: and the Levites and the priests praised the Lord day by day, *singing* with loud instruments unto the Lord.

Loud instruments.—Literally, *instruments of strength* or *instruments of praise.* At the command of Hezekiah the passover was kept at Jerusalem, and that was a suitable occasion for special joy and praise. The usual instruments, and especially the powerful ones, were probably employed.

II Chronicles xxxiv. 12.

And the men did the work faithfully: and the overseers of them *were* Jahath and Obadiah, the Levites, of the sons of Merari: and Zechariah and Meshullam, of the sons of the Kohathites, to set *it* forward; and *other of* the Levites, all that could skill of instruments of music.

Under the reign of Manasseh and Ammon the temple had been desecrated, the altars overthrown, and the worship of the living God almost abandoned. Josiah repaired the sacred edifice, appointed Levites as musicians, and restored the worship of Jehovah.

All that could skill of instruments of music.—This is a badly translated phrase. It signifies, literally, *every one skilled in the instruments of song.*

II Chronicles xxxv. 15, 25.

15 And the singers the sons of Asaph *were* in their place, according to the commandment of David, and Asaph, and Heman, and Jeduthun the

king's seer; and the porters *waited* at every gate; they might not depart from their service; for their brethren the Levites prepared for them.

25 And Jeremiah lamented for Josiah: and all the singing men and the singing women spake of Josiah in their lamentations to this day, and made them an ordinance in Israel: and, behold, they *are* written in the lamentations.

Verse 15 has reference to the celebration of the passover by Josiah the king. The mention of singers indicates that there was vocal as well as instrumental music on such occasions.

Singing men and singing women spake of Josiah in their lamentations (v. 25).—This indicates that females as well as males sometimes took part in musical performances. This was the case in the tabernacle and temple service. Heman had fourteen sons and three daughters, who were skilled in music, and Ezra, when enumerating those who returned from the Babylonish captivity, names 200 singing men and singing women (vid. Ezra ii. 65).

THE BOOK OF EZRA.

INTRODUCTORY REMARKS.

THE books of Ezra and Nehemiah were anciently called the first and second book of Ezra. As the author of the former speaks in the first person, it is evident that he witnessed the events which he describes. The composition was originally written in the Hebrew language, excepting from the eighth verse of the fourth chapter to the eighteenth verse of the sixth chapter, and from the twelfth to the twenty-sixth verse of the seventh chapter, which were written in Chaldee. We have here a history of God's chosen people during the time which elapsed from the edict of Cyrus until the twentieth year of Artaxerxes Longimanus, about seventy, or, as some suppose, one hundred years. The return of the Jews from Babylon, under Zerubbabel, and the reformation of religion under Ezra, are described. There are a few references to music.

EZRA ii. 41, 65, 70.

41 The singers: the children of Asaph, an hundred twenty and eight.

65 Besides their servants and their maids, of whom *there were* seven thousand three hundred thirty and seven: and *there were* among them two hundred singing men and singing women.

70 So the priests, and the Levites, and *some* of the people, and the singers, and the porters, and

the Nethinims, dwelt in their cities, and all Israel in their cities.

This chapter narrates the numbering of the Israelites in each tribe and department, and their return from their captivity in Babylon.

There were 128 singers, children of Asaph (v. 41), and, in the whole congregation, 200 singing men and singing women (v. 65). The captivity occurred, according to the usual computation, 587 B. C., or A. M. 3416. While the Israelites were in Egypt (which they left about 1491 B. C., or A. M. 2513) they undoubtedly became acquainted with Egyptian music, and adopted it to some extent, as we have shown in the introduction to this work. When they were captives in Babylonia, their music was probably modified by that of their oppressors, as they were in bondage seventy years, returning to Judæa about 517 B. C. This was about half a century after the flourishing period of Solomon's reign, when the arts had reached a high degree of improvement for that age. The glory of the temple, the splendor of its ornaments and services, had passed away—the favored people of God had worn, for a long time, the galling chains of slavery, and were emerging from the clouds of darkness which had so long enshrouded them. They had returned to the land of their fathers, and were preparing to restore the worship of God in their deserted temple. In numbering their singing men and singing women, instead of having 4000, as in the days of Solomon, they found that they had only 200.

EZRA iii. 10–13.

10 And when the builders laid the foundation of the temple of the Lord, they set the priests in their apparel with trumpets, and the Levites the sons of Asaph with cymbals to praise the Lord,

after the ordinance of David king of Israel. 11
And they sung together by course, in praising and
giving thanks unto the Lord; because he is good,
for his mercy *endureth* for ever toward Israel.
And all the people shouted with a great shout,
when they praised the Lord, because the founda-
tion of the house of the Lord was laid. 12 But
many of the priests and Levites and chief of the
fathers, *who were* ancient men, that had seen the
first house, when the foundation of this house was
laid before their eyes, wept with a loud voice; and
many shouted aloud for joy; 13 So that the peo-
ple could not discern the noise of the shout of joy
from the noise of the weeping of the people: for
the people shouted with a loud shout, and the noise
was heard afar off.

These verses refer to the ceremony of laying the foundation of the second temple. The one built by Solomon was desolated, and finally burned by Nebuchadnezzar, who carried the Israelites into captivity. By a decree of the Persian monarch, that oppressed people had been permitted now to return to Judæa, and commence building another temple under the direction of Zerubbabel. It was erected upon the site of the first; but was inferior to that edifice in splendor. The ark of the covenant and mercy seat, the Shekinah or manifestation of the divine presence in the holy of holies, the sacred fire on the altar kindled from on high, the Urim and Thummim and the spirit of prophecy, which adorned and made sacred the first, were entirely wanting in this; still the glory of the latter, in one respect, excelled that of the former. The Saviour graced it with his presence and holy teachings. The foundations of this new temple were laid amid great rejoicings. Some *shouted* in triumph, while the aged, who had in by-gone days entered the courts of the former temple with thanksgiving, *wept* with a *loud voice* (verses 11, 12, 13). As they reflected upon their former prosperity, when they worshipped unmolested in that splendid edifice where Jehovah vouchsafed his presence—while contemplating its utter desolation, their fearful bondage in Babylonia, and the cheering prospect now before them of rearing another house of God upon the site of the former one, and once more entering its gates with praise,—they were overwhelmed with mingled emotions of grief and joy.

Trumpets (v. 10).—These were *straight trumpets.*

Cymbals (v. 10) *m'tsiltayim.*—The same instruments as those mentioned in I Chron. xvi. 5, 42, and II Chron. xxix. 25.

Ezra vii. 7, 24.

7 And there went up *some* of the children of Israel, and of the priests, and the Levites, and the singers, and the porters, and the Nethinims, unto Jerusalem, in the seventh year of Artaxerxes the king.

24 Also we certify you, that touching any of the priests and Levites, singers, porters, Nethinims, or ministers of this house of God, it shall not be lawful to impose toll, tribute, or custom, upon them.

Artaxerxes, king of Persia, favored the project of rebuilding the temple at Jerusalem, and addressed a letter to Ezra upon the subject, assuring him that the priests, Levites, *singers*, porters, and Nethinims, should not be required to pay tribute, toll, or custom.

EZRA X. 24.

Of the singers also; Eliashib: and of the porters; Shallum, and Telem, and Uri.

Singers.—After the Israelites had returned to the land of Judæa, they brought down upon themselves the indignation of Jehovah, by taking strange wives, and the judgments of heaven began to descend upon them. The *singers* were among the number of transgressors, and at the solicitation of Ezra, they put away their wives, humbled themselves before God, and secured again his favor.

THE BOOK OF NEHEMIAH.

INTRODUCTORY REMARKS.

In some versions this is called the second book of Ezra. Nehemiah was born at Babylon during the captivity, was honored by Artaxerxes Longimanus, king of Persia, and finally became his cup-bearer. Though elevated to a high rank, he did not forget his kindred the Hebrews, and obtained permission of the king to assist them in rebuilding the walls of Jerusalem and the temple. He was appointed governor of the province of Judæa, and entered the holy city about thirteen years after the arrival of Ezra. The book contains an account of the rebuilding of Jerusalem and the temple, the opposition of Sanballat, and the first and second reformation, in respect to the Jews, accomplished by Nehemiah.

NEHEMIAH iv. 18–20.

18 For the builders, every one had his sword
girded by his side, and *so* builded. And he that
sounded the trumpet *was* by me. 19 And I said
unto the nobles, and to the rulers, and to the rest
of the people, The work *is* great and large, and
we are separated upon the wall, one far from an-
other. 20 In what place *therefore* ye hear the
sound of the trumpet, resort ye thither unto us:
our God shall fight for us.

These verses refer to the expected attack of Israel's foes while the former were building the walls of Jerusalem. They were obliged to hold their weapon of warfare in one hand and build with the other.

Trumpet (vs. 18–20).—This was the *shophar* or crooked trumpet, used to sound an alarm. These verses in the Hebrew Bible are numbered 12, 13, and 14. The division into chapters and verses being of comparatively late origin, and not of divine authority, translators and revisers have felt at liberty to use their own judgment in making the divisions, thus causing some diversity in different versions and editions.

Nehemiah vii. 1, 44, 67, 73.

1 Now it came to pass, when the wall was built,
and I had set up the doors, and the porters and the
singers and the Levites were appointed.
44 The singers: the children of Asaph, an hun-
dred forty and eight.
67 Beside their man-servants and their maid-
servants, of whom *there were* seven thousand three
hundred thirty and seven: and they had two hun-
dred forty and five singing men and singing wom-
en.
73 So the priests, and the Levites, and the por-
ters, and the singers, and *some* of the people, and
the Nethinims, and all Israel, dwelt in their cities;
and when the seventh month came, the children of
Israel *were* in their cities.

Singers (verses 1, 44, 73).—The children of Asaph were 148 in number. Some of these singers may have been more distant descendants of that eminent musician, than sons. When the Israelites first came from Babylon, they had 128 singers; and now, having completed the repairs of the temple, they appointed a larger choir.

Singing men and singing women (v. 67).—Here were forty-five more than those mentioned in Ezra ii. 65, as having just come from Babylon.

NEHEMIAH x. 28.

And the rest of the people, the priests, the Levites, the porters, the singers, the Nethinims, and all they that had separated themselves from the people of the lands unto the law of God, their wives, their sons, and their daughters, every one having knowledge, and having understanding.

Singers.—These were a part of the number who took a solemn oath to walk in accordance with God's law.

NEHEMIAH xi. 22, 23.

22 The overseer also of the Levites at Jerusalem *was* Uzzi the son of Bani, the son of Hashabiah, the son of Mattaniah, the son of Micha. Of the sons of Asaph, the singers *were* over the business of the house of God. 23 For *it was* the king's commandment concerning them, that a certain portion should be for the singers, due for every day.

Singers.—It seems by verse 23, that a portion of the singers were appointed to perform each day, and only on the most important public occasions did they all perform at once.

NEHEMIAH xii. 27–47.

27 And at the dedication of the wall of Jerusa-
lem they sought the Levites out of all their places,
to bring them to Jerusalem, to keep the dedication
with gladness, both with thanksgivings, and with
singing, *with* cymbals, psalteries, and with harps.
28 And the sons of the singers gathered them-
selves together, both out of the plain country
round about Jerusalem, and from the villages of
Netophathi; 29 Also from the house of Gilgal,
and out of the fields of Geba and Azmaveth: for
the singers had builded them villages round about
Jerusalem. 30 And the priests and the Levites
purified themselves, and purified the people, and
the gates, and the wall. 31 Then I brought up
the princes of Judah upon the wall, and appointed
two great *companies of them that gave* thanks,
whereof one went on the right hand upon the wall
toward the dung gate: 32 And after them went
Hoshaiah, and half of the princes of Judah, 33
And Azariah, Ezra, and Meshullam, 34 Judah,
and Benjamin, and Shemaiah, and Jeremiah, 35
And *certain* of the priests' sons with trumpets;
namely, Zechariah the son of Jonathan, the son of
Shemaiah, the son of Mattaniah, the son of Mich-
aiah, the son of Zaccur, the son of Asaph: 36
And his brethren, Shemaiah, and Azarael, Milalai,
Gilalai, Maai, Nethaneel, and Judah, Hanani, with
the musical instruments of David the man of God,

and Ezra the scribe before them. 37 And at the
fountain gate, which was over-against them, they
went up by the stairs of the city of David, at the
going up of the wall, above the house of David,
even unto the water gate eastward. 38 And the
other *company of them that gave* thanks went over
against *them*, and I after them, and the half of the
people upon the wall, from beyond the tower of
the furnaces even unto the broad wall; 39 And
from above the gate of Ephraim, and above the
old gate, and above the fish gate, and the tower of
Hananeel, and the tower of Meah, even unto the
sheep gate: and they stood still in the prison gate.
40 So stood the two *companies of them that gave*
thanks in the house of God, and I, and the half of
the rulers with me: and the priests; 41 Eliakim,
Maaseiah, Miniamin, Michaiah, Elioenai, Zechariah,
and Hananiah, with trumpets; 42 And Maaseiah,
and Shemaiah, and Eleazar, and Uzzi, and Jehoha-
nan, and Malchijah, and Elam, and Ezer. And the
singers sang loud, with Jezrahiah *their* overseer.
43 Also that day they offered great sacrifices, and
rejoiced: for God had made them rejoice with
great joy: the wives also and the children re-
joiced: so that the joy of Jerusalem was heard
even afar off.

44 And at that time were some appointed over
the chambers for the treasures, for the offerings,
for the first-fruits, and for the tithes, to gather into
them, out of the fields of the cities, the portions

of the law for the priests and Levites: for Judah
rejoiced for the priests and for the Levites that
waited. 45 And both the singers and the porters
kept the ward of their God, and the ward of the
purification, according to the commandment of
David, *and* of Solomon his son. 46 For in the
days of David and Asaph of old, *there were* chief
of the singers, and songs of praise and thanksgiv-
ing unto God. 47 And all Israel, in the days of
Zerubbabel, and in the days of Nehemiah, gave
the portions of the singers and the porters, every
day his portion; and they sanctified *holy things*
unto the Levites; and the Levites sanctified *them*
unto the children of Aaron.

These verses refer to the dedication of the walls of Jerusalem. Probably all of the different kinds of instruments in use were employed. *Cymbals*, *psalteries*, and *harps* are named (v. 27)—the same as those used on former occasions.

Priests' sons with trumpets (v. 35).—The expression, *priests' sons*, is similar to *sons of the prophets*, meaning those instructed by the prophets, and in many cases their *natural* sons. So it was undoubtedly in reference to *sons of the priests*.

Musical instruments of David (v. 36).—The expression indicates those which he had ordained to be used, and it was possible that some of the very same instruments employed in the time of that monarch, had been preserved.

Nehemiah xiii. 5, 10.

5 And he had prepared for him a great chamber, where aforetime they laid the meat-offerings, the frankincense, and the vessels, and the tithes

of the corn, the new wine, and the oil, which was commanded *to be given* to the Levites, and the singers, and the porters; and the offerings of the priests.

10 And I perceived that the portions of the Levites had not been given *them:* for the Levites and the singers, that did the work, were fled every one to his field.

Singers.—Ordinary performers in the temple service.

POETICAL BOOKS OF THE OLD TESTAMENT.

INTRODUCTORY REMARKS.

THE poetical books of the Old Testament are five in number, viz: Job, Psalms, Proverbs, Ecclesiastes, and Canticles, or the Song of Solomon. They are almost entirely written in Hebrew rhythm, and are therefore usually classed by themselves, though some of them, in point of date, are anterior to the historical books. As long ago as the time of Gregory Nazianzen, they were called by him the *five metrical books* (vid. Greg. Naz. Carm. xxxiii. v. 16). They are also mentioned by Amphilochius, Bishop of Iconium, in an iambic poem which he addressed to Seleucus (Op. Tom. ii., p. 98; Paris, 1611). Also Epiphanius and Cyril of Jerusalem refer to them (Epiph. de Pond. et Mens., p. 533; Suicer's Thesaurus, Tom. ii). In our Hebrew Bibles they are placed in the *Hagiographa* (*holy writings*), between Malachi and the book of Esther; but in our English version between the historical and prophetic writings.

These books are important for our present purpose, as they contain numerous allusions to music, and as they had, in many cases, at least, during their recital, musical accompaniments. We shall therefore consider them rather more fully than the other books of the sacred volume.

HEBREW POETRY.

GENERAL VIEW OF HEBREW POETRY.

Of all poetry, that of the Hebrews is the most ancient on record which has reached our times in any language, and to determine its origin we are obliged to go back nearly to the commencement of the human race. Instrumental music was, in all probability, practised as early as 160 years after the creation of Adam, and vocal music undoubtedly preceded that. When the human voice first began to utter musical sounds, or certainly very soon after, words must have been employed, and expressed in a kind of poetry, though imperfect and rude. Dr. Jahn informs us that "poetry had its origin in the first ages of the world, when undisciplined feelings and a lively imagination naturally supplied strong expressions, giving an expressive modulation to the voice, and motion to the limbs" (Jahn's Biblical Arch. § 90). The word *poetry* is derived from the Greek term Ποιησις *poiesis*, signifying the *production* or *creation* of anything, referring undoubtedly to the creative power necessary for a poet. Although the term which now indicates poetry is of comparatively modern origin; yet poetic effusions were uttered long anterior to the existence of the Greek language or nation, and even before the national existence of the Hebrews, although, as we have said, their writings contain the earliest authoritative record of the art extant. In India, refined poetry existed in the sacred books of the Hindoos, 1000 years B. C., and probably rude specimens 3000 years B. C. The Egyptians cultivated music, and probably poetry, more than 3000 years B. C. Some other nations cultivated the latter nearly as early; but we have a rude specimen in the Jewish scriptures recorded by Moses, and represented as having been uttered by Lamech, the father of

Jubal, to his two wives in reference to a heinous crime of which he was guilty. In the excited state of his mind he exclaims:

"Adah and Zillah, hear my voice,
Ye wives of Lamech, hearken unto my speech;
For I have slain a man to my wounding,
And a young man to my hurt:
If Cain shall be avenged sevenfold,
Truly Lamech seventy and sevenfold."

Vid. Gen. iv. 23, 24.

This passage, occurring in immediate connection with the mention of Jubal, and having been uttered by his father, must have been spoken as early as 150 or 160 years after the creation of Adam, and about 1496 or 1506 before the deluge. It is a remarkable circumstance that we have the mention of music and a specimen of poetry in immediate connection, though they are not named as accompanying each other. The name of Jubal is recorded as the father of instrumental music, and Lamech, his natural father, presents a specimen of rude poetry, from the excitement produced by reflecting upon a revolting crime which he had committed. Here we have proof positive that poetry was coeval with music. Dr. Jahn asserts that poetry, music, and dancing were contemporaneous in origin (Jahn's Biblical Arch. § 90). It is not necessary to suppose that there was a musical accompaniment to the recital of Lamech's poetry. It is probable that there was not, though very often, subsequently, there were such accompaniments. This specimen of early versification is called by biblical scholars *prosaic* poetry. It has the imagination, pathos, passion, and striking expression of poetry, but not faultless versification nor metaphorical language. It is *natural* in distinction from artificial and finished poetry.

Another specimen may be found in Gen. ix. 25, 26, 27, where the patriarch Noah, awaking from his wine and ascertaining the shameful conduct of Ham and Canaan, and the commendable course of Shem and Japheth, is represented as exclaiming, under the excitement of his feelings, in oriental verse:

"Cursed be Canaan;
A servant of servants shall he be unto his brethren.
And he said,
Blessed be the Lord God of Shem;
And Canaan shall be his servant.
God shall enlarge Japheth, and he shall dwell in the tents of Shem;
And Canaan shall be his servant."

This was an important prophecy in reference to the settlement and government of mankind upon the earth, which has been terribly fulfilled in respect to the descendants of Ham and Canaan, who are even now in bondage in this and other countries. The prediction has also been remarkably fulfilled in respect to the descendants of Shem and Japheth, who have extended their borders to almost all parts of the globe.

Another instance occurs in Gen. xxvii. 27, 28, 29:

And he came near, and kissed him: and he smelled the smell of his raiment, and blessed him, and said,

"See, the smell of my son is as the smell of a field which the Lord hath blessed;
Therefore God give thee of the dew of heaven,
And the fatness of the earth, and plenty of corn and wine:
Let people serve thee, and nations bow down to thee:
Be lord over thy brethren, and let thy mother's sons bow down to thee:
Cursed be every one that curseth thee, and blessed be he that blesseth thee."

Isaac blessed his son Jacob while he supposed he was blessing Esau. This occurred in consequence of the duplicity of Rebekah, in endeavoring to secure the blessing for her son Jacob the younger, and to deprive Esau, the elder, of his birthright. When the latter returned with his venison, and found that his younger brother had taken away his birth-right, he wept bitterly, and called upon his father to bless *him* also. Isaac did so in the following poetic effusion contained in Gen. xxvii. 39, 40:

And Isaac his father answered, and said unto him,

"Behold, thy dwelling shall be the fatness of the earth,
And of the dew of heaven from above;
And by the sword shalt thou live, and shalt serve thy brother:
And it shall come to pass, when thou shalt have the dominion,
That thou shalt break his yoke from off thy neck."

These prophecies were remarkably fulfilled in the posterity of the two brothers.

We find similar specimens of poetry in Ex. xxxii. 18, and last clause of v. 17 (vid. Rem. on Ex. xxxii. 17, 16, *supra*).

17 And when Joshua heard the noise of the people as they shouted, he said unto Moses,

There is a noise of war in the camp.

18 And he said,

It is not the voice of *them that* shout for mastery,
Neither *is it* the voice of *them that* cry for being overcome:
But the noise of *them that* sing do I hear.

The specimens which we have presented, it will be readily perceived, are not the most elevated kind of poetry, and may properly be called *poetic prose.* They were uttered about 1800 years B. C.

We have another specimen in Gen. xlix. 2–27 inclusive:

"Gather yourselves together and hear, ye sons of Jacob;
And hearken unto Israel your father.
Reuben, thou art my first-born,
My might, and the beginning of my strength,
The excellency of dignity, and the excellency of power:
Unstable as water, thou shalt not excel;
Because thou wentest up to thy father's bed;
Then defiledst thou it: he went up to my couch.
Simeon and Levi are brethren;
Instruments of cruelty are in their habitations.
O my soul, come not thou into their secret;
Unto their assembly, mine honor, be not thou united:
For in their anger they slew a man,
And in their self-will they digged down a wall.
Cursed be their anger, for it was fierce;
And their wrath, for it was cruel:
I will divide them in Jacob,
And scatter them in Israel.
Judah, thou art he whom thy brethren shall praise;
Thy hand shall be in the neck of thine enemies:
Thy father's children shall bow down before thee.
Judah is a lion's whelp:
From the prey, my son, thou art gone up:
He stooped down, he couched as a lion,
And as an old lion; who shall rouse him up?
The sceptre shall not depart from Judah,
Nor a lawgiver from between his feet,
Until Shiloh come;
And unto him shall the gathering of the people be:

Binding his foal unto the vine,
And his ass' colt unto the choice vine;
He washed his garments in wine,
And his clothes in the blood of grapes:
His eyes shall be red with wine,
And his teeth white with milk.
Zebulun shall dwell at the haven of the sea;
And he shall be for an haven of ships,
And his border shall be unto Zidon.
Issachar is a strong ass,
Couching down between two burdens:
And he saw that rest was good,
And the land that it was pleasant;
And bowed his shoulder to bear,
And became a servant unto tribute.
Dan shall judge his people,
As one of the tribes of Israel.
Dan shall be a serpent by the way,
An adder in the path,
That biteth the horse-heels,
So that his rider shall fall backward.
I have waited for thy salvation, O Lord.
Gad, a troop shall overcome him;
But he shall overcome at the last.
Out of Asher his bread shall be fat,
And he shall yield royal dainties.
Naphtali is a hind let loose:
He giveth goodly words.
Joseph is a fruitful bough,
Even a fruitful bough by a well;
Whose branches run over the wall.
The archers have sorely grieved him,
And shot at him, and hated him;
But his bow abode in strength,

And the arms of his hands were made strong
By the hands of the mighty God of Jacob:
(From thence is the Shepherd, the stone of Israel):
Even by the God of thy father, who shall help thee;
And by the Almighty, who shall bless thee
With blessings of heaven above,
Blessings of the deep that lieth under,
Blessings of the breasts, and of the womb:
The blessings of thy father have prevailed
Above the blessings of my progenitors,
Unto the utmost bound of the everlasting hills:
They shall be on the head of Joseph,
And on the crown of the head of him
That was separate from his brethren.
Benjamin shall raven as a wolf:
In the morning he shall devour the prey,
And at night he shall divide the spoil."

This is a little more elevated than the other passages quoted; but it is far from being the highest kind of Hebrew poetry. Good old Jacob, just before he left the world, called his sons together, and uttered this remarkable prophecy in respect to the varied scenes through which they would be called to pass during their earthly career. In Hebrew poetry there are evidently various kinds of verse, though we have an imperfect knowledge in respect to the subject. We are ignorant even of the manner in which the ancient Hebrews *pronounced* their most common words. But from the way in which Josephus, Origen, and Jerome speak of Hebrew poetry, it would seem that it was well understood in their time. Josephus asserts that Moses wrote in Hexameter verse, and David in trimeters and pentameters (Josep. Ant. ii., xvi. 4; iv., viii. 44; vii., xii. 3). Jerome thought he discovered iambic, alcaic, and sapphic verses in the Psalms; hexameters and pentameters in Deuteronomy, Isaiah, Job, and the writings of Solomon (Hieron. Præf.

in Chron. Epist. 135 ad Paul. et Epist. Urb. ad Paulin. Comment. in Ezek. c. 30). But at this day we cannot determine with certainty the different kinds of verse in which the Hebrews wrote, nor is it certain that even Origen, Jerome, Eusebius, or Josephus fully understood the subject. It is obvious, however, to a casual observer, that many parts of the sacred volume were written in verse of different metres. Bishop Lowth, one of the ablest writers upon this subject, informs us that there are four characteristics of Hebrew poetry: 1. The acrostical or alphabetical commencement of lines or stanzas; 2. The admission of foreign words and certain particles which seldom are found in prose, and thus form a distinct poetical dialect; 3. Sententious, figurative, and sublime expressions; 4. Parallelism. But it has justly been doubted by Bishop Jebb and other distinguished biblical scholars, whether any of these, considered as general characteristics, excepting the last (Parallelism), really exist. By parallelism we mean a certain resemblance or relationship between two members of a sentence adjusted in such a manner that, in two lines or members of a period, words shall answer to words and things to things as though they were fitted to each other according to some rule or measure. There may be said to be four kinds of Parallelism, viz., Parallel lines *Gradational, Antithetic, Synthetic, and Introverted.*

In *Gradational* Parallel lines, the responsive clause generally rises above the preceding one, sometimes by a descending scale in the value of the related terms and periods, but always with a distinction in meaning. This is very common in the Psalms and Isaiah.

In Parallel lines *Antithetic*, two correspond with each other by opposition of terms and sentiments. For instance, the second line is contrasted with the first, in expression or sense. This is not of very frequent occurrence, especially in the higher kinds of poetry. The Proverbs of Solomon receive much of their force and elegance from this species of parallelism.

In Parallel lines *Synthetic*, or *Constructive*, the Parallelism consists only in a resemblance of construction, and such a resemblance that word does not answer to word, nor sentence to sentence, as equivalent or opposite. There is, however, a correspondence between the different propositions in reference to the turn of the whole sentence. For instance, noun answers to noun, verb to verb, interrogative to interrogative, negative to negative, member to member. This kind of parallelism is extensively employed by the sacred writers, though sometimes it is with difficulty apparent.

In Parallel lines *Introverted*, whatever may be their number, the first is parallel with the last, the second with the next to the last, and so on. An abundance of these different species of parallelism may be found in the Old Testament, and Bishop Jebb has shown that the same characteristics appear in the New Testament. The latter is supplementary to and perfective of the Old Testament, having been composed in like manner by native Jews, in Hellenistic or Hebraic Greek, under the same divine influence, and we should naturally expect the same kinds of parallelism, and other similar indications of poetic effusion.

Jebb remarks, that the poetry of the New Testament consists,—1. In simple and direct quotations of single passages from the poetic parts of the Old Testament. 2. In quotations of a more complex kind when fragments are combined from different parts of the poetical Scriptures, and formed into one connected whole. 3. In quotations mingled with original matter, in which one passage or more is derived from the Hebrew Scriptures and so connected with what is original that the compound forms a homogeneous whole.

The different kinds of *original Parallelism* in the New Testament are, according to the same distinguished scholar,—I. *Parallel couplets;* II. *Parallel triplets;* III. *Quatrains*, of which the lines are either directly, alternately, or inversely parallel; IV. Stanzas of five lines; V. Stanzas of six lines; VI. Stanzas of more than six parallel lines.

Parallel lines gradational, or *Cognate Parallelisms* are also found in the New as well as the Old Testament, as in II Thess.

ii. 8; Matt. x. 5, 6, etc. *Introverted Parallelism* is also found, and the *Epanodos*, as Jebb calls it.

We discover in the Sacred Scriptures seven different kinds of poetic composition, viz: *Prophetic*, *Elegiac*, *Didactic*, *Lyric*, the *Idyl* or short pastoral poem, *Dramatic* poetry, and the *Acrostic* or *Alphabetical* poems. Oriental poetry is full of strong expressions, striking metaphors, lively descriptions, and glowing sentiments, expressed in the most vivid manner.

In addition to the passages already presented, which may be called *poetic prose*, there are a few other specimens of poetry before coming to the poetic books. We have already noticed some, and find in them a higher kind of poetry than that which we have been considering. They are the following: The Song of Moses and the Israelites, uttered after their deliverance from the Egyptians at the Red Sea, contained in Ex. xv. 1–18 (vid. p. 102, *supra*); the Song of Miriam, contained in Ex. xv. 21 (vid. p. 106, *supra*); also a song of the Israelites, contained in Num. xxi. 17, 18 (a part of the verse) (vid. p. 127, *supra*).

These are specimens of Lyric poetry. Another instance is found in Num. xxi. 27–30. It is a triumphal ode, in which Israel exults, after a sanguinary battle, in view of her victory over Sihon, king of the Amorites. We give Herder's translation of it (Marsh's Ed.):

A SONG OF TRIUMPH OVER THE AMORITES, WHO HAD BEEN THE CONQUERORS OF MOAB.

27 Come ye into Heshbon,
Build and strengthen Sihon,
28 A fire went out of Heshbon.
A flame from the city Sihon,
Which consumed the mountains of Moab,
The dwellers in the high places of Arnon.
29 Woe unto thee, Moab,
Thou art undone, people of Chemosh.
Thy sons must be fugitives,

Thy daughters become captives
To Sihon, king of the Amorites.
30 Their yoke is now broken
From Heshbon unto Dibon.
We laid waste unto Nophah,
We laid them waste unto Medbah.

The Israelites here invite their enemies to come into the cities which they had just subdued, and extol, in the keenest irony, the achievements of the conqueror.

We find, also, other instances, as follows:

Numbers xxiii. 7–10.

7 And he took up his parable, and said,
Balak the king of Moab hath brought me from Aram,
Out of the mountains of the east, *saying*,
Come, curse me Jacob,
And come, defy Israel.
8 How shall I curse, whom God hath not cursed?
Or how shall I defy, *whom* the Lord hath not defied?
9 For from the top of the rocks I see him,
And from the hills I behold him:
Lo, the people shall dwell alone,
And shall not be reckoned among the nations.
10 Who can count the dust of Jacob,
And the number of the fourth *part* of Israel?
Let me die the death of the righteous,
And let my last end be like his!

Numbers xxiii. 18–24.

18 And he took up his parable, and said,
Rise up, Balak, and hear;
Hearken unto me, thou son of Zippor:

19 God *is* not a man, that he should lie;
Neither the son of man, that he should repent:
Hath he said, and shall he not do *it?*
Or hath he spoken, and shall he not make it good?
20 Behold, I have received *commandment* to bless:
And he hath blessed; and I cannot reverse it.
21 He hath not beheld iniquity in Jacob,
Neither hath he seen perverseness in Israel:
The Lord his God *is* with him,
And the shout of a King *is* among them.
22 God brought them out of Egypt;
He hath as it were the strength of an unicorn.
23 Surely *there is* no enchantment against Jacob,
Neither *is there* any divination against Israel:
According to this time it shall be said
Of Jacob and of Israel, What hath God wrought!
24 Behold, the people shall rise up as a great lion,
And lift up himself as a young lion:
He shall not lie down until he eat *of* the prey,
And drink the blood of the slain.

Numbers xxiv. 3–9.

3 And he took up his parable, and said,
Balaam the son of Beor hath said,
And the man whose eyes are open hath said:
4 He hath said, which heard the words of God,
Which saw the vision of the Almighty,
Falling *into a trance*, but having his eyes open:

From verse 5 to 9 we copy Dr. Hales' beautiful translation, as follows:

5 How goodly are thy tents, O Jacob,
And thy tabernacles, O Israel!
6 As streams do they spread forth,

As gardens by the river side;
As sandal trees which the Lord hath planted,
As cedar trees beside the waters.
7 There shall come forth a man of his seed,
And shall rule over many nations:
And his king shall be higher than Gog,
And his kingdom shall be exalted.
8 (God brought him forth out of Egypt,
He is to him as the strength of a unicorn).
He shall devour the nations, his enemies,
And shall break their bones.
And pierce them through with arrows.
9 He lieth down as a lion,
He coucheth as a lioness,
Who shall rouse him?
Blessed is he that blesseth thee,
And cursed is he that curseth thee.

Verses 15–24 of the same chapter, refer to other prophecies of Balaam.

15 And he took up his parable, and said,
Balaam the son of Beor hath said,
And the man whose eyes are open hath said:
16 He hath said, which heard the words of God,
And knew the knowledge of the Most High,
Which saw the vision of the Almighty,
Falling *into a trance*, but having his eyes open:
17 I shall see him, but not now:
I shall behold him, but not nigh:
There shall come a Star out of Jacob.
And a Sceptre shall rise out of Israel,
And shall smite the corners of Moab,
And destroy all the children of Sheth.
18 And Edom shall be a possession,

Seir also shall be a possession for his enemies;
And Israel shall do valiantly.
19 Out of Jacob shall come he that shall have dominion,
And shall destroy him that remaineth of the city.
20 And when he looked on Amalek, he took up his parable, and said,
Amalek *was* the first of the nations;
But his latter end *shall be* that he perish for ever.
21 And he looked on the Kenites, and took up his parable, and said,
Strong is thy dwelling-place,
And thou puttest thy nest in a rock.
22 Nevertheless the Kenite shall be wasted,
Until Asshur shall carry thee away captive.
23 And he took up his parable, and said,
Alas, who shall live when God doeth this!
And ships *shall come* from the coast of Chittim,
24 And shall afflict Asshur, and shall afflict Eber,
And he also shall perish forever.

These are remarkable instances of prophetic poetry by an irreligious man. Balaam, the son of Beor, was called by Balak, king of Moab, to curse Israel. It is a disputed point whether he was a true prophet of the Lord, or only a magician. The most probable supposition is that he was a Chaldæan priest, magician, and astrologist, and distinguished throughout Asia in his profession. At the same time, he had a knowledge of the Supreme Being, and worshipped him, though his religious notions and services were mingled with superstition and error. It is evident from the account given of him by Moses, that he was, occasionally at least, inspired, and uttered prophetic poetry, though probably a wicked man. It is obvious, from Matt. vii. 22, that those who had the gift of prophecy were not, in all cases, truly pious persons. It seems that Balaam was desirous to curse the Israelites; but dared not do it without authority from Jehovah. Thus he blessed them three times, in elevated Hebrew poetry, with language abounding in gay and splendid imagery, drawn directly from nature. The figures are remarkably diversified, and the style glowing and elegant.

The next instance which we shall present, is found in Deuteronomy xxxii. 1–43. We give Herder's translation of it (Marsh's Ed.):

SONG OF MOSES TO THE ASSEMBLED ISRAELITES BEFORE HIS DEATH.

1 Give ear, O ye heavens, to my speech,
Hear, O earth, the words of my mouth.
2 My doctrine shall drop as the rain,
My words shall distil as the dew,
As rain upon the tender herb,
And as showers upon the grass;
3 For I will publish the name of Jehovah—
Ascribe ye greatness to Jehovah our God.
4 He is a rock, his work is perfect,
And all his dealings are right;
A God of truth, without iniquity,
Sincere and righteous is he.
5 They only are no longer his children,
Their iniquity hath turned them from him,
A faithless and perverse generation.
6 Is this your requital to Jehovah,
O foolish people and unwise?
Is he not thy father, he that hath bought thee?
That hath made thee, and established thee?
7 Call to remembrance the ancient days,
The years from generation to generation.
Ask thy father, and he will shew thee,
The aged men, and they will tell it thee.
8 When the Almighty gave the nations their lands,
When he separated the children of men,

He limited the bounds of the nations,
That the numbers of Israel might have room;
9 For the portion of God is his people,
Jacob, the lot of his inheritance.
10 He found him in a desert land,
In a waste and howling wilderness;
He took him in his arms and taught him;
He guarded him as the apple of his eye.
11 As the eagle covers her nest around,
And hovers over her young,
Spreads her wings, takes them thereon,
And bears them aloft upon her wings;
12 So did Jehovah lead him, himself alone,
There was no strange God with him.
13 He bore him to the mountain heights,
And fed him with the fruits of the earth;
He made him to suck honey from the rock,
And oil out of the flinty rock,
14 Butter of kine, and milk of sheep,
The fat of lambs, and of the rams of Bashan,
The fat kidneys of goats, and bread of wheat,
And thou didst drink the blood of the grape.
15 Then Jeshurun waxed stout, and rebelled,
Thou wast too fat, too satiate, too full,
Thou didst forsake the God that made thee,
And lightly esteem the rock of thy salvation.
They moved his jealousy with strange gods,
16 They provoked his anger with abominations,
They sacrificed to demons, not to God,
17 To idols, of whom they had no knowledge,
To new gods, that were newly invented,
Before whom your fathers trembled not;
18 Of Him that begat thee—the Rock—thou wast forgetful,
And didst forget the God that formed thee.

19 This Jehovah saw, and cast away in anger,
Those who were his sons and daughters.
20 He said, "I will turn my face from them,
I will see to what end they will come.
For they are a perverse generation,
Children of a base and faithless sort.
21 They moved me to jealousy with their no-god,
They provoked me to anger with their idols;
I also will move their jealousy with a no-people,
With a foolish nation I will provoke their anger.
22 For the fire of my wrath is kindled,
And shall burn even to the deep abyss,
It shall consume the earth and her fruits,
And fire the foundations of the mountains.
23 I will heap up afflictions upon them,
And my arrows will I send upon them,
24 Consumed with hunger, and burned with heat,
Devoured with bitter destruction,
I will send upon them the teeth of wild beasts,
With the poison of serpents from the dust.
25 The sword shall be without, and terror within,
And shall destroy both the young man and virgin,
The suckling, and the man of gray hairs.
26 I had almost said, I will destroy them,
And blot out their name among men;
27 Had I not feared the pride of the enemy,
That their oppressors would mistake it,
And say, "our own high hand,
And not Jehovah hath done this."
28 For they are a nation void of counsel,
There is no understanding in them.
29 O that they were wise, to understand this,
That they would consider their latter end.
30 How is it, that one can chase a thousand,

And two of them put ten thousand to flight?
Is it not, that their rock hath forsaken them,
That Jehovah hath given them for a prey?
31 Else their rock were not like our rock,
Our enemies themselves being judges.
32 Their vine is from the vine of Sodom,
Their grapes from the fields of Gomorrah,
Grapes of gall, their clusters are bitter,
33 Their juice is the poison of dragons,
The deadly venom of serpents.
34 Have I not already my secret counsel,
Sealed and laid up in my treasures?
35 "Vengeance is mine and the day of recompense,
Their foot is even now ready to slide,
The day of their calamity is at hand,
Their destiny is soon coming upon them."
36 Jehovah is now the judge of his people,
It repents him that they are his children,
He seeth, that their power is departed,
That nothing is left to them more.
37 He asked them, where are now their gods,
The guardian God, in whom they trusted?
38 Which did eat the fat of their sacrifices,
And drank the wine of their drink-offerings?
Let them now rise up and help you,
Let them now be your protection.
39 See now, that I, even I am he,
And there are no Gods with me.
I am he, that killeth and maketh alive,
I am he, that woundeth and healeth,
And none can deliver out of my hand.
40 For I lift up my hand to heaven,
And say, I am, the living one
From eternity to eternity.

41 If I whet my glittering sword,
And my hand take hold on judgment,
I will render vengeance to mine enemies,
And will reward them that hate me.
42 I will make mine arrows drunk with blood,
My sword shall satiate itself with flesh,
The blood of the slain, and of the captives,
With the head of the chief of my enemy.
43 Rejoice, ye Gentiles, now his people,
He will avenge the blood of his servants,
And render vengeance to his enemies,
And purify his land and people.

Another instance occurs in

Deuteronomy xxxiii. 1–29.

1 And this *is* the blessing, wherewith Moses the
man of God blessed the children of Israel before
his death. And he said,
2 The Lord came from Sinai,
And rose up from Seir unto them;
He shined forth from Mount Paran,
And he came with ten thousands of saints:
From his right hand *went* a fiery law for them.
3 Yea, he loved the people:
All his saints *are* in thy hand:
And they sat down at thy feet;
Every one shall receive of thy words.
4 Moses commanded us a law,
Even the inheritance of the congregation of Jacob.
5 And he was king in Jeshurun
When the heads of the people
And the tribes of Israel were gathered together.
6 Let Reuben live, and not die;

And let *not* his men be few.

7 And this *is the blessing* of Judah: and he said,
Hear, Lord, the voice of Judah,
And bring him unto his people:
Let his hands be sufficient for him;
And be thou an help *to him* from his enemies.

8 And of Levi he said,
Let thy Thummim and thy Urim *be* with thy holy one,
Whom thou didst prove at Massah,
And with whom thou didst strive at the waters of Meribah:

9 Who said unto his father, and to his mother, I have not seen him:
Neither did he acknowledge his brethren, nor knew his own children:
For they have observed thy word, and kept thy covenant.

10 They shall teach Jacob thy judgments, and Israel thy law:
They shall put incense before thee, and whole burnt sacrifices upon thine altar.

11 Bless, Lord, his substance,
And accept the work of his hands;
Smite through the loins of them that rise against him,
And of them that hate him, that they rise not again.

12 *And* of Benjamin he said,
The beloved of the Lord shall dwell in safety by him;
And the Lord shall cover him all the day long,
And he shall dwell between his shoulders.

13 And of Joseph he said,
Blessed of the Lord *be* his land,
For the precious things of heaven, for the dew,
And for the deep that coucheth beneath,

14 And for the precious fruits brought forth by the sun,
And for the precious things put forth by the moon,
15 And for the chief things of the ancient mountains,
And for the precious things of the lasting hills,
16 And for the precious things of the earth and fullness thereof,
And *for* the good-will of him that dwelt in the bush:
Let *the blessing* come upon the head of Joseph,
And upon the top of the head of him that was separated from his brethren.
17 His glory *is like* the firstling of his bullock,
And his horns *are like* the horns of unicorns;
With them he shall push the people together to the ends of the earth:
And they *are* the ten thousands of Ephraim,
And they *are* the thousands of Manasseh.

18 And of Zebulun he said,
Rejoice, Zebulun, in thy going out;
And, Issachar, in thy tents.
19 They shall call the people unto the mountain;
There they shall offer sacrifices of righteousness:
For they shall suck *of* the abundance of the seas,
And *of* treasures hid in the sand.

20 And of Gad he said,
Blessed be he that enlargeth Gad:
He dwelleth as a lion,
And teareth the arm with the crown of the head.
21 And he provided the first part for himself,
Because there, *in* a portion of the lawgiver, *was he* seated;
And he came with the heads of the people,
He executed the justice of the Lord,
And his judgments with Israel.

22 And of Dan he said,

Dan *is* a lion's whelp:
He shall leap from Bashan.
23 And of Naphtali he said,
O Naphtali, satisfied with favor,
And full with the blessing of the Lord:
Possess thou the west and the south.
24 And of Asher he said,
Let Asher *be* blessed with children;
Let him be acceptable to his brethren,
And let him dip his foot in oil.
25 Thy shoes *shall be* iron and brass;
And as thy days, *so shall* thy strength *be*.
26 *There is* none like unto the God of Jeshurun,
Who rideth upon the heaven in thy help,
And in his excellency on the sky.
27 The eternal God *is thy* refuge,
And underneath *are* the everlasting arms:
And he shall thrust out the enemy from before thee;
And shall say, Destroy *them*.
28 Israel then shall dwell in safety alone:
The fountain of Jacob *shall be* upon a land of corn and wine;
Also his heavens shall drop down dew.
29 Happy *art* thou, O Israel:
Who *is* like unto thee, O people saved by the Lord,
The shield of thy help, and who *is* the sword of thy excellency:
And thine enemies shall be found liars unto thee;
And thou shalt tread upon their high places.

This seems to have been the valedictory poem of the great Lawgiver of Israel. He had premonitions of his approaching departure, and was borne down with anxiety in reference to his disobedient people. In his prophetic description of God's dealings with them, the most vivid and striking images are em ployed. We see before us the flaming mountain, the pillars of fire, and hear the voice of the Eternal, directing his chosen people. It is a lyric ode, but plaintive, exciting, and beautiful.

Another instance appears in Joshua x. 12, in which the leader of Israel's forces exclaims:

> "Sun, stand thou still upon Gibeon,
> And thou, Moon, in the valley of Ajalon."

This is a remarkable instance in which nature obeyed the mandate of a human being. Rationalism may attempt to show that no miracle was wrought in this case—that it is a mere poetic license—that Joshua only *wished* the sun not to go down, as Herder asserts; but we believe that the Almighty interposed, and that the earth stopped in her diurnal revolution, or that the laws of refraction were so changed that the sun was visible about a day longer than usual. In either case it was a miracle. The passage is a striking instance of bold, animated poetry.

The Song of Deborah (Judges v. 2–31) we have already considered (vid. pp. 143–147, *supra*).

In I Sam. ii. 1–10, we have the prayer of a mother in Israel, expressed in antithetic parallel lines, as follows:

1 And Hannah prayed, and said,
My heart rejoiceth in the Lord,
Mine horn is exalted in the Lord:
My mouth is enlarged over mine enemies;
Because I rejoice in thy salvation.
2 *There is* none holy as the Lord:
For *there is* none beside thee:
Neither *is there* any rock like our God.
3 Talk no more so exceeding proudly;
Let *not* arrogancy come out of your mouth:
For the Lord *is* a God of knowledge,

And by him actions are weighed.
4 The bows of the mighty men *are* broken,
And they that stumbled are girded with strength.
5 *They that were* full have hired out themselves for bread;
And *they that were* hungry ceased:
So that the barren hath born seven;
And she that hath many children is waxed feeble.
6 The Lord killeth, and maketh alive:
He bringeth down to the grave, and bringeth up.
7 The Lord maketh poor, and maketh rich:
He bringeth low, and lifteth up.
8 He raiseth up the poor out of the dust,
And lifteth up the beggar from the dunghill,
To set *them* among princes,
And to make them inherit the throne of glory:
For the pillars of the earth *are* the Lord's,
And he hath set the world upon them.
9 He will keep the feet of his saints,
And the wicked shall be silent in darkness;
For by strength shall no man prevail.
10 The adversaries of the Lord shall be broken to pieces;
Out of heaven shall he thunder upon them:
The Lord shall judge the ends of the earth;
And he shall give strength unto his King,
And exalt the horn of his anointed.

Hannah rises in a kind of triumphal climax from her own domestic happiness to that of her fellow-men at large. She returns thanks to God, in an impressive manner, for the birth of Samuel, who was destined to be a renowned prophet of the Lord.

In II Sam. i. 19–27, we have an admirable specimen of elegiac poetry from the sweet singer of Israel. We present Herder's translation (Marsh's Ed.):

DAVID'S LAMENTATION FOR JONATHAN, HIS FRIEND.

19 Beautiful Roe, thou pride and glory of Israel!
Thus then art thou wounded upon thy high places!
CHORUS. Fallen, fallen are the heroes!
How are the heroes fallen?
20 Tell ye it not in Gath,
Publish it not in the streets of Askelon,
Lest the daughters of the Philistines rejoice,
Lest the daughters of the uncircumcised leap for joy.
21 Ye mountains of Gilboa, on you henceforth
Let no more rain nor dew descend forever.
No more on you, ye mountains blighted with a curse,
For there the shield of heroes was struck down,
The shield of Saul, as of one unconsecrated with oil.
22 From the blood of the slain, from the fat of the strong,
The bow of Jonathan never turned backward,
The sword of Saul returned not empty. (It reached the blood of the slain).
23 Saul and Jonathan, dear to each other in life,
They went undivided in love to the realm of shades:
Swifter than eagles, bolder were they than lions.
24 Daughters of Israel, weep ye for Saul,
No more will he clothe you in garments of purple,
Nor deck your apparel with ornaments of gold.
25 CHORUS. *Ah! how are the heroes fallen in the midst of battle,*
Jonathan, thou lovely Roe, slain on thy high places.
26 I am afflicted for thee, my brother Jonathan,
Lovely wast thou to me, exceeding lovely,
Yea, my love for thee surpassed the love of women.
27 CHORUS. *Ah! how are the heroes fallen,*
And their weapons of war perished.

These lines are tender, plaintive, and exceedingly touching. David loved Jonathan as he did his own soul, and not without reason, for the latter, though a prince, and the lawful heir to the throne of Israel, allowed the son of Jesse to be anointed king. Saul had disregarded the divine command, and was rejected of God; but when the shepherd-boy was made king in his place, he sought to take his life. Jonathan continued to be a true friend to the young king, and often shielded him from the darts of his father Saul. In a battle on Mount Gilboa Saul and Jonathan were slain, and in view of that mournful fact, David breaks forth in this splendid elegy, in honor of both.

In II Sam. iii. 33, 34, David utters five lines of the same kind of poetry, in honor of Abner, the leader of the party opposed to him. The following is Herder's translation of it (Marsh's Ed.):

"Abner died not as a coward dieth!
Thy hands were not bound,
Nor thy feet put in fetters.
As one falleth before wicked men,
So fellest thou."

The soul of David was full of tender and lofty emotions, and when his friends or even his enemies were in mourning, or were swept away by the rude hand of the destroyer, he was always ready to pour forth the overflowing sympathies and benevolence of his nature, in plaintive and elegant rhythm.

His triumphal song, recorded in II Sam. xxii. 2–51, and xxiii. 2–7, we have already considered (vid. pp. 180–185, *supra*).

In II Kings xix. 21–34, there is a terrific denunciation by Jehovah, through his servant, Isaiah, against Sennacherib, the Assyrian monarch, as follows:

21 This *is* the word that the Lord hath spoken concerning him;

The virgin the daughter of Zion
Hath despised thee, *and* laughed thee to scorn;

The daughter of Jerusalem hath shaken her head at thee.
22 Whom hast thou reproached and blasphemed?
And against whom hast thou exalted *thy* voice,
And lifted up thine eyes on high?
Even against the Holy *One* of Israel.
23 By thy messengers thou hast reproached the Lord,
And hast said, With the multitude of my chariots
I am come up to the height of the mountains,
To the sides of Lebanon,
And will cut down the tall cedar-trees thereof,
And the choice fir-trees thereof:
And I will enter into the lodgings of his borders,
And into the forest of his Carmel.
24 I have digged and drunk strange waters,
And with the sole of my feet
Have I dried up all the rivers of besieged places.
25 Hast thou not heard long ago *how* I have done it,
And of ancient times that I have formed it?
Now have I brought it to pass,
That thou shouldest be to lay waste fenced cities *into* ruinous heaps.
26 Therefore their inhabitants were of small power,
They were dismayed and confounded;
They were *as* the grass of the field,
And *as* the green herb, *as* the grass on the house-tops,
And *as corn* blasted before it be grown up.
27 But I know thy abode,
And thy going out,
And thy coming in,
And thy rage against me.
28 Because thy rage against me
And thy tumult is come up into mine ears,
Therefore I will put my hook in thy nose,

And my bridle in thy lips,
And I will turn thee back by the way by which thou camest.
29 And this *shall be* a sign unto thee,
Ye shall eat this year such things as grow of themselves,
And in the second year that which springeth of the same;
And in the third year sow ye and reap,
And plant vineyards, and eat the fruits thereof.
30 And the remnant that is escaped of the house of Judah
Shall yet again take root downward, and bear fruit upward.
31 For out of Jerusalem shall go forth a remnant,
And they that escape out of mount Zion:
The zeal of the Lord *of hosts* shall do this.
32 Therefore thus saith the Lord concerning the king of Assyria,
He shall not come into this city,
Nor shoot an arrow there,
Nor come before it with shield,
Nor cast a bank against it.
33 By the way that he came,
By the same shall he return,
And shall not come into the city,
Saith the Lord.
34 For I will defend this city, to save it,
For mine own sake, and for my servant David's sake.

Sennacherib had come up against Hezekiah, king of Judah, and determined to destroy Jerusalem. The latter monarch prayed earnestly to God, who interposed in a wonderful manner, in answer to the supplications of his servant. He directs the son of Amoz to utter in the ears of Hezekiah the exalted effusions, which we have presented above, predicting the discomfiture and ruin of the haughty Assyrian. The passage is replete with sharp rebuke to Sennacherib, derision and fearful denunciation. The same evening, the inspired writer informs us, an angel of the Lord smote an hundred fourscore and five thousand of the Assyrians. The remnant retreated, and finally Sennacherib was murdered at Nineveh by his own sons.

David's Psalm of thanksgiving, found in I Chron. xvi. 8–36, has already been considered (vid. pp. 200–202, *supra*).

THE BOOK OF JOB.

INTRODUCTORY REMARKS.

THIS book receives its title from the person described in its pages. It has been questioned, however, by biblical scholars, whether the name of Job refers to a real personage. That it does not, is maintained by Maimonides, LeClerc, Michaelis, Semler, Stock, and others. That there is reference to a real personage is supported by Calmet, Heidegger, Spanheim, Moldenhawer, Schultens, Carpzof, Magee, Lowth, Kennicott, Hales, Taylor, and by evangelical divines generally. The improbability that Satan would be represented as accusing Job, the inconsistency of the idea that God should permit such grievous temptations and sufferings to be experienced by a just man, and the artificial regularity of the numbers used in describing the patriarch's possessions, are presented as proofs that the name does not indicate a real personage. On the other hand, the manner in which different inspired writers have spoken of Job (cf. Eze. xiv. 14; James v. 11, etc.), and the fact that he is expressly mentioned as a real personage by various ancient historians, leave but little doubt that such a man existed.

The learned Dr. Hales has shown by astronomical calculations that Job's trial must have occurred 818 years after the deluge, 184 before the birth of Abraham, and 689 before the exodus of the Israelites from Egypt, or B. C. 2337 (2130 according to the usual computation). The fact that the exodus is not mentioned in the book of Job, nor the destruction of Sodom and Gomorrah, the great length of the patriarch's life, the allusion to Sabianism, one of the most ancient superstitions, also the fact that all of the speakers use the Hebrew language, though Idumæans or Arabians, and other considerations, confirm the great antiquity of the poem, and critics and commentators agree that it is the most ancient book extant.

The scene of this composition is laid in Uz, which seems to have been Idumæa (cf. Lam. iv. 21), located between Egypt and Philistia (cf. Jer. xxv. 20). The poem contains a description of a great sufferer. Though Job was a just man, he was lamentably afflicted with a loathsome disease, as well as with the loss of his property and friends. He was an Emir or Arabian prince of great wealth, authority, and distinction, and probably his friends Eliphaz, Bildad, and Zophar were Emirs of important cities. It is believed that the Patriarch had the *Elephantiasis* or *leprosy* of the Arabians, which the ancient medical writer, Paul of Ægineta, characterized as an universal ulcer. It was named Elephantiasis by the Greeks, because it rendered the skin like that of an elephant, scabrous, dark colored, furrowed with tubercles, and extremely loathsome to the patient as well as to others. The good man seemed to be reduced to the lowest depths of human misery, and his mournful condition called forth the strongest feelings of the heart, and suggested the highest kind of poetic numbers.

That the Book of Job was composed by a single author is evident from the remarkable unity which is apparent throughout its pages, and from the references in the peroration to the exordium and to other parts of the poem. There is a difference of opinion, however, in reference to the question, who that author was? It must have been either Job himself, or a contemporary of his. Had it been Moses, as some suppose, there would undoubtedly have been frequent allusions to the customs, manners, and history of the Israelites; but there is not one such reference. The grand object presented to our contemplation, is the example of a devotedly pious man, suddenly precipitated from the highest pinnacle of earthly prosperity to the most abject misery and ruin, yet sustaining his bereavements and sorrows with entire resignation to the divine will.

The book is a kind of elegiac drama. Bishop Lowth considers it, "to some extent, a dramatic poem, as the parties are introduced as speaking with great fidelity of character, and as it deviates from strict historical accuracy for the sake of effect." But this is questioned by others. The book has been called by different critics, a didactic, an ethic, an epic, and a dramatic poem. It may have some of the qualities of all. It is unique in its character, differing in some respects from all the other specimens of poetry in the sacred Scriptures.

The circumstances under which it was composed are exciting in the highest degree. A mortal is suddenly reduced from princely affluence to the most distressing poverty and misery imaginable—enduring, without a murmur, apparently more than human nature could bear—his relatives, of great influence and power, visiting him for the avowed purpose of consolation, but reproaching him, and uttering unjust suspicions in reference to the motives by which he was actuated—Job in his wretchedness appealing to the Almighty, and the Eternal, from his throne, condescending to hold conversation with him. This accumulation of mournful circumstances is adapted to arouse all the energies of the soul, and produce, in the mind, the sublimest emotions.

The power of lifelike description here exhibited is far superior to that of any other of the sacred poets. As we read, we feel that we are in the midst of the wild sublimities of nature, where the lightnings play and the thunders roll. We see the parched desert, and then the dashing, whirling tempest. We hear the tiger's growl and the lion's roar. We behold nature in her simplest, roughest, and yet grandest form; we seem to be grappling with the terrific war-horse, the monster behemoth, and the powerful leviathan; and then we are listening to the strange, wild music of nature. How vivid is Eliphaz's description of a vision of the night. Darkness surrounds him. He is alone on his bed. Suddenly a shuddering comes over him. A kind of indefinite shadow moves before him. He fears and trembles until every bone shakes. At length he perceives, more distinctly, a spirit passing. His hair is erect. It is a form without a marked outline—a messenger from another world—and then a still, small voice is heard. "How can man be more just than God, or mortal man more just than his Maker?"

This is a masterly description, excelling even Milton's representation of chaos. The whole poem is full of oriental rudeness, beauty, and grandeur.

Elegiac, as well as lyric poetry, was often accompanied by plaintive music. Some of the Psalms of David are sacred elegies, and their recital was doubtless accompanied by plaintive notes from his enchanting harp. The original recital of the book of Job was not probably accompanied by either instrumental or vocal music, as the occasion did not seem to require it. Its metrical arrangement, however, is adapted to musical accompaniments.

The commencement and close of the book are written in prose. The exordium contains a description of Job's wealth, domestic prosperity and happiness. Then follows an account of a remarkable conversation between the Great Creator and the arch-Deceiver of mankind, in reference to a just man called Job. Jehovah directs the attention of Satan to him as "perfect and upright above any other person upon the earth." The Deceiver replies, and utters the suspicion that Job exhibits apparent piety from the fact that he had been continually blessed and never afflicted. Then God permits him to sift the good man, as wheat, that his faith may be thoroughly tried. The Devil retires from the presence of the Lord, and the sad tidings are speedily brought to the old patriarch that his oxen and asses had been carried away by the Sabæans, and that some of his servants had been slain. Next, his sheep, and other servants are consumed by fire from heaven. Then his camels are captured by the Chaldæans, and finally it is announced that his sons are buried beneath the ruins of the house in which they had assembled. These accumulated and terrible afflictions deeply afflicted the man of God; but he did not murmur. He arose, rent his mantle, shaved his head, and falling upon the earth, worshipped God, exclaiming, in plaintive, poetic strains,

"Naked came I out of my mother's womb,
And naked shall I return thither:
The Lord gave, and the Lord hath taken away;
Blessed be the name of the Lord."

Vid. Job i. 21.

The second chapter of the book is written in prose, in the first part of which is found a continuation of the conversation between Deity and Satan. Jehovah descants upon the perseverance of the patriarch in his integrity though in so great distress, while the latter intimates, that if the good man should be attacked by disease, he would curse his Maker. God permits the Devil to afflict him still more severely, and the fiend smites him with sore boils upon every part of his body, and he sits in ashes. His wife, perceiving his anguish, advises him to curse God, and die; but he reproves her, and still maintains his integrity. His three friends, Eliphaz the Temanite, Bildad the Shuhite, and Zophar the Naamathite, also visit him, and beholding his great affliction, mingle their tears with his, rend their mantles, sprinkle dust upon their heads, and sit with him in silence upon the ground, during seven days and seven nights. Finally, Job's distress is so aggravated that human nature is overwhelmed, and he breaks the sad silence by bitter asseverations, in the following plaintive strains of elegiac poetry.

JOB'S PLAINTIVE ADDRESS.

Job iii. 2–26.

2 And Job spake, and said,
3 Let the day perish wherein I was born,
And the night *in which* it was said,
There is a man-child conceived.
4 Let that day be darkness;
Let not God regard it from above,
Neither let the light shine upon it.
5 Let darkness and the shadow of death stain it;
Let a cloud dwell upon it;
Let the blackness of the day terrify it.
6 *As for* that night, let darkness seize upon it;
Let it not be joined unto the days of the year,
Let it not come into the number of the months.
7 Lo, let that night be solitary,
Let no joyful voice come therein.
8 Let them curse it that curse the day,
Who are ready to raise up their mourning.
9 Let the stars of the twilight thereof be dark;

Let it look for the light, but *have* none;
Neither let it see the dawning of the day:
10 Because it shut not up the doors of my *mother's* womb,
Nor hid sorrow from mine eyes.
11 Why died I not from the womb?
Why did I *not* give up the ghost when I came out of the belly?
12 Why did the knees prevent me?
Or why the breasts that I should suck?
13 For now should I have lain still and been quiet,
I should have slept; then had I been at rest,
14 With kings and counsellors of the earth,
Which built desolate places for themselves;
15 Or with princes that had gold,
Who filled their houses with silver:
16 Or as an hidden untimely birth I had not been;
As infants *which* never saw light.
17 There the wicked cease *from* troubling;
And there the weary be at rest.
18 *There* the prisoners rest together;
They hear not the voice of the oppressor.
19 The small and great are there;
And the servant *is* free from his master.
20 Wherefore is light given to him that is in misery,
And life unto the bitter *in* soul;
21 Which long for death, but it *cometh* not;
And dig for it more than for hid treasures;
22 Which rejoice exceedingly, *and* are glad,
When they can find the grave?
23 *Why is light given* to a man whose way is hid,
And whom God hath hedged in?
24 For my sighing cometh before I eat,
And my roarings are poured out like the waters.
25 For the thing which I greatly feared is come upon me,

And that which I was afraid of is come unto me.
26 I was not in safety, neither had I rest,
Neither was I quiet; yet trouble came.

In this complaint of the patriarch, he utters passionate exclamations and execrations of the day of his birth.

Here properly begins the plot of the poem. The friends of Job, who had professedly come to administer consolation in this trying hour, had, thus far, remained in silence. On hearing his vehement complaints, however, they seemed to be exasperated. They had unholy suspicions in reference to his integrity, and finally reproached him with severity. This cruel treatment added tenfold to the load of sorrow which was crushing his spirit.

Eliphaz first raised his warning voice and condemned Job's impatience, distrusting his integrity, and, intimating that the chastisement of God had justly come upon him, a fact which he should not despise. The miserable comforter speaks in the following vindictive manner:

REPLY OF ELIPHAZ TO JOB.

Job iv. 1–21.

1 Then Eliphaz the Temanite, answered and said,
2 *If* we assay to commune with thee, wilt thou be grieved?
But who can withhold himself from speaking?
3 Behold, thou hast instructed many,
And thou hast strengthened the weak hands.
4 Thy words have upholden him that was falling,
And thou hast strengthened the feeble knees.
5 But now it is come upon thee, and thou faintest;
It toucheth thee, and thou art troubled.
6 *Is* not *this* thy fear, thy confidence,
Thy hope, and the uprightness of thy ways?

7 Remember, I pray thee, who *ever* perished, being innocent?
Or where were the righteous cut off?
8 Even as I have seen, they that plow iniquity,
And sow wickedness, reap the same.
9 By the blast of God they perish,
And by the breath of his nostrils are they consumed.
10 The roaring of the lion, and the voice of the fierce lion,
And the teeth of the young lions, are broken.
11 The old lion perisheth for lack of prey,
And the stout lion's whelps are scattered abroad.
12 Now a thing was secretly brought to me,
And mine ear received a little thereof.
13 In thoughts from the visions of the night,
When deep sleep falleth on men,
14 Fear came upon me, and trembling,
Which made all my bones to shake.
15 Then a spirit passed before my face;
The hair of my flesh stood up:
16 It stood still, but I could not discern the form thereof;
An image *was* before mine eyes,
There was silence, and I heard a voice, *saying*,
17 'Shall mortal man be more just than God?
Shall a man be more pure than his Maker?
18 Behold, he put no trust in his servants;
And his angels he charged with folly:
19 How much less *in* them that dwell in houses of clay,
Whose foundation *is* in the dust, *which* are crushed before the moth?
20 They are destroyed from morning to evening:
They perish for ever without any regarding *it*.
21 Doth not their excellency *which is* in them go away?
They die, even without wisdom.'

FARTHER REPLY OF ELIPHAZ TO JOB.

Job v. 1–27.

1 Call now, if there be any that will answer thee;
And to which of the saints wilt thou turn?
2 For wrath killeth the foolish man,
And envy slayeth the silly one.
3 I have seen the foolish taking root:
But suddenly I cursed his habitation.
4 His children are far from safety,
And they are crushed in the gate,
Neither *is there* any to deliver *them*.
5 Whose harvest the hungry eateth up,
And taketh it even out of the thorns,
And the robber swalloweth up their substance.
6 Although affliction cometh not forth of the dust,
Neither doth trouble spring out of the ground;
7 Yet man is born unto trouble,
As the sparks fly upward.
8 I would seek unto God,
And unto God would I commit my cause:
9 Which doeth great things and unsearchable;
Marvellous things without number:
10 Who giveth rain upon the earth,
And sendeth waters upon the fields:
11 To set up on high those that be low;
That those which mourn may be exalted to safety.
12 He disappointeth the devices of the crafty,
So that their hands cannot perform *their* enterprise.
13 He taketh the wise in their own craftiness:
And the counsel of the froward is carried headlong.
14 They meet with darkness in the day-time,
And grope in the noon-day as in the night.
15 But he saveth the poor from the sword,

From their mouth, and from the hand of the mighty.
16 So the poor hath hope,
And iniquity stoppeth her mouth.
17 Behold, happy *is* the man whom God correcteth:
Therefore despise not thou the chastening of the Almighty:
18 For he maketh sore, and bindeth up:
He woundeth, and his hands make whole.
19 He shall deliver thee in six troubles:
Yea, in seven there shall no evil touch thee.
20 In famine he shall redeem thee from death:
And in war from the power of the sword.
21 Thou shalt be hid from the scourge of the tongue:
Neither shalt thou be afraid of destruction when it cometh.
22 At destruction and famine thou shalt laugh:
Neither shalt thou be afraid of the beasts of the earth.
23 For thou shalt be in league with the stones of the field:
And the beasts of the field shall be at peace with thee.
24 And thou shalt know that thy tabernacle *shall be* in peace;
And thou shalt visit thy habitation, and shalt not sin.
25 Thou shalt know also that thy seed *shall be* great,
And thine offspring as the grass of the earth.
26 Thou shalt come to *thy* grave in a full age,
Like as a shock of corn cometh in in his season.
27 Lo this, we have searched it, so it *is*;
Hear it, and know thou *it* for thy good.

Job answered by referring to his severe trials, and complained of the unkindness of his friends, calling upon God and man to witness that he was unjustly oppressed; but he knew that he could not contend with his Maker.

The address is full of enthusiasm and poetic beauty. It is the following:

REPLY OF JOB TO ELIPHAZ.

Job vi. 1–30.

1 But Job answered, and said,
2 O that my grief were thoroughly weighed,
And my calamity laid in the balances together!
3 For now it would be heavier than the sand of the sea:
Therefore my words are swallowed up.
4 For the arrows of the Almighty *are* within me,
The poison whereof drinketh up my spirit:
The terrors of God do set themselves in array against me.
5 Doth the wild ass bray when he hath grass?
Or loweth the ox over his fodder?
6 Can that which is unsavory be eaten without salt?
Or is there *any* taste in the white of an egg?
7 The things *that* my soul refused to touch
Are as my sorrowful meat.
8 O that I might have my request;
And that God would grant *me* the thing that I long for!
9 Even that it would please God to destroy me;
That he would let loose his hand, and cut me off!
10 Then should I yet have comfort;
Yea, I would harden myself in sorrow:
Let him not spare; for I have not concealed the words of the Holy One.
11 What *is* my strength, that I should hope?
And what *is* mine end, that I should prolong my life?
12 *Is* my strength the strength of stones?
Or *is* my flesh of brass?
13 *Is* not my help in me?
And is wisdom driven quite from me?
14 To him that is afflicted, pity *should be showed* from his friend;

But he forsaketh the fear of the Almighty.
15 My brethren have dealt deceitfully as a brook,
And as the stream of brooks they pass away;
16 Which are blackish by reason of the ice,
And wherein the snow is hid:
17 What time they wax warm, they vanish:
When it is hot, they are consumed out of their place.
18 The paths of their way are turned aside;
They go to nothing, and perish.
19 The troops of Tema looked,
The companies of Sheba waited for them.
20 They were confounded because they had hoped;
They came thither, and were ashamed.
21 For now ye are nothing;
Ye see *my* casting down, and are afraid.
22 Did I say, Bring unto me?
Or, Give a reward for me of your substance?
23 Or, Deliver me from the enemy's hand?
Or, Redeem me from the hand of the mighty?
24 Teach me, and I will hold my tongue:
And cause me to understand wherein I have erred.
25 How forcible are right words!
But what doth your arguing reprove?
26 Do ye imagine to reprove words,
And the speeches of one that is desperate,
Which are as wind?
27 Yea, ye overwhelm the fatherless,
And ye dig *a pit* for your friend.
28 Now therefore be content, look upon me;
For *it is* evident unto you if I lie.
29 Return, I pray you, let it not be iniquity;
Yea, return again, my righteousness *is* in it.
30 *Is* there iniquity in my tongue?
Cannot my taste discern perverse things?

FARTHER REPLY OF JOB TO ELIPHAZ.

Job vii. 1–21.

1 *Is there* not an appointed time to man upon earth?
Are not his days also like the days of an hireling?
2 As a servant earnestly desireth the shadow,
And as an hireling looketh for *the reward of* his work:
3 So am I made to possess months of vanity,
And wearisome nights are appointed to me.
4 When I lie down, I say, When shall I arise, and the night be gone?
And I am full of tossings to and fro unto the dawning of the day.
5 My flesh is clothed with worms and clods of dust;
My skin is broken, and become loathsome.
6 My days are swifter than a weaver's shuttle,
And are spent without hope.
7 Oh! remember that my life *is* wind:
Mine eye shall no more see good.
8 The eye of him that hath seen me shall see me no *more:*
Thine eyes *are* upon me, and I *am* not.
9 *As* the cloud is consumed and vanisheth away:
So he that goeth down to the grave shall come up no *more.*
10 He shall return no more to his house,
Neither shall his place know him any more.
11 Therefore I will not refrain my mouth;
I will speak in the anguish of my spirit;
I will complain in the bitterness of my soul.
12 *Am* I a sea, or a whale, that thou settest a watch over me?
13 When I say, My bed shall comfort me,
My couch shall ease my complaint;

14 Then thou scarest me with dreams,
And terrifiest me through visions:
15 So that my soul chooseth strangling,
And death rather than my life.
16 I loathe *it;* I would not live alway:
Let me alone; for my days *are* vanity.
17 What *is* man, that thou shouldest magnify him?
And that thou shouldest set thine heart upon him?
18 And *that* thou shouldest visit him every morning,
And try him every moment?
19 How long wilt thou not depart from me,
Nor let me alone till I swallow down my spittle?
20 I have sinned: what shall I do unto thee,
O thou preserver of men? why hast thou set me as a mark against thee,
So that I am a burden to myself?
21 And why dost thou not pardon my transgressions,
And take away mine iniquity?
For now shall I sleep in the dust;
And thou shalt seek me in the morning, but I *shall* not *be.*

Bildad next speaks, in the same overbearing manner, severely reproving the patriarch. Zophar is still more inveterate, openly upbraiding Job with arrogance, vanity, and falsehood. The good man expostulates with his friends, and they reply with still greater acerbity, employing splendid oriental imagery. Finally, Elihu, offended with both parties, descants with great energy, pathos, and power. He reproves Job for justifying himself before God, and blames the three friends because they condemn the patriarch without any evidence of his guilt.

The several addresses of Elihu, to which Job made no reply, are the following:

ADDRESS OF ELIHU TO JOB. EXORDIUM.

Job xxxii. 6–22.

6 And Elihu the son of Barachel the Buzite answered and said,
I *am* young, and ye *are* very old;
Wherefore I was afraid, and durst not show you mine opinion.
7 I said, Days should speak,
And multitude of years should teach wisdom.
8 But *there is* a spirit in man:
And the inspiration of the Almighty giveth them understanding.
9 Great men are not *always* wise:
Neither do the aged understand judgment.
10 Therefore I said, Hearken to me;
I also will show mine opinion.
11 Behold, I waited for your words;
I gave ear to your reasons, whilst ye searched out what to say.
12 Yea, I attended unto you,
And, behold, *there was* none of you that convinced Job,
Or that answered his words:
13 Lest ye should say, We have found out wisdom:
God thrusteth him down, not man.
14 Now he hath not directed *his* words against me:
Neither will I answer him with your speeches.
15 They were amazed, they answered no more:
They left off speaking.
16 When I had waited, (for they spake not,
But stood still, *and* answered no more);
17 *I said*, I will answer also my part,
I also will show mine opinion.
18 For I am full of matter,

The spirit within me constraineth me.
19 Behold, my belly *is* as wine *which* hath no vent;
It is ready to burst like new bottles.
20 I will speak, that I may be refreshed:
I will open my lips and answer.
21 Let me not, I pray you, accept any man's person,
Neither let me give flattering titles unto man.
22 For I know not to give flattering titles;
In so doing my maker would soon take me away.

OPENING OF THE ARGUMENT.

Job xxxiii. 1–33.

1 Wherefore, Job, I pray thee, hear my speeches,
And hearken to all my words.
2 Behold, now I have opened my mouth,
My tongue hath spoken in my mouth.
3 My words *shall be of* the uprightness of my heart:
And my lips shall utter knowledge clearly.
4 The Spirit of God hath made me,
And the breath of the Almighty hath given me life.
5 If thou canst answer me,
Set *thy words* in order before me, stand up.
6 Behold, I *am* according to thy wish in God's stead:
I also am formed out of the clay.
7 Behold, my terror shall not make thee afraid,
Neither shall my hand be heavy upon thee.
8 Surely thou hast spoken in mine hearing,
And I have heard the voice of *thy* words, *saying*,
9 I am clean without transgression,
I *am* innocent; neither *is there* iniquity in me.
10 Behold, he findeth occasions against me,
He counteth me for his enemy,
11 He putteth my feet in the stocks,

He marketh all my paths.
12 Behold, *in* this thou art not just:
I will answer thee, that God is greater than man.
13 Why dost thou strive against him?
For he giveth not account of any of his matters.
14 For God speaketh once, yea twice,
Yet man perceiveth it not.
15 In a dream, in a vision of the night,
When deep sleep falleth upon men,
In slumberings upon the bed;
16 Then he openeth the ears of men,
And sealeth their instruction,
17 That he may withdraw man *from his* purpose,
And hide pride from man.
18 He keepeth back his soul from the pit,
And his life from perishing by the sword.
19 He is chastened also with pain upon his bed,
And the multitude of his bones with strong *pain:*
20 So that his life abhorreth bread,
And his soul dainty meat.
21 His flesh is consumed away, that it cannot be seen;
And his bones *that* were not seen, stick out.
22 Yea, his soul draweth near unto the grave,
And his life to the destroyers.
23 If there be a messenger with him,
An interpreter, one among a thousand,
To show unto man his uprightness:
24 Then he is gracious unto him,
And saith, deliver him from going down to the pit:
I have found a ransom.
25 His flesh shall be fresher than a child's:
He shall return to the days of his youth:
26 He shall pray unto God,
And he will be favorable unto him:

And he shall see his face with joy:
For he will render unto man his righteousness.
27 He looketh upon men,
And *if any* say, I have sinned,
And perverted *that which was* right, and it profited me not;
28 He will deliver his soul from going into the pit,
And his life shall see the light.
29 Lo, all these *things* worketh God oftentimes with man,
30 To bring back his soul from the pit,
To be enlightened with the light of the living.
31 Mark well, O Job, hearken unto me:
Hold thy peace, and I will speak.
32 If thou hast any thing to say, answer me:
Speak, for I desire to justify thee.
33 If not, hearken unto me:
Hold thy peace, and I shall teach thee wisdom.

DEFENCE OF GOD'S GOVERNMENT.

JOB xxxiv. 1–37.

1 Furthermore Elihu answered and said,
2 Hear my words, O ye wise *men;*
And give ear unto me, ye that have knowledge.
3 For the ear trieth words,
As the mouth tasteth meat.
4 Let us choose to us judgment:
Let us know among ourselves what *is* good.
5 For Job hath said, I am righteous:
And God hath taken away my judgment.
6 Should I lie against my right?
My wound is incurable without transgression.
7 What man *is* like Job,
Who drinketh up scorning like water?

8 Which goeth in company with the workers of iniquity,
And walketh with wicked men.
9 For he hath said, It profiteth a man nothing
That he should delight himself with God.
10 Therefore hearken unto me, ye men of understanding:
Far be it from God, *that he should do* wickedness;
And *from* the Almighty, *that he should commit* iniquity.
11 For the work of a man shall he render unto him,
And cause every man to find according to *his* ways.
12 Yea, surely God will not do wickedly,
Neither will the Almighty pervert judgment.
13 Who hath given him a charge over the earth?
Or who hath disposed the whole world?
14 If he set his heart upon man,
If he gather unto himself his spirit and his breath;
15 All flesh shall perish together,
And man shall turn again unto dust.
16 If now *thou hast* understanding, hear this:
Hearken to the voice of my words.
17 Shall even he that hateth right govern?
And wilt thou condemn him that is most just?
18 *Is it fit* to say to a king, *Thou art* wicked?
And to princes, *Ye are* ungodly?
19 *How much less to him* that accepteth not the persons of princes,
Nor regardeth the rich more than the poor?
For they all *are* the work of his hands.
20 In a moment shall they die,
And the people shall be troubled at midnight, and pass away:
And the mighty shall be taken away without hand.
21 For his eyes *are* upon the ways of man,
And he seeth all his goings.

22 *There is* no darkness, nor shadow of death,
Where the workers of iniquity may hide themselves.
23 For he will not lay upon man more *than right;*
That he should enter into judgment with God.
24 He shall break in pieces mighty men without number,
And set others in their stead.
25 Therefore he knoweth their works,
And he overturneth *them* in the night,
So that they are destroyed.
26 He striketh them as wicked men
In the open sight of others;
27 Because they turned back from him,
And would not consider any of his ways:
28 So that they cause the cry of the poor to come unto him,
And he heareth the cry of the afflicted.
29 When he giveth quietness, who then can make trouble?
And when he hideth *his* face, who then can behold him?
Whether *it be done* against a nation, or against a man only:
30 That the hypocrite reign not,
Lest the people be ensnared.
31 Surely it is meet to be said unto God,
I have borne *chastisement*, I will not offend *any more;*
32 *That which* I see not, teach thou me:
If I have done iniquity, I will do no more.
33 *Should it be* according to thy mind? he will recompense it,
Whether thou refuse, or whether thou choose;
And not I: therefore speak what thou knowest.
34 Let men of understanding tell me,
And let a wise man hearken unto me.
35 Job hath spoken without knowledge,
And his words *were* without wisdom.
36 My desire *is that* Job may be tried unto the end,

Because of *his* answers for wicked men.
37 For he addeth rebellion unto his sin,
He clappeth *his hands* among us,
And multiplieth his words against God.

MAN'S RIGHTEOUSNESS VAIN.

Job xxxv. 1–16.

1 Elihu spoke moreover, and said,
2 Thinkest thou this to be right,
That thou saidst, My righteousness *is* more than God's?
3 For thou saidst, What advantage will it be unto thee?
And, What profit shall I have, *if I be cleansed* from my sin?
4 I will answer thee,
And thy companions with thee.
5 Look unto the heavens, and see;
And behold the clouds *which* are higher than thou.
6 If thou sinnest, what doest thou against him?
Or *if* thy transgressions be multiplied, what doest thou unto him?
7 If thou be righteous, what givest thou him?
Or what receiveth he of thine hand?
8 Thy wickedness *may hurt* a man as thou *art;*
And thy righteousness *may profit* the son of man.
9 By reason of the multitude of oppressions they make *the oppressed* to cry:
They cry out by reason of the arm of the mighty.
10 But none saith, where *is* God my maker,
Who giveth songs in the night;
11 Who teacheth us more than the beasts of the earth,
And maketh us wiser than the fowls of heaven?
12 There they cry, but none giveth answer,
Because of the pride of evil men.

13 Surely God will not hear vanity,
Neither will the Almighty regard it.
14 Although thou sayest thou shalt not see him,
Yet judgment *is* before him;
Therefore trust thou in him.
15 But now, because *it is* not *so*, he hath visited in his anger;
Yet he knoweth it not in great extremity:
16 Therefore doth Job open his mouth in vain;
He multiplieth words without knowledge.

FARTHER DEFENCE OF GOD'S DEALINGS.

Job xxxvi. 1–33.

1 Elihu also proceeded, and said,
2 Suffer me a little, and I will show thee
That *I have* yet to speak on God's behalf.
3 I will fetch my knowledge from afar,
And will ascribe righteousness to my Maker.
4 For truly my words *shall* not *be* false;
He that is perfect in knowledge *is* with thee.
5 Behold, God *is* mighty, and despiseth not *any:*
He is mighty in strength *and* wisdom.
6 He preserveth not the life of the wicked:
But giveth right to the poor.
7 He withdraweth not his eyes from the righteous:
But with kings *are they* on the throne;
Yea, he doth establish them for ever, and they are exalted.
8 And if *they be* bound in fetters,
And be holden in cords of affliction;
9 Then he showeth them their work,
And their transgressions that they have exceeded.
10 He openeth also their ear to discipline,

And commandeth that they return from iniquity.
11 If they obey and serve *him*,
They shall spend their days in prosperity,
And their years in pleasures.
12 But if they obey not,
They shall perish by the sword,
And they shall die without knowledge.
13 But the hypocrites in heart heap up wrath:
They cry not when he bindeth them.
14 They die in youth,
And their life *is* among the unclean.
15 He delivereth the poor in his affliction,
And openeth their ears in oppression.
16 Even so would he have removed thee out of the strait
Into a broad place, where *there is* no straitness;
And that which should be set on thy table *should be* full of fatness.
17 But thou hast fulfilled the judgment of the wicked:
Judgment and justice take hold *on thee*.
18 Because *there is* wrath,
Beware lest he take thee away with *his* stroke:
Then a great ransom cannot deliver thee.
19 Will he esteem thy riches?
No, not gold, nor all the forces of strength.
20 Desire not the night,
When people are cut off in their place.
21 Take heed, regard not iniquity:
For this hast thou chosen rather than affliction.
22 Behold, God exalteth by his power:
Who teacheth like him?
23 Who hath enjoined him his way?
Or who can say, Thou hast wrought iniquity?
24 Remember that thou magnify his work,
Which men behold.

25 Every man may see it;
Man may behold *it* afar off.
26 Behold, God *is* great, and we know *him* not,
Neither can the number of his years be searched out.
27 For he maketh small the drops of water:
They pour down rain according to the vapor thereof:
28 Which the clouds do drop
And distil upon man abundantly.
29 Also can *any* understand the spreadings of the clouds,
Or the noise of his tabernacle?
30 Behold, he spreadeth his light upon it,
And covereth the bottom of the sea.
31 For by them judgeth he the people;
He giveth meat in abundance.
32 With clouds he covereth the light;
And commandeth it *not to shine* by *the cloud* that cometh betwixt.
33 The noise thereof showeth concerning it,
The cattle also concerning the vapor.

SUBLIME PERORATION.

Job xxxvii. 1–24.

1 At this also my heart trembleth,
And is moved out of his place.
2 Hear attentively the noise of his voice,
And the sound that goeth out of his mouth.
3 He directeth it under the whole heaven,
And his lightning unto the ends of the earth.
4 After it a voice roareth:
He thundereth with the voice of his excellency;
And he will not stay them when his voice is heard.
5 God thundereth marvellously with his voice:
Great things doeth he, which we cannot comprehend.
6 For he saith to the snow, Be thou *on* the earth;

Likewise to the small rain, and to the great rain of his strength.
7 He sealeth up the hand of every man;
That all men may know his work.
8 Then the beasts go into dens,
And remain in their places.
9 Out of the south cometh the whirlwind:
And cold out of the north.
10 By the breath of God frost is given:
And the breadth of the waters is straitened.
11 Also by watering he wearieth the thick cloud:
He scattereth his bright cloud:
12 And it is turned round about by his counsels:
That they may do whatsoever he commandeth them
Upon the face of the world in the earth.
13 He causeth it to come, whether for correction,
Or for his land, or for mercy.
14 Hearken unto this, O Job:
Stand still, and consider the wondrous works of God.
15 Dost thou know when God disposed them,
And caused the light of his cloud to shine?
16 Dost thou know the balancings of the clouds,
The wondrous works of him which is perfect in knowledge?
17 How thy garments *are* warm,
When he quieteth the earth by the south *wind*?
18 Hast thou with him spread out the sky,
Which is strong, *and* as a molten looking-glass?
19 Teach us what we shall say unto him;
For we cannot order *our speech* by reason of darkness.
20 Shall it be told him that I speak?
If a man speak, surely he shall be swallowed up.
21 And now *men* see not the bright light which *is* in the clouds;

But the wind passeth, and cleanseth them.
22 Fair weather cometh out of the north:
With God *is* terrible majesty.
23 *Touching* the Almighty, we cannot find him out;
He is excellent in power, and in judgment, and in plenty of justice:
He will not afflict.
24 Men do therefore fear him:
He respecteth not any *that are* wise of heart.

Then Jehovah deigns to interfere and speak to his servant Job. The very idea that the Supreme Ruler of the universe should condescend to address one of his fallen creatures is morally sublime. He disdains to enter into any particular explication of his counsels; but describes, with intense vividness and splendor, the stupendous results of his power. He reproves the temerity of Job, shows his ignorance in not understanding the works of creation, the structure of the earth, the sea, light, and the animal kingdom. He then calls upon the patriarch to exert his power, and equal a single act of divine energy. He asks Job how he could contend with Omnipotence if he could not stand before the violence of irrational animals, many of which far surpass him in strength. The Almighty proceeds by a series of questions and descriptions adapted to convince his complaining servant that he was incapable of judging how the moral government of God should be administered. The grandeur and sublimity of this address perhaps never was equalled by human language. The following is Herder's translation of it (Marsh's Ed.):

ADDRESS OF THE ALMIGHTY TO JOB.

Job xxxviii. 1–41.

1 Jehovah spoke to Job from out of the tempest, and said to him,
2 Who is it, that darkeneth the counsels of God

By words without knowledge?
3 Gird up thy loins like a man;
I will ask thee, teach thou me.
4 Where wast thou,
When I founded the earth?
Tell me, if thou knowest.
5 Who fixed the measure of it? dost thou know?
Who stretched the line upon it?
6 Whereon stand its deep foundations?
Who laid the corner-stone thereof,
7 When the morning stars sang in chorus,
And all the sons of God shouted for joy?
8 Who wrapped up the sea in swaddling-clothes,
When it broke forth from the mother's womb?
9 I gave it the clouds for garments,
I swathed it in mists and darkness,
10 I fixed my decrees upon it,
And placed them for gates and bars
11 I said, Thus far shalt thou come, and no further,
Here shalt thou dash thy stormy waves.
12 Hast thou in thy lifetime commanded the dawn?
And taught the day-spring to know its place,
13 That it seize on the far corners of the earth,
And scatter the robbers before it?
14 Like clay the form of things is changed by it,
They stand forth, as if clothed with ornament.
15 From the wicked their light is taken away,
Their haughty arm is broken.
16 Hast thou entered into the caverns of the sea?
Hast thou explored the hollow depths of the abyss?
17 Have the gates of death opened for thee?
And hast thou seen the doors of non-existence?
18 Is thy knowledge as broad as the earth?
Show me, if thou knowest it all.

19 Where dwelleth the light? where is the way to it?
And the darkness, where is its place?
20 That thou mayest reach even the limits thereof,
For thou knowest the path to its house,
21 Thou knowest, for thou wast already born,
And the number of thy days is great.
22 Hast thou been into the storehouse of the snow?
And seen the treasury of the hail,
23 Which I have laid up for the time of need,
For the day of war and of slaughter?
24 Where doth the light divide itself,
When the east wind streweth it upon the earth?
25 Who divided the water-courses of heaven?
And traced a path for the storms of thunder?
26 To bring rain upon lands, where no man dwelleth,
Upon deserts, which no man inhabiteth,
27 To refresh the wilderness, and the barren place,
And cause the tender herb to spring forth.
28 Who is the father of the rain?
The drops of dew, who hath generated them?
29 From whose womb came forth the ice?
The hoar-frost of heaven, who gave it birth?
30 The waters hide themselves and become as stone,
The surface of the abyss is confined as in chains.
31 Canst thou bind together the brilliant Pleiades?
Or canst thou loose the bands of Orion?
32 Canst thou bring the stars of the Zodiac in their season?
And lead forth the Bear with her young?
33 Knowest thou the laws of the heavens above?
Or hast thou given a decree to the earth beneath?
34 Canst thou lift up thy voice to the clouds,
And enter into them clothed with floods?
35 Canst thou send the lightnings, that they shall go,
And say to thee, "Here are we?"

36 Who gave understanding to the flying clouds?
Or intelligence to the meteors of the air?
37 Who by his wisdom hath numbered the drops of rain?
Hath sent down the gentle showers from heaven,
38 And watered the dust, that it might unite,
And the clods of the earth cleave together?
39 Dost thou hunt for the lion his prey?
The hunger of the young lions dost thou satisfy,
40 When they lie in wait in their dens,
And couch under covert in ambush?
41 Who provideth for the raven his food,
When his young cry unto God,
And wander for lack of meat?

CLOSE OF GOD'S ADDRESS TO JOB.

Job xxxix. 1–39.

1 Dost thou know when the chamois-goat brings forth?
And mark the birth-throes of the hind?
2 Dost thou number the months they fulfill,
And know the period of their bringing forth?
3 They bow themselves, and give birth to their young,
They cast forth the offspring of their pains.
4 Their young ones increase in strength;
They grow up in the wilderness;
They go from them, and return no more.
5 Who sent forth the wild ass free,
And broke from him his slavish bonds?
6 The wilderness have I made an house for him,
And the barren desert his dwelling.
7 He scoffs at the uproar of the city;
The cry of the driver, he heedeth it not.
8 He spieth out in the mountains his pasture;
He searcheth after every green thing.

9 Will the buffalo be willing to serve thee,
And abide through the night at thy crib?
10 Wilt thou bind him with his band in the furrow,
And will he harrow the valleys after thee?
11 Wilt thou trust him because he is strong,
And commit unto him thy labor?
12 Believest thou in him, that he will gather thy harvest,
And that thy threshing-floor shall be filled?
13 A wing with joyous cry is uplifted yonder;
Is it the wing and feather of the ostrich?
14 When she commits her eggs to the earth,
And leaves them to be warmed on the sand,
15 She heeds it not, that the foot may crush them,
And the wild beasts trample upon them.
16 She casts off her young for none of hers;
In vain is her travail, but she regards it not;
17 For God hath made her forgetful of wisdom,
And hath not imparted to her reflection.
18 At once she is up, and urges herself forward.
She laughs at the horse and his rider.
19 Hast thou given the horse his strength,
And clothed his neck with its flowing mane?
20 Dost thou make him leap like the locust?
The pomp of his neighing is terrible;
21 He paweth the earth and joyeth in his strength,
When he goeth against the weapons of war.
22 He scoffeth at fear, and is nothing daunted,
And turneth not back from facing the sword.
23 Above him is the rattling of the quiver,
The lightning of the spear and the lance.
24 With vehemence and rage he devoureth the ground,
And believeth not that the trumpet is sounding.
25 The trumpet sounds louder; he cries—aha!
And from afar he snuffeth the slaughter,

The war-cry of the captains, and the shout of battle.
26 Is it by thy understanding that the hawk flieth,
And spreadeth his wings to the south wind?
27 Is it at thy word that the eagle is lifted up,
And buildeth his nest on high?
28 He inhabiteth the rock, and all night is there,
High upon the cliff, his rocky fortress.
29 From this he spieth out his prey,
His eye searcheth it out from afar.
30 His young ones are greedy of blood,
And where the carcasses are, there is he.

Job listens to this unearthly eloquence, and is overwhelmed with a sense of his own imperfection and sinfulness. He abhors himself, and repents in dust and ashes.

We should love to dwell longer upon the poetical splendor of this wonderful oriental composition; but it would be contrary to the design of this work to pursue the subject further.

There are a few allusions to music in the book.

Job xvii. 6

He hath made me also a byword of the people:
And aforetime I was as a tabret.

This passage occurs in Job's answer to the second part of Eliphaz's address. The patriarch speaks of his present loathsome, afflictive state, and the contempt exhibited towards him by his friends. He had become a "byword," though formerly, according to our common English version, he was "*as a tabret*," it being a figurative expression, indicating that he was formerly in prosperous, joyful circumstances.

As a tabret.—This instrument is a symbol of joy. The Hebrew term, translated *tabret*, is תֹּפֶת *topheth*, which, according to Gesenius and other biblical critics, signifies *spittle*, being derived from תּוּף *tuph*, *to spit upon*, and not, as the translators of our common version supposed, from תֹּף *toph, a tabret.* The translators of the Septuagint did not employ a musical term, but, also mistaking the true meaning of the word, used γελως *gelows*, signifying *joy, mirth*. The idea, no doubt, which the patriarch wished to convey by תֹּפֶת *topheth*, was, that derision was then heaped upon him by his pretended friends, *gelows* signifying *joy*. We have already shown that the trial of Job occurred, according to Dr. Hales, 2337 years B. C., (2130 according to the usual computation), 818 years after the deluge, 184 before the birth of Abraham, and 689 after the exodus from Egypt, or about 532 years after music is known to have been cultivated in Egypt (vid. pp. 56, 60, *supra*), and that was about 1850 years after Jubal's music.

Job xxi. 11, 12.

11 They send forth their little ones like a flock,
And their children dance.
12 They take the timbrel and harp,
And rejoice at the sound of the organ.

These verses occur in Job's answer to Zophar, in which he strongly reproves his miserable comforters. He describes the wicked in a clear and vivid manner, plainly intimating that his pretended friends were among their number. He shows that the prosperity of the ungodly continues only for a time.

Their children dance.—This indicates *rejoicing*. The term translated *dance*, is יְרַקְּדוּן *y^{e}raqqedhun*, from the verb רָקַד *raqadh, to leap, to skip, to dance.* The term in the Septuagint signifies *to play like a child.*

In verse 12, we have three instruments mentioned, viz: the *timbrel, harp*, and *organ*. The first is a percussion instrument, the Hebrew term being תֹּף *toph*. The same word is used in Gen. xxxi. 27, and translated *tabret*, which indicates the same instrument as *timbrel* (vid. Rem. on that passage, *supra*). The Septuagint has ψαλτηριον *psalterion, psaltery*, which is a stringed instrument. The LXX must have been mistaken, as the Hebrew term clearly indicates a percussion instrument.

Harp.—This is the *kinnor* to which reference is made in Gen. iv. 21.

Organ.—This is the *ugabh* found also in Gen. iv. 21. The Septuagint has, for the last two terms, *κιθαραν kitharan*, *cithara*, and *ψαλμοῦ psalmou*, *psalm*, or *song*. Sometimes the LXX use *psalterion* for *kinnor* (vid. Rem. on Gen. iv. 21, *supra*). Evidently, the Alexandrine translators did not have correct ideas in respect to those ancient instruments, and perhaps scholars at the present day are too confident in reference to their knowledge in these matters. Here we perceive that one of each kind of the three grand classes is mentioned, viz: percussion, stringed, and wind instruments.

Job xxix. 13.

The blessing of him that was ready to perish came upon me:
And I caused the widow's heart to sing for joy.

This is a part of the answer of Job to Bildad the Shuhite, in justification of his conduct. He shows that he assisted the poor, the fatherless, and the widow.

To sing.—The original is אַרְנִן *arnin*, *I caused to sing*, the Hiphil conjugation of רָנַן *ranan*. In the Septuagint there is no allusion to singing, but it is merely an expression indicating joy on the part of the widow.

Job xxx. 9, 31.

9 And now am I their song,
Yea, I am their byword.
31 My harp also is *turned* to mourning,
And my organ into the voice of them that weep.

These passages occur in Job's eloquent reply to Bildad. He complains that those who were much younger than himself, and whose fathers he would disdain to place with the dogs of his flock, reproach him, and make him their *song*. The original, נְגִינָתָם *n'gînathām, their song* (v. 9), signifies *music of stringed instruments*, and may mean *song*, in derision, as it does here. The LXX translate it thus: *I am their cithara.* The meaning, however, is the same.

In the 31st verse, Job appears to speak, in a figurative manner, of his *harp* and *organ*. He wished to express the sad idea that his joy was turned into mourning and weeping; still the fact that he used the names of those instruments, shows that he was acquainted with them, and that in all probability he performed upon them before the dreadful trial which he was then enduring. The same terms in the original are employed which occur in Job. xxi. 12, also in Gen. iv. 21. The instruments are the *kinnor* and *ugabh*.

Job xxxviii. 7.

When the morning stars sang together,
And all the sons of God shouted for joy?

This language occurs in the sublime address of the Almighty to his servant Job. In recounting the wonders of creation, Jehovah refers to the time when he laid the foundations of the earth—when the mighty forces of the material universe were ushered into being—when suns, planets, and satellites were hurled into their splendid orbits. In celebration of that event, the choirs of heaven raised their pæan of praise to the Great Creator.

The morning stars sang together.—These, it is thought, could not have been *men*, as it is generally admitted that this language refers to a period anterior to the creation of Adam. They are supposed to have been *angels*. *Sons of God*, in the same verse are thought to refer to the same holy beings. But would it not be more natural to suppose that there is a difference of signification in the two phrases? The first, *morning stars*, may indicate the thousand voices of nature. The stars and the whole material universe raised their notes of praise, and then, in unison with this choir, were that of the *sons of God*—the angels burning around the throne. These last may represent the universe of created intelligent existences at that remote period. This is, of course, the language of elevated oriental poetry, and highly figurative; but not more so than some of the Psalms of David, in which inanimate nature is represented as praising God. At the celebration of so grand an event, certainly it would seem admissible, if under any circumstances, to personify nature, and represent her as breaking forth in songs of praise.

Sang.—The original word is a derivative of רָנַן *ranan*, signifying *a tremulous, creaking sound*, as of a pole in the wind' also *a roaring sound*, as of a torrent.

Shouted for joy.—This is a figurative expression, of similar import to the one which we have just considered.

Job xxxix. 24, 25.

24 He swalloweth the ground with fierceness and rage;
Neither believeth he that *it is* the sound of the trumpet.
25 He saith among the trumpets, Ha, ha!
And he smelleth the battle afar off,
The thunder of the captains, and the shouting.

These verses also occur in the memorable address of Deity to Job, and refer to the fierceness and fury of the war-horse.

Trumpet, trumpets.—These are the *shophars* (vid. Rem. on 5; Ex. xix. 16, where reference is made to the sameJosh. vi. instruments).

THE BOOK OF PSALMS.

INTRODUCTORY REMARKS.

We come now to the lays of the sweet singer of Israel, who chanted upon his harp those joyous or mournful strains of music, which indicated the depression or elevation of his spirit while contemplating the prosperous or adverse circumstances of his country, the advancement or declension of true piety among that people who once hung their harps upon the willows in a strange land.

The Psalms have been admired by Christians in all ages, as affording consolation in every event of life, and as valuable helps to devotion. Among the Fathers, Basil considered them as a compendium of all theology, and Athanasius, as an epitome of the entire sacred volume. Among the Reformers, Melancthon declared that they were the most elegant writings in the whole world, and Luther called them a little Bible, the summary of the old Testament. Prefixed to the Reformers' Bible is the following just and beautiful tribute to the Psalms:

"The book of Psalms is set forth unto us by the Holy Ghost, to be esteemed as a most precious treasure; wherein all things are contained that appertain to true felicity, as well in this present life as in the life to come: for the riches of true knowledge and heavenly wisdom are set open for us, to take thereof most abundantly. If we would know the great and high Majesty of God, here we may see the brightness thereof shine most clearly. If we would seek this incomprehensible wisdom, here is the school of the same profession. If we would comprehend his inestimable bounty, and approach near thereunto, and fill our hands with that treasure, here we may have a most lively and comfortable taste thereof. If we would know wherein standeth our salvation, and how to attain to life everlasting, here is Christ, our only Redeemer and Mediator, most evidently described. The rich man may learn the true use of riches: the poor man may find full contentment. He that will rejoice shall know the true joy, and how to keep measure therein. They that are afflicted and oppressed, shall see wherein standeth their comfort, and how they ought to praise God when he sendeth them deliverance. The wicked, and the persecutors of the children of God, shall see how the hand of God is ever against them; and though he suffer them to prosper for a while, yet he bridleth them, insomuch that they cannot touch a hair of one's head, except he permit them; and how in the end their destruction is most miserable. Briefly, here we may have present remedies against all temptations, and troubles of mind and conscience; so that, being well practised herein, we may be assured against all dangers in this life, live in the true fear and love of God, and at length attain to that incorruptible crown of glory, which is laid up for all them that love the coming of our Lord Jesus Christ."

This book, in Hebrew, is entitled, *Book of Hymns or Praises*, in the Septuagint, simply *Psalms*, and in the Syriac, *Book of Psalms of David, the King and Prophet*. Origen, Chrysostom, Ambrose, and other ancient Fathers, believed that David was the sole author of that composition; but a careful perusal of it will show that it was written by various persons, some earlier and some later than the time of David. The great Hebrew poet reduced the Jewish service relating to music to a regular system, and was an excellent composer as well as performer in the art. He received the divine approval in appointing a select company of singers to celebrate the praises of God in the tabernacle.

This book contains every variety of Hebrew poetry. We find in it elegiac, historical, moral, and lyric verse. Indeed, it may *all* be considered as lyric poetry, since it is adapted to music, but it is extremely varied in style, extending from the dignified ode, with its ornate beauty, to the grave ethical or simple didactic rhythm. De Wette, in his admirable *Einleitung in die Psalmen*, remarks: "They are lyric in the proper sense; for among the Hebrews, as among the ancients generally, poetry, singing, and music were united, and the inscriptions to most of the Psalms determine their connection with music, though in a way not always intelligible to us. Also, as works of taste these compositions deserve to be called lyric. The essence of lyric poetry is the immediate expression of feeling; and feeling is the sphere in which most of the Psalms move. Pain, grief, fear, hope, joy, trust, gratitude, submission to God, everything that moves and elevates the heart, is expressed in these songs. Most of them are the lively effusions of the excited susceptible heart, the fresh offspring of inspiration and elevation of thought; while only a few are spiritless imitations and compilations, or unpoetic forms of prayer, temple hymns, and collections of proverbs."

We find occasional pastoral idyls and enigmatical poems; but a kind of dramatic ode in the form of a dialogue, is most prevalent. Bishop Horseley remarks: "The persons are frequently the psalmist himself, or the chorus of priests and Levites, or the leader of the Levitical band, opening the ode with a proem declarative of the subject, and very often closing the whole with a solemn admonition drawn from what the other persons say. The other persons are,

Jehovah, sometimes as one, sometimes as another of the three persons; Christ in his incarnate state, sometimes before, sometimes after his resurrection; the human soul of Christ, as distinguished from the divine essence. Christ, in his incarnate state, is personated sometimes as a priest, sometimes as a king, sometimes as a conqueror; and in those psalms in which he is introduced as a conqueror, the resemblance is very remarkable between this conqueror in the book of Psalms, and the warrior on the white horse in the book of Revelations, who goes forth with a crown on his head and a bow in his hand, conquering and to conquer. And the conquest in the Psalms is followed, like the conquest in the Revelations, by the marriage of the conqueror. These are circumstances of similitude, which, to any one versed in the prophetic style, prove beyond a doubt that the mystical conqueror is the same personage in both."—(Horseley's Psalms, vol. 1, p. 16).

The authors of this book, as we have already intimated, are various, and lived at different periods, embracing about nine hundred years. Jewish writers suppose that there were ten authors, viz: Adam, Melchisedec, Abraham (whom they call Ethan), Moses, Asaph, Heman, Jeduthun, and the three sons of Korah. They strangely exclude David, and assert that he merely collected them into one book. But this opinion is alike contrary to scripture and fact. It will be found that, in all probability, the Psalms were composed by Moses, David, Solomon, Asaph, Heman, Ethan, Jeduthun, and the three sons of Korah. This opinion is generally maintained by modern biblical critics. We shall mention the authors of individual psalms as we consider them separately.

It is difficult to determine with certainty who collected these poems into one book, and when the compilation was made. David, undoubtedly, in his time collected many of them; but, from an examination of their contents, it seems quite evident that the book of Psalms was compiled by various persons at different times. Psalm cxxvi was obviously composed while the second temple was being built, so that the collection must have been made before that time. In very ancient versions, like the Syriac, the collection is divided into five books, to correspond, it is thought, with the Pentateuch. This division is proved to have been in existence before the Septuagint Greek version was made, and certainly existed more than 200 years before the Christian era. The first book extended from Psalm i. to xli.; the second from Psalm xlii. to lxxii.; the third from Psalm lxxiii. to lxxxix.; the fourth from xc. to cvi.; and the fifth from cvii. to cl. It is generally believed that Ezra formed the different collections into one volume at the time that the Jewish canon of scripture was completed. Ewald (Poetic Books ii. 205) remarks that it must have been as early as 450 B. C. The number of psalms admitted into the canon, was one hundred and fifty. Another, however, describing the combat of David with Goliath, appears in the Septuagint version, also in the Syriac, Arabic, and Æthiopic translations. But it is not found in the Hebrew, has always been rejected by the Fathers, and is evidently spurious, though very ancient.

Various instruments of music are mentioned in the book, which Herder (vid. Herder's Heb. Poet. by Marsh, vol. ii. p. 265) divides into *ruling* and *accompanying* ones. The latter are the common instruments, and do not appear in any superscriptions of the Psalms. There are many grand choruses represented in this book, which were performed by multitudes, and generally accompanied by the more common instruments, such as flutes, castanets, the adufa, and different kinds of trumpets.

There is not that boldness in the poetry and music of

the Psalms which is found in more ancient compositions The lyric poetry of the Hebrews was much refined, and the music elevated and improved, under the influence of David. At the same time, it lost some of that native originality and pathetic grandeur which it possessed in the times of Moses and Deborah. The highly figurative language of ancient poetry, possessed, under David, less natural vigor, freshness, and energy, but was more polished and scientific. The poetry and music of David and Solomon were tame compared with the same in the hands of the ancient prophets. The real difference was, that David's seers were not natural but artificial poets, while the old prophets were the Homers and Miltons of the age in which they lived. They could thunder, lighten, raise tempests, shake the earth, and cause all nature to quake in terror. But David's seers move in a humbler sphere, though there are some exceedingly fine touches in the sweet singer's beautiful lays. In some of the Psalms, indeed, we find most admirable specimens of the morally sublime. Some of them, which we shall examine individually, are far more ancient than others, and represent different periods of Hebrew poetry.

The Psalms may be classed under the following divisions:

I. *Prayers.*

1. Prayers for pardon of sin, Psal. vi. xxv. xxxviii. li. cxxx. Psalms styled penitential, vi. xxii. xxxviii. li. cii. cxxx. cxliii.

2. Prayers, composed when the Psalmist was deprived of an opportunity of the public exercise of religion, Psal. xlii. xliii. lxiii. lxxxiv.

3. Prayers, in which the Psalmist seems extremely dejected, though not totally deprived of consolation, under

his afflictions, Psal. xiii. xxii. lxix. lxxvii. lxxxviii. cxliii.

4. Prayers, in which the Psalmist asks help of God, in consideration of his own integrity, and the uprightness of his cause, Psal. vii. xvii. xxvi. xxxv.

5. Prayers, expressing the firmest trust and confidence in God under afflictions, Psal. iii. xvi. xxvii. xxxi. liv. lvi. lvii. lxi. lxii. lxxi. lxxxvi.

6. Prayers, composed when the people of God were under affliction or persecution, Psal. xliv. lx. lxxiv. lxxix. lxxx. lxxxiii. lxxxix. xciv. cii. cxxiii. cxxxvii.

7. The following are likewise prayers in time of trouble and affliction, Psal. iv. v. xi. xxviii. xli. lv. lix. lxiv. lxx cix. cxx. cxl. cxli. cxliii.

8. Prayers of intercession, Psal. xx. lxvii. cxxii. cxxxii. cxliv.

II. *Psalms of Thanksgiving.*

1. Thanksgivings for mercies vouchsafed to particular persons, Psal. ix. xviii. xxii. xxx. xxxiv. xl. lxxv. ciii. cviii. cxvi. cxviii. cxxxviii. cxliv.

2. Thanksgivings for mercies vouchsafed to the Israelites in general, Psal. xlvi. xlvii. lxv. lxvi. lxviii. lxvi. lxxxi. lxxxv. xcviii. cv. cxxiv. cxxvi. cxxix. cxxxv. cxxxvi. cxlix.

III. *Psalms of Praise and Adoration, displaying the Attributes of God.*

1. General acknowledgments of God's goodness and mercy, and particularly his care and protection of good men, Psal. xxiii. xxiv. xxxvi. xci. c. ciii. cvii. cxvii. cxxi. cxlv. cxlvi.

2. Psalms displaying the power, majesty, glory, and other attributes of the Divine Being, Psal. viii. xix. xxiv. xxix. xxxiii. xlvii. l. lxv. lxvi. lxxvi. lxxvii. xciii. xcv.

xcvi. xcvii. xcix. civ. cxi. cxiii. cxiv. cxv. cxxxiv. cxxxix. cxlvii. cxlviii. cl.

IV. *Instructive Psalms.*

1. The different characters of good and bad men,—the happiness of the one, and the misery of the other,—are represented in the following psalms:—i. v. vii. ix. x. xi. xii. xiv. xv. xvii. xxiv. xxv. xxxii. xxxiv. xxxvi. xxxvii. l. lii. liii. lviii. lxxii. lxxv. lxxxiv. xci. xcii. xciv. cxii. cxix. cxvi. cxxv. cxxvii. cxxviii. cxxxiii.
2. The excellence of God's laws, Psal. xix. cxix.
3. The vanity of human life, Psal. xxxix. xlix. xc.
4. Advice to magistrates, Psal. lxxxii. ci.
5. The virtue of humility, Psal. cxxxi.

V. *Psalms more eminently and directly Prophetical.*

Psal. ii. xvi. xxii. xl. xlv. lxviii. lxxii. lxxxvii. cx. cxviii.

VI. *Historical Psalms.*

Psal. lxxviii cv. cvi.
(Vid. Horne's Intro. P. v., c. iii., Sec. ii. xi).

Psalm i. 1–6.

1 Blessed *is* the man,
That walketh not in the counsels of the ungodly,
Nor standeth in the way of sinners,
Nor sitteth in the seat of the scornful:
2 But his delight *is* in the law of the Lord;
And in his law does he meditate day and night.
3 And he shall be like a tree planted by the rivers of water,
That bringeth forth his fruit in his season;

His leaf also shall not wither;
And whatsoever he doeth shall prosper.
4 The ungodly *are* not so:
But *are* like the chaff which the wind driveth away.
5 Therefore the ungodly shall not stand in the judgment,
Nor sinners in the congregation of the righteous.
6 For the Lord knoweth the way of the righteous:
But the way of the ungodly shall perish.

This psalm is evidently a kind of preface to the book, giving an admirable view of the truly happy man, both in this life and in that which is to come. The description is brief, but clear, vivid, and comprehensive. The poem contains a compendium of the doctrines inculcated in the book of Psalms. It is supposed to have been written about 444 years B. C., but its date is somewhat uncertain. From the fact that it is intimately connected with the second psalm, and corresponds very nearly with it in style, we conclude that it must have been composed by the same person who wrote that, the author of which we know to have been David. Some suppose that Ezra composed it when he completed the collection; but this opinion is obviously incorrect. The poetry is not of the most elevated kind, and can only be distinguished by its lively figures, from ornate prose. Bishop Jebb gives this psalm as an example of *Parallel lines gradational*, or those in which some clauses are responsive to others, and rise above them in a regular gradation. The first line is an exclamation which belongs equally to each of the three following: In the triplet, not only does the general sense of each successive line rise by a regular gradation above the preceding one, but each is divided into three members, and the sense of each successive member rises above the preceding one. This is the most common kind of parallelism, and sometimes the gradation is by a *descending* scale. "To *walk*," says Jebb, "implies no more than casual intercourse; to *stand*, closer intimacy; to *sit*, fixed and permanent connection; the *counsel*, the ordinary place of meeting, or public resort; the *way*, the select and chosen foot-path; the *seat*, the habitual and final resting-place; the *ungodly*, negatively wicked; *sinners*, positively wicked; the *scornful*, scoffers at the very name or notion of piety and goodness (vid. Jebb's Sacred Literature, p. 41). There is no allusion to music or musical instruments in the poem.

Psalm ii. 1–12.

1 What tumult reigns among the nations!
Why do they clamor with empty noise?
2 The kings of the earth rise up,
The princes build projects together
Against Jehovah and his anointed.
3 "Let us break their bands asunder,
And cast away their fetters from us."
4 He, that is throned in heaven, shall laugh,
Jehovah holdeth them in derision.
5 He speaketh to them in his wrath,
And scattereth them in his fierce anger.
6 "I have set my king upon my throne,
Upon my holy mountain Zion."
7 I will also declare the divine decree,
Jehovah said unto me,
"Thou art my son,
So be it from this day forth."
8 Ask of me,
And nations shall be thine inheritance,
The utmost parts of the earth thy possession.
9 Thou shalt smite them with an iron sceptre,
And dash them as a potter's vessel.
10 Be wise now, therefore, O ye kings,
Be instructed, ye judges of the earth.
11 Obey Jehovah with fear,
And honor him with trembling,

12 Do homage to the son, lest he be angry,
And bring destruction on you by the way,
For soon his wrath will be kindled,
And happy they, who are faithful to him.

The above is the translation of Herder. This psalm, like Ps. i., is anonymous, though, as we have already intimated, it was evidently composed by David, the imagery being clearly taken from the warlike times of that Hebrew monarch, and closely resembling several of the following psalms bearing his name: Luke (vid. Acts iv. 25) ascribes it to him. It is supposed to have been written about 1044 B. C. Herder calls it a royal psalm, the crown of the book (vid. Herder's Heb. Poetry, translated by Marsh, vol. ii., p. 264). This is the first prophetic psalm in which the promise made to David in respect to the Messiah is presented in lyric poetry. The style is rather more lively than that of the first psalm. "Among the perfect specimens," says Herder, "which have not only variety and contrast, but a progressive lyric action, I venture to name the Second Psalm (Ibid vol ii., p. 233).

The poet presents a striking view of the nations who had renounced their allegiance to Jehovah; but a glance from the Eternal, as he sits upon his throne, or a smile of derision, blasts all of their most lofty anticipations. God speaks to them in thunder, and scatters them with his lightnings. The psalm consists of four strophes or stanzas, of three verses each. The conduct of the wicked nations is described in the *first* (including the first three verses). The *second* (including verses 4, 5, and 6), contains the reply of Deity. The *third* (including verser 7, 8, and 9), contains the declaration of the Messiah regarding the divine decree in respect to himself. In the *fourth* (including verses 10, 11, and 12), earthly potentates are exhorted to submission, and, in case of refusal, the threatenings of divine wrath are denounced against them. The parallelisms are regular, and the number of verses and stanzas is just double that of the first psalm. There are in it no allusions to music.

Psalm iii. 1–8.

A Psalm of David when he fled from Absalom, his son.

1 Lord, how are they increased that trouble me!
Many *are* they that rise up against me.
2 Many *there be* which say of my soul,
There is no help for him in God. Selah.
3 But thou, O Lord, *art* a shield for me;
My glory, and the lifter up of mine head.
4 I cried unto the Lord with my voice,
And he heard me out of his holy hill. Selah.
5 I laid me down and slept;
I awaked: for the Lord sustained me,
6 I will not be afraid of ten thousands of people
That have set *themselves* against me round about.
7 Arise, O Lord; save me, O my God!
For thou hast smitten all mine enemies upon the cheek-bone;
Thou hast broken the teeth of the ungodly.
8 Salvation *belongeth* unto the Lord;
Thy blessing *is* upon thy people. Selah.

This psalm contains an energetic description of the numerous foes and dangers that encompassed the writer. Yet he confided in his Heavenly Father to deliver him, as he had done on former occasions. This was probably among the first poetic effusions from David's pen. It is merely called *mizmōr* (מזמור), meaning *Psalm*,* and seems to have been composed after David had been driven from Jerusalem by Absalom, about 1023 B.C. It consists of four double verses, exclusive of the title. There has been much controversy among scholars in respect to

* There are 45 psalms called *mizmor*, viz: 3, 4, 5, 6, 8, 9, 12, 13, 15, 19, 20, 21, 22, 23, 24, 29, 31, 38, 39, 40, 41, 47, 49, 50, 51, 62, 63, 64, 73, 75, 77, 79 80, 82, 84, 85, 98, 100, 101 109, 110, 139, 140, 141, 143.

the question, whether the titles to the psalms are of equal authority with the other parts of the book. The ancient critics generally admit them to be genuine; but most modern critics either reject them as not canonical, *entirely* or in *part*. The titles are obviously very ancient, as they are found in the Septuagint; and it is probable that they are older even than that version, as the LXX in many cases have transferred the Hebrew words, not being able to translate them, and when they have attempted a translation it is in some cases entirely unintelligible. This, however, may have been owing to the fact that the translators resided in Egypt, and were unacquainted with the psalmody of the temple service at Jerusalem. From the fact that these appendages are found in the Septuagint, they must be as ancient as the time of Ezra. All critics agree that they are very obscure. Several of them do not appear in the original Hebrew, having been added in the Septuagint and other Greek versions. Many of them are probably conjectural additions, made by the collectors of the psalms at different periods, and some, no doubt, are of equal authority with the text. A few refer to music, which we shall consider in their proper places. The object of the title is generally to name the author, the chief singer, the instrument of music to be used, or style of music, the kind of poetry, or the subject or occasion of the psalm. In our English version the Hebrew words are generally retained without attempting a translation. Luther translated them as well as his knowledge of their meaning would allow; but Coverdale omitted them altogether, excepting the names of the authors.

In this psalm (iii) the word *Selah* occurs at the end of the second, fourth, and eighth verses. There is a variety of opinions in respect to its signification. It occurs seventy three times in the Book of Psalms, and three times in the prophecy of Habakkuk. It occurs still more frequently in the Septuagint, and is there translated by ΔΙΑΨΑΛΜΑ *diapsalma*, signifying a rest or pause, referring to music. Suidas thinks that *diapsalma* signifies a *change* of the *song*, or *modulation*. Some suppose that it refers to the *time* of the music, and corresponds to *slow* among us. Others believe that it denotes a *repetition* of the last *strain* by a *chorus;* others still that it indicates a change of *metre*, and others suppose that it calls particular attention to a *remarkable passage*. Jerome asserts that it connects what follows with what precedes, and that the clause with which it is connected is of great importance. Jahn and others think that it is similar to the Italian *Da Capo;* Buxtorf and others that it is a note of ancient music, and that its use is now lost. Calmet and others believe that it was put in the margin to denote the end of a strain, and indicated the time when the whole choir were to suspend their voices, or commence again. Rabbi Kimchi affirms that it probably refers both to music and the sense, denoting something specially important. A. F. Pfeiffer, Rosenmüller, and others suppose it to denote a rest for the vocal performers, while the instruments are sounding. Ewald and De Wette derive it from סלה or סלל, *to raise*, and suppose that it means a *raising* of the voice or *music*. Gesenius, Rosenmüller, Hengstenberg, Tholuck, and others derive it from סלה, *to be silent*, and suppose that it signifies *a pause* in the singing. Herder maintains that it corresponds neither with pauses, da capo, nor intermezzo, but must mean *change of tone*, expressed by increase of force, or transition into another time and mode (Herd. Spir. Heb. Poet. vol. ii., p. 267, Marsh's transl.). Nearly all critics agree that the principal use of Selah was in music, while *some* suppose that it had reference both to the sense and to music. Is it not highly probable that it *did* refer to both? Professor Wilson, late of Oxford, has presented an ingenious and perhaps correct explanation of the term, at least in many cases where it occurs. He says, "The root of the word appears, evidently, to lie in the two first letters, סל, which are in contraction for סלל, *to raise, to exalt, to magnify*." He supposes ה to be an abbreviation for יהוה, and *Selah* would thus be a contracted form for סלויה, *celebrate ye Jehovah, exalt the Lord*, viz: in songs of praise, accompanied by instruments of music. Thus it indicates about the same as הללויה, our *Halleluyah*, meaning *Praise ye the Lord.* This view is confirmed by the latter part of verse fourth of the sixty-eighth psalm, which is translated thus: Extol Him that rideth upon the heavens with *the name Jah* (vid. Wilson's Heb. Gram., pp. 315, 316, 4th edition, as quoted by T. H. Horne, Intro. P. v., c. iii., Sec. ii. viii). Still, judging from the connection in which it is employed, we believe that in many cases it signifies *silence*, or a *pause* in the music.

Psalm iv. 1–8.

To the Chief Musician on Neginoth. A Psalm of David.

1 Hear me when I call, O God of my righteousness:
Thou hast enlarged me *when I was* in distress;
Have mercy upon me, and hear my prayer.
2 O ye sons of men, how long *will ye turn* my glory into shame? [Selah.
How long will ye love vanity, *and* seek after leasing?
3 But know, that the Lord
Hath set apart him that is godly for himself:
The Lord will hear when I call unto him.
4 Stand in awe, and sin not;
Commune with your own heart upon your bed, and be still. Selah.
5 Offer the sacrifices of righteousness;
And put your trust in the Lord.
6 *There be* many that say, Who will show us any good?
Lord, lift thou up the light of thy countenance upon us.
7 Thou hast put gladness in my heart,
More than in the time *that* their corn and their wine increased.
8 I will both lay me down in peace, and sleep:
For thou, Lord, only makest me dwell in safety.

This Psalm seems to be a prayer of David, and is believed to have been composed about 1023 B. C. He calls upon God to deliver him from his present and past troubles, and defends himself, in the possession of his kingdom, from the assaults of his foes. The composition is dedicated to the chief musician or superintendent of the temple music. The Hebrew term translated *to the chief musician* is לַמְנַצֵּחַ *lamnatseahh*, derived from נָצַח *natsahh*, signifying *to shine, to conquer*, and, in the Peal conjugation, *to lead in music*. The chief musician was to superintend the recital of the poetry and the accompanying music. This psalm was doubtless prepared for the use of the temple service, and not for any private purpose. The title further indicates how the stanzas were to be recited.

On Neginoth (נְגִינוֹת *n^eginoth*).—The Hebrew word, it will be perceived, is not translated, but transferred, in our English version, and appears in the titles of five other psalms (viz: vi. liv. lv. lxi. lxxvi). It is derived from נְגִינָה *n^eginah*, signifying *music of stringed instruments*. According to Gesenius, this term means simply *instruments of music*. Prof. Alexander, in his excellent commentary on the Psalms, supposes that it denotes *stringed instruments*, and that it "may either qualify *chief musician*, as denoting the leader in that particular style of performance, or direct him to perform this psalm with that kind of accompaniment" (vid. J. A. Alexander's Comment. on Psal. vol. i. p. 27). The verb נָגַן *nagan*, from which the nouns *n^egina* and *n^eginoth* are derived, means *to strike a chord*, thus clearly showing that the reference is to stringed instruments. T. H. Horne supposes that it signifies stringed instruments to be played on with the fingers (cf. p. 80, *supra*). Calmet proposes to translate the title thus: "A Psalm of David, to the master of music who presides over the stringed instruments." The term *Selah* occurs at the end of verses 2 and 4. The last occurrence of it seems to the writer to be a pretty clear case in which it signifies *silence*, a pause in the music. Otherwise it would do violence to the sense. There are no other allusions to music in this psalm.

Psalm v. 1–12.

To the Chief Musician upon Nehiloth. A Psalm of David.

1 Give ear to my words, O Lord;
Consider my meditation.
2 Hearken unto the voice of my cry, my King,
And my God: for unto thee will I pray.
3 My voice shalt thou hear in the morning, O Lord;
In the morning will I direct *my prayer* unto thee, and will look up.
4 For thou *art* not a God that hath pleasure in wickedness;
Neither shall evil dwell with thee.
5 The foolish shall not stand in thy sight:
Thou hatest all workers of iniquity.
6 Thou shalt destroy them that speak leasing:
The Lord will abhor the bloody and deceitful man.
7 But as for me, I will come *into* thy house in the multitude of thy mercy;
And in thy fear will I worship toward thy holy temple.
8 Lead me, O Lord, in thy righteousness,
Because of mine enemies; make thy way straight before my face.
9 For *there is* no faithfulness in their mouth;
Their inward part *is* very wickedness;
Their throat *is* an open sepulchre;
They flatter with their tongue.
10 Destroy thou them, O God;
Let them fall by their own counsels:
Cast them out in the multitude of their transgressions:
For they have rebelled against thee,
11 But let all those that put their trust in thee rejoice:
Let them ever shout for joy because thou defendest them;

Let them also that love thy name be joyful in thee.
12 For thou, Lord, wilt bless the righteous;
With favor wilt thou compass him as with a shield.

This Psalm also, in the title, is ascribed to David. The poet pleads for divine assistance, that he may be delivered from his enemies, who were ready to devour him. The composition seems to be a kind of *double* psalm, the same considerations being repeated in the lost part of it, as occur in the first. The two preceding psalms form a pair, repeating, in a similar manner, essentially the same truths. This, like the fourth psalm, is addressed to the *chief musician.*

On N^{e}hhïloth (נְחִילוֹת).—This is a very obscure term, and is untranslated in our English version. The LXX translate it by *κληρονομούσης kleronomouses*, derived from the verb *κληρονομεω kleronomeo*, signifying, *to get, or obtain by lot.* Hengstenberg supposes that the Hebrew word signifies *lots* or *heritages*, being derived from the verb נָחַל *nahhal, to possess*, and that the LXX have translated it correctly. Most of the ancient versions explain it in a similar manner, referring it to the subject of the psalm. Calmet supposes that it is derived from the verb חָלַל *hhalal, to perforate*, and means *pipes* or *flutes.* De Wette and others take the same view, while Rosenmüller supposes that the *organ* was intended. Gesenius intimates, that, in the singular number, (נְחִילָה *n^{e}hhïlah*), the term means *an instrument of music*, probably the *tibia, pipe* or *flute.* Modern critics generally suppose that the word relates to music, and to some kind of wind instrument. This is probably its signification. If it refer to a flute, then we must understand that the psalm was to be sung to an accompaniment of that instrument; but the fact that flutes are not mentioned as a part of the temple instrumental music, has led some to suppose that it signifies the *name* of a *tune* or of *another song* to the melody of which this psalm was to be adapted (vid. J. A.

Alexander's Com. on this Psalm). It is by no means certain, however, that flutes were not used in the temple service. We know that wind instruments were employed, and Nehiloth may include flutes among others of that class.

In verse 11 we have a reference to music. *Shout* (יְרַנְּנוּ) *y^e^rannenu*, from רָנַן *runan, to give forth a tremulous sound.* Peal conjugation, *to shout.*

Psalm vi. 1–10.

The following is Herder's translation (Marsh's Ed.)

To the Chief Musician on Neginoth upon Sheminith. A song of David.

1 O Lord, rebuke me not in thy wrath,
Nor chasten me in thy fierce anger.
2 Be merciful to me, O Jehovah! for I am weak.
Heal me, O Jehovah, for my bones tremble;
3 My whole soul is in terrors.
And thou, Jehovah? O how long!
4 Return, O Jehovah, deliver my soul.
O save me for thy mercies' sake.
5 For in death there is no remembrance of thee,
In the grave, who shall give thee thanks?
6 I am weary with my groaning,
All night my bed is wet with tears.
With tears I make my couch to swim,
7 Mine eye is consumed with sorrow,
It looks but feebly upon all mine enemies.
8 Depart from me, ye workers of iniquity!
For God hath heard the voice of my weeping.
9 Jehovah hath heard my supplication,
Jehovah hath accepted my prayer.
10 Ashamed, confounded, shall be my enemies,
They shall fall back, and be ashamed suddenly.

In this psalm, the writer prays that God would deliver him from his severe affliction, intimating that he cannot endure them longer without assistance, and implores divine interposition. He is sure of aid, and certain that his enemies, the originators of his distress, will be overthrown. This is called the first of the *penitential* psalms. It is ascribed to David, by whom it was evidently written, near the close of his life. Like Psalms iv. and v., it is addressed to the chief musician, and, like Psalm iv., was to be performed on *n^egînoth*, (for an explanation of this term, vid. Rem. on Psalm iv. *supra*). The title further adds, *on Shĕmînîth* (שְׁמִינִית). The same term is used in the title of Psalm xii. The LXX translate it by ογδοης *ogdoes*, from ογδοος *ogdoos*, meaning *eighth*. Gesenius, De Wette, Hengstenberg, Tholuck, and others consider that rendering as correct, and suppose the term to refer to music in the lower notes or bass. Horne and others think it refers to a harp with eight strings. Prof. Alexander remarks that the term corresponds exactly to our octave. Some suppose that it has no reference to instrumental music. The most reasonable supposition is, that it refers to the lower notes or bass, whether performed by instruments or the voice. In I Chronicles xv. 20, 21, we have an instance in which *sheminith* evidently denotes the lowest part (our bass—an octave below), in opposition to *alamoth*, which denotes the higher part (our treble), (vid. Rem. on I Chron. xv. 20, 21).

Psalm vii. 1–18.

Shiggaion of David, which he sang unto the Lord, concerning Cush the Benjaminite.

1 O Lord, my God, in thee do I put my trust:
Save me from all them that persecute me, and deliver me.
2 Lest he tear my soul like a lion,
Rending it in pieces while there is none to deliver.

3 O Lord, my God, if I have done this;
If there be iniquity in my hands;
4 If I have rewarded evil unto him that was at peace with me;
(Yea I have delivered him that without cause is mine enemy);
5 Let the enemy persecute my soul and take it;
Yea, let him tread down my life upon the earth,
And lay mine honor in the dust. Selah.
6 Arise, O Lord, in thine anger,
Lift up thyself, because of the rage of mine enemies;
And awake for me to the judgment *that* thou hast commanded.
7 So shall the congregation of the people compass thee about;
For their sakes, therefore, return thou on high.
8 The Lord shall judge the people:
Judge me, O Lord, according to my righteousness,
And according to mine integrity *that is* in me.
9 Oh! let the wickedness of the wicked come to an end;
But establish the just:
For the righteous God trieth the hearts and reins.
10 My defence *is* of God, which saveth the upright in heart.
11 God judgeth the righteous, and God is angry *with the wicked* every day.
12 If he turn not, he will whet his sword;
He hath bent his bow, and made it ready.
13 He hath also prepared for him the instruments of death;
He ordaineth his arrows against the persecutors.
14 Behold, he travaileth with iniquity,
And hath conceived mischief,
And brought forth falsehood.

15 He made a pit, and digged it,
And is fallen into the ditch *which* he made.
16 His mischief shall return upon his own head,
And his violent dealings shall come down upon his own pate.
17 I will praise the Lord according to his righteousness;
18 And will sing praise to the name of the Lord most high.

This psalm is ascribed to David, and is supposed to have been composed by him a little before his death. The author here, as in the preceding one, prays for deliverance from his malicious foes. He speaks not as an individual, but as the representative of the righteous, and justifies the latter through himself. He believes that the vengeance of God will be exhibited against the impenitent—that they will even be their own destroyers. In the title, the term, *shiggayon* (שִׁגָּיוֹן) which is not translated in our English version, signifies, according to Gesenius, *a song, a psalm*, and is derived from שָׁגָה *shagah, to be great.* In the Peal conjugation, if used, it would mean to *magnify, to extol with praises, to utter a song under the greatest excitement. Shiggayon* is a noun, translated by the LXX by *ψαλμος psalmos, psalm.* De Wette, Tholuck, Rosenmüller, Calmet, Dr. Kennicott, and others suppose that it signifies *a plaintive song* or *elegy.* Ewald, Hengstenberg, and others maintain that it refers to the errors or abberations of the wicked, and includes the subject discussed in the poem. They call it a *wandering* psalm. Houbigant, Parkhurst, and others also think that it signifies *a wandering song*, referring to the fact that David had fled as a fugitive from Saul. They derive it from an Arabic root. Should we not arrive nearer the truth by uniting the opinion of Houbigant with that of Rosenmüller and others, thus making it a *plaintive, wandering song*, composed by David while in the deepest distress, fleeing from his persecutor Saul?

The title further informs us that the psalm relates to the words of *Cush*, the Benjaminite. Some suppose this Cush to have been a person, nowhere else appearing in history. Others think that Shimei, who cursed David, is the individual indicated; and others still, with more probability, we think, maintain that it refers to Saul, as Cush is the Hebrew name of Æthiopia, and would apply to Saul, whose character was morally black, like an Æthiopian.

In the fifth verse the word *Selah* occurs, and gives effect to the preceding solemn appeal to God, by indicating *silence*.

I will sing אֲזַמְּרָה *azamm^erah* (v. 17), future tense from זָמַר *zamar*, to *prune*.

Psalm viii. 1-9.

To the Chief Musician upon Gittith. A Psalm of David.

1 O Lord, our Lord, how excellent is thy name in all the earth!
Who hast set thy glory above the heavens.
2 Out of the mouths of babes and sucklings
Hast thou ordained strength, because of thine enemies;
That thou mightest still the enemy and the avenger.
3 When I consider thy heavens,
The work of thy fingers,
The moon and the stars,
Which thou hast ordained;
4 What *is* man, that thou art mindful of him?
And the son of man, that thou visitest him?
5 For thou hast made him a little lower then the angels,
And hast crowned him with glory and honor.
6 Thou madest him to have dominion over the works of thy hands;

Thou hast put all *things* under his feet;
7 All sheep and oxen,
Yea, and the beasts of the field;
8 The fowl of the air, and the fish of the sea,
And whatsoever passeth through the paths of the seas.
9 O Lord our Lord, how excellent *is* thy name in all the earth!

This psalm is ascribed to David, and is supposed to have been written about 1015 B. C. It extols the excellence of Deity as displayed in animate and inanimate creation. It is addressed to the chief musician upon *Gittith*. This term is untranslated in our version. The same expression appears also in Ps. lxxxi. and lxxxiv. The Hebrew is גִּתִּית *gittith*, feminine from the noun גַּת *Gath*, the name of one of the principal cities of the Philistines. Or it may signify a *wine-press*. Gesenius supposes that the feminine form, *gittith*, indicates an instrument of music, so called either because it was common among the Gittites, or belonged to the wine-press, and was used to accompany the songs of the vintage. Rabbi Jarchi, Tholuck, De Wette, Hengstenberg, Rosenmüller, Ewald, and others suppose it to signify an instrument brought from Gath. The Septuagint has ὑπέρ τῶν ληνῶν *huper tōn lēnōn*, referring to a wine-press. Calmet thinks that it is an *air* or *song* sung at the time of vintage. The etymology of the word evidently refers to the wine-press, and the most probable opinion is that it was an instrument of music used by the Gittites and adopted by the Hebrews (David having once resided at Gath), and afterwards used by the Jews as a favorite instrument during the festivities of the vintage. What kind of an instrument it was we have no means of ascertaining. Some suppose that it resembled the wine-press in shape; but nothing can be determined with certainty upon the subject. There are no further allusions to music in the psalm.

Psalm ix. 1–20.

To the Chief Musician upon Muth-labben. A Psalm of David.

1 I will praise *thee*, O Lord, with my whole heart;
I will show forth all thy marvellous works.
2 I will be glad and rejoice in thee:
I will sing praise to thy name, O thou Most High.
3 When mine enemies are turned back,
They shall fall and perish at thy presence.
4 For thou hast maintained my right and my cause;
Thou sattest in the throne judging right.
5 Thou hast rebuked the heathen, thou hast destroyed the wicked,
Thou hast put out their name for ever and ever.
6 O thou enemy! destructions are come to a perpetual end;
And thou hast destroyed cities:
Their memorial is perished with them.
7 But the Lord shall endure for ever:
He hath prepared his throne for judgment;
8 And he shall judge the world in righteousness,
He shall minister judgment to the people in uprightness.
9 The Lord also will be a refuge for the oppressed,
A refuge in times of trouble.
10 And they that know thy name will put their trust in thee:
For thou, Lord, hast not forsaken them that seek thee.
11 Sing praises to the Lord, which dwelleth in Zion;
Declare among the people his doings.
12 When he maketh inquisition for blood, he remembereth them:
He forgetteth not the cry of the humble.

13 Have mercy upon me, O Lord;
Consider my trouble *which I suffer* of them that hate me,
Thou that liftest me up from the gates of death;
14 That I may show forth all thy praise
In the gates of the daughter of Zion:
I will rejoice in thy salvation.
15 The heathen are sunk down in the pit *that* they made:
In the net which they hid is their own foot taken.
13 The Lord is known *by* the judgment *which* he executeth:
The wicked is snared in the work of his own hands.
Higgaion. Selah.
17 The wicked shall be turned into hell,
And all the nations that forget God.
18 For the needy shall not alway be forgotten:
The expectation of the poor shall *not* perish forever.
19 Arise, O Lord, let not man prevail;
Let the heathen be judged in thy sight.
20 Put them in fear, O Lord;
That the nations may know themselves *to be but* men.
Selah.

This Psalm is supposed to have been written by David after his victory over Goliath. He expresses his thankfulness for past mercies, and full confidence in God, that he would continue to bless him. The psalm is addressed to the chief musician, and there is added, in the title, the expression *al-müth-làbben* עַל-מוּת לַבֵּן literally, *upon death to the son*. There are various readings in different manuscripts. Some have *Alamoth* or *Alamuth*, which means *virgins*, and probably relates to that part in music usually performed by females, which is our treble (vid. Rem. on I Chron., xv. 20, *supra*). Some critics suppose that *Müth-labben* refers to the *occasion* which called forth the psalm; but most refer it to a musical accompaniment. Gesenius maintains that it relates to music performed by a choir of boys in the treble. Calmet supposes a choir of virgins to be indicated, taking *Alamụth* for the true reading; *labben* he considers as two words, *La Ben, to Ben* or *Benaiah.* Professor Alexander inclines to the opinion that *Mụth-labbe̱n* indicates the title, first words, or a prominent expression of some other poem, in the style or to the air of which this psalm was composed. The term is very obscure, but probably relates to music, perhaps of a mournful kind, or to some accompanying instrument.

Sing (v. 2).—The same Hebrew word is here used as in Ex. xv. 2. The same term is also translated *sing* in verse 11 of this psalm. *Cry* (v. 12) signifies a call for help, and does not relate to music.

Higgaion-selah (v. 16).—The Hebrew term is הִגָּיוֹן סֶלָה *higgạyōn se̱lạh.* Gesenius defines *Higgaion* to signify a *murmur —sound of the harp or cithara.* But in this place he considers the two words, *higgaion selah*, as musical terms, indicating that the instruments were to strike up a symphony while the vocal performers should pause. *Higgạyon* (הִגָּיוֹן) is probably derived from הָגָה *hạgạh, to murmur, to mutter, to growl;* evidently referring to a low sound, if not to entire silence. In connection with *selah*, there is more reason in supposing that a *pause, silence, meditation*, are indicated, as that term is undoubtedly often used to denote *silence* (vid. Rem. on Ps. iii. *supra*). Tholuck, Hengstenberg, and others, think that the terms in conjunction mean that the vocal performers were to meditate while the music should cease. The LXX translate the phrase by ᾠδὴ διαψάλματος, *ode diapsalmatos*, signifying a pause in the music. *Selah* occurs again in verse 20, and probably indicates *silence.*

PSALM X. 1–18.

1 Why standest thou afar off, O Lord?
Why hidest thou *thyself* in times of trouble?

2 The wicked in *his* pride doth persecute the poor:
Let them be taken in the devices that they have imagined.
3 For the wicked boasteth of his heart's desire,
And blesseth the covetous, *whom* the Lord abhorreth.
4 The wicked, through the pride of his countenance, will not seek *after God:*
God *is* not in all his thoughts.
5 His ways are always grievous;
Thy judgments *are* far above out of his sight:
As for all his enemies, he puffeth at them.
6 He hath said in his heart, I shall not be moved:
For *I shall* never *be* in adversity.
7 His mouth is full of cursing, and deceit, and fraud;
Under his tongue *is* mischief and vanity.
8 He sitteth in the lurking-places of the villages;
In the secret places doth he murder the innocent:
His eyes are privily set against the poor.
9 He lieth in wait secretly as a lion in his den;
He lieth in wait to catch the poor:
He doth catch the poor, when he draweth him into his net.
10 He croucheth, *and* humbleth himself,
That the poor may fall by his strong ones.
11 He hath said in his heart, God hath forgotten:
He hideth his face; he will never see *it.*
12 Arise, O Lord; O God, lift up thine hand:
Forget not the humble.
13 Wherefore doth the wicked contemn God?
He hath said in his heart, Thou wilt not require *it.*
14 Thou hast seen *it;* for thou beholdest
Mischief and spite, to requite *it* with thy hand:
The poor committeth himself unto thee:
Thou art the helper of the fatherless.

15 Break thou the arm of the wicked, and the evil *man:*
Seek out his wickedness, *till* thou find none.
16 The Lord *is* king for ever and ever:
The heathen are perished out of his land.
17 Lord, thou hast heard the desire of the humble;
Thou wilt prepare their heart, thou wilt cause thine ear to hear;
18 To judge the fatherless and the oppressed,
That the man of the earth may no more oppress.

This psalm has no title, but was evidently composed by David during the Babylonish captivity. The Vulgate and Septuagint unite this with the ninth, and make of the two *a pair*, or *double-psalm.* The first part of this poem is ascribed to David, and the latter part bears strong evidence that it was from the same pen.

The king of Israel asserts that he is neglected by Jehovah. He also avers that he is hated by his foes, and prays for deliverance.

PSALM xii. 1–8.

To the Chief Musician upon Sheminith. A Psalm of David.

1 Help, Lord, for the godly man ceaseth;
For the faithful fail from among the children of men.
2 They speak vanity every one with his neighbor:
With flattering lips, *and* with a double heart, do they speak.
3 The Lord shall cut off all flattering lips,
And the tongue that speaketh proud things;
4 Who have said, With our tongue will we prevail;
Our lips *are* our own: who *is* lord over us?
5 For the oppression of the poor, for the sighing of the needy,
Now will I arise saith the Lord;

I will set *him* in safety *from him* that puffeth at him.
6 The words of the *Lord are* pure words;
As silver tried in a furnace of earth
Purified seven times.
7 Thou shalt keep them, O Lord,
Thou shalt preserve them from this generation for ever.
8 The wicked walk on every side,
When the vilest men are exalted.

In the first part of this psalm of David the author speaks of the prevalence of wickedness and the declension of piety, and in the latter part he expresses his confidence that he should receive assistance from on high. In the title, the psalm is directed to the chief musician *on Sheminith*, meaning, probably, on the octave below, or on a bass instrument of music (vid. Remarks on I Chron., xv. 21, and Ps. vi). There is no other reference to music in the poem.

Psalm xiii. 1–6.

To the Chief Musician. A Psalm of David.

1 How long wilt thou forget me, O Lord, forever?
How long wilt thou hide thy face from me?
2 How long shall I take counsel in my soul,
Having sorrow in my heart daily?
How long shall mine enemy be exalted over me?
3 Consider and hear me, O Lord my God:
Lighten mine eyes, lest I sleep the sleep of death;
4 Lest mine enemy say, I have prevailed against him;
And those that trouble me rejoice when I am moved.
5 But I have trusted in thy mercy;
My heart shall rejoice in thy salvation.
6 I will sing unto the Lord,
Because he hath dealt bountifully with me.

This psalm of David is supposed to have been composed during the Babylonish captivity, as the writer speaks of great afflictions, and earnestly implores Jehovah, in whom he puts his trust, to deliver him. There is an allusion to music in the last verse.

I will sing.—The original is a derivative of *shîr, song.* There is an addition to the last verse in the Septuagint, the translation of which is: *Yea, I will praise the name of the Lord Most High.* This does not occur in any Hebrew manuscript (vid. J. A. Alexander's Com. on this Ps). In psalm xv. 49, *sing* occurs in the usual sense.

Psalm xvi. 1–11.

Michtam of David.

1 Preserve me, O God; for in thee do I put my trust.
2 O *my soul*, thou hast said unto the Lord,
Thou *art* my Lord:
My goodness *extendeth* not to thee;
3 *But* to the saints that *are* in the earth,
And *to* the excellent, in whom is all my delight.
4 Their sorrows shall be multiplied *that* hasten *after* another God:
Their drink-offerings of blood will I not offer,
Nor take up their names into my lips.
5 The Lord *is* the portion of mine inheritance and of my cup:
Thou maintainest my lot.
6 The lines are fallen unto me in pleasant *places*,
Yea, I have a goodly heritage.
7 I will bless the Lord who hath given me counsel;
My reins also instruct me in the night seasons.
8 I have set the Lord always before me:
Because *he* is at my right hand I shall not be moved.
9 Therefore my heart is glad and my glory rejoiceth;

My flesh also shall rest in hope:
10 For thou wilt not leave my soul in hell;
Neither wilt thou suffer thine Holy One to see corruption.
11 Thou wilt show me the path of life:
In thy presence is fullness of joy:
At thy right hand there are pleasures for ever more.

This psalm is called *Miktam* (מִכְתָּם) of David, and is thought to have been composed about 1044 B. C. The term *miktam* is found in the titles of five other psalms (vid. Psalms lvi., lvii., lviii., lix., and lx), and appears to be a substitute for *psalm* or *song*. Aben-Ezra and other critics derive it from כֶּתֶם, *kethem*, meaning *gold*, and would translate the term *golden psalm*. T. H. Horne favors the opinion which he derived from D'Herbelot, that the psalms to which *Miktam* is attached were so called on account of having been written on some occasion in letters of gold, and hung up in the sanctuary (Horne's Intro. P. v., ch. iii., sec. ii., 7—vol. ii., p. 242, Phil. ed.). The LXX translate the word by Στηλογραφια, *stelographia*, signifying *inscription*, supposing the psalm to have been engraved on a monument. Hengstenberg thinks that it means *mystery*, indicating that the psalms to which it is prefixed have an occult meaning. Prof. Alexander supposes that it "probably indicates the depth of doctrinal and spiritual import" of the poems to which it is prefixed. Gesenius believes that the final letter of the word was originally ב, and was gradually changed to ם. The ancient form of the word appears over Hezekiah's song, in Isa. xxxviii., 9. Thus the word would be מִכְתָּב *miktabh*, *a writing*, *a poem*, *a song*, instead of מִכְתָּם, *miktam*. Rosenmüller, Tholuck, De Wette, and others take this view, which is probably the correct one; as those letters, by the carelessness of transcribers, were often, in ancient times, interchanged with each other. There is no allusion to music in the psalm.

Psalm xviii.

This psalm has already been considered in our remarks on II Sam. xxii. above, to which the reader is referred. The title is a lengthy one, presenting simply the subject of the psalm. There is an allusion to music in the 49th verse, in which the term *sing* is employed similarly to its use in previous psalms.

Psalm xx.

There is no allusion to music in this psalm, excepting the occurrence of the word *Selah* in the third verse, probably in the sense of *Halleluya.*

Psalm xxi. 1–13.

To the Chief Musician. A Psalm of David.

1 The King shall joy in thy strength, O Lord;
And in thy salvation how greatly shall he rejoice!
2 Thou hast given him his heart's desire, [Selah.
And hast not withholden the request of his lips.
3 For thou preventest him with the blessings of goodness;
Thou settest a crown of pure gold on his head.
4 He asked life of thee,
And thou gavest *it* him,
Even length of days for ever and ever.
5 His glory *is* great in thy salvation:
Honor and majesty hast thou laid upon him.
6 For thou hast made him most blessed for ever:
Thou hast made him exceeding glad with thy countenance,
7 For the king trusteth in the Lord;
And, through the mercy of the Most High, he shall not be moved.

8 Thine hand shall find out all thine enemies:
Thy right hand shall find out those that hate thee.
9 Thou shalt make them as a fiery oven in the time of thine anger:
The Lord shall swallow them up in his wrath, and the fire shall devour them.
10 Their fruit shalt thou destroy from the earth,
And their seed from among the children of men.
11 For they intended evil against thee;
They imagined a mischievous device, *which* they are not able to *perform*.
12 Therefore shalt thou make them turn their back,
When thou shalt make ready *thine arrows* upon thy strings, against the face of them.
13 Be thou exalted, Lord, in thine own strength;
So will we sing and praise thy power.

This psalm represents the chosen people of God as rendering thanksgiving to the Great Creator. In verse 2, *selah* occurs, probably meaning *halleluya*. In verse 13, the word *sing* occurs, but in the usual form.

PSALM xxii. 1–31.

We present Herder's translation (Marsh's Ed.).

THE SUFFERER.

To the Chief Musician, at the Dawn of Morning. A Psalm of David.

1 My God, my God! wherefore dost thou forsake me?
Why art thou far from helping me, and from my cry?
2 My God, by day I call, but thou hearest not,
I cry by night, and find no time of rest!
3 And yet art thou the adorable one,
Who is enthroned amid the praises of Israel.

4 In thee our fathers trusted,
They trusted, and thou didst save them,
5 They cried to thee, and were delivered,
Trusted in thee, and were not confounded.
6 But I am but a worm, and no man,
Contemned of men, the people's scorn.
7 All they that see me, scoff at me,
They pout the lips, and shake the head.
8 "He calls upon Jehovah; let him save him,
Let him deliver him, since he delights in him."
9 Yet thou didst take me from my mother's womb,
And wast my hope upon my mother's breasts.
10 While laid upon the lap, I hung on thee,
And from my mother's womb thou wast my God!
11 Be therefore, even now, not far from me,
For trouble comes, and there is none to help!
12 Many bulls have compassed me about,
Strong bulls of Bashan have beset me round.
13 They rushed with open mouth upon me,
Like ravening and roaring lions.
14 Like water am I poured out,
And all my bones are loosed.
My heart is melted like wax within me,
15 My strength dried up like a potsherd.
My tongue too cleaveth to the roof of my mouth,
And thou hast laid me in the dust of death.
16 Dogs have encompassed me around,
And gangs of wicked men enclose me,
They pierce my hands and feet.
17 I might count over all my bones,
They see it, and with joy they gaze upon me.
18 They even now divide my garments,
And cast lots upon my vesture.
19 But be not thou, Jehovah, far from me,

My strong deliverer, haste and help me,
20 Deliver my life from the sword,
My soul from the power of the dog.
21 Rescue me from the lion's mouth,
And save me from the bullock's horns,
22 Among my brethren then will I extol thee,
And praise thee in the congregation.
23 Ye, that fear Jehovah, praise him!
All ye offspring of Jacob, glorify him,
And reverence him, ye seed of Israel,
24 For he contemneth not nor despiseth
The mournful cry of the afflicted,
Nor hath he hid his face from him,
But when he cried to him, he heard.
25 My song shall praise thee in the congregation,
Before thy servants will I pay my vows.
26 Eat, and be satisfied, ye humble sufferers,
Ye, that seek him, praise Jehovah,
Your heart shall be revived forever,
27 And all inhabitants of the earth,
Remembering, shall turn to Jehovah,
And all the tribes of men worship him.
28 For to Jehovah doth the kingdom pertain,
And he is ruler among the nations.
29 Let them that eat the fat of the earth worship him,
And them that are humble, bow before him,
Whose souls are vexed with care!
30 The future generations shall revere him,
And shall be counted as his people.
31 They come to make his kindness known,
And what he hath performed, to future times!

This Psalm of David describes a righteous person in deep affliction from the cruelties of his foes. His final deliverance from them is delineated, and its effect upon others. There is an affecting allusion to the vicarious sufferings of Jesus Christ. The psalm is addressed, in the title, to the chief musician upon *Ayyeleth hashahhar* (אַיֶּלֶת הַשַּׁחַר), signifying *hinds of the morning*, or, as Herder translates it, *at the dawn of morning.* Harmer supposes that these terms have no reference to musical instruments, but that they refer to the *tune*, in accordance with which the words were arranged. Aben-Ezra and other critics think that they designate *a song*, bearing this name or commencing with it, to the melody of which the psalm was to be sung. Tholuck and others suppose that it relates to the subject of the psalm. Prof. Alexander takes the same view. Gesenius translates it, *hind of the dawn*, and supposes, with the first named critics, that the expression indicates the name of some other poem or song, to the measure of which this psalm was to be chanted. This seems to be the most reasonable conclusion. There is no other reference in it to music.

PSALM xxiv. 1–10.

We present Herder's translation :

The Entrance of God upon Mount Zion.

1 ALL. Jehovah's is the earth and its fullness,
The world and they that dwell therein,
2 For he hath founded it upon the seas,
He hath established it upon the floods.
3 1. Who shall ascend the mountain of Jehovah?
Who dares to stand in his most holy place?
4 2. He that hath clean hands, and a pure heart,
That hath not bound his soul with perfidy,
Nor ever sworn deceitfully.
5 He shall receive a blessing from Jehovah,
The approbation of his guardian God.

6 1. This is the people, that seek after him,
That seek thy face, O God of Jacob.
7 CHORUS. Lift up your heads, O ye gates,
And be ye lifted up, ye everlasting doors,
For the king of glory will come in.
8 1. Who is the king of glory?
Jehovah strong and mighty,
2. Jehovah mighty in battle.
9 CHORUS. Lift up your heads, O ye gates,
And be ye lifted up, ye everlasting doors,
For the king of glory will come in.
10 1. Who is the king of glory?
CHORUS. Jehovah, God of gods! he is the king of glory.

According to Herder's arrangement, the whole assembly perform the first part of this ode. Then a single person sings, "Who shall ascend," etc. The answer is performed by two voices. Then one begins, "This is the people," etc. Next the chorus proclaims: "Lift up your heads," etc. One then asks, "Who is the king of glory?" etc. Then follow two voices, and then the chorus again: "Lift up your heads," etc. Finally one asks: "Who is the king of glory?" and the chorus proclaim the answer. Bishop Jebb presents this as an instance of *parallel lines gradational.* The gradation in sentiment is ascending. Whether the poem was performed by answering choirs, as Herder thinks, or not, we have no means of determining with certainty. Its recital was probably accompanied by all of the instruments of music known to the Israelites, as the occasion was an important one, being no less than the removal of the ark of the covenant to Mount Zion, described in II Sam. vi. and I Chron. xv (vid. Rem. on those passages).

The word *Selah* occurs in verses 6 and 10, probably in the sense of *halleluyah.*

PSALM XXV. 1–22.

A Psalm of David.

1 Unto thee, O Lord, do I lift up my soul.
2 O my God, I trust in thee:
Let me not be ashamed;
Let not mine enemies triumph over me.
3 Yea, let none that wait on thee be ashamed,
Let them be ashamed which transgress without cause.
4 Show me thy ways, O Lord;
Teach me thy paths.
5 Lead me in thy truth, and teach me;
For thou *art* the God of my salvation:
On thee do I wait all the day.
6 Remember, O Lord, thy tender mercies,
And thy loving-kindnesses;
For they *have been* ever of old.
7 Remember not the sins of my youth, nor my transgressions:
According to thy mercy, remember thou me,
For thy goodness' sake, O Lord.
8 Good and upright *is* the Lord:
Therefore will he teach sinners in the way.
9 The meek will he guide in judgment,
And the meek will he teach his way.
10 All the paths of the Lord *are* mercy and truth
Unto such as keep his covenant and his testimonies.
11 For thy name's sake, O Lord,
Pardon mine iniquity; for it *is* great.
12 What man *is* he that feareth the Lord?
Him shall he teach in the way *that* he shall choose:
13 His soul shall dwell at ease;
And his seed shall inherit the earth.
14 The secret of the Lord *is* with them that fear him:

And he will show them his covenant.
15 Mine eyes *are* ever toward the Lord:
For he shall pluck my feet out of the net.
16 Turn thee unto me, and have mercy upon me:
For I *am* desolate and afflicted.
17 The troubles of my heart are enlarged;
O bring thou me out of my distresses.
18 Look upon mine affliction and my pain;
And forgive all my sins.
19 Consider mine enemies: for they are many,
And they hate me with cruel hatred.
20 O keep my soul, and deliver me:
Let me not be ashamed;
For I put my trust in thee.
21 Let integrity and uprightness preserve me;
For I wait on thee.
22 Redeem Israel, O God, out of all his troubles.

David here seeks deliverance from his enemies, and implores pardon for his own sins. This is the first of the alphabetical psalms. The others are the xxxiv. xxxvii. cxi. cxii. cxix. and cxlv. Also Prov. xxxi. 10–31, and Lam. i. ii. iii. iv., are of the same character. This species of poetry consists of twenty-two lines, says Lowth, or twenty-two systems of lines, periods, or stanzas, corresponding with the number of the Hebrew alphabet. Every line, or every stanza, begins with each letter, generally in the order in which it stands in the alphabet. It is thought that the object of this arrangement was to assist the memory, as the alphabetical psalms are composed of detached sentences or aphorisms on moral and religious subjects. Psalms cxi. cxii. and Lam. iii. are *perfectly* alphabetical, every line being marked by a letter of the alphabet in its regular order. The others are *imperfectly* so, every stanza only commencing with a letter of the alphabet in its regular order. Psalm xxv. consists of stanzas of two lines each. Psalms xxxiv. cxix.

cxlv., Prov. xxxi., and Lam. iv., are arranged in a similar manner. These stanzas are divided each into lines, as is evident from the sense. The first line or first stanza of the poem, begins with *Aleph* (א), the second with *Beth* (ב), and so on in the order of the alphabet. In the psalm under consideration, the first two verses begin with *Aleph* (א), the third verse with *Gemel* (ג), passing over *Beth*, the second letter of the alphabet. Verse fourth begins with *Daleth* (ד), and so on. Verses 18 and 19 begin with the same letter (*Resh* ר).

Psalm xxx. 1–12.

A Psalm and a Song at the Dedication of the house of David.

1 I will extol thee, O Lord;
For thou hast lifted me up,
And hast not made my foes to rejoice over me.
2 O Lord my God, I cried unto thee, and thou hast healed me.
3 O Lord, thou hast brought up my soul from the grave;
Thou hast kept me alive, that I should not go down to the pit.
4 Sing unto the Lord, O ye saints of his,
And give thanks at the remembrance of his holiness.
5 For his anger *endureth but* a moment;
In his favor *is* life:
Weeping may endure for a night,
But joy *cometh* in the morning.
6 And in my prosperity I said, I shall never be moved.
7 Lord, by thy favor thou hast made my mountain to stand strong:
Thou didst hide thy face, *and* I was troubled.
8 I cried to thee, O Lord;
And unto the Lord I made supplication.
9 What profit *is there* in my blood, when I go down to the pit?

Shall the dust praise thee? shall it declare thy truth?
10 Hear, O Lord, and have mercy upon me:
Lord, be thou my helper.
11 Thou hast turned for me my mourning into dancing:
Thou hast put off my sackcloth, and girded me with gladness;
12 To the end that *my* glory may sing praise to thee, and not be silent.
O Lord my God, I will give thanks unto thee forever.

The title of this psalm seems to indicate that it was prepared with special reference to the dedication of the house or *altar* of God, referring, probably, to the place which David purchased (vid. II Sam. xxiv; I Chron. xxi), and on which he erected an altar for sacrifice. It was the spot on which the temple was subsequently built. The psalmist praises God for his deliverance from ruin, and calls upon others to join in ascriptions of adoration.

Verse 4. *Sing.*—The writer, in this verse, calls upon the righteous to sing praises to God. There is nothing peculiar in the expression.

Verse 11. *Dancing.*—The Hebrew term is מָחוֹל *mahhol.* Another form of the word is used in Ex. xv. 20. In the last verse the word *sing* is used in a similar manner as in verse 4.

Psalm xxxii. 1–11.

A Psalm of David. Maschil.

1 Blessed *is he whose* transgression *is* forgiven,
Whose sin *is* covered.
2 Blessed *is* the man unto whom the Lord imputeth not iniquity,
And in whose spirit *there is* no guile.
3 When I kept silence, my bones waxed old
Through my roaring all the day long,

4 (For day and night thy hand was heavy upon me)
My moisture is turned into the drought of summer.
Selah.

5 I acknowledged my sin unto thee;
And mine iniquity have I not hid.
I said, I will confess my transgressions unto the Lord:
And thou forgavest the iniquity of my sin. Selah.
6 For this shall every one that is godly
Pray unto thee, in a time when thou mayest be found;
Surely in the floods of great waters, they shall not come nigh unto him.
7 Thou *art* my hiding-place;
Thou shalt preserve me from trouble:
Thou shalt compass me about with songs of deliverance. Selah.
8 I will instruct thee, and teach thee in the way which thou shalt go;
I will guide thee with mine eye.
9 Be ye not as the horse, *or* as the mule,
Which have no understanding;
Whose mouth must be held in with bit and bridle,
Lest they come near unto thee.
10 Many sorrows *shall be* to the wicked:
But he that trusteth in the Lord, mercy shall compass him about.
11 Be glad in the Lord, and rejoice, ye righteous:
And shout for joy, all *ye that are* upright in heart.

A contrast is made in this psalm between the lamentable condition of the sinner while unpardoned, and his happy state when forgiven. The term *Maskil* (מַשְׂכִּיל) occurs in the title. The same word is employed in eleven other psalms (vid. Ps. xxxii, xlii, xliv, lii, liii, liv, lv, lxxiv, lxxviii, lxxxix, cxliii). It is a participial noun in the Hiphil conjugation, signifying *poem, song.* It is derived from שָׂכַל *sakal, to look at, to behold.* How the term came to signify *song*, is uncertain. Gesenius supposes that it originally indicated a DIDACTIC *song*, and subsequently different kinds of verse. De Wette, Calmet, and others take a similar view. Hengstenberg, Tholuck, and others maintain that it signifies a *didactic poem;* but they derive it from הִשְׂכִּיל *haskil, to teach, to make wise.* Rosenmüller considers it as a generic term for a particular kind of poem, though he agrees with Calmet in respect to its use in this psalm. The word *selah* occurs in verse 4, probably in the sense of *silence*, and in verses 5 and 7 in the sense of *halleluyah.*

Shout (v. 11)—a general expression of rejoicing without any particular reference to music.

PSALM xxxiii. 1–22.

1 Rejoice in the Lord, O ye righteous;
For praise is comely for the upright.
2 Praise the Lord with harp;
Sing unto him with the psaltery, *and* an instrument of ten strings.
3 Sing unto him a new song;
Play skillfully with a loud noise;
4 For the word of the Lord *is* right;
And all his works *are done* in truth.
5 He loveth righteousness and judgment;
The earth is full of the goodness of the Lord.
6 By the word of the Lord were the heavens made;
And all the host of them by the breath of his mouth.
7 He gathereth the waters of the sea together as an heap;
He layeth up the depth in storehouses.
8 Let all the earth fear the Lord;
Let all the inhabitants of the world stand in awe of him:
9 For he spake, and it was *done;*

He commanded, and it stood fast.
10 The Lord bringeth the counsel of the heathen to nought:
He maketh the devices of the people of none effect.
11 The counsel of the Lord standeth for ever,
The thoughts of his heart to all generations.
12 Blessed *is* the nation whose God *is* the Lord;
And the people *whom* he hath chosen for his own inheritance.
13 The Lord looketh from heaven;
He beholdeth all the sons of men.
14 From the place of his habitation he looketh
Upon all the inhabitants of the earth.
15 He fashioneth their hearts alike;
He considereth all their works.
16 There is no king saved by the multitude of an host;
A mighty man is not delivered by much strength.
17 An horse *is* a vain thing for safety:
Neither shall he deliver *any* by his great strength.
18 Behold, the eye of the Lord *is* upon them that fear him,
Upon them that hope in his mercy;
19 To deliver their soul from death,
And to keep them alive in famine.
20 Our soul waiteth for the Lord;
He *is* our help and our shield.
21 For our heart shall rejoice in him;
Because we have trusted in his holy name.
22 Let thy mercy, O Lord, be upon us,
According as we hope in thee.

This psalm is intimately connected with the preceding, and enlarges upon the closing sentiment of that poem, thus furnishing a reason why no title is prefixed in the Hebrew text. The

LXX ascribe it to David. Its object seems to be to excite confidence in God.

Harp (v. 2).—This is the *kinnor* mentioned in Gen iv. 21, for a full explanation of which vid. remarks above on that passage. *Cithara* is used in the Septuagint.

Psaltery (v. 2).—This is the *nebhel* which occurs in I Sam. x. 5, and II Sam. vi. 5. The LXX use *psalterion*, *psaltery*.

An instrument of ten strings.—Gesenius supposes that עָשׂוֹר *asor*, translated *an instrument of ten strings* in our English version, is to be taken with נֶבֶל *nebhel*, and that they mean a *ten-stringed lyre*. The LXX translate it *ten-stringed psaltery* (vid. Rem on I Sam. x. 5. *supra*, where it is shown that the *nehbel* was probably a kind of *guitar*).

Sing—a new song—play skillfully with a loud noise (v. 3).—The usual term for *song* and *sing* (*shîr*) is used as in Ex. xv. i. The original for *play* means *to do good*, and sometimes *to be joyful*, *to play*. The whole verse is intended as an expression of joy and praise.

In Psalm xxxv. 27 the word *shout* is used, but with no particular reference to music.

Psalm xxxvii. 1–40.

A Psalm of David.

1 Fret not thyself because of evil-doers,
Neither be thou envious against the workers of iniquity.
2 For they shall soon be cut down like the grass,
And wither as the green herb.
3 Trust in the Lord, and do good;
So shalt thou dwell in the land, and verily thou shalt be fed.
4 Delight thyself also in the Lord;
And he shall give thee the desires of thine heart.

5 Commit thy way unto the Lord;
Trust also in him, and he shall bring *it* to pass.
6 And he shall bring forth thy righteousness as the light,
And thy judgment as the noon-day.
7 Rest in the Lord, and wait patiently for him:
Fret not thyself because of him who prospereth in his way,
Because of the man who bringeth wicked devices to pass.
8 Cease from anger, and forsake wrath;
Fret not thyself in any wise to do evil.
9 For evil-doers shall be cut off:
But those that wait upon the Lord, they shall inherit the earth.
10 For yet a little while, and the wicked *shall* not *be:*
Yea, thou shall diligently consider his place, and it *shall* not *be.*
11 But the meek shall inherit the earth;
And shall delight themselves in the abundance of peace.
12 The wicked plotteth against the just,
And gnasheth upon him with his teeth.
13 The Lord shall laugh at him:
For he seeth that his day is coming.
14 The wicked have drawn out the sword,
And have bent their bow,
To cast down the poor and needy,
And to slay such as be of upright conversation.
15 Their sword shall enter into their own heart,
And their bows shall be broken.
16 A little that a righteous man hath
Is better than the riches of many wicked.
17 For the arms of the wicked shall be broken:
But the Lord upholdeth the righteous.

18 The Lord knoweth the days of the upright:
And their inheritance shall be forever.
19 They shall not be ashamed in the evil time.
And in the days of famine they shall be satisfied.
20 But the wicked shall perish,
And the enemies of the Lord *shall be* as the fat of lambs:
They shall consume; into smoke shall they consume away.
21 The wicked borroweth, and payeth not again:
But the righteous showeth mercy, and giveth.
22 For *such as be* blessed of him shall inherit the earth;
And *they that be* cursed of him shall be cut off.
23 The steps of a *good* man are ordered by the Lord:
And he delighteth in his way.
24 Though he fall, he shall not be utterly cast down:
For the Lord upholdeth *him with* his hand.
25 I have been young, and *now* am old;
Yet have I not seen the righteous forsaken,
Nor his seed begging bread.
26 *He is* ever merciful, and lendeth;
And his seed *is* blessed.
27 Depart from evil, and do good;
And dwell for evermore.
28 For the Lord loveth judgment,
And forsaketh not his saints;
They are preserved for ever:
But the seed of the wicked shall be cut off.
29 The righteous shall inherit the land,
And dwell therein for ever.
30 The mouth of the righteous speaketh wisdom,
And his tongue talketh of judgment.
31 The law of his God *is* in his heart;
None of his steps shall slide.

32 The wicked watcheth the righteous,
And seeketh to slay him.
33 The Lord will not leave him in his hand,
Nor condemn him when he is judged.
34 Wait on the Lord, and keep his way,
And he shall exalt thee to inherit the land:
When the wicked are cut off, thou shalt see *it*.
35 I have seen the wicked in great power,
And spreading himself like a green bay-tree:
36 Yet he passed away, and lo, he *was* not;
Yea, I sought him, but he could not be found.
37 Mark the perfect *man*, and behold the upright:
For the end of *that* man *is* peace.
38 But the transgressors shall be destroyed together;
The end of the wicked shall be cut off.
39 But the salvation of the righteous *is* of the Lord;
He is their strength in the time of trouble.
40 And the Lord shall help them, and deliver them:
He shall deliver them from the wicked, and save them,
Because they trust in him.

This is an alphabetical poem like psalm xxv., describing the sinner as a self-destroyer, and assuring the righteous that he need not fear from his enemies as God will sustain him. The psalm much resembles the book of proverbs from its aphoristic character, and may have been the model, Prof. Alexander thinks, according to which that book was constructed. There is no allusion to music in the psalm.

Psalm xxxix. 1–13.

To the Chief Musician, even to Jeduthun. A Psalm of David.

1 I said, I will take heed to my ways, that I sin not with
my tongue:

I will keep my mouth with a bridle,
While the wicked is before me.
2 I was dumb with silence, I held my peace,
Even from good: and my sorrow was stirred.
3 My heart was hot within me,
While I was musing the fire burned:
Then spake I with my tongue.
4 Lord, make me to know mine end,
And the measure of my days, what it *is;*
That I may know how frail I *am.*
5 Behold, thou hast made my days *as* an hand-breadth;
And mine age *is* as nothing before thee:
Verily every man at his best state *is* altogether vanity. Selah.
6 Surely every man walketh in a vain show:
Surely they are disquieted in vain;
He heapeth up *riches*, and knoweth not who shall gather them.
7 And now, Lord, what wait I for?
My hope *is* in thee.
8 Deliver me from all my transgressions:
Make me not the reproach of the foolish.
9 I was dumb, I opened not my mouth,
Because thou didst *it.*
10 Remove thy stroke away from me:
I am consumed by the blow of thine hand.
11 When thou with rebukes dost correct man for iniquity,
Thou makest his beauty to consume away like a moth:
Surely every man *is* vanity. Selah.
12 Hear my prayer, O Lord,
And give ear unto my cry;
Hold not thy peace at my tears:
For I *am* a stranger with thee,
And a sojourner, as all my fathers *were.*

13 O spare me, that I may recover strength,
Before I go hence and be no more.

The psalmist here expresses his past and present feelings in respect to the providences of God. David composed this poem for the chief musician named Jeduthun, signifying *praise-giver.* Jeduthun, Asaph, Heman, and Ethan were the king's leading musicians or choristers. None but the Levites were allowed to sing, or play on instruments of music, in the tabernacle or temple. Those who belonged to other tribes were permitted, on secular occasions, though not in the temple, to use all kinds of musical instruments, excepting the silver trumpets, which the priests only could blow. The Hebrew monarchs also had their private music. Asaph was master of David's royal band of musicians. Two other psalms seem to have been composed for Jeduthun (vid. Ps. lxii. and lxxvii).

In verses 5 and 11 the word *selah* is used, probably meaning *silence.*

In psalm xl. the usual term (shir) is employed and translated *song.*

Psalm xlii. 1-11.

To the Chief Musician, Maschil, for the Sons of Korah.

1 As the hart panteth after the water-brooks,
So panteth my soul after thee, O God.
2 My soul thirsteth for God, for the living God:
When shall I come and appear before God?
3 My tears have been my meat day and night,
While they continually say unto me, Where *is* thy God?
4 When I remember these *things*, I pour out my soul in me:
For I had gone with the multitude,
I went with them to the house of God,

With the voice of joy and praise,
With a multitude that kept holy-day.
5 Why art thou cast down, O my soul?
And *why* art thou disquieted in me?
Hope thou in God: for I shall yet praise him
For the help of his countenance.
6 O my God, my soul is cast down within me:
Therefore will I remember thee from the land of Jordan,
And of the Hermonites, from the hill Mizar.
7 Deep calleth unto deep at the noise of thy water-spouts:
All thy waves and thy billows are gone over me.
8 *Yet* the Lord will command his loving-kindness in the day-time,
And in the night his song *shall be* with me,
And my prayer unto the God of my life.
9 I will say unto God my rock, Why hast thou forgotten me?
Why go I mourning because of the oppression of the enemy?
10 *As* with a sword in my bones, mine enemies reproach me;
While they say daily unto me, Where is thy God?
11 Why art thou cast down, O my soul?
And why art thou disquieted within me?
Hope thou in God: for I shall yet praise him,
Who is the health of my countenance, and my God.

This psalm is ascribed to the Sons of Korah. Prof. Alexander supposes that they did not compose the poem, being merely "performers" of it, but that David was the writer, as the experience of that monarch is evidently described, and probably that part of his experience which transpired when he was excluded from the sanctuary on account of Absalom's rebellion. Calmet thinks that it was composed during the captivity. We are inclined to believe, with Rosenmüller and other eminent critics, that it was written by one of the sons of Korah, as the title indicates. The expression *by the Sons of Korah*, is entirely separate from *chief musician*, and is in the place which the author's name usually occupies.

This is the first sacred song ascribed to the sons of Korah. The forty-one psalms preceding were evidently from David's pen. Others which follow are obviously his composition. Seventy-one psalms in all are ascribed to him in the Hebrew text, and eleven others in the Septuagint; but not all which bear his name were really composed by him, and some which do not bear his name are obviously his composition. Calmet, after a careful examination, concludes that forty-five were written by that monarch. The Sons of Korah were Levites, employed in the temple music. Prof. Stuart supposes that they were descendants of that Korah who was destroyed in the rebellion described in Num. xvi., some of whose posterity presided over the tabernacle music. Overseers of the tabernacle are mentioned by that name (vid. Num. xvi. 8; I Chron. vi. 22, 37; ix. 19; xxvi. 1; II Chron. xx. 19). This poem is designated as a *Maskil*, or *didactic* psalm, being intended for permanent use.

The only allusion to music is in the eighth verse (ninth in Hebrew, the title being reckoned as one verse), where the usual term for *song* is employed.

Psalm xliii. 1–5.

1 Judge me, O God, and plead my cause against an ungodly nation:
O deliver me from the deceitful and unjust man.
2 For thou *art* the God of my strength:
Why dost thou cast me off?
Why go I mourning because of the oppression of the enemy?
3 O send out thy light and thy truth:

Let them lead me;
Let them bring me unto thy holy hill, and to thy tabernacles.
4 Then will I go unto the altar of God,
Unto God my exceeding joy;
Yea, upon the harp will I praise thee, O God my God,
5 Why art thou cast down, O my soul?
And why art thou disquieted within me?
Hope in God: for I shall yet praise him,
Who is the health of my countenance, and my God.

This and the preceding psalm are united into one poem in more than thirty Hebrew manuscripts. The two compositions closely resemble each other, and the most probable opinion is that the latter is supplementary to the former, and composed by the same individual who wrote that. Hence the omission of the title. The subject of the psalm is the description of a person in sorrow, seeking deliverance from his enemies.

Harp (v. 4).—This is the *Kinnor* (כִּנּוֹר), probably the instrument on which David played so beautifully. The same term occurs in Gen. iv. 21, in our remarks upon which, above, it is particularly explained; also in our remarks on I Sam. x. 5; I Kings, x. 12. It is translated *cithara* in the Septuagint.

PSALM xliv. 1–26.

To the Chief Musician for the Sons of Korah.

1 We have heard with our ears, O God, our fathers have told us,
What work thou didst in their days, in the times of old.
2 *How* thou didst drive out the heathen with thy hand, and plantedst them;
How thou didst afflict the people and cast them out.
3 For they got not the land in possession by their own sword.

Neither did their own arm save them;
But thy right hand, and thine arm,
And the light of thy countenance, because thou hadst a favor unto them.
4 Thou art my king, O God:
Command deliverances for Jacob.
5 Through thee will we push down our enemies:
Through thy name we will tread them under that rise up among us.
6 For I will not trust in my bow,
Neither shall my sword save me.
7 But thou hast saved us from our enemies,
And hast put them to shame that hated us.
8 In God we boast all the day long,
And praise thy name forever. Selah.
9 But thou hast cast off, and put us to shame:
And goest not forth with our armies.
10 Thou makest us to turn back from the enemy:
And they which hate us spoil for themselves.
11 Thou hast given us like sheep *appointed* for meat;
And hast scattered us among the heathen.
12 Thou sellest thy people for nought,
And dost not increase *thy wealth* by their price.
13 Thou makest us a reproach to our neighbors,
A scorn and a derision to them that are round about us.
14 Thou makest us a byword among the heathen,
A shaking of the head among the people.
15 My confusion *is* continually before me,
And the shame of my face hath covered me,
16 For the voice of him that reproacheth and blasphemeth;
By reason of the enemy and avenger.
17 All this is come upon us; yet have we not forgotten thee,
Neither have we dealt falsely in thy covenant.

18 Our heart is not turned back,
Neither have our steps declined from thy way;
19 Though thou hast sore broken us in the place of dragons,
And covered us with the shadow of death.
20 If we have forgotten the name of our God,
Or stretched out our hands to a strange god;
21 Shall not God search this out?
For he knoweth the secrets of the heart.
22 Yea, for thy sake are we killed all the day long;
We are counted as sheep for the slaughter.
23 Awake, why sleepest thou, O Lord?
Arise, cast *us* not off forever.
24 Wherefore hidest thou thy face,
And forgettest our affliction and our oppression?
25 For our soul is bowed down to the dust:
Our belly cleaveth unto the earth.
26 Arise for our help,
And redeem us for thy mercies' sake.

This, like the forty-second psalm, is ascribed to the sons of Korah, and was probably composed by one of them. The poet speaks of God as having been the deliverer of his people in ancient times; but intimates that now they are given up to their enemies. Still Israel trusts in Him. This is a *Maskil* or *didactic* psalm, being intended for permanent use. At the end of the eighth verse the word *selah* occurs, probably in the sense of *halleluyah*.

Psalm xlv. 1–17.

To the Chief Musician upon Shoshannim for the Sons of Korah, Maschil.—A song of loves.

1 My heart is inditing a good matter:
I speak of the things which I have made touching the king:

My tongue *is* the pen of a ready writer.
2 Thou art fairer than the children of men:
Grace is poured into thy lips:
Therefore God hath blessed the forever.
3 Gird thy sword upon *thy* thigh, O *most* mighty,
With thy glory and thy majesty.
4 And in thy majesty ride prosperously,
Because of truth and meekness *and* righteousness;
And thy right hand shall teach thee terrible things.
5 Thine arrows *are* sharp in the heart of the king's enemies:
Whereby the people fall under thee.
6 Thy throne, O God, *is* for ever and ever:
The sceptre of thy kingdom *is* a right sceptre.
7 Thou lovest righteousness, and hatest wickedness:
Therefore God, thy God, hath anointed thee
With the oil of gladness above thy fellows.
8 All thy garments *smell* of myrrh, and aloes, *and* cassia,
Out of the ivory palaces,
Whereby they have made thee glad.
9 Kings' daughters *were* among thy honorable women:
Upon thy right hand did stand the queen in gold of Ophir.
10 Hearken, O daughter, and consider, and incline thine ear;
Forget also thine own people, and thy father's house;
11 So shall the king greatly desire thy beauty:
For he *is* thy Lord; and worship thou him.
12 And the daughter of Tyre *shall be there* with a gift;
Even the rich among the people shall entreat thy favor.
13 The king's daughter *is* all glorious within:
Her clothing *is* of wrought gold.

14 She shall be brought unto the king in raiment of needlework;
The virgins her companions that follow her shall be brought unto thee.
15 With gladness and rejoicing shall they be brought:
They shall enter into the king's palace.
16 Instead of thy fathers shall be thy children,
Whom thou mayest make princes in all the earth.
17 I will make thy name to be remembered in all generations:
Therefore shall the people praise thee forever and ever.

This Psalm is also ascribed to the sons of Korah, and was probably written by one of them.

Upon Shoshannim.—This expression in the title is supposed by some to refer to a *musical instrument*, and by others to a particular *tune*. The Hebrew term is שֹׁשַׁנִּים the plural of שׁוּשַׁן *shushan*, usually signifying *lily*. Hengstenberg and some others suppose that it refers to the *subject* of the Psalm, and indicates a cheerful theme. Gesenius thinks that it refers to a *musical instrument*, resembling a lily in shape. The same term is used in Psalms lx. lxix. and lxxx. In Psalms lx. and lxxx. עֵדוּת *edhuth* is joined with *shushan*, and Gesenius supposes the two words united to signify *pipe of song* or *a lyric pipe*, probably referring to the *cymbal*. This opinion is confirmed from the fact that there is one kind of lily called the *martabon lily*, or *Turkish cap*, which very much resembles the cymbal in form. Indeed, the name of *cymbal* was sometimes given to this species of lily. The flower and stock bear a strong resemblance to several kinds of wind instruments, and may refer to them.

This is a *Maskil*, or *didactic* psalm. It is also called *a song of loves*, referring probably to the connection between Jesus

Christ and the church represented as bridegroom and bride. Such a remarkable accumulation of titles would seem to indicate that the psalm is one of vital importance to the people of God.

Psalm xlvi. 1–11.

To the Chief Musician for the Sons of Korah.—A song upon Alamoth.

1 God *is* our refuge and strength,
A very present help in trouble.
2 Therefore will not we fear, though the earth be removed,
And though the mountains be carried into the midst of the sea;
3 *Though* the waters thereof roar *and* be troubled,
Though the mountains shake with the swelling thereof. Selah.
4 *There is* a river, the streams whereof shall make glad the city of God,
The holy *place* of the tabernacles of the Most High.
5 God *is* in the midst of her; she shall not be moved:
God shall help her, *and that* right early.
6 The heathen raged, the kingdoms were moved:
He uttered his voice, the earth melted.
7 The Lord of hosts *is* with us;
The God of Jacob *is* our refuge. Selah.
8 Come, behold the works of the Lord,
What desolations he hath made in the earth.
9 He maketh wars to cease unto the end of the earth;
He breaketh the bow, and cutteth the spear in sunder;
He burneth the chariot in the fire.
10 Be still, and know that I *am* God:
I will be exalted among the heathen,
I will be exalted in the earth.

11 The Lord of hosts *is* with us;
The God of Jacob *is* our refuge. Selah.

This psalm describes the righteous as safe under the protection of their Heavenly Father. It is ascribed to the *sons of Korah*, and was probably composed by one of them.

On Alamoth.—This term occurs in the title, and refers probably to female voices, or the *treble* (vid. Rem. on I Chron. xv, *supra*). This psalm is divided into three strophes, as indicated by the word *selah* after verses 3, 7, and 11.

Psalm xlvii. 1–9.

To the Chief Musician.—A Psalm for the Sons of Korah.

1 O clap your hands, all ye people;
Shout unto God with the voice of triumph.
2 For the Lord Most High is terrible;
He is a great King over all the earth.
3 He shall subdue the people under us,
And the nations under our feet.
4 He shall choose our inheritance for us,
The excellency of Jacob whom he loved. Selah.
5 God is gone up with a shout,
The Lord with the sound of a trumpet.
6 Sing praises to God, sing praises:
Sing praises unto our King, sing praises.
7 For God is the King of all the earth:
Sing ye praises with understanding.
8 God reigneth over the heathen:
God sitteth upon the throne of his holiness.
9 The princes of the people are gathered together,
Even the people of the God of Abraham:
For the shields of the earth *belong* unto God:
He is greatly exalted.

This psalm expresses great joy on account of some remarkable deliverance of the chosen people of God. It is generally thought, by critics, to refer to the sanguine contest between the Israelites under Jehoshaphat, and the Ammonites and Edomites, in which Israel was victorious (vid. II Chron. xx. 18–29). It seems that singers on that occasion went before the army, and shouted forth the praises of God.

Shout (v. 1).—This refers to the ancient method of going to war with loud vociferations (vid. Rem. on Ex. xxxii. 18 *supra*). The soldiers were called upon to clap their hands, to *sing* (verses 6 and 7). In verse 5 the writer exclaims, *God is gone up with the sound of a trumpet.* This is thought, by some eminent commentators, to be an exclamation indicating that God, after the victory, had gone up to heaven with shouting and great pomp. But it seems more natural to consider the writer as intending to say, that God was present, by his approbation at least, with the soldiers as they went up to the battle, attended by singing, the blast of the trumpet, and the shout of war. We have not room to examine this view critically, but present it as more natural than the other. The whole psalm seems to refer to some great conflict and victory. The people of God triumphed and praised Jehovah, because he went up with them and effected a victory. The word translated *trumpet* (v. 5), is the *shophar* or *crooked one* (vid. Rem. on Ex. xix. 16 *supra*).

Selah occurs at the end of verse 4, probably in the sense of *Halleluyah.* It also occurs in psalm xlviii. 8 in the same sense.

Psalm xlix. 1–20.

To the Chief Musician.—A Psalm for the Sons of Korah.

1 Hear this, all ye people:
Give ear, all ye inhabitants of the world:
2 Both low and high, rich and poor together.
3 My mouth shall speak of wisdom;
And the meditation of my heart *shall* be of understanding.

4 I will incline mine ear to a parable:
I will open my dark saying upon a harp.
5 Wherefore should I fear in the days of evil,
When the iniquity of my heels shall compass me about?
6 They that trust in their wealth,
And boast themselves in the multitude of their riches;
7 None of *them* can by any means redeem his brother,
Nor give to God a ransom for him.
8 (For the redemption of their soul is precious, and it ceaseth forever);
9 That he should still live forever, *and* not see corruption.
10 For he seeth *that* wise men die,
Likewise the fool and the brutish person perish,
And leave their wealth to others.
11 Their inward thought *is*, *that* their houses *shall continue* forever,
And their dwelling-places to all generations;
They *call* their lands after their own names.
12 Nevertheless, man *being* in honor abideth not:
He is like the beasts *that* perish.
13 This their way *is* their folly:
Yet their posterity approve their sayings. Selah.
14 Like sheep they are laid in the grave;
Death shall feed on them;
And the upright shall have dominion over them in the morning;
And their beauty shall consume in the grave from their dwelling.
15 But God will redeem my soul from the power of the grave:
For he shall receive me. Selah.
16 Be not thou afraid when one is made rich,
When the glory of his house is increased;

17 For when he dieth he shall carry nothing away:
His glory shall not descend after him.
18 Though while he lived he blessed his soul:
And *men* will praise thee, when thou doest well to thyself.
19 He shall go to the generation of his fathers;
They shall never see light.
20 Man *that is* in honor, and understandeth not,
Is like the beasts *that* perish.

This psalm describes the trials of the righteous arising from the success and hatred of the wicked. Sources of comfort to the people of God, under such circumstances, are mentioned. It was probably written by one of the Sons of Korah, as its title indicates. Its exact date cannot be ascertained; but the obscurity of the style refers it to a high antiquity.

Harp (v. 4).—This is the *kinnor*, the same which is mentioned in Gen. iv. 21. The LXX translate it by ψαλτηρίῳ (*psalterio*), *psaltery*. *Selah* occurs in verse 13, probably in the sense of *silence*, or *meditation*. It also occurs in verse 15, probably in the sense of *Halleluyah*.

Psalm l. 1–23.

A Psalm of Asaph.

1 The mighty God, even the Lord, hath spoken,
And called the earth, from the rising of the sun unto the going down thereof.
2 Out of Zion, the perfection of beauty,
God hath shined.
3 Our God shall come, and shall not keep silence:
A fire shall devour before him, and it shall be very tempestuous round about him.
4 He shall call to the heavens from above,
And to the earth, that he may judge his people.

5 Gather my saints together unto me;
Those that have made a covenant with me by sacrifice.
6 And the heavens shall declare his righteousness:
For God *is* judge himself. Selah.
7 Hear, O my people, and I will speak;
O Israel, and I will testify against thee:
I *am* God, *even* thy God.
8 I will not reprove thee for thy sacrifices,
Or thy burnt-offerings, *to have been* continually before me.
9 I will take no bullock out of thy house,
Nor he-goats out of thy folds,
10 For every beast of the forest *is* mine,
And the cattle upon a thousand hills.
11 I know all the fowls of the mountains;
And the wild beasts of the field *are* mine.
12 If I were hungry, I would not tell thee:
For the world *is* mine, and the fullness thereof.
13 Will I eat the flesh of bulls,
Or drink the blood of goats?
14 Offer unto God thanksgiving;
And pay thy vows unto the Most High:
15 And call upon me in the day of trouble:
I will deliver thee, and thou shalt glorify me.
16 But unto the wicked God saith,
What hast thou to do to declare my statutes,
Or *that* thou shouldest take my covenant in thy mouth?
17 Seeing thou hatest instruction,
And castest my words behind thee.
18 When thou sawest a thief, then thou consentedst with him,
And hast been partaker with adulterers.
19 Thou givest thy mouth to evil,
And thy tongue frameth deceit,

20 Thou sittest *and* speakest against thy brother;
Thou slanderest thine own mother's son.
21 These *things* hast thou done, and I kept silence;
Thou thoughtest that I was altogether *such an one* as thyself:
But I will reprove thee, and set *them* in order before thine eyes
22 Now consider this, ye that forget God,
Lest I tear *you* in pieces, and *there be* none to deliver.
23 Whoso offereth praise glorifieth me:
And to him that ordereth *his* conversation *aright* will I show the salvation of God.

In this psalm God is represented as condemning formalists, on the ground that they are deceitful. He calls upon them to worship their Creator. This is the first psalm which is ascribed to Asaph. From I Chron. xxv. 1, 2, it appears that he was an inspired prophet, as well as one of David's chief singers. Twelve psalms, viz: l., and lxxii.–lxxxiii., are ascribed to him. He was a distinguished Levite, and a celebrated musician and composer. It is thought that the seventy-fourth and seventy-ninth psalms can hardly be his composition, as they speak of the destruction of Jerusalem and the burning of the temple. The style seems to be very similar to that of the lamentations of Jeremiah. It is believed either that the poem is incorrectly ascribed to Asaph, or that it was composed by another person by the same name, living at the time of the captivity. There is a deep vein of *thought* pervading Asaph's psalms. He dwells upon doctrines. His style is more bold and vehement than that of David, and sometimes reaches the morally sublime.

In verse 6 *selah* occurs, probably in the sense of *silence*.

In the fourteenth verse of the fifty-first chapter the word *sing* is employed, referring to the utterance of the praises of God. In verses 3 and 5 of chapter lii., *selah* occurs in the sense of *silence*.

Psalm liii. 1–6.

To the Chief Musician upon Mahhalath, Maschil.—A Psalm of David.

1 The fool hath said in his heart, *There is* no God.
Corrupt are they, and have done abominable iniquity:
There is none that doeth good.
2 God looked down from heaven upon the children of men,
To see if there were *any* that did understand, that did seek God.
3 Every one of them is gone back;
They are altogether become filthy;
There is none that doeth good, no, not one.
4 Have the workers of iniquity no knowledge?
Who eat up my people *as* they eat bread:
They have not called upon God.
5 There were they in great fear, *where* no fear was:
For God hath scattered the bones of him that encampeth *against* thee:
Thou hast put *them* to shame, because God hath despised them.
6 O that the salvation of Israel *were come out* of Zion!
When God bringeth back the captivity of his people,
Jacob shall rejoice, *and* Israel shall be glad.

This is a psalm of David, and similar to the fourteenth. It is thought by the best critics that both psalms were written by him, and that the latter is simply the former rewritten and revised, in order to elucidate some points without intending to supersede the use of the original composition. This is a *Maskil*, or didactic psalm.

On Măhhălath.—This term (מַחֲלַת) occurs in the title. It is derived from the verb חָלָה *hhạlạ, to be smooth* or *soft, to be sick.* Some critics believe that *mahhalath*, in this place, signifies *disease*, referring to the subject of the psalm. Others, with more reason we think, adopt the former signification, and derive from it the meaning *to sing.* Gesenius supposes that it means a *stringed instrument*, a *lute* or *guitar.* In the Æthiopic version it is translated *song.* Fürst supposes it to mean a *tune*, and that it is the first word of some popular song. Calmet translates the title of this psalm thus: "*An instructive psalm of David for the chief master of dancing: or for the chorus of singers and dancers.*" Horne thinks it refers to some peculiar dance used at festivals. The LXX, contrary to their usual course, leave the term untranslated. The general belief is that it relates, in some manner, to music; and this is probably its true meaning. It occurs in only one other psalm, viz., the 88th, with probably a similar signification. It is impossible to ascertain what kind of an instrument is intended: but the etymology of the word would indicate the softer kind, perhaps the *lute* or *guitar.*

Psalm liv. 1–7.

To the Chief Musician on Neginoth, Maschil, A Psalm of David, when the Ziphims came and said to Saul, Doth not David hide himself with us?

1 Save me, O God, by thy name,
And judge me by thy strength.
2 Hear my prayer, O God;
Give ear to the words of my mouth.
3 For strangers are risen up against me,
And oppressors seek after my soul:
They have not set God before them. Selah.
4 Behold, God *is* mine helper:
The Lord *is* with them that uphold my soul.
5 He shall reward evil unto mine enemies:
Cut them off in thy truth.

6 I will freely sacrifice unto thee:
I will praise thy name, O Lord, for *it is* good.
7 For he hath delivered me out of all trouble:
And mine eye hath seen *his desire* upon mine enemies.

In this psalm the writer prays for deliverance from his enemies. The term *n'ginoth* (נְגִינוֹת) occurs in the title, meaning stringed instruments of music, as in psalm iv (vid. Rem. on the same, *supra*). *Selah* occurs at the end of verse 4, probably in the sense of *silence*. *N'ginoth* also occurs in the title of Psalm lv, with a similar meaning as in Ps. liv. At the end of verse 7, and in the middle of verse 19, *selah* is found, meaning *silence*.

Psalm lvi. 1–6.

To the Chief Musician upon Jonath-Elem Rechokim, Michtam of David, when the Philistines took him in Gath.

1 Be merciful unto me, O God;
For man would swallow me up:
He fighting daily oppresseth me.
2 Mine enemies would daily swallow *me* up:
For *they be* many that fight against me, O thou Most High.
3 What time I am afraid,
I will trust in thee.
4 In God I will praise his word;
In God I have put my trust:
I will not fear what flesh can do unto me.
5 Every day they wrest my words;
All their thoughts are against me for evil.
6 They gather themselves together, they hide themselves.

In this psalm David asks to be delivered from the malice and oppression of his foes, and trusts in the Almighty arm to rescue him. This is addressed to the chief musician, and is a *miktam* or *didactic* psalm.

On *yonath ēlem r^ehhoqīm* (יוֹנַת אֵלֶם רְחֹקִים). *Yonath* signifies a *dove*; *ēlem*, *dumb*, *silent*, and *r^ehhoqīm*, *far distant*. Prof. Alexander supposes that this phrase refers to David, and represents him as an innocent and uncomplaining sufferer among strangers (vid. his Comment. on this Ps.). Gesenius translates it thus: "*the silent dove among strangers*," and supposes that it may refer to the people of Israel in exile. There seems to be no allusion to music in this expression, excepting that it is part of the title to a lyric poem.

Psalm lvii. 1–11.

To the Chief Musician, Al-taschith, Michtam of David, when he fled from Saul in the cave.

1 Be merciful unto me, O God, be merciful unto me:
For my soul trusteth in thee:
Yea, in the shadow of thy wings will I make my refuge,
Until *these* calamities be overpast.
2 I will cry unto God most high;
Unto God that performeth *all things* for me.
3 He shall send from heaven, and save me
From the reproach of him that would swallow me up. Selah.
God shall send forth his mercy and his truth.
4 My soul *is* among lions:
And I lie *even among* them that are set on fire,
Even the sons of men, whose teeth *are* spears and arrows,
And their tongue a sharp sword.
5 Be thou exalted, O God, above the heavens:
Let thy glory *be* above all the earth.

6 They have prepared a net for my steps;
My soul is bowed down:
They have digged a pit before me,
Into the midst whereof they are fallen *themselves.*

7 My heart is fixed, O God, my heart is fixed:
I will sing and give praise.
8 Awake up, my glory; awake, psaltery and harp:
I *myself* will awake early.
9 I will praise thee, O Lord, among the people:
I will sing unto thee among the nations.
10 For thy mercy *is* great unto the heavens,
And thy truth unto the clouds.
11 Be thou exalted, O God, above the heavens:
Let thy glory *be* above all the earth.

In this psalm the writer describes his sufferings, and seeks for deliverance from his enemies.

Al-taschheth (אַל־תַּשְׁחֵת).—This obscure term, which occurs in the title, means *destroy not.* Some critics maintain that it relates to music. Prof. Alexander adopts the explanation suggested by the Chaldee Paraphrase, viz: that the psalm belongs to that period in David's life when he was under the necessity of saying constantly, *Destroy not.* Gesenius supposes, with more reason, we think, that this expression contains the "first words or title of a song, to the melody of which this psalm was to be sung." This view is generally received as correct. Psalms lviii, lix, and lxxv, have the same term in their titles.

Miktam is also employed in the title, probably meaning *psalm* or *song* (vid. Rem. on Ps. xvi, *supra*).

In verses 3 and 6, *selah* occurs, probably in the sense of *silence.*

In verse 7, the expression, *I will sing and give praise,* is translated by Prof. Alexander thus: *I will sing and play,* thus intimating that there was probably not only *vocal,* but *instru-*

mental music. The original word translated sing in verses 7 and 8, has the same derivation as that in Ex. xv. 2 (vid Rem. on the same above.)

Psaltery (v. 8).—*Nebhel* is used here in the same sense as in I Sam. x. 5, and II Sam. vi. 5.

Harp (v. 8).—This is the *kinnor*, the same as in Gen. iv. 21. The Septuagint has *cithara*. The literal translation of the last clause of the verse is, *I will awaken morning*. A beautiful idea. The writer was going to awaken the dawn instead of being awakened by it.

Psalm lix. 1–17.

To the Chief Musician, Al-taschith, Michtam of David, when Saul sent, and they watched the house to kill him.

1 Deliver me from mine enemies, O my God:
Defend me from them that rise against me.
2 Deliver me from the workers of iniquity,
And save me from bloody men.
3 For lo, they lie in wait for my soul:
The mighty are gathered against me;
Not *for* my transgression, nor *for* my sin, O Lord.
4 They run and prepare themselves without *my* fault:
Awake to help me, and behold.
5 Thou, therefore, O Lord God of hosts,
The God of Israel, awake to visit all the heathen:
Be not merciful to any wicked transgressors. Selah.
6 They return at evening;
They make a noise like a dog,
And go round about the city.
7 Behold, they belch out with their mouth:
Swords *are* in their lips;
For who, (*say they*,) doth hear?
8 But thou, O Lord, shalt laugh at them;
Thou shalt have all the heathen in derision.

9 *Because of* his strength will I wait upon thee;
For God *is* my defence.
10 The God of my mercy shall prevent me;
God shall let me see *my desire* upon mine enemies.
11 Slay them not, lest my people forget:
Scatter them by thy power;
And bring them down, O Lord our shield.
12 *For* the sin of their mouth, *and* the words of their lips,
Let them even be taken in their pride:
And for cursing and lying *which* they speak.
13 Consume *them* in wrath, consume *them*, that they *may* not *be*:
And let them know that God ruleth in Jacob unto the ends of the earth. Selah.
14 And at evening let them return;
And let them make a noise like a dog,
And go round about the city.
15 Let them wander up and down for meat,
And grudge if they be not satisfied.
16 But I will sing of thy power;
Yea, I will sing aloud of thy mercy in the morning:
For thou hast been my defence and refuge in the day of my trouble.
17 Unto thee, O my strength, will I sing:
For God *is* my defence, *and* the God of my mercy.

This Psalm contains a description of the sufferings of a pious man, from implacable foes. He prays for deliverance, and confides in God to accomplish what he so much desires. The latter part of the poem forms a parallelism with the first part, the same subject being repeated. The title is the same as those of the two preceding psalms. *Selah* occurs in verses 5 and 13, probably in the sense of *silence*.

I will sing (verses 16 and 17).—In verse 16 a derivative of

the same word, in the original, is used, as in Gen. xxxi. 27 and Ex. xv. 1, and in verse 17 a derivative of the same word as is found in Ex. xv. 2, remarks on which see.

Psalm lx. 1–12.

To the Chief Musician upon Shushan-eduth, Michtam of David, to teach; when he strove with Aram-naharaim, and with Aram-zobah, when Joab returned, and smote of Edom in the valley of Salt, twelve thousand.

1 O God, thou hast cast us off,
Thou hast scattered us, thou hast been displeased;
O turn thyself to us again.
2 Thou hast made the earth to tremble; thou hast broken it:
Heal the breaches thereof; for it shaketh.
3 Thou hast showed thy people hard things:
Thou hast made us to drink the wine of astonishment.
4 Thou hast given a banner to them that fear thee,
That it may be displayed because of the truth. Selah.
5 That thy beloved may be delivered;
Save *with* thy right hand, and hear me.
6 God hath spoken in his holiness;
I will rejoice, I will divide Shechem,
And mete out the valley of Succoth.
7 Gilead *is* mine, and Manasseh *is* mine;
Ephraim also *is* the strength of mine head;
Judah *is* my lawgiver;
8 Moab *is* my wash-pot;
Over Edom will I cast out my shoe:
Philistia, triumph thou because of me.
9 Who will bring me *into* the strong city?
Who will lead me into Edom?
10 *Wilt* not thou, O God, *which* hadst cast us off?

And *thou*, O God, *which* didst not go out with our armies?
11 Give us help from trouble;
For vain *is* the help of man.
12 Through God we shall do valiantly:
For he *it is that* shall tread down our enemies.

This psalm is divided into three equal strophes of four verses each. The writer pleads earnestly for the people of God.

Shushan-edhuth (שׁוּשַׁן עֵדוּת).—This expression in the title signifies *lily of the testimony*. The first part of it occurs in the plural in Psalm xlv (שֹׁשַׁנִּים *shoshannīm*). This expression probably indicates some kind of wind instrument of music resembling a lily in shape (vid. Rem. on Ps. xlv. *supra*). *Miktam*, meaning *song*, also appears in the title. At the end of verse 4, *selah* occurs, probably in the sense of *halleluyah*. In Psalm lxi, *n^egīnoth* is used as in Psalms iv, vi, liv, lv, signifying *stringed instruments of music*. At the end of verse 4, in the same Psalm (lxi), *selah* is found, probably in the sense of *halleluyah*.

I will sing (Ps. lxi. 8), would be more correctly translated, *I will celebrate*, i. e., both by vocal and instrumental music. Psalm lxii. is ascribed to Jeduthun like psalm xxxix, which see. *Selah* at the end of verse 4 in Ps. lxii, probably means *silence*, and in verse 8, *halleluyah*. In Psalm lxv, verse 13, *sing* is used. The same original word is employed as in Gen. xxxi. 27, remarks on which see.

PSALM lxvi. 1–20.

To the Chief Musician.—A song or psalm.

1 Make a joyful noise unto God, all ye lands:
2 Sing forth the honor of his name:
Make his praise glorious.
3 Say unto God, How terrible *art thou in* thy works!

Through the greatness of thy power
Shall thine enemies submit themselves unto thee.
4 All the earth shall worship thee, and shall sing unto thee;
They shall sing *to* thy name. Selah.
5 Come and see the works of God:
He is terrible *in his* doing toward the children of men.
6 He turned the sea into dry *land:*
They went through the flood on foot:
There did we rejoice in him.
7 He ruleth by his power for ever;
His eyes behold the nations:
Let not the rebellious exalt themselves. Selah.
8 O bless our God, ye people,
And make the voice of his praise to be heard:
9 Which holdeth our soul in life,
And suffereth not our feet to be moved.
10 For thou, O God, hast proved us:
Thou hast tried us, as silver is tried.
11 Thou broughtest us into the net;
Thou laidest affliction upon our loins.
12 Thou hast caused men to ride over our heads:
We went through fire and through water:
But thou broughtest us out into a wealthy *place.*
13 I will go into thy house with burnt-offerings:
14 I will pay thee my vows, which my lips have uttered,
And my mouth hath spoken, when I was in trouble.
15 I will offer unto thee burnt-sacrifices of fatlings,
With the incense of rams; I will offer bullocks with goats. Selah.
16 Come *and* hear, all ye that fear God,
And I will declare what he hath done for my soul.
17 I cried unto him with my mouth,
And he was extolled with my tongue.

18 If I regard iniquity in my heart,
The Lord will not hear *me:*
19 *But* verily God hath heard *me;*
He hath attended to the voice of my prayer.
20 Blessed *be* God, which hath not turned away my prayer,
Nor his mercy from me.

God's wonderful works, and his dealings with the righteous are here recorded.

Sing (verses 2, 4).—A similar term in the original is used as in Ex. xv. 2, remarks on which see. *Selah*, at the end of verses 4 and 15, probably means *halleluyah*, and in verse 7, *silence*. In the title of Psalm lxvii. *neginoth* occurs, meaning *stringed instruments*. *Selah* in the first verse probably means *silence*, and in verse 4, *halleluyah*.

Sing (verse 4).—The original word has the same derivation as that used in Lev. ix. 24, and translated *shouted*, remarks on which see.

Psalm lxviii. 1–4; 13–35.

1 Let God arise, let his enemies be scattered:
Let them also that hate him flee before him,
2 As smoke is driven away, *so* drive *them* away:
As wax melteth before the fire,
So let the wicked perish at the presence of God.
3 But let the righteous be glad; let them rejoice before God:
Yea, let them exceedingly rejoice.
4 Sing unto God, sing praises to his name:
Extol him that rideth upon the heavens
By his name *Jah*, and rejoice before him.
13 Though ye have lien among the pots,

Yet shall ye be as the wings of a dove covered with silver,
And her feathers, with yellow gold.
14 When the Almighty scattered kings in it,
It was *white* as snow in Salmon.
15 The hill of God *is as* the hill of Bashan;
An high hill, *as* the hill of Bashan.
16 Why leap ye, ye high hills?
This is the hill *which* God desireth to dwell in;
Yea, the *Lord* will dwell *in it* forever:
17 The chariots of God *are* twenty thousand, *even* thousands of angels;
The Lord *is* among them *as* in Sinai, in the holy place.
18 Thou hast ascended on high,
Thou hast led captivity captive:
Thou hast received gifts for men;
Yea, *for* the rebellious also,
That the Lord God might dwell *among them.*
19 Blessed *be* the Lord, *who* daily loadeth us *with benefits,*
Even the God of our salvation. Selah.
20 *He that is* our God *is* the God of salvation;
And unto God the Lord *belong* the issues from death.
21 But God shall wound the head of his enemies,
And the hairy scalp of such an one as goeth on still in his trespasses.
22 The Lord said, I will bring again from Bashan,
I will bring *my people* again from the depths of the sea:
23 That thy foot may be dipped in the blood of *thine* enemies,
And the tongue of thy dogs in the same.
24 They have seen thy goings, O God,

Even the goings of my God, my King, in the sanctuary:
25 The singers went before,
The players on instruments *followed* after;
Among *them were* the damsels playing with timbrels.
26 Bless ye God in the congregations,
Even the Lord, from the fountain of Israel.
27 There *is* little Benjamin *with* their ruler,
The princes of Judah *and* their council,
The princes of Zebulun, *and* the princes of Naphtali.
28 Thy God hath commanded thy strength:
Strengthen, O God, that which thou hast wrought for us.
29 Because of thy temple at Jerusalem
Shall kings bring presents unto thee.
30 Rebuke the company of spearmen,
The multitude of the bulls, with the calves of the people,
Till every one submit himself with pieces of silver:
Scatter thou the people *that* delight in war.
31 Princes shall come out of Egypt;
Æthiopia shall soon stretch out her hands unto God.
32 Sing unto God, ye kingdoms of the earth;
O sing praises *unto* the Lord; **Selah.**
33 To him that rideth upon the heavens of heavens *which were* of old;
Lo, he doth send out his voice, *and that* a mighty voice.
34 Ascribe ye strength unto God;
His excellency *is* over Israel, and his strength *is* in the clouds.
35 O God, *thou art* terrible out of thy holy places:
The God of Israel *is* he that giveth strength and power unto *his* people.
Blessed *be* God.

In this psalm David utters ascriptions of praise to God for some celebrated victory. It is thought that reference is made to a war near the close of his reign, mentioned in II Sam. xii. 26–31. A history of the dealings of God with Israel, in different ages, follows.

Sing (v. 4).—A derivative of *shīr*, is the original, as in Ex. xv. 1.

Sing (in the same verse).—The original in this case is a derivative of *zamar*, as in Ex. xv. 2, remarks on which see. *Selah* occurs in verse 7, probably in the sense of *silence*, and in verses 19 and 32, in the sense of *halleluyah*.

The singers (v. 25).—The original is the plural of *shīr*, as in verse 4.

Players on instruments (v. 25).—The original is נֹגְנִים *nogᵉnīm*, the general term for *stringed instruments*, from *nagan*, *to play on stringed instruments* (vid. Rem. on Gen. iv. 21 *supra*). Probably different kinds of instruments of that class were employed.

Timbrels (v. 25).—These were *tophs*, as in Ex. xv. 20, remarks on which see above. It seems by this that not only stringed, but pulsatile instruments were employed, and that by females. The original indicates that the singers and those performing on stringed instruments were surrounded by females playing on their timbrels.

In verse 32, *sing* occurs in the ordinary sense. The kingdoms of the earth are called upon to sing praises to God. In psalm lxix., *shoshannīm* is used in the title, and probably means a *wind instrument* somewhat resembling a *lily*, as in psalm xlv, remarks on which see. . In verse 30, *song* occurs, for which the usual word *shīr* is used in the original.

Psalm lxxi. 1–24.

1 In thee, O Lord, do I put my trust:
Let me never be put to confusion.

2 Deliver me in thy righteousness, and cause me to escape:
Incline thine ear unto me, and save me.
3 Be thou my strong habitation, whereunto I may continually resort:
Thou hast given commandment to save me;
For thou *art* my rock and my fortress.
4 Deliver me, O my God, out of the hand of the wicked,
Out of the hand of the unrighteous and cruel man.
5 For thou *art* my hope, O Lord God:
Thou art my trust from my youth.
6 By thee have I been holden up from the womb:
Thou art he that took me out of my mother's bowels:
My praise *shall be* continually of thee.
7 I am as a wonder unto many:
But thou *art* my strong refuge.
8 Let my mouth be filled *with* thy praise,
And with thy honor all the day.
9 Cast me not off in the time of old age;
Forsake me not when my strength faileth.
10 For mine enemies speak against me;
And they that lay wait for my soul take counsel together,
11 Saying, God hath forsaken him:
Persecute and take him;
For *there is* none to deliver *him*.
12 O God, be not far from me;
O my God, make haste for my help.
13 Let them be confounded *and* consumed that are adversaries to my soul;
Let them be covered *with* reproach and dishonor that seek my hurt.
14 But I will hope continually,
And will yet praise thee more and more.

15 My mouth shall show forth thy righteousness *and* thy
salvation all the day;
For I know not the numbers *thereof*.
16 I will go in the strength of the Lord God;
I will make mention of thy righteousness, *even* of thine
only.
17 O God, thou hast taught me from my youth:
And hitherto have I declared thy wondrous works.
18 Now also, when I am old and grey-headed, O God, forsake me not;
Until I have showed thy strength unto *this* generation,
And thy power to every one *that* is to come.
19 Thy righteousness also, O God, *is* very high,
Who hast done great things:
O God, who *is* like unto thee!
20 *Thou*, which hast showed me great and sore troubles,
shalt quicken me again,
And shalt bring me up again from the depths of the
earth.
21 Thou shalt increase my greatness,
And comfort me on every side.
22 I will also praise thee with the psaltery,
Even thy truth, O my God:
Unto thee will I sing with the harp,
O thou holy one of Israel.
23 My lips shall greatly rejoice when I sing unto thee;
And my soul, which thou hast redeemed.
24 My tongue also shall talk of thy righteousness all the
day long:
For they are confounded, for they are brought unto
shame, that seek my hurt.

This psalm resembles the 22d, 35th, 38th, and 40th, and appears to have a part of the last prefixed to it, which circumstance is supposed to be the reason why it has no title. The theme of the psalm seems to be the sufferings of the righteous and their plea for deliverance.

Psaltery—harp (v. 22).—These are the *nebhel* and *kinnor* (vid. Rem. on I Sam. x. 5; II Sam. vi. 5, and Gen. iv. 21). Prof. Alexander translates thus: "Also *I will thank thee with a harp-instrument*, i. e., with a harp or lyre as the instrument of praise." In the 23d verse, the two verbs translated, in our English version, *rejoice* and *sing*, may refer, though not necessarily, to both instrumental and vocal music. In the title of Psalm lxxv. *Al-tascheth* occurs, signifying *destroy not* (vid. Rem. on Ps. lvii, and lviii, *supra*).

Sing (v. 9), occurs in the usual sense.

Selah is found in verse 5, probably in the sense of *silence*. *Sing* occurs in verse 9, referring to the praises of God. In the title of psalm lxxvi, *neginoth*, meaning *stringed instruments*, occurs, for an explanation of which see remarks on Gen. iv. 21; Job xxx. 9; Ps. iv.

Selah is found in verses 3 and 9, probably in the sense of *silence*. In psalm lxxvii. 7, *sing* occurs, the original of which is *neginathiy*, and may be translated, *I will play on stringed instruments*.

In verses 3, 9, and 15, *selah* is found. In the 15th verse it probably signifies *halleluyah*, and in the other two, *silence*. In Psalm lxxx, *shoshannim eduth* appear in the title, meaning *song of the lily*. See remarks on Psalms xlv, and lx, where the same terms occur.

PSALM lxxxi. 1–16.

To the Chief Musician upon Gittith.—A Psalm of Asaph.

1 Sing aloud unto God our strength:
Make a joyful noise unto the God of Jacob.
2 Take a psalm, and bring hither the timbrel,
The pleasant harp with the psaltery.

3 Blow up the trumpet in the new moon,
In the time appointed, on our solemn feast-day.
4 For this *was* a statute for Israel,
And a law of the God of Jacob.
5 This he ordained in Joseph *for* a testimony,
When he went out through the land of Egypt;
Where I heard a language *that* I understood not.
6 I removed his shoulder from the burden:
His hands were delivered from the pots.
7 Thou calledst in trouble, and I delivered thee;
I answered thee in the secret place of thunder:
I proved thee at the waters of Meribah. **Selah.**
8 Hear, O my people, and I will testify unto thee:
O Israel, if thou wilt hearken unto me;
9 There shall no strange god be in thee;
Neither shalt thou worship any strange god.
10 I *am* the Lord thy God,
Which brought thee out of the land of Egypt:
Open thy mouth wide, and I will fill it.
11 But my people would not hearken to my voice;
And Israel would none of me.
12 So I gave them up unto their own hearts' lust:
And they walked in their own counsels.
13 O that my people had hearkened unto me,
And Israel had walked in my ways!
14 I should soon have subdued their enemies,
And turned my hand against their adversaries.
15 The haters of the Lord should have submitted themselves unto him:
But their time should have endured for ever.
16 He should have fed them also with the finest of the wheat:
And with honey out of the rock should I have satisfied thee.

The Psalmist exhorts Israel to praise God for deliverance from her enemies in Egypt, and the poem is supposed to have been prepared in order to be sung at the Passover.

Gittith, probably meaning *instruments of music*, though it is uncertain what kind, occurs in the title, for an explanation of which vid. remarks on Psalm viii. *supra*.

Sing aloud (v. 1).—The original of this is a derivative of *ranan* (רָנַן) *to utter a tremulous sound.* In Ps. v. 11 (v. 12 in Heb.), the same word is translated *shout.* The idea is, to utter exalted songs of praise to God. The parallel verb in the same verse, is, according to Alexander, a generic term, referring both to *shouting*, and to the sound of the *trumpet.*

Timbrel, harp, psaltery (v. 2).—These are the *toph*, *kinnor*, and *nebhel*, for an explanation of which see Rem. on Ex. xv. 20; Gen. iv. 21; and I Sam. x. 5.

Blow up the trumpet (v. 3).—This is the *shophar* (vid. Rem. on Ex. xix. 16 *supra*). In verse 7 *selah* occurs, probably meaning *halleluyah.* In Psalm lxxxii, *selah* is found in verse 2, probably in the sense of *silence.* In the same sense also it occurs in Psalm lxxxiii. 8. In the title of Psalm lxxxiv, *gittith* is found, meaning probably *instruments of music* (vid. Rem. on Ps. viii. *supra*). In verses 4 and 8 *selah* occurs, probably in the sense of *halleluyah.* In Psalm lxxxv, verse 2, *selah* is found in the sense of *halleluyah.*

Psalm lxxxvii. 1–7.

A Psalm or Song for the Sons of Korah.

1 His foundation *is* in the holy mountains.
2 The Lord loveth the gates of Zion
More than all the dwellings of Jacob.
3 Glorious things are spoken of thee, O city of God.
Selah.
4 I will make mention of Rahab and Babylon to them
that know me:

Behold Philistia, and Tyre, with Æthiopia;
This *man* was born there.
5 And of Zion it shall be said, This and that man was
born in her,
And the Highest himself shall establish her.
6 The Lord shall count, when he writeth up the people,
That this *man* was born there. Selah.
7 As well the singers as the players on instruments *shall
be there:*
All my springs *are* in thee.

This Psalm seems to have been composed in commemoration of the fact, that Hezekiah had been delivered from the power of the Assyrians.

Singers — players on instruments (verse 7.) — The term translated *singers* is *shạrim*, the usual term employed. The word translated *players on instruments*, is the plural of *hạhlil* (חָלִיל), meaning *pipers*. This refers probably to the Hebrew flute, for a full explanation of which see Rem. on I Sam. x. 5, and I Kings i. 40. Alexander correctly translates the verse thus: "*And singers as well as players* (shall be heard saying), *All my springs are in thee.*" The poet seems to have had a vision of the nations, preceded by musicians, moving in solemn procession to Mount Zion. The reference is to vocal and instrumental music in praise of Jehovah. *Selah* is found in verses 3 and 6, probably in the sense of *halleluyah*. They are also, doubtless, intended to mark the divisions of the poem.

Psalm lxxxviii. 1-18.

A Song or Psalm for the Sons of Korah, to the Chief Musician upon Mahhalath Leannoth, Maschil of Heman the Ezrahite.

1 O Lord God of my salvation,
I have cried day *and* night before thee:
2 Let my prayer come before thee;

Incline thine ear unto my cry;
3 For my soul is full of troubles:
And my life draweth nigh unto the grave.
4 I am counted with them that go down into the pit:
I am as a man *that hath* no strength:
5 Free among the dead like the slain that lie in the grave,
Whom thou rememberest no more:
And they are cut off from thy hand.
6 Thou hast laid me in the lowest pit,
In darkness, in the deeps.
7 Thy wrath lieth hard upon me,
And thou hast afflicted *me* with all thy waves. Selah.
8 Thou hast put away mine acquaintance far from me;
Thou hast made me an abomination unto them:
I am shut up, and I cannot come forth.
9 Mine eye mourneth by reason of affliction:
Lord, I have called daily upon thee,
I have stretched out my hands unto thee.
10 Wilt thou show wonders to the dead?
Shall the dead arise *and* praise thee? Selah.
11 Shall thy loving-kindness be declared in the grave?
Or thy faithfulness in destruction?
12 Shall thy wonders be known in the dark?
And thy righteousness in the land of forgetfulness?
13 But unto thee have I cried, O Lord;
And in the morning shall my prayer prevent thee.
14 Lord, why castest thou off my soul?
Why hidest thou thy face from me?
15 I *am* afflicted and ready to die from *my* youth up:
While I suffer thy terrors I am distracted.
16 Thy fierce wrath goeth over me;
Thy terrors have cut me off.
17 They came round about me daily like water;
They compassed me about together.

18 Lover and friend hast thou put far from me,
And mine acquaintance into darkness.

This Psalm is a mournful lamentation, and probably constitutes, with Psalm lxxxix, really one poem. The first part is plaintive, and the last joyous. The long title of Psalm lxxxviii, is probably intended for both compositions. It is ascribed to Heman. He was one of David's chief singers, as appears from I Chron. xv. 19. He is called, in the title, the Ezrahite, and in I Chron. vi. 33–38 a Kohathite. He was also probably a Korahite, as the former were reckoned in the line of Korah (I Chron. vi. 22, 37, 38). Heman, then, must have been a descendant of some person by the name of Ezra, who was a descendant of Korah. It is generally believed that Psalm lxxxviii, was written by Heman, as its title indicates; but some have doubts upon the subject. *Mahhălath lĕannoth* (לְעַנּוֹת מַחֲלַת) in the title, mean *sickness*, to *afflict—afflictive sickness*. The term is generally believed to refer to music. *Mahhalath* probably means *lute* or *guitar*. Thus the whole expression would be *mournful lute*, referring to the character of the Psalm (vid. Rem. on Ps. liii, *supra*). *Selah* in the sense of *silence*, occurs in verses 7 and 10.

PSALM lxxxix. 1–27.

Maschil of Ethan the Ezrahite.

1 I will sing the mercies of the Lord forever:
With my mouth will I make known thy faithfulness to all generations.
2 For I have said, Mercy shall be built up forever:
Thy faithfulness shalt thou establish in the very heavens.
3 I have made a covenant with my chosen,
I have sworn unto David my servant.
4 Thy seed will I establish forever,

And build up thy throne to all generations. Selah.

5 And the heavens shall praise thy wonders, O Lord:
Thy faithfulness also in the congregation of the saints.

6 For who in the heavens can be compared unto the Lord?
Who among the sons of the mighty can be likened unto the Lord?

7 God is greatly to be feared in the assembly of the saints.
And to be had in reverence of all *them that are* about him.

8 O Lord God of hosts, who *is* a strong Lord like unto thee?
Or to thy faithfulness round about thee?

9 Thou rulest the raging of the sea:
When the waves thereof arise, thou stillest them.

10 Thou hast broken Rahab in pieces, as one that is slain;
Thou hast scattered thine enemies with thy strong arm.

11 The heavens *are* thine, the earth also *is* thine:
As for the world and the fullness thereof, thou hast founded them.

12 The north and the south thou hast created them:
Tabor and Hermon shall rejoice in thy name.

13 Thou hast a mighty arm:
Strong is thy hand, *and* high is thy right hand.

14 Justice and judgment *are* the habitation of thy throne:
Mercy and truth shall go before thy face.

15 Blessed *is* the people that know the joyful sound:
They shall walk, O Lord, in the light of thy countenance.

16 In thy name shall they rejoice all the day:
And in thy righteousness shall they be exalted.

17 For thou *art* the glory of their strength:
And in thy favor our horn shall be exalted.

18 For the Lord is our defence;
And the Holy One of Israel is our King.
19 Then thou spakest in vision to thy holy one, and saidst,
'I have laid help upon *one that is* mighty;
I have exalted *one* chosen out of the people.
20 I have found David my servant;
With my holy oil have I anointed him:
21 With whom my hand shall be established:
Mine arm also shall strengthen him.
22 The enemy shall not exact upon him;
Nor the son of wickedness afflict him.
23 And I will beat down his foes before his face,
And plague them that hate him.
24 But my faithfulness and my mercy *shall be* with him:
And in my name shall his horn be exalted.
25 I will set his hand also in the sea,
And his right hand in the rivers.
26 He shall cry unto me, Thou *art* my Father,
My God, and the rock of my salvation.
27 Also I will make him *my* first-born,
Higher than the kings of the earth.

This Psalm seems to be a continuation of the eighty-eighth. It is of a cheerful character, referring to blessed promises. The name of Ethan is inserted in the title as the author. He was an Ezrahite (I Kings iv. 31; I Chron. ii. 6), and a leader in the temple music. The word *sing* occurs in the first verse, in the usual sense. *Selah* is found in verses 4 and 37, in the sense of *silence*, and in verses 45 and 48 in the sense of *halleluyah.*

PSALM xcii. 1–15.

A Psalm or Song for the Sabbath Day.

1 *It is a* good *thing* to give thanks unto the Lord,
And to sing praises unto thy name, O most High:

2 To show forth thy loving-kindness in the morning,
And thy faithfulness every night,
3 Upon an instrument of ten strings, and upon the psaltery;
Upon the harp with a solemn sound.
4 For thou, Lord, hast made me glad through thy work:
I will triumph in the works of thy hands.
5 O Lord how great are thy works!
And thy thoughts are very deep.
6 A brutish man knoweth not,
Neither doth a fool understand this
7 When the wicked spring as the grass,
And when all the workers of iniquity do flourish;
It is that they shall be destroyed forever.
8 But thou, Lord, *art most* high for evermore.
9 For lo, thine enemies, O Lord,
For lo, thine enemies shall perish;
All the workers of iniquity shall be scattered.
10 But my horn shalt thou exalt like the *horn of* an unicorn:
I shall be anointed with fresh oil.
11 Mine eyes also shall see *my desire* on mine enemies,
And mine ears shall hear *my desire* of the wicked that rise up against me.
12 The righteous shall flourish like the palm-tree:
He shall grow like a cedar in Lebanon.
13 Those that be planted in the house of the Lord
Shall flourish in the courts of our God.
14 They shall still bring forth fruit in old age;
They shall be fat and flourishing;
15 To show that the Lord *is* upright:
He is my Rock, and *there is* no unrighteousness in him.

This is a Psalm of praise in commemoration of the wisdom and power of God, manifested in his dealings with both the righteous and wicked. The last part of the title informs us that the psalm was intended *for the Sabbath.* *Sing* occurs in the first verse. The original is a derivative of *zamar*, meaning *to prune*, and in the Peal conjugation, *to sing*, or *make music.* Alexander translates it *to make music* (vid. Rem. on Ps. xxxiii. 2, *supra*).

Instrument of ten strings (v. 3).—The Hebrew (עָשׂוֹר *asor*), signifies *ten, a decade.* It doubtless here refers to an instrument of music, and seems to indicate one of ten strings. The Septuagint unites the psaltery with this word, and translates the two, *ten-stringed psaltery.* But the two words are separated in the Hebrew, each having a preposition before it, and obviously referring to different instruments (vid. Rem. on Ps. xxxiii. 2, *supra*).

Psaltery (v. 3).—This is the *nebhel* (vid. Rem. on I Sam. x. 5; II Sam. vi. 5).

Harp (v. 3).—This is the *kinnor* (in the Septuagint, *cithara,* vid. Rem. on Gen. iv. 21).

In Psalm xcv. 1, general expressions of joy and triumph appear. In Psalm xcvi. 1 and 2, occur several expressions of exultation.

Psalm xcviii. 1–9.

A Psalm.

1 O Sing unto the Lord a new song;
For he hath done marvellous things:
His right hand, and his holy arm,
Hath gotten him the victory.
2 The Lord hath made known his salvation:
His righteousness hath he openly showed in the sight of the heathen.

3 He hath remembered his mercy and his truth toward the house of Israel:
All the ends of the earth have seen the salvation of our God.
4 Make a joyful noise unto the Lord, all the earth;
Make a loud noise, and rejoice, and sing praise.
5 Sing unto the Lord with the harp;
With the harp, and the voice of a psalm.
6 With trumpets and sound of cornet,
Make a joyful noise before the Lord, the King.
7 Let the sea roar, and the fullness thereof;
The world, and they that dwell therein.
8 Let the floods clap *their* hands;
Let the hills be joyful together
9 Before the Lord;
For he cometh to judge the earth:
With righteousness shall he judge the world,
And the people with equity.

This Psalm is filled with expressions of praise to God. Its title is simply *mizmor*, meaning *song* or *poem*. This word occurs in the titles of several psalms; but in no other does it compose the whole title. In verses 1, 4, and 5, general expressions of praise and triumph, with an allusion to song, occur. In verse 5, the *kinnor*, translated *harp*, is twice found (vid. Rem. on Gen. iv. 21, *supra*).

Trumpets (v. 6).—These were *hătsotseras*, or straight trumpets (vid. Rem. on Num. x. 2; II Chron. vii. 6).

Cornet (v. 6).—This is the *shophar* or *crooked trumpet*. The cornet was a wind instrument; but we know of no good reason why the *crooked trumpet* should be thus designated. The Septuagint has σαλπιγγος κερατινης, *salpinggos keratines*, meaning a trumpet made of horn (vid. Rem. on Ex. xix. 16; Lev. xxv. 9).

In Psalms c. 2; ci. 1; cv. 2; cvi. 12, there is a general reference to singing as employed in praising God. In Psalm cviii. 1, 3, a similar reference to vocal music occurs. In verse 2, the *nebhel* and *kinnor* are translated *psaltery* and *harp;* see remarks on I Sam. x. 5; II Sam. vi. 5; Gen. iv. 21. In Psalm cxviii. 14, *song* occurs. A derivative of *zamar* is used (vid. Rem. on Ex. xv. 2).

Psalm cxix.1-8; 169-176.

ALEPH.

1 Blessed *are* the undefiled in the way,
Who walk in the law of the Lord.
2 Blessed *are* they that keep his testimonies,
And that seek him with the whole heart.
3 They also do no iniquity:
They walk in his ways.
4 Thou hast commanded *us*
To keep thy precepts diligently.
5 O that my ways were directed
To keep thy statutes!
6 Then shall I not be ashamed
When I have respect unto all thy commandments.
7 I will praise thee with uprightness of heart,
When I shall have learned thy righteous judgments.
8 I will keep thy statutes:
O forsake me not utterly.

TAU.

169 Let my cry come near before thee, O Lord:
Give me understanding according to thy word.
170 Let my supplication come before thee:
Deliver me according to thy word.
171 My lips shall utter praise,
When thou hast taught me thy statutes.

172 My tongue shall speak of thy word:
For all thy commandments *are* righteousness.
173 Let thine hand help me;
For I have chosen thy precepts.
174 I have longed for thy salvation, O Lord:
And thy law *is* my delight.
175 Let my soul live, and it shall praise thee;
And let thy judgments help me.
176 I have gone astray like a lost sheep;
Seek thy servant; for I do not forget thy commandments.

Various opinions exist in respect to the object of this remarkable Psalm; but the most probable supposition is that it was intended as a manual of instruction for youth after the return of the Israelites from their exile. It is the most perfect specimen of an alphabetical psalm which we have; being divided into twenty-two paragraphs, corresponding with the letters of the Hebrew alphabet, and each paragraph consists of eight verses, all beginning with the same Hebrew letter (vid. Rem. on Ps. xxv, *supra*). In verse 54 there is a reference to vocal music.

Psalm cxx. 1–7.

A Psalm of Degrees.

1 In my distress I cried unto the Lord,
And he heard me.
2 Deliver my soul, O Lord,
From lying lips, *and* from a deceitful tongue.
3 What shall be given unto thee?
Or what shall be done unto thee, thou false tongue?
4 Sharp arrows of the mighty,
With coals of juniper.

5 Woe is me, that I sojourn in Mesech,
That I dwell in the tents of Kedar?
6 My soul hath long dwelt with him that hateth peace.
7 I *am for* peace: but when I speak, they *are* for war.

This and the fourteen following Psalms are designated in the titles as *Songs of Degrees*. The Hebrew term is שִׁיר הַמַּעֲלוֹת *shîr hămmuᵃhloth*, literally *song of the steps*, translated in our English version *song of degrees*. The LXX translate the term by ᾠδὴ τῶν ἀναβαθμῶν, *ode of the steps*, and the Vulgate has *carmen graduum*, *song of the steps*. In accordance with this idea the ancient Jewish writers supposed that these Psalms were sung on fifteen stairs of the temple, leading from the court of Israel to the court of the women (vid. Mishna Sucah, cap. v. 4). But that explanation is not now received among critics as satisfactory. Luther translated the term *a song in the higher choir*, supposing that the poem was sung either in an elevated position, or with a loud voice. Tholuck takes the same view. Gesenius thinks that it indicates a certain number or rhythm, by which the sense ascends as it were by degrees or steps. De Wette and Winer take the same view (De Wette Einl. in das A. T. p. 289). But this characteristic is not obvious in all of this species of poetry. The most probable explanation is that of Ewald, Herder, and others, who suppose that the expression means *song of the ascents*, or *pilgrim song*, sung during the journeyings of the Israelites to Jerusalem, either from Babylon, or as they repaired to that city statedly to attend their national solemnities. Jerusalem, and especially the temple, were elevated and, going up to them was called *an ascent* (vid. Ez. vii. 9; xxxiv. 24; 1 Kings xii. 27, 28).

In Ps. cxxvi. 2, *singing* occurs. The original is a derivative of *ranan*, signifying to *sing aloud*, to *shout* (vid. Rem. on Lev. ix. 24). In Ps. cxxxii. 9, 16, *shout* is employed. In both cases a derivative of *ranan* is found in the original. In Ps. cxxxv. 2, the term *sing* occurs. The original word is a derivative of *zamar*, to *prune*, in Peal conjugation, *to sing* (vid. Rem. on Ex. xv. 2).

Psalm cxxxvi. 1–26.

1 O give thanks unto the Lord: for *he is* good:
For his mercy *endureth* forever.
2 O give thanks unto the God of gods:
For his mercy *endureth* forever.
3 O give thanks to the Lord of lords:
For his mercy *endureth* forever.
4 To him who alone doeth great wonders:
For his mercy *endureth* forever.
5 To him that by wisdom made the heavens:
For his mercy *endureth* forever.
6 To him that stretched out the earth above the waters:
For his mercy *endureth* forever.
7 To him that made great lights:
For his mercy *endureth* forever:
8 The sun to rule by day:
For his mercy *endureth* forever:
9 The moon and stars to rule by night:
For his mercy *endureth* forever:
10 To him that smote Egypt in their first-born:
For his mercy *endureth* forever:
11 And brought out Israel from among them:
For his mercy *endureth* forever:
12 With a strong hand, and with a stretched-out arm:
For his mercy *endureth* forever.
13 To him which divided the Red Sea into parts:
For his mercy *endureth* forever:
14 And made Israel to pass through the midst of it:
For his mercy *endureth* forever:

15 But overthrew Pharaoh and his host in the Red Sea:
For his mercy *endureth* forever:
16 To him which led his people through the wilderness:
For his mercy *endureth* forever.
17 To him which smote great kings:
For his mercy *endureth* forever:
18 And slew famous kings:
For his mercy *endureth* forever:
19 Sihon king of the Amorites:
For his mercy *endureth* forever:
20 And Og the king of Bashan:
For his mercy *endureth* forever:
21 And gave their land for an heritage:
For his mercy *endureth* forever:
22 *Even* an heritage unto Israel his servant:
For his mercy *endureth* forever.
23 Who remembered us in our low estate:
For his mercy *endureth* forever:
24 And hath redeemed us from our enemies:
For his mercy *endureth* forever.
25 Who giveth food to all flesh:
For his mercy *endureth* forever.
26 O give thanks unto the God of heaven:
For his mercy *endureth* forever.

This Psalm is remarkable from the fact that a *burden* or *refrain*, as it is called, occurs regularly at the end of every verse. Some biblical critics suppose that alternate or responsive choirs are indicated by it. Others think that the singers sometimes answered their own questions, and others still, that the people united in a kind of chorus. The latter is probably the correct view. The choir repeated the first part of the verse, and then the multitude joined in a chorus, and repeated the latter part of each verse.

Psalm cxxxvii. 1–9.

We give Herder's translation:

THE CAPTIVITY IN BABYLON.

1 By the rivers of Babylon we sat down,
And wept, when we remembered Zion.
2 We hanged our harps upon their willows.
3 For they, that held us in captivity,
Required of us a song,
Our oppressors required of us mirth.
"Sing us one of the songs of Zion."
4 How shall we sing Jehovah's song
In a foreign land!
5 If I forget thee, O Jerusalem!
Let my right hand forget me,
Let my tongue cleave to the roof of my mouth.
6 If I do not remember thee,
If I prefer not Jerusalem
Above my highest joy.
7 Remember, O Lord, the children of Edom.
In the day of Jerusalem's affliction,
When they cried "Raze it,
Raze it, even to its foundation."
8 Daughter of Babylon, the desolate,
Blessed be he that requiteth thee,
That requiteth thee, as thou hast done to us.
9 Happy shall he be that seizeth thy little ones,
And casteth them upon the rocks.

This is a beautiful Psalm of the plaintive kind. It refers directly to the captivity of the Hebrews in Babylonia. As they thought of their religious privileges in Palestine, they could not be cheerful. They could not sing the songs of Zion, nor play upon their instruments of music. They hung their harps upon the willows. Here seems to be a difficulty, as history informs us that no willows grow in Babylonia. We must then suppose that the language is figurative, and merely indicates that the Jews could neither sing, nor play on instruments. The willow tree usually grows on the banks of rivers, hence that particular tree is mentioned. This is a beautiful and pathetic elegy, flowing in the most tender and mournful strains.

Harps (v. 2).—These were *kinnors*, probably somewhat similar to *harps* at this day, for, at the time of the Babylonish captivity, when this Psalm is supposed to have been written, that instrument had been much improved. Its number of strings had been multiplied from three to an indefinite number. More than 500 years earlier, during the reign of David in Jerusalem, the harp had reached a high state of improvement, and, in the hands of that monarch, chanted forth elevated strains of music (vid. Rem. on Gen. iv. 21).

In verses 2 and 3, *sing* and *song* are used, but are derivatives of the usual term (*shīr*).

In Psalm cxxxviii. 1 and 5, *sing* occurs. In verse 1, a derivative of *zạmar* is used, meaning *to sing with vociferation, to shout.* In verse 5, a derivative of the usual term (*shīr*) is employed. In Psalm cxl. 3, 5, and 8, *selah* occurs, probably in the sense of *silence.* In Psalm cxliii. 6, *selah* occurs, probably in the sense of *halleluyah.*

PSALM cxliv. 1–15.

A Psalm of David.

1 Blessed *be* the Lord my strength,
Which teacheth my hands to war,
And my fingers to fight;
2 My goodness, and my fortress;
My high tower, and my deliverer;
My shield, and *he* in whom I trust;
Who subdueth my people under me.

3 Lord, what *is* man, that thou takest knowledge of him?
Or the son of man, that thou makest account of him?
4 Man is like to vanity:
His days *are* as a shadow that passeth away.
5 Bow thy heavens, O Lord, and come down:
Touch the mountains, and they shall smoke.
6 Cast forth lightning, and scatter them:
Shoot out thine arrows, and destroy them.
7 Send thine hand from above;
Rid me, and deliver me out of great waters.
From the hand of strange children;
8 Whose mouth speaketh vanity,
And their right hand *is* a right hand of falsehood.
9 I will sing a new song unto thee, O God:
Upon a psaltery *and* an instrument of ten strings
Will I sing praises unto thee.
10 *It is he* that giveth salvation unto kings,
Who delivereth David his servant from the hurtful sword.
11 Rid me, and deliver me from the hand of strange children,
Whose mouth speaketh vanity.
And their right hand *is* a right hand of falsehood:
12 That our sons *may be* as plants grown up in their youth;
That our daughters *may be* as corner-stones,
Polished *after* the similitude of a palace:
13 *That* our garners *may be* full,
Affording all manner of store;
That our sheep may bring forth thousands
And ten thousands in our streets:
14 *That* our oxen *may be* strong to labor;

That there be no breaking in, nor going out:
That *there be* no complaining in our streets.
15 Happy *is that* people that is in such a case;
Yea, happy *is that* people whose God *is* the Lord.

In verse 9, the Psalmist, in exultation, declares that he will *sing a new song* to the Lord his deliverer, upon the *psaltery* and *an instrument of ten strings*. *Shîr* is the original, translated *song*, and a derivative of the same is translated *sing*, in the same verse. The expression, *a new song*, indicates, probably, a new occasion for singing praises to God.

Upon the psaltery and an instrument of ten strings will I sing praises unto thee.—Prof. Alexander translates the passage thus: *With a lyre of ten* (strings) *I will play* (or *make music*) *to thee.* This is certainly the literal meaning of the original, and we perceive no good reason why *a̤sor* (עָשׂוֹר) translated in our English version, *an instrument of ten strings*, should not be referred to the *ne̱bhel* (נֵבֶל) rendered *psaltery*. Gesenius and other eminent scholars take the same view. We should prefer to translate *ne̱bhel* by *guitar* rather than *lyre* (vid. Rem. on I Sam. x. 5). This instrument in very early times had five, and subsequently ten and twelve, strings. The last verb in the verse is from *za̤mar*, which signifies *to shout*, *to make a tremulous vociferation* or *sound*, and may refer to the voice, or to a musical instrument. The same Hebrew word is used in Psalm cxlvi. 2, translated *sing*, and indicates the exultation by which the Psalmist would praise Jehovah.

In Psalm cxlvii. 1, 7, *za̤mar* is translated *sing* once in each verse.

In the first part of verse 7 the original for *sing* is *'nṳ* (עֱנוּ) and indicates a *shout*, or *song of triumph* (vid. Rem. on Ex. xxxii. 18).

Harp (v. 7).—This is the *kinnor* (vid. Rem. on Gen. iv. 21).

Psalm cxlix. 1–9.

1 Praise ye the Lord.
Sing unto the Lord a new song,
And his praise in the congregation of saints.
2 Let Israel rejoice in him that made him;
Let the children of Zion be joyful in their King.
3 Let them praise his name in the dance:
Let them sing praises unto him with the timbrel and harp.
4 For the Lord taketh pleasure in his people:
He will beautify the meek with salvation.
5 Let the saints be joyful in glory:
Let them sing aloud upon their beds.
6 *Let* the high *praises* of God *be* in their mouth,
And a two-edged sword in their hand;
7 To execute vengeance upon the heathen,
And punishments upon the people;
8 To bind their kings with chains,
And their nobles with fetters of iron;
9 To execute upon them the judgment written:
This honor have all his saints.
Praise ye the Lord.

This Psalm is full of expressions of triumph and praise to God, in view of the fact that Jerusalem and the Jewish nation, under the administration of Nehemiah, had been fortified and made secure from the attacks of their foes.

Song (v. 1).—*Shîr* is here used. The *verb* also appears in the first part of the verse. *Dance* (v. 3), a derivative of *hhụl* (חוּל), the usual term, is employed (vid. Rem. on Ex. xv. 20). *Sing* (v. 3), properly *play* in this place, as the term (a derivative of *zạmar*) relates to the performance on the *toph* and *kinnor*, mentioned in immediate connection. The *toph* is a percussion instrument, sometimes called *tabret*, *tabor*, and *tambou-*

rine (vid. Rem. on Gen. xxxi. 27). The *kinnor* is our *harp* (vid. Rem. on Gen. iv. 21).

Psalm cl. 1–6.

1 Praise ye the Lord.
Praise God in his sanctuary:
Praise him in the firmament of his power.
2 Praise him for his mighty acts:
Praise him according to his excellent greatness.
3 Praise him with the sound of the trumpet:
Praise him with the psaltery and harp.
4 Praise him with the timbrel and dance:
Praise him with stringed instruments and organs.
5 Praise him upon the loud cymbals:
Praise him upon the high-sounding cymbals.
6 Let everything that hath breath praise the Lord.
Praise ye the Lord.

This brief poem contains a remarkably simple, yet pathetic and sublime burst of triumphant praise to Jehovah. It is a kind of halleluyah psalm or doxology, elegantly closing the beautiful melodies of the book.

Sound of the trumpet.—This is the *shophar*, or crooked trumpet. The phrase might be rendered *blast of the trumpet.* The original of *blast* is a derivative of *taqa* (תָּקַע). By this peculiar sound, the Israelites were called together on important occasions, and but one blast was given. The Psalmist, by a bold personification, would seem to indicate that one tremendous blast was to be made to call all animate and inanimate nature together, for the purpose of uttering the praises of Almighty God.

Psaltery and harp (v. 3.)—These are the *nebhel* (*guitar*) and *kinnor.*

Timbrel (v. 4).—This is the *toph*, a pulsatile instrument (vid. Rem. on Gen. xxxi. 27).

Dance (v. 4).—For this the same Hebrew word is employed as in Psalm cxlix. 3 (ibid).

Stringed instruments (v. 4).—Literally *strings.* The Hebrew term is מִנִּים (*minnim*), from מֵן (*men*), meaning a *part* or *portion*, and in the plural *strings*, evidently indicating all kinds of stringed instruments (vid. Rem. on Gen. iv. 21; Job xxx. 9; Ps. iv. title). The Septuagint has χορδαις (*chordais*), *chords*, *strings.*

Organs (v. 4).—It should be *organ* or *pipe*, as the original *ugabh* is in the singular number (vid. Rem. on Gen. iv. 21).

Loud Cymbals (v. 5).—These were pulsatile instruments. The Hebrew term is צִלְצְלֵי (*tsiltseley*), meaning literally *cymbals of sound*, probably referring to the smaller instrument of this kind (vid. Rem. on II Sam. vi. 5).

High-sounding cymbals (v. 5).—The same word for cymbals is used in the original as in the first part of the verse. The term translated *high-sounding* is תְרוּעָה (*t'ruah*), and signifies *a loud noise*, *a tumult*, indicating that these cymbals were the larger kind, as explained in our remarks on II Sam. vi. 5. The three classes of musical instruments—wind, stringed, and pulsatile—are here mentioned. The writer undoubtedly intended to include all kinds of musical instruments of every description. He finally closes the poem by calling upon everything that hath breath to praise the Lord, thus elegantly completing this admirable collection of the songs of Zion.

The Septuagint contains another psalm numbered cli. Dr. A. Clarke's translation of it is the following:

Psalm cli. 1–8.

"*A Psalm, in the hand-writing of David, beyond the number of the Psalms, composed by David, when he fought in single combat with Goliath.*"

1 I was the least among my brethren,
And the youngest in my father's house;

And I kept also my father's sheep.
2 My hands made the organ,
And my fingers jointed the psaltery.
3 And who told it to my Lord?
(*Arab.* And who is he who taught me?)
The Lord himself, he is my Master,
And the hearer of all that call upon him.
4 He sent his angel and took me away from my father's sheep:
And anointed me with the oil of his anointing.
5 My brethren were taller and more beautiful than I:
Nevertheless the Lord delighted not in them.
6 I went out to meet the Philistine,
And he cursed me by his idols.
7 (In the strength of the Lord I cast three stones at him.
I smote him in the forehead, and felled him to the earth. *Arab.*)
8 And I drew out his own sword from its sheath, and cut off his head,
And took away the reproach from the children of Israel.

This Psalm is found in the Syriac, Arabic, and Æthiopic versions of the scriptures. David's contest with Goliath is the subject of the poem. It is evidently very ancient, as it is found in the Codex Alexandrinus, which is a production of the sixth century. It has never been inserted, however, in the Hebrew scriptures, and has been invariably rejected by the Fathers. Furthermore, it is not written in the style of David, though ascribed to him, and is evidently spurious. Every Council held in the Christian church has rejected it, and scholars almost universally consider it as of little account. There is an allusion to music in the second verse. *Organ* and *psaltery* occur. *Οργανον organon*, and *ψαλτηριον psalterion*, are the original words, indicating, doubtless, the *ṳgabh* or organ, and *ne̮bhel* or guitar.

THE BOOK OF PROVERBS.

INTRODUCTORY REMARKS.

THIS book is ascribed to Solomon. Probably he did not compose the whole of it, but collected a portion from different sources. All, after the beginning of the twenty-fifth chapter, we are informed, was added by order of King Hezekiah. It is generally believed by biblical scholars, that the collection, as we now have it, was arranged by different persons; but mostly composed and arranged by Solomon. There are numerous quotations from the book in the New Testament, thus clearly establishing its canonicity. This kind of composition is very ancient, and adapted to the rudest state of society. The inhabitants of Palestine and other oriental nations were accustomed to utter aphorisms, or brief, sententious sayings. Subsequently metaphors and other embellishments of style were employed. The teachers of religion, in many cases, rather commanded than reasoned. Bishop Lowth mentions three characteristics of the proverbial style, viz: brevity, obscurity, and elegance. The first is obviously striking, and universal in this kind of writing. It is apparent from the etymology of the word *proverbia*, meaning *for words*, i. e., one word for many. *Obscurity* is a characteristic of some proverbs, but is not universal in that kind of composition. *Elegance* of diction is sometimes found, though it is by no means universal. Another striking characteristic of proverbial writings is *concentration of thought—point.* This is found probably in every proverb, and sometimes takes the antithetic form. The brevity, pointed character, and boldness of this species of composition, make it a very favorable medium for conveying thought.

The object of the Book of Proverbs is to instruct mankind in the principles of true wisdom, which is the knowledge and fear of the Lord. It contains an immense variety of choice sayings, embracing various principles of morality, doctrine, and practical considerations in respect to our duties to God, our fellow-men, and ourselves.

Bishop Lowth considers this book as didactic poetry. It abounds with that remarkable characteristic of Hebrew poetry, parallelism, consisting in a resemblance as to thought or form, or both, between the members of a period. Lowth divides the parallelism of Proverbs into *synonymous*, or that in which there are but two members, the latter repeating the idea contained in the former; and *antithetic*, or that in which the last member is an antithetic expression commencing with *but*. An instance of the first kind is found in Prov. ii. 1–5:

"My son, if thou wilt receive my words,
And hide my commandments with thee;
So that thou incline thine ear to wisdom,
And apply thy heart to understanding;
Yea, if thou criest after knowledge,
And liftest up thy voice for understanding;
If thou seekest her as silver,
And searchest for her as for hid treasures;
Then shalt thou understand the fear of the Lord,
And find the knowledge of God."

An instance of the second kind is found in Prov. x. 27–29:

"The fear of the Lord prolongeth days;
But the years of the wicked shall be shortened.
The hope of the righteous shall be gladness;

But the expectation of the wicked shall perish.
The way of the Lord is strength to the upright;
But destruction shall be to the workers of iniquity."

The first nine chapters of Proverbs are very different from the other parts of the book, and seem to be a kind of proem, or exordium, containing a continuous discourse, and are supposed to have been committed to writing, while the more disconnected aphorisms of the other parts were merely uttered verbally. The first part of the book abounds with beautiful figures and illustrations, and ranks with the highest style of poetry. The personification of wisdom is truly elegant, and is one of the finest specimens of Prosopopeia to be found in the scriptures. From chapter x. to xxii. 17, the style is entirely different. That part of the poem consists of pointed, but disconnected, aphorisms of a varied character. From chapter xxii. 17, to chapter xxv. the style is more ornate, though not so elegant as in the exordium. The remainder of the book consists of detached maxims, with the exception of the thirtieth and thirty-first chapters, which are ascribed to Agur and the mother of king Lemuel. The thirtieth chapter consists principally of enigmas. This species of poetry is frequent in the scriptures.* These sayings are supposed to have been composed about 1000 years B. C.

There are but few allusions to music in the book. In Prov. xi. 10, *shouting* occurs, referring to the destruction of the wicked. The original is a derivative of *ranan*, indicating a tremulous, exciting sound.

Singeth songs (xxv. 20).—The usual terms are here employed. In Prov. xxix. 6, a derivative of *ranan* is employed, and translated *sing*, denoting the triumph of the righteous.

* Vid. Judges xiv. 12-18; Ezra xvii. in which the king of Babylon is compared to an eagle; Jer. xiii. 1-11; xviii. 1-6; xxiv. 1-10.

THE BOOK OF ECCLESIASTES.

INTRODUCTORY REMARKS.

THE name of this book in Hebrew is *Qoheleth* (קֹהֶלֶת) which is generally considered as an epithet of Solomon. It is translated in the Septuagint by Ἐκκλησιαστής (*Ekklesiastes*), which is the term employed in our English Bible, and signifies a *preacher*, or one who addresses a public assembly. The book is a kind of philosophical treatise, and was evidently composed by Solomon, though it does not bear his name (cf. Eccl. i. 12, 16; xi. 4–9; xii. 9, 10). That monarch probably found that the Hebrew language was not sufficient to express his ideas, and made use, to some extent, of the popular Chaldaic dialect. Solomon seems to have prepared this composition in his old age, after having tried the pleasures, honors, and riches of the world, and become thoroughly convinced that nothing but true piety was really valuable. Ecclesiastes is classed by Bishop Lowth among the didactic poems of the Hebrews. He afterwards, however, assents to the view of Des Voeux, who considers it as a philosophical discourse interspersed with poetry.

The book possesses, in a small degree, the characteristics of poetry, and partakes of the conversational style. The following is a synopsis of it, by G. Holden.

PART I. THE VANITY OF ALL EARTHLY CONDITIONS, OCCUPATIONS, AND PLEASURES.

SECT. I. The vanity of all earthly things (i. 2).

SECT. II. The unprofitableness of human labor, and the transitoriness of human life (i. 3–11).

SECT. III. The vanity of laborious inquiries into the ways and works of man (i. 12–18).

SECT. IV. Luxury and pleasure are only vanity and vexation of spirit (ii. 1–11).

SECT. V. Though the wise excel fools, yet, as death happens to them both, human learning is but vanity (ii. 12–17).

SECT. VI. The vanity of human labor, in leaving it they know not to whom (ii. 18–23).

SECT. VII. The emptiness of sensual enjoyments (ii. 24–26).

SECT. VIII. Though there is a proper time for the execution of all human purposes, yet are they useless and vain; the divine counsels, however, are immutable (iii. 1–14).

SECT. IX. The vanity of human pursuits proved from the wickedness prevailing in courts of justice, contrasted with the righteous judgment of God (iii. 15–17).

SECT. X. Though life, considered in itself, is vanity, for men die as well as beasts, yet in the end it will be very different with the spirit of man and that of beasts (iii. 18–22).

SECT. XI. Vanity is increased unto men by oppression (iv. 1–3).

SECT. XII. The vanity of prosperity (iv. 4).

SECT. XIII. The vanity of folly, or of preferring the world to True Wisdom (iv. 5, 6).

SECT. XIV. The vanity of covetousness (iv. 7, 8).

SECT. XV. Though society has its advantages, yet dominion and empire are but vanity (iv. 9–16).

SECT. XVI. Errors in the performance of divine worship, which render it vain and unprofitable (v. 1–7).

SECT. XVII. The vanity of murmuring at injustice;

for, though the oppression of the poor and the perversion of judgment greatly prevail, they do not escape the notice of the Almighty (v. 8, 9).

SECT. XVIII. The vanity of riches; with an admonition as to the moderate enjoyment of them (v. 10–20).

SECT. XIX. The vanity of avarice (vi. 1–9).

PART II. THE NATURE, EXCELLENCE, AND BENEFICIAL EFFECTS OF WISDOM OR RELIGION.

SECT. XX. Since all human designs, labors, and enjoyments are vain, it is natural to inquire, What is good for man? What is his supreme good? (vi. 10–12). The answer is contained in the remainder of the book.

SECT. XXI. The praise of character and reputation (vii. 1).

SECT. XXII. Affliction improves the heart, and exalts the character of the wise (vii. 2–10).

SECT. XXIII. The excellence of Wisdom (vii. 11–14).

SECT. XXIV. An objection, with the answer (vii. 15; viii. 7).

SECT. XXV. The evil of wickedness shows the advantage of True Wisdom (viii. 8–13).

SECT. XXVI. An objection, with the answer (viii. 14; ix. 1).

SECT. XXVII. An objection, with the answer (ix. 2; x. 17).

SECT. XXVIII. The banefulness of sloth (x. 18).

SECT. XXIX. The power of wealth (x. 19).

SECT. XXX. An exhortation against speaking evil of dignities (x. 20).

SECT. XXXI. Exhortation to charity and benevolence (xi. 1–10).

SECT. XXXII. An exhortation to the early cultivation of Religious Habits (xiii. 1–7).

SECT. XXXIII. The conclusion (xii. 8–14).

The allusions to music in the book are very few.

ECCLESIASTES ii. 8.

I gathered me also silver and gold, and the peculiar treasure of kings and of the provinces; I gat me men-singers and women-singers, and the delights of the sons of men, *as* musical instruments, and that of all sorts.

Men-singers—women-singers.—The plural masculine and feminine of the usual term *shir*, are here employed.

Musical instruments, and that of all sorts.—The original of this signifies simply *wife* and *wives*. Gesenius remarks that the singular noun may refer to the queen, and the plural to the king's other wives and concubines. The word here employed denotes, in the Talmud, *a woman's camel saddle*. In the Arabic it signifies the same. The Septuagint has οινοχοος (*oinochoos*), *a cup-bearer*. It is a very obscure term, and scholars have expressed various opinions in respect to its derivation. From the context it is evident that it refers to some kind of enjoyment, and its etymology would indicate that that enjoyment was connected in some way with females. As music was often practised by them, there may be a remote reference to the art. The word translated *delights*, may include music, among other things adapted to produce enjoyment.

In Eccl. iii. 4, *dance* occurs. The original is a derivative of רָקַד (*raqadh*), signifying *to skip, to play, to dance*. In Eccl. xii. 4, the word *music* occurs. It is literally, *daughters of the song*. The usual term for song is employed. The expression is a general one, indicating all the sources of pleasure, and among them, music as one of the most important.

THE SONG OF SOLOMON.

INTRODUCTORY REMARKS.

THE Hebrew title of the book is שיר השירים (*shîr hashîrîm*), signifying literally *song of the songs*, indicating that the poem is an elevated one. It seems to be an allegory, representing the church of God and her glorious Head under the similitude of two lovers. It is ascribed to Solomon, and contains obvious internal marks that he was the author (vid. Song of Solomon i. 5, 9; iii. 9, 10; vi. 12). It must have been composed by a contemporary, and, it is in the highest degree probable, by that monarch himself, for there are references in the book to nearly all of the leading circumstances in his life. About two centuries before Christ a Greek translation of it was made by the Jewish authors of the Septuagint, and is now found in the Alexandrian version. Aquila, Symmachus, and Theodotion also translated it into Greek, in the second century of the Christian era. Origen inserted it in his Hexapla in the third century. The allegorical signification attached to it by the Chaldee paraphrasts, shows that the ancient Jews considered it as inspired. Josephus, Eusebius, Melito, of the second century, Ignatius, Athanasius, and others mention it as one of the books of the Jewish scriptures. From these and other proofs, it is generally received as canonical.

All commentators agree that the *song of songs* is a *poem*, but they differ in respect to the class of poetry to which it belongs.

Harmer regards it as a *nuptial song;* Bossuet, Calmet,

Percy, and others as a regular *drama*. As the Jews were accustomed to celebrate their nuptials seven days in succession, some critics divide the book into seven parts corresponding to each day. Bishop Lowth considers it as a *sacred pastoral drama*, though he does not agree with Bossuet in considering it a *regular* one. Bauer, Jahn, and others regard it as an idyl, or perhaps more correctly, several idyls. Dr. Good maintains that it consists of a series of poems, which he calls *sacred idyls*. Accordingly, he divides the book as follows:

IDYL 1	CHAP. i. 1–8.
2	i. 9–ii. 7.
3	ii. 8–17.
4	iii. 1–5.
5	iii. 6–iv. 7.
6	iv. 8–v. 1.
7	v. 2–vi. 10.
8	vi. 11–13.
9	vii. 1–9.
10	vii. 10–viii. 4.
11	viii. 5–7.
12	viii. 8–14.

This view is adopted by other eminent critics, and is probably the correct one. Dr. Wright presents an interesting analysis of the book, drawn probably from Jahn, which we here copy (vid. Kitto's Cyclop. Bib. Lit. Art. Canticles).

1. An innocent country maiden makes an undisguised profession of her attachment, and her lover, a shepherd, replies to it with equal protestations of affection (i. 2, ii. 7). Some prefer concluding this dialogue at i. 11, and making i. 12–ii. 7, a soliloquy, in which the maiden is supposed to repeat some compliments of her lover. But this is without sufficient reason.—2. A maiden sings of

her lover, who is seeking her everywhere, and she also confesses her warm affection (ii. 8–iii. 5). Some suppose that ii. 8–14 is a dream, and that in verse 15 the maiden awakes, who dreams again in iii. 1–5. But if these places are similar to dreams, it ought to be remembered that waking dreams are not uncommon with lovers. This the poet, true to nature, has here presented.—3. A maiden in a litter, surrounded by Solomon's soldiers, is brought to the harem of the king. The lover prefers, far before all the royal beauties, his own beloved, in whose society he declares that he is happier than the king himself (iii. 6–v. 1). Some choose to make iv. 8–v. 1, a distinct poem: but they can hardly offer any sufficient reason for separating this portion from the other. Nevertheless the distribution of the work into its several parts must be left very much to the reader's own taste and feeling.—4. A maiden beloved sings of her lover. He had come to her door at night, and had fled away before she opened it. She seeks him; is beaten by the watch, and stripped of her veil. She describes the beauty of her lover, who at length answers, celebrating her loveliness, with a contemptuous glance at the multitude of the king's wives (v. 2–vi. 19). —5. Shulamith recounts, in few words, the allurements of the courtiers, whom she has met with unexpectedly in the garden, and her rejection of them, and celebrates her affection for her lover (vi. 10–viii. 3).—6. Protestation and praises of constant affection (viii. 4–7).—7. A discourse between two brothers, about guarding and giving away their sister in marriage; who replies with scorn, that she would be her own guardian (viii. 8–12).—8. A fragment. A lover wishes to hear his beloved. She replies by persuading him to fly. Perhaps her parents or relations were near, who, in the East, never permit such meetings (viii. 13, 14).

Ewald supposes that the book was composed about 920 B. C. Pareau, De Wette, and scholars generally agree that it must have been written in the age of Solomon.

There is one allusion to music in chapter ii. verse 12, *singing.* A derivative of *zāmar* is used in the Hebrew, meaning *to prune*, and in the Peal conjugation, *to cut off discourse at regular intervals*, *to sing* (vid. Rem. on Ex. xv. 2).

THE BOOK OF ISAIAH.

INTRODUCTORY REMARKS.

THE *prophetical* writings are mostly in poetry, and contain some of the highest flights of the Hebrew bards. This species of poetry is different, in some respects, from all other kinds found in the sacred volume. The sententious parallelism is remarkably prevalent, and the ornaments are more numerous and far more elegant. The imagery is taken from natural objects as well as from sacred history; its metaphors, comparisons, and allegories, are abundant and exceedingly rich. The seers, inspired from on high, manifest the most exalted enthusiasm. They seem to be entirely absorbed in the subject before them: their diction is sententious and energetic—even electric in its effect—and often rises to the highest degree of the morally sublime (vid. Bishop Lowth's Lect. on Heb. Poet., Lectures xviii, xix, xx). The Bishop presents Balaam's prophecy in Num. xxiv. 5–9, as one of the most elegant specimens of this kind of poetry extant, as it is distinguished for charming imagery, the figures being diversified, and the language glowing and elegant. We have already presented Dr. Hale's translation of it (vid. p. 243 *supra*). Some of the prophetical poetry is plaintive. The Lamentations of Jeremiah, for instance, furnish probably the most perfect and beautiful specimen of elegiac Hebrew poetry ever written. (For further general Rem. on Hebrew poetry, see Rem. on I Chron. xxv. 1, *supra*).

Isaiah is justly distinguished for the energy, beauty, and

grandeur of his conceptions and style. For this reason, among other considerations, the book of Isaiah, though the fifth in the order of time, is placed first among the prophetical writings. It appears from his own account, that this prophet was the son of Amos, and flourished from 810–698 B. C., during the reigns of Uzziah, Jotham, Ahaz, and Hezekiah. Some suppose that he was brother of Uzziah, king of Judah, but this is not certain. The prophets Amos, Hosea, Joel, and Micah, were his contemporaries.

Isaiah was a bold, original, and splendid writer. His language, in some instances, is in the highest degree exalted and sublime. He rises upon the mount of vision, his conceptions are intensely vivid, and his style full of energy and pathos. The terrific and joyous scenes which were to transpire in future ages, seem to have been really before him. He is in the midst of commotions, wars, and triumphs. He hears the cannon's roar, beholds the thousands slain, listens to the groans of the dying, and then to the songs of victory. He is the "*matchless*" Hebrew bard, and is justly styled, by Lowth, "the prince of all the prophets."

Dœderlein, Hoppe, Bauer, Eichhorn, Justi, Rosenmüller, and others have undertaken to show that Isaiah did not compose the whole book ascribed to him, but Jahn and others have triumphantly refuted their arguments.

The object of the prophet in writing this book, was to show the Israelites as well as the Gentile nations, the turpitude of their iniquities, and to call down upon them, unless they should repent, the judgments of an offended God. The writer warns them to repent, and avert impending wrath. He also comforts the godly in view of their severe afflictions. There are in the book numerous and unmistakable prophecies concerning the advent of the

Messiah, some of which are exceedingly beautiful and sublime. There are a few allusions to music in the book.

Isaiah iii. 16–18.

16 Moreover the Lord saith,
Because the daughters of Zion are haughty,
And walk with stretched-forth necks and wanton eyes,
Walking and mincing *as* they go, and making a tinkling with their feet:
17 Therefore the Lord will smite with a scab
The crown of the head of the daughters of Zion,
And the Lord will discover their secret parts.
18 In that day the Lord will take away the bravery of *their* tinkling ornaments *about their feet,*
And *their* cauls, and *their* round tires like the moon.

Tinkling (vs. 16, 18).—This does not refer to music; but to a clinking sound caused by chains attached to the ankles of ladies, who thus attracted the attention of the populace. The austere prophet condemns this custom as indicative of pride.

Isaiah v. 1, 12.

1 Now will I sing to my well-beloved
A song of my beloved touching his vineyard.
My well-beloved hath a vineyard in a very fruitful hill:
12 And the harp, and the viol, the tabret,
And pipe, and wine, are in their feasts:
But they regard not the work of the Lord,
Neither consider the operation of his hands.

Sing—song (v. 1).—The usual term is employed here for *sing* (vid. Rem. on Ex. xv. 1).

Harp—viol—tabret—pipe (v. 12).—*Kinnor* is the original for *harp* (vid. Rem. on Gen. iv. 21), and *nebhel* for *viol*. The *nebhel*, we have already shown, resembled our guitar more nearly than any other instrument. *Viol* is a general term, including the guitar and other instruments of that class (vid. Rem. on I Sam. x. 5; II Sam. vi. 5). *Toph* is the original for *tabret* (vid. Rem. on Gen. xxxi. 27; Ex. xv. 20), and *halil* for *pipe*. The latter was evidently a wind instrument, probably resembling a flute, and should not be confounded with the *ugabh* or *organ*, which was a much more ancient instrument (vid. Rem. on I Sam. x. 5; I Kings i. 40).

Isaiah xii. 2, 5, 6.

2 Behold, God *is* my salvation;
I will trust, and not be afraid:
For the Lord Jehovah *is* my strength and *my* song;
He also is become my salvation.
5 Sing unto the Lord;
For he hath done excellent things:
This *is* known in all the earth.
6 Cry out and shout, thou inhabitant of Zion:
For great *is* the Holy One of Israel in the midst of thee.

Song (v. 2).—In the original, a derivative of *zamar* is used, also in verse 5, the term translated *sing* is similarly derived (vid. Rem. on Ex. xv. 20). In verse 6, *cry out* and *shout* is simply an expression of joy. In Isa. xiii. 21, the word *dances* is found. The original of it is a derivative of *raqadh* (vid. Rem. on Eccl. iii. 4).

The language here employed is highly figurative and terrific. The writer is speaking of the destruction of Babylon, and his predictions have been literally and dreadfully fulfilled.

Isaiah xiv. 4–19.

We present Noyes' translation.

4 Then shalt thou utter this song over the king of
Babylon, and say,
"How hath the tyrant fallen!
The tribute ceased!
5 Jehovah hath broken the staff of the wicked,
The rod of the tyrants,
6 That smote the people in anger
With a continual stroke,
That lorded it over the nations in wrath
With unremitted oppression.
7 The whole earth is at rest, is quiet;
They break forth into singing.
8 Even the cypress trees exult over thee,
And the cedars of Lebanon;
'Since thou art fallen,
No feller cometh up against us.'
9 Hades beneath is in commotion on account of thee,
To meet thee at thy coming;
He stirreth up before thee the shades, all the mighty
of the earth;
He arouseth from their thrones all the kings of the
nations;
10 They all accost thee, and say,
'Art thou, too, become weak as we?
Art thou become like us?'
11 Thy pomp is brought down to the grave,
And the sound of thy harps.
Vermin have become thy couch,
And earth-worms thy covering.
12 How art thou fallen from heaven!
Howl, son of the morning!

How art thou cast down to the ground,
Thou that didst trample upon the nations!
13 Thou saidst in thy heart, 'I will ascend to heaven!
Above the stars of God will I exalt my throne;
I will sit upon the mount of assembly in the farthest north.
14 I will ascend above the height of the clouds;
I will be like the Most High.'
15 But thou art brought down to the grave,
To the depths of the pit;
16 They that see thee gaze upon thee, and view thee attentively, (and say,)
'Is this the man that made the earth tremble?
That did shake kingdoms?
17 That made the world a wilderness,
And laid waste its cities,
And dismissed not his captives to their homes?'
18 All the kings of the nations, yea, all of them,
Lie down in glory, each in his own sepulchre;
19 But thou art cast forth without a grave,
Like a worthless branch;
Covered with the slain, who are pierced by the sword,
Who go down to the stones of the pit,
Like a carcass, trampled under foot."

This chapter is considered as one of the most beautiful and sublime specimens of Hebrew poetry found in the sacred volume, or in any other book. Bishop Lowth uses the following language in respect to it:

"How forcible is this imagery, how diversified, how sublime! how elevated the diction, the figures, the sentiments!—The Jewish nation, the cedars of Lebanon, the ghosts of departed kings, the Babylonish monarch, the travelers who find his corpse, and last of all Jehovah himself, are the characters which support this beautiful lyric drama. One continued action is kept up, or rather a series of interesting actions are connected together in an incomparable whole; this, indeed, is the principal and distinguished excellence of the sublimer ode, and is displayed in its utmost perfection in this poem of Isaiah, which may be considered as one of the most ancient, and certainly one of the most finished, specimens of that species of composition which has been transmitted to us. The personifications here are frequent, yet not confused; bold, yet not improbable: a free, elevated, and truly divine spirit pervades the whole; nor is there any thing wanting in this ode to defeat its claim to the character of perfect beauty and sublimity. If, indeed, I may be indulged in the free declaration of my own sentiments on this occasion, I do not know a single instance, in the whole compass of Greek and Roman poetry, which, in every excellence of composition, can be said to equal, or even to approach it."

Singing (v. 7).—The original is a derivative of *ranan*, signifying to utter a *tremulous sound, to shout*, referring to exultation, triumph. In verse 11, the term *viols* occurs. The original is the plural of *nebhel*, indicating an instrument resembling the *guitar*, and often translated *psaltery* in our English version of the scriptures. The term here seems to be a general one, referring to the viol class of stringed instruments (vid. Rem. on I Sam. x. 5; II Sam. vi. 5).

In chapter xvi. verse 9, *shouting* is used, referring to the custom of rejoicing in view of gathering in the harvest. The same word occurs in verse 10, referring to joy in the time of vintage. *Singing* also occurs in the same verse. A derivative of *ranan* is used (vid. Rem. on Isa. xiv. 7). In verse 11, *kinnor*, translated *harp*, is employed in a peculiarly figurative and striking manner.

In chapter xviii, verse 3, *trumpet* is employed. This is the *shophar* or *crooked trumpet* (vid. Rem. on Ex. xix. 16; Lev. xxv. 9), used principally in war. The prophet here declares the fact, that a powerful army would come from beyond the Euphrates, and spread desolation in every direction. This prophecy is exceedingly obscure, and it is impossible to ascertain beyond a doubt from what country the warriors were to emerge. Vitringa and others suppose that they were Assyrians, while Bishop Lowth thinks that they were Egyptians. Rosenmüller and others maintain that they were Æthiopians.

In Isaiah xxiii. 15, *sing* occurs. The original is a derivative of the usual form *shïr*. In verse 16, *kinnor*, translated *harp*, is found. *Sing* occurs in the same verse. The original word is נַגֵּן *naggen*, meaning *to play on stringed instruments*. Reference is probably made to instruments of the viol kind (vid. Rem. on Gen. iv. 21; Job xxx. 9). In chapter xxiv. 8, a derivative of *toph*, translated *tabrets*, is used. Also the *kinnor*, *harp*. In verse 14, *sing* occurs—from a derivative of *ranan* (vid. Rem. on Lev. iv. 24). In verse 16, the word *songs* is found—a derivative of *zamar* (vid. Rem. on Ex. xv. 2).

Chapter xxvi. 1, *song—sung*.—The usual term is employed here; but in verse 19, a derivative of *ranan*. The prophetic denunciations and encouragements contained in Isaiah xxiv, xxv, and xxvi, are supposed to have been delivered in the beginning of Hezekiah's reign. In chapter xxiv, a terrible destruction by the invasion of some powerful chieftain is announced. Commentators are not agreed whether it was Shalmaneser, Nebuchadnezzar, or the leader of the Romans, who was to make the attack. Lowth supposes that there may be reference to all three. Finally, the prophet, in chapters xxv, and xxvi, breaks forth into beautiful and sublime songs of adoration. In chapter xxvii. 2, *sing* occurs. The original is a derivative of *anah*, meaning *to sing, to shout, the cry of victory* (vid. Rem. on Ex. xxxii. 18).

Great trumpet (v. 13).—This is the *shophar* or *crooked trumpet*. Here is a beautiful reference to that custom of the Jews, by which they blew the trumpet or *shophar* to call the people together for their holy solemnities, for war, or to suppress a rebellion. The Israelites, though scattered and oppressed, shall return to the holy city at the blast of the *great trumpet*, and three worship the God of their fathers.

Song (Isa. xxx. 29).—The usual Hebrew term is here employed (vid. Rem. on Ex. xv. 1).

Pipe (v. 29).—This is the *halil* or *flute* kind of wind instruments, different from the *ugabh* or organ (vid. Rem. on I Sam. x. 5; I Kings i. 40).

Tabrets and harps (v. 32).—These were *tophs* and *kinnors* (vid. Rem. on Gen. iv. 21; xxxi. 27).

Isaiah xxxv. 1–10.

1 The wilderness and the solitary place shall be glad for them;
And the desert shall rejoice, and blossom as the rose.
2 It shall blossom abundantly, and rejoice even with joy and singing:
The glory of Lebanon shall be given unto it, the excellency of Carmel and Sharon.
They shall see the glory of the Lord, *and* the excellency of our God.
3 Strengthen ye the weak hands, and confirm the feeble knees.
4 Say to them *that are* of a fearful heart, Be strong, fear not;
Behold, your God will come *with* vengeance,
Even God *with* a recompense;
He will come and save you.
5 Then the eyes of the blind shall be opened,
And the ears of the deaf shall be unstopped.
6 Then shall the lame *man* leap as an hart,
And the tongue of the dumb sing:
For in the wilderness shall waters break out,
And streams in the desert.
7 And the parched ground shall become a pool,
And the thirsty land springs of water:
In the habitations of dragons, where each lay,

Shall be grass with reeds and rushes.
8 And an highway shall be there, and a way,
And it shall be called the way of holiness;
The unclean shall not pass over it; but it *shall be* for those:
The wayfaring men, though fools, shall not err *therein.*
9 No lion shall be there;
Nor *any* ravenous beast shall go up thereon,
It shall not be found there;
But the redeemed shall walk *there:*
10 And the ransomed of the Lord shall return,
And come to Zion with songs, and everlasting joy upon their heads.

Singing (v. 2), *sing* (v. 6), *songs* (v. 10).—In these three cases derivatives of *ra̤nan* are employed (vid. Rem. on Lev. ix. 24). Chapter xxxv is an elegant poem, and refers in the plainest terms to the incarnation and sufferings of the Messiah. The previous chapter is intimately connected with this, the two containing an entire prophecy.

We will sing my songs to the stringed instruments (Isa. xxxviii. 20).—This expression indicates rejoicing in consequence of the recovery of King Hezekiah from a dangerous illness. נְנַגֵּן (*n*^{e}*naggen*), translated *sing my songs*, also נְגִינוֹתַי (*n*^{e}*gīnothay*), translated *stringed instruments*, are both derived from *na̤gan, to strike a chord or string* (vid. Rem. on Job xxx. 9; Ps. iv. title). The LXX designate the particular stringed instrument used, calling it the psaltery, but there is nothing in the original to show that the inspired writer intended to indicate any particular stringed instrument. The expression is obviously a general one, indicating praise and rejoicing with instrumental, as well as vocal, music. Chap. xlii. 10, 11, *sing—song—shout.* The prophet here speaks of the infinite goodness of

God in providing a Saviour, and calls upon all men to rejoice and praise the Lord in view of the wonderful fact. In verse 10, derivatives of *shīr* are used for *sing* and *song*, and in verse 11, for *sing*, a derivative of *ranan* (vid. Rem. on Ex. xv. 1; Lev. ix. 24). Chap. xliv. 23. Here the prophet calls upon the heavens and earth to praise Jehovah, because he had redeemed his people. A derivative of *ranan* is used in both cases in which reference is made to music. In chap. xlviii. 20, a derivative of the same word is employed and translated *singing*. The same is true of the references to music in chap. xlix. 13.

Chap. li. 3, *melody.*—The original of this is a derivative of *zamar* (vid. Rem. on Ex. xv. 2). It is usually translated *song*. In v. 11, a derivative of *ranan* is employed for *singing*. Chap. lii. 8, 9, *sing*, a derivative of *ranan*, is used in both cases. The same is true of the references to music in chap. liv. 1. The same is true also in chap. lv. 12. In chap. lviii. 1, *trumpet*. This was the *shophar*, or *crooked trumpet* (vid. Rem. on Ex. xix. 16; Lev. xxv. 9). In chap. lxv. 14, a derivative of *ranan* is employed.

BOOK OF THE PROPHET JEREMIAH.

INTRODUCTORY REMARKS.

THE object of the writer in this book is to exhibit the great wickedness and apostasy of the people of Judah, to show that they would be punished by judgments from heaven, and, upon repentance, be finally restored to the divine favor. Jeremiah was sensitive, naturally timid, and retiring; still, in the discharge of his duty he did not shrink from publicity, danger, or even death itself. He was remarkably susceptible to sorrowful emotions, and utters many plaintive and thrilling lays. His style is highly pathetic and beautiful. He speaks the truth with boldness and fidelity, but with the utmost tenderness. He beholds in prophetic vision the judgments of heaven descending upon his people. He deeply sympathizes with them, and exhorts them to avert impending destruction by turning to the Lord. Bishop Lowth considers Jeremiah as nearly equalling Isaiah in sublimity of thought and diction.

The canonicity of this book is well-established, though some German critics have raised objections against detached passages. There seems to be a disarrangement in the chronological order of the different prophecies of Jeremiah, and various conjectures have been suggested to account for it, but we have not a sufficient number of facts at present to enable us to decide with certainty the cause. Dr. Blaney has arranged the prophecies in the following manner:

1. *The prophecies delivered in the reign of Josiah*, containing chapters i–xii, inclusive.

2. *The prophecies delivered in the reign of Jehoiakim,* comprising chapters xiii–xx, xxii, xxiii, xxxv, xxxvi, xlv–xlviii, and xlix, 1–33.

3. *The prophecies delivered in the reign of Zedekiah,* including chapters xxi, xxiv, xxvii–xxxiv, xxxvii–xxxix, xlix, 34–39, and l, and li.

4. *The prophecies delivered under the government of Gedaliah,* from the taking of Jerusalem to the retreat of the people into Egypt, and the prophecies of Jeremiah delivered to the Jews in that country; comprehending chapters xl–xliv, inclusive.

This book is believed to have been written at different times between 628 and 583 B. C., and is consequently very ancient. There are occasional allusions to music. Indeed, nearly the whole book consists of beautiful poems, which were probably set to music. As a specimen of the plaintive, pathetic, sublime lays of this poet, we present a part of the fourth chapter (verses 19–26). It is the following. as translated by Herder:

19 My bowels, my bowels! I'm filled with pain,
My very heart is full of anguish,
And yet I cannot hold my peace.
My soul hath heard the sound of trumpets,
The shout and alarm of war.
20 Destruction, desolation, is cried,
For all the land is desolate,
My tents are suddenly spoiled.
21 How long shall I yet see the standard,
And hear the sound of trumpets?
22 My foolish nation understand me not,
Unwise children and void of sense,
Wise to do evil, but never to do good.
23 I look abroad upon the earth,

And lo! it is desolate and waste,
Upon the heavens, and they have no light,
24 I see the mountains, and they tremble,
And all the hills are in commotion.
25 I behold, and lo! there is no man,
And all the birds of heaven are fled.
26 I look, and lo! Carmel is a desert,
And all its cities are laid waste
Before the presence of Jehovah,
Before the blast of his fierce anger.

In this passage we have references to music in verses 5, 19 and 21. The *shophar, crooked trumpet,* is used (vid. Rem. on Ex. xix. 16; Lev. xxv. 9). The prophet elegantly describes, in prophetic vision, the invasion of Judæa by the Babylonians, Chaldæans, Assyrians, and Medes, the awful ravages of the country by the enemy, and their victory over the disobedient, though favored people of the Lord. The writer's lamentation over the sorrows of his people is truly elegant. The Hebrews are commanded to *blow* the *trumpet*—to call the warriors to the combat. In chapter vi. 1, 17, a similar expression is employed. Judah and Jerusalem are called upon to sound the *shophar* in view of an attack by the Babylonians and Chaldæans. Chapter xx. 13, *sing.* Pashur, the chief governor of the house of the Lord, persecuted Jeremiah, smote him, and put his feet in the stocks. The prophet made his complaint, and exulted in God as the deliverer of his people from the hands of evil-doers. A derivative of *shir* is used, and translated *sing* (vid. Rem. on Ex. xv. 1). In verse 16 *shouting* occurs. The original is *teruah,* indicating triumph (vid. Rem. on Num. x. 5; xxix. 1). Chapter xxxi. 4, *tabrets.* The original is a derivative of *toph,* a pulsatile instrument (vid. Rem. on Gen. xxxi. 27; Ex. xv. 20; I Sam. xviii. 6). The prophet is speaking of the restoration of Israel to the favor of God. In the same verse it is said that they *shall go forth in dances of them that make merry.* The whole indicates joy and triumph. In verse 7, Israel is called upon to *sing* and *shout.* In one case the original is a derivative of *ranan*, and in the other *simha* is employed, all indicative of great joy (vid. Rem. on Gen. xxxi. 27; Lev. ix. 24). In verse 12, a derivative of *ranan* is employed, indicating extreme joy "on the heights of Zion." In verse 13, it is said that Israel shall unite in *dances* as well as *singing.*

Trumpet (Jer. xlii. 14).—This is the *shophar* or *crooked trumpet* (vid. Rem. on Ex. xix. 16). Reference is here made to the *war-blast.* The Israelites thought they should not hear the sound of that terrible instrument if they should go down into Egypt. In chap. xlviii. 33, *shouting* occurs three times. The original is הֵידָד *hedhadh*, from the verb, הָדַד *hadhadh*, *to break forth into joy, to shout for joy.* The reference is to the exultation of those whose wine-presses are full of wine from an abundant harvest. The joy usually characteristic of such occasions was to be turned into mourning. In verse 36, of the same chapter, the prophet declares that his heart should *sound* like *pipes* for Moab and Kir-heres. *Pipes* were used particularly at funerals to aid in mournful demonstrations. So there should be similar mourning for Moab and Kir-heres. The original is a derivative of חָלַל (*hhalal*), *to pierce, to bore through, to play on the pipe.* This was evidently a wind instrument, probably a flute, and as it appears in the plural form, it is supposed to refer to the double flute (vid. Rem. on I Sam. x. 5; I Kings, i. 40.) In chap. li. 27, the *shophar* or crooked trumpet is mentioned. The allusion is to the terrible destruction of Babylon predicted by the prophet. In prophetic vision he beholds the great and wicked city attacked by surrounding nations—he hears the blast of the war-trumpet, and sees Babylon fall. Then in verse 48, he represents the heavens and earth as *rejoicing*, and *singing* in triumph at her overthrow. A derivative of *ranan* is employed (vid. Rem. on Lev. ix. 24).

LAMENTATIONS OF JEREMIAH.

INTRODUCTORY REMARKS.

In this part of the prophet's writings we find his sweetest and most exalted elegiac lays. He is a mourner. The kingdom of Judah is rent by a foreign foe, the beloved city of Jerusalem is destroyed, and Israel overwhelmed in sorrow. The prophet is borne down with inconsolable grief. He appears upon the ruins of that city, once prosperous, and beholds the fearful desolation around him,—the dear homes of his people demolished, the streets flowing with blood, his own relatives slain or carried to Babylon into hopeless captivity; and, worse than all, he views the sacred temple, where God had vouchsafed his presence, leveled to the ground and burned with fire—its altars, sanctuary, and holy of holies desecrated and laid in utter desolation. Its beauty and splendor were no more—the plaintive or joyous tones of its vocal and instrumental music reverberated within its walls no longer; its solemn assemblies had ceased to witness, in its holy portals, the divine manifestations; and its priesthood had fallen by the sword or been carried into captivity. Not only are the city and temple destroyed, but the whole land is laid waste. With this overwhelming view before him, the inspired seer utters his plaintive strains. He strikes his lyre, and from its quivering strings proceed those tones which are in unison with the deep emotions of his soul. He is in tears, and the bitterest pang which heaves his bosom is caused by the fact that Israel is *guilty*—that she has inflicted upon *herself* this dread calamity.

This part of the book consists of five distinct elegies, all of which are plaintive funeral dirges. Each elegy contains twenty-two periods, corresponding with the number of letters in the Hebrew alphabet. In the first four chapters the several periods begin with the different letters in alphabetical order, thus marking the metre more precisely. In the third chapter each period contains three verses, all having the same initial letter. There seems to be nothing artificial or methodical in the arrangement of these elegies; yet there is no incoherency or abrupt transition. There is a great variety of beautiful and pathetic images, all clad in the habiliments of mourning. There are some allusions to music,—indeed, the whole piece is a musical composition. As a specimen, we present the following:

Lamentations iii. 31–66.

31 For the Lord will not cast off for ever:
32 But though he cause grief, yet will he have compassion according to the multitude of his mercies.
33 For he doth not afflict willingly nor grieve the children of men.
34 To crush under his feet all the prisoners of the earth,
35 To turn aside the right of a man before the face of the Most High,
36 To subvert a man in his cause, the Lord approveth not.
37 Who *is* he *that* saith, and *it* cometh to pass, *when* the Lord commandeth *it* not?
38 Out of the mouth of the Most High proceedeth not evil and good?
39 Wherefore doth a living man complain, a man for the punishment of his sins?
40 Let us search and try our ways, and turn again to the Lord.

41 Let us lift up our heart with *our* hands unto God in the heavens.

42 We have transgressed and rebelled: thou hast not pardoned.

43 Thou hast covered with anger, and persecuted us: thou hast slain, thou hast not pitied.

44 Thou hast covered thyself with a cloud, that *our* prayer should not pass through.

45 Thou hast made us *as* the offscouring and refuse in the midst of the people.

46 All our enemies have opened their mouths against us.

47 Fear and a snare is come upon us, desolation and destruction.

48 Mine eye runneth down with rivers of water for the destruction of the daughter of my people.

49 Mine eye trickleth down, and ceaseth not, without any intermission,

50 Till the Lord look down, and behold from heaven.

51 Mine eye affecteth mine heart because of all the daughters of my city.

52 Mine enemies chased me sore, like a bird, without cause.

53 They have cut off my life in the dungeon, and cast a stone upon me.

54 Waters flowed over my head; *then* I said, I am cut off.

55 I called upon thy name, O Lord, out of the low dungeon.

56 Thou hast heard my voice: hide not thine ear at my breathing, at my cry.

57 Thou drewest near in the day *that* I called upon thee: thou saidst, Fear not.

58 O Lord, thou hast pleaded the causes of my soul; thou hast redeemed my life.

59 O Lord, thou hast seen my wrong; judge thou my cause.
60 Thou hast seen all their vengeance *and* all their imaginations against me:
61 Thou hast heard their reproach, O Lord, *and* all their imaginations against me;
62 The lips of those that rose up against me, and their device against me all the day.
63 Behold their sitting down, and their rising up; I *am* their music.
64 Render unto them a recompense, O Lord, according to the work of their hands.
65 Give them sorrow of heart, thy curse unto them.
66 Persecute and destroy them in anger from under the heavens of the Lord.

The whole chapter is a beautiful elegy upon the afflictions which the prophet was experiencing in view of the grievous calamities which had fallen upon his people. In verse 14, *song* is used. The original word is a derivative of *nagan*, signifying *to strike the strings*. The *noun*, which is here employed, signifies, music of stringed instruments. The same word, in Lam. v. 14, is translated *music*. In the former instance the prophet refers to the derision which his enemies heaped upon him. The idea in the original is, that his foes *shouted*, and not only employed their *voices*, but *stringed instruments*, in triumphing over him. The same term is used in the 63d verse of the same chapter in a similar sense, and translated *music*. In Lam. v. 14, Jeremiah speaks of the sadness of his afflicted people. Even the young men had ceased to be joyful, and the cheering sound of their harps could no longer be heard.

BOOK OF THE PROPHET EZEKIEL.

INTRODUCTORY REMARKS.

THIS prophet was one of those whom Nebuchadnezzar, king of Babylon, carried captive into his own dominions, after the destruction of Jerusalem and the Temple, so beautifully and pathetically described by Jeremiah in his inimitable Lamentations. Ezekiel resided at some distance from Babylon, on the river Chebar, and there commenced his career as an inspired prophet of God. He had many remarkable visions, which cast a shade of obscurity over some parts of his writings. With great vehemence he reproves the sins of his people.

Some critics of late have raised doubts in reference to the canonicity of the book, and endeavored to show that some parts of it were not written by Ezekiel; but their objections have been unanswerably refuted, and the composition is now almost universally received as authoritative and canonical. The chief objection of the prophet is to administer consolation to his afflicted people. His style is much more bold and denunciatory than that of Jeremiah. Ezekiel is oftener in the tempest—amid the raging of the elements. He delights in the terrific—the awful. He was a person of extensive information and great genius. Bishop Lowth describes him thus (Lowth's Sac. Poet. of the Heb., Lect. 22): "Ezekiel is much inferior to Jeremiah in elegance; in sublimity he is not even excelled by Isaiah; but his sublimity is of a totally different kind. He is deep, vehement, tragical; the only sensation he affects to excite, is the terrible; his sentiments are elevated, fervid, full of fire, indignant; his imagery is crowded, magnificent, terrific sometimes almost to disgust; his language is pompous, solemn, austere, rough, and at times unpolished: he employs frequent repetitions, not for the sake of grace or elegance, but from the vehemence of passion and indignation. Whatever subject he treats of, that he sedulously pursues, from that he rarely departs, but cleaves as it were to it; whence the connection is in general evident and well preserved. In many respects he is perhaps excelled by the other prophets; but in that species of composition to which he seems by nature adapted,—the forcible, the impetuous, the great and solemn,—not one of the sacred writers is superior to him. His diction is sufficiently perspicuous; all his obscurity consists in the nature of the subject. Visions (as for instance, among others, those of Hosea, Amos, and Jeremiah) are necessarily dark and confused. The greater part of Ezekiel, towards the middle of the book especially, is poetical, whether we regard the matter or the diction."

Michaelis and others intimate that Lowth is probably a little too enthusiastic in his praise of Ezekiel. Still, he was a splendid prophet and poet—the Homer of the Hebrews. As a beautiful specimen of his poetry, read the glowing and sublime description of his vision of Jehovah enthroned above the cherubim (Ezek. i. 4–14, 22–28), as translated by Herder.

Ezekiel's vision of God enthroned above the Cherubim.

4 I looked, and lo! a whirlwind from the North
Came sweeping onward, a vast cloud, that rolled
Its volumes, charged with gleaming fire, along,
And cast its dazzling splendors all around.
Now from within shone forth, what seemed the glow
Of gold and silver, molten in the flame,

5 And in the midst thereof the form expressed,
As of a four-fold living thing—a shape,
That yet contained the semblance of a man.
6 With four-fold visage each, and each four wings,
7 On upright limbs and cloven feet they stood,
And shone with splendor as of burnished brass.
Withdrawn beneath their wings, on every side
8 Were human hands, for each four-sided seemed,
And four-fold had their faces and their wings.
9 Then, wing to wing, and each to each close joined,
They turned not in their going, but went forth,
Advancing each with look and course unchanged.
10 In all the four-fold visaged four was seen
The face of man; the right a lion, and an ox
The left distinguished, and to all the four
Belonged an eagle's visage. By itself
11 Distinct, their faces and their wings they each
Extended upward, joining thus, it seemed,
Two wings for flight, while two their bodies veiled,
12 With course direct, and forward each advanced,
Whither the spirit-moved they went, nor ever turned.
13 The several living forms, like glowing coals
Appeared. What seemed the flame of torches played
Between them, and the dazzling light of fire.
From out the fire went gleaming lightnings forth;
14 And quick, as lightnings flash, the living forms
Were here and there, went forth and back returned.

22 Above their heads, high over-arching, seemed
An azure firmament outspread, like clear
Transparent crystal, that inspired with awe.
23 Approaching near the firmament, their wings,
Extending wing to wing, were upward spread.
With two they bore themselves aloft, with two

24 They veiled their bodies round. And as they went,
I heard the rushing sound of wings, like rush
Of mighty waters, or the distant sound
Of thunder, the dread voice of Shaddai.
They went with sound of tumult, like an host,
And when they stopped, they closed again their wings,
25 For when, from the o'er-arching firmament
Above a voice was uttered forth, they stood
With wings depending, and close veiled around.
26 And high upraised above the firmament
There seemed the sapphire splendor of a throne,
And on the throne there sat, what seemed the form
27 Of man. It shone with amber glow of gold
And silver intermixed, as burning fire.
Both inward and without, and from the loins
Above and underneath it seemed like fire,
And shone with radiant lustre all around.
28 As shines the rainbow in the day of rain,
So seemed the lustre of that radiant form.
The aspect of Jehovah's Majesty
I saw in this, and fell upon my face
And heard the voice of one that spake

There are, in the book of Ezekiel, some allusions to music. The poem was written about 595–536 B. C. *To blow the trumpet* (Ezek. vii. 14). The writer here employs two derivatives of תָּקַע (*taqa*), the verb and noun meaning *to blow a blast.* The prophet is describing the afflictions of his people, and intimates that none go up to battle when they are *called*, evidently referring to the *war trumpet.* The Septuagint has *σαλπίσατε σάλπιγγι salpisate salpingi*, *blow the trumpet.* In chap. xxvi. 13, occur *songs*, *harps.* The writer in prophetic vision beholds the multitudes of Nebuchadnezzar's warriors coming up with fury against Tyre, to slay her inhabitants, and cause her songs of joy and instrumental music to cease. The usual term for songs is employed, viz: *shîr* (vid. Rem. on Ex. xv. 1). The term translated *harp* is the *kinnor* (vid. Rem. on Gen. iv. 21). Chap. xxvii. 25, *sing*. The ordinary term is here used. Chap. xxviii. 13, *tabrets, pipes*. The prophet is here speaking of the beauty and glory of Tyre, and warning the inhabitants of the appalling calamities which were sure to fall upon them. Among other things he speaks of their musical instruments. *Tabrets*. This is the *toph* (vid. Rem. on Gen. xxxi. 27; Ex. xv. 20). *Pipes*. The original of this is a noun derived from נָקַב *naqabh, to hollow out, to excavate, to bore*. The noun נֶקֶב (*neqebh*) means *a cavity, a pipe*, and sometimes refers to musical instruments, T. H. Horne supposes that it was the *hautboy*. *Halil* is the usual word denoting the flute (vid. Rem. on 1 Sam. x. 5; 1 Kings, 1. 40). Some suppose that *neqebh* does not refer to music in this place (vid. Gesen. Heb. Lex. under נֶקֶב). We incline to the opinion that there is reference here to a wind instrument of music. At least the etymology of the word strongly favors that idea. Chap. xxxiii. 3, 4, 5, 6. *Trumpet*. This is the *shophar* or *crooked trumpet* (vid. Rem. on Ex. xix. 16). *Song—instruments* (Ezek. xxxiii. 32). God is represented here as declaring to the prophet, that the children of Israel are deceptive —listening to the preacher's voice and being apparently delighted with his exhortations, but considering them as a *song* and an *instrument*, and not performing the duties enjoined. For *song*, the usual word *shîr* is employed. A derivative of *nagan* is translated *instrument*. It refers to a stringed instrument (vid. Rem. on Ps. iv. title). Chap. xl. 44, *singers*. The original is the plural of *shîr*, referring to the singers in the temple.

THE BOOK OF DANIEL.

INTRODUCTORY REMARKS.

This prophet was carried a captive to Babylon 606 years B. C., which was seven years before Ezekiel shared a similar fate. The former was learned in Chaldæan literature, and highly honored by the Babylonian monarchs, having been promoted to an elevated official position. From the fact that he often speaks in the first person, it is evident that he wrote the book ascribed to him, though his name is not prefixed. The first part relates to his own history and that of the Jews. The second part contains important prophecies relating to the various kingdoms of the world, in reference to the advent of Jesus Christ, and other important events extending from the establishment of the Persian empire to the final judgment and consummation of all things. The writings of Daniel are considered as less obscure than those of the other prophets. His style is clear, simple, and not as lofty and figurative as that of the others.

The evidence of the canonicity of the book, external and internal, is abundant. Various neological writers have objected to this view, but they have been ably refuted by Dr. Hengstenberg of Berlin.

This book is not so highly poetical as some other prophetical writings, still it contains fine specimens of the beautiful and sublime. Take, for instance, the description of Deity in Dan. vii. 9, 10, as translated by Herder (vid. Herder's Heb. Poetry by Marsh, vol. ii. pp. 41, 42.)

9 This I saw, until the thrones were raised,
And the ancient of days enthroned,
His garment was white as snow,
The hair of his head like pure wool.
His throne was like the fiery flame,
Its wheels like burning fire.
10 A fiery stream issued forth,
And went before his face,
A thousand thousand ministered to him,
Ten thousand times ten thousand stood before him.
The judgment was set,
And the Books were opened.

Daniel iii. 5, 10, 15.

5 So *that* at what time ye hear the sound of the cornet, flute, harp, sackbut, psaltery, dulcimer, and all kinds of music, ye fall down and worship the golden image that Nebuchadnezzar the king hath set up:

10 Thou, O king, hast made a decree, that every man that shall hear the sound of the cornet, flute, harp, sackbut, psaltery, and dulcimer, and all kinds of music, shall fall down and worship the golden image.

15 Now if ye be ready that at what time ye hear the sound of the cornet, flute, harp, sackbut, psaltery, and dulcimer, and all kinds of music, ye fall down and worship the image which I have made; *well:* but if ye worship not, ye shall be cast the same hour into the midst of a burning fiery

furnace; and who *is* that God that shall deliver you out of my hands?

There are a few allusions to music in this book.

Cornet, flute, sackbut, harp, psaltery, dulcimer.—Here is an account of a remarkable concert of instruments belonging to the Babylonish royal band of musicians. Nebuchadnezzar had caused a golden image to be constructed, and had called together the magnates of his realm, commanding them, when they should hear the music of his band, to fall down and worship the image. The best performers, undoubtedly, and the most important instruments in his dominions, were employed on that great occasion.

Cornet.—This is the *qeren* (we have here the Chaldee form קַרְנָא *qarna*), *horn*. In the most ancient times, this instrument was made of the horn of an ox, and subsequently of a ram's-horn. *Yobhel*, meaning *jubel* or *jubilee*, generally accompanies *qeren*, though it is not found here. *Menaănîm* (מְנַעַנְעִים) is rendered *cornets* in II Sam. vi. 5, but incorrectly, as it is obviously a *pulsatile*, and the cornet a *wind*, instrument. The *qeren* might more properly be translated *cornet*, as the latter is a musical tube increasing in diameter from the mouth-piece to the lower end, and is a sort of *horn* (vid. Rem. on II Sam. vi. 5; I Chron. xiii. 8). The Septuagint has *salpinx*, *trumpet*. *Flute* (מַשְׁרוֹקִיתָא *mashroqîytha*).—This word occurs four times in the book of Daniel (Dan. iii. 5, 7, 10, 15), and in no other part of the sacred writings. It is a noun from the verb שָׁרַק (*sharaq*), signifying *to hiss, to whistle.* Some suppose that the noun was the name of a modified form of the Hebrew *ugabh* or *organ;* but it is generally and with more probability, thought to be the *double flute*, or flute with two reeds (vid. a representation of it on p. 161). The Septuagint has συριγξ (*syrinx*), signifying, the *pipe of Pan*. The term for the single flute is *halîl* (vid. Rem. on I Sam. x. 5).

Sackbut.—According to the order of the Hebrew, *harp* should precede *sackbut.* The original for the latter is סַבְּכָא (*sabb*[e]*ka̤*). But the *sackbut* is a *horn*, one species of which is the *trombone.*

Sabb[e]*ka̤* evidently refers to a stringed instrument, and is incorrectly translated *sacbut.* The Septuagint renders it *σαμβυκης* (*sambukēs, sambuke*). Gesenius supposes it to have been similar to the *ne̱bhel*, which he believes to be the *harp* or *lyre.* The next term is *harp*, קִיתְרֹס (*qayth*[e]*ros*), *cithara*, meaning *harp.* The Greek *cithara* was derived from this Chaldee term. The Hebrew word for *harp* is *kinnor* (vid. Rem. on Gen. iv. 21).

Psaltery פְּסַנְתְּרִין *p*[e]*sant*[e]*rīn.*—This Chaldee term is supposed to represent the Hebrew *ne̱bhel.* It probably indicates a stringed instrument, but its precise form we cannot ascertain. The word occurs also in verses 7, 10, and 15, of the same chapter, and in no other part of the scriptures.

Dulcimer סוּמְפֹּנְיָה *sṳmpon*[e]*ya̤h.*—A Chaldee word, meaning a *double pipe with a sack, a bagpipe.* The Greek term is *συμφωνια sumphonia, symphony, harmony.* It was undoubtedly a wind instrument made of reeds. The Syrians called it *sambonja.* In the seventh verse of the same chapter the same musical terms occur with the exception of the last, which is omitted in the Chaldee. The Septuagint omits that word in verse 5. In verse 10, the same terms occur as in verse 5. The same also in verse 15.

Chapter vi. 18, *instruments of music.* These words refer to a remarkable occasion. It seems that Daniel had been promoted by Darius to the highest office in his kingdom: but the princes who were inferior to Daniel in authority, moved by envy, drew from the king a decree, that whoever should make a petition to any god or man except Darius, for thirty days, should be cast into the lion's den. Daniel heeded not the king's command, and prayed to his God three times a day. Consequently, the terrible penalty of disobedience was inflicted upon him. Darius, however, was in great affliction in view of the dangerous situation of the prophet. He spent the night in fasting, and would not allow any *instruments of music* to be brought before him. The Chaldee term for *instruments of music* is דַּחֲוָן *dahhᵃvạn*, signifying, *concubine*, from דְּחָה *dạhhạh, to thrust, to push, to strike.* Hence some suppose that it refers to music. The passage evidently indicates that the king would not indulge in any kind of pleasure while Daniel was in the den of lions.

THE BOOK OF HOSEA.

INTRODUCTORY REMARKS.

THE prophecies contained in this book are supposed to have been made and committed to writing between the years 810 and 725 B. C. The object of the prophet is to reprove the Jews for their aggravated transgressions, and especially for the sin of idolatry. He speaks of their grievous captivity by the Assyrians, and calls upon them to repent of their iniquities. The style of the composition exhibits marks of great antiquity. It is concise, abrupt, vehement, and was, undoubtedly, at first in a metrical form, though the precise arrangement is now lost. This book seems to contain only some of Hosea's leading prophecies, and is consequently, in some parts, very obscure. One grand idea pervades the whole book, and absorbs the mind of the prophet. It is the estrangement of Israel and Judah from Jehovah, and the question how they can be restored to the favor of God. In his bold earnestness, Hosea, in prophetic vision, beholds the righteous reduced to the lowest extremities of want and distress, and then raised, as it were, to heaven by the bestowment of the divine blessing. In the vehemence of his emotions he seems to be bewildered and almost overwhelmed, uttering broken metaphors and unfinished sentences, and passing from one subject to another with the greatest precipitancy. The first part of the book is rather repulsive, but the last part closes with great beauty. The abruptness and agitation of the writer are succeeded by a heavenly calmness. His furious and incoherent declarations are changed into sweet, consoling, elevated musical strains of unearthly eloquence. Take, for example, the last chapter, from verse 4 to the close, as translated by Noyes:

4 "I will heal their rebellion; I will love them freely;
For my anger is turned away from them.
5 I will be as the dew to Israel;
He shall bloom as the lily,
And strike his roots like Lebanon.
6 His branches shall spread,
And his beauty shall be as the olive-tree,
And his fragrance as Lebanon.
7 They that dwell under his shadow, shall gather strength;
They shall revive as the corn;
They shall shoot forth as the vine,
Their name shall be like the wine of Lebanon.
8 Ephraim shall say, What have I more to do with idols?
I will hear him; I will care for him;
I will be like a green olive-tree;
From me shall thy fruit be found."
9 Who is wise, that he may understand these things:
Prudent, that he may know them?
For the ways of Jehovah are right,
And the righteous walk in them;
But in them transgressors stumble.

Sing (Hosea ii. 15; v. 17 in Heb.). The original is a derivative of *anah, to sing* (vid. Rem. on Ex. xxxii. 18).

Cornet, trumpet (Hos. v. 8). These are the *shophar* or *crooked trumpet*, and *hatsotsera* or *straight trumpet* (vid. Rem. on Ex. xix. 16; Lev. xxv. 9; Num. x. 2; II Chron. vii. 6). For the sake of variety in expression, one of these words is translated *cornet*, as that instrument is one species of the trumpet. The prophet is speaking of the aggravated sins of Israel, and threatens the infliction upon her of the divine wrath. The trumpet shall be sounded, war will ensue, and Israel be overthrown.

Trumpet (Hos. viii. 1). This is the *shophar* or *war trumpet* (vid Rem. on Ex. xix. 16).

THE BOOK OF JOEL.

INTRODUCTORY REMARKS.

THE prophecies contained in this book were written about 810–660 B. C. Various opinions have been advanced by scholars in respect to the time when Joel lived; but it is now generally admitted that he was a contemporary of Amos and Hosea. The prophet graphically describes the sins of the priesthood and laity, calling upon both to repent, to fast and pray. Finally, in glowing, beautiful language, he speaks of the conversion and return of God's favored people to the land of their fathers. His style is highly poetic, solemn, vehement, elegant, and sublime. In speaking of the judgments which were to fall upon the Jews, he represents a vast army of locusts led on by Deity himself, rushing with vengeance upon those who had incurred the Divine displeasure. In describing the final contest between idolatry and Christianity, he speaks of great multitudes assembled in one place. Darkness covers them. Mount Olivet is suddenly in a blaze, from whose brilliant light the countenances of the wicked are visible. A voice from Zion shakes the heavens and the earth, and Jehovah appears in behalf of his people.

The style of Joel is sombre, and often terrific and sublime. Take for example chapter ii. 1–11, as translated by Noyes:

1 Blow ye the trumpet in Zion;
Sound an alarm in my holy mountain!
Let all the inhabitants of the land tremble!
For the day of Jehovah cometh; for it is near!

2 A day of darkness, and gloominess;
A day of clouds, and thick darkness.
As the morning light spreadeth itself upon the mountains,
There cometh a numerous people and a strong;
Like them there have been none of old time,
And after them there shall not be,
Even to the years of many generations.
3 A fire devoureth before them,
And behind them a flame burneth;
The land is as the garden of Eden before them,
And behind them a desolate wilderness!
Yea, nothing escapeth them.
4 Their appearance is like the appearance of horses,
And like horsemen do they run;
5 Like rattling chariots they leap on the tops of the mountains;
Like the crackling flame of fire, which devoureth stubble;
Like a mighty host set in battle array.
6 Before them the people tremble,
And all faces gather blackness.
7 They run like mighty men;
They climb the wall like warriors;
They march every one on his way;
They change not their paths.
8 One doth not trust another;
They march every one in his path;
And if they rush against the sword, they are not wounded.
9 They run through the city;
They run upon the wall;
They climb up upon the houses;
They enter in at the windows, like a thief.

10 The earth quaketh before them,
And the heavens tremble:
The sun and the moon are darkened,
And the stars withdraw their shining.
11 Jehovah uttereth his voice before his army;
His camp is very great;
He is strong that executeth his word;
The day of Jehovah is great, and very terrible;
Who shall be able to bear it?

Compare this with chapter iii. 9–21.

9 Proclaim ye this among the nations,
"Prepare war! Stir up the mighty ones!
Let all the warriors draw near; let them come up!"
10 Beat your ploughshares into swords,
And your pruning-hooks into spears;
Let the weak say, I am strong!
11 Assemble yourselves and come, all ye nations round about;
Gather yourselves together!
Yet there will Jehovah bring low your mighty ones.
12 Let the nations rise and come up to the valley of Jehoshaphat!
For there will I sit to Judge all the nations around.
13 Put ye in the sickle, for the harvest is ripe;
Come and tread, for the wine-press is full;
The vats overflow;
For their wickedness is great!
14 The multitudes, the multitudes, in the valley of judgment!
For the day of Jehovah is near in the valley of Jehoshaphat;
15 The sun and the moon are darkened,
And the stars withdraw their shining.

16 Jehovah also roareth from Zion,
And uttereth his voice from Jerusalem;
The heavens and the earth shake.
Jehovah is a refuge to his people;
A strong-hold to the sons of Israel.
17 Then shall ye know that I am Jehovah your God,
Dwelling in Zion, my holy mountain;
And Jerusalem shall be holy;
Strangers shall pass through her no more.
18 In that day shall the mountains drop down new wine,
And the hills shall flow with milk,
And all the streams of Judah shall flow with water.
A fountain shall come forth from the house of Jehovah,
That shall water the valley of Shittim.
19 Egypt shall be a waste,
And Edom a desolate wilderness,
For their violence against the sons of Judah;
For they shed innocent blood in their land.
20 But Judah shall be inhabited forever,
And Jerusalem from generation to generation.
21 And I will avenge their blood, which I have not avenged,
And Jehovah will dwell upon Zion.

There are only two allusions to music in the book, and they are found in chapter ii. 1 and 15.

Blow the trumpet.—The same expression is used in both cases. This is the *shophar* or *crooked war trumpet* (vid. Rem. on Ex. xix. 16; Lev. xxv. 9).

THE BOOK OF AMOS.

INTRODUCTORY REMARKS.

THIS book is supposed to have been written B. C. 810–785. Amos informs us that he was not a prophet, neither the son of a prophet, indicating that he was not educated in the schools of the prophets. He was called to the prophetic office from the occupation of a herdsman and gatherer of sycamore fruit. He was contemporary with Hosea, and predicted the overthrow of the nations surrounding Judæa. He condemns the wickedness of the favored people of God, and encourages them with prospective deliverance from their foes if they should repent of their sins.

Jerome, Calmet, and others have regarded the book of Amos as rude, and sadly wanting in all the characteristics of an elevated and finished style; but Bishop Lowth declares that, "in sublimity and magnificence, he is almost equal to the greatest, so in splendor of diction and clearness of expression, he is scarcely inferior to any."

It is certain that his conceptions were exceedingly vivid. In prophetic vision he was often in the midst of terrific scenes, and his mind was consequently in the highest state of excitement. He was full of the fury of the Lord, and uttered with vehemence, abruptness, and severity, the fiercest and most awful denunciations against the enemies of righteousness. He deals with disobedient Israel in a summary, startling, and indignant manner. His language is not so smooth, beautiful, and elegant as that of some other prophets, but it is so energetic, and his thoughts so original, elevated, and sublime, that the reader is awed, excited, and charmed. His imagery is pastoral, and some of it exceedingly fine. As a sample of his terrific denunciations, we present the first part of chapter ix., v. 1–8, Noyes' translation.

1 I saw the Lord standing upon the altar; and he said,
Smite the capitals, so that the pillars shall tremble;
Break them in pieces upon the heads of all of them!
And their residue will I slay with the sword.
He that fleeth of them shall not flee from danger,
And he that escapeth of them shall not escape into safety.
2 Though they dig down to the lower world,
Thence shall my hand take them;
Though they climb up to heaven,
Thence will I bring them down.
3 Though they hide themselves on the top of Carmel,
I will search for them, and thence will I take them away;
Though they hide themselves from mine eyes in the bottom of the sea,
There will I command the serpent, and he shall bite them.
4 Though they go into captivity before their enemies,
There will I command the sword, and it shall slay them;
I will set mine eyes upon them for evil, and not for good.
5 For the Lord Jehovah of hosts
Is he, that toucheth the earth, and it shall melt,
And all that dwell therein shall mourn;
All of it shall rise in waves like a river,
And shall be overflowed, as by the river of Egypt;

6 He that buildeth his upper rooms in the heavens,
And foundeth his arch upon the earth;
That calleth up the waters of the sea,
And poureth them out upon the face of the earth;
Jehovah is his name.
7 Are ye not as the Æthiopians to me, O children of Israel, saith Jehovah?
Did I not bring Israel from the land of Egypt,
And the Philistines from Caphtor, and the Syrians from Kir?
8 Behold the eyes of the Lord Jehovah are upon the sinful kingdom,
And I will destroy it from the face of the earth;
Yet will I not utterly destroy the house of Jacob, saith Jehovah.

As a specimen of his less sublime but beautiful style, read, in the same chapter vs. 11–15, as translated by Noyes.

11 In that day I will raise up the fallen tabernacle of David,
And I will close up the breaches thereof,
And raise up its ruins,
And I will build it, as in the days of old.
12 That they, who are called by my name, may possess the remnant of Edom,
And all the nations.
Thus saith Jehovah, who doeth this.
13 Behold the days come, saith Jehovah,
That the plougher shall draw near to the reaper,
And the treader of grapes to the sower of the seed;
And the mountains shall drop new wine,
And all the hills shall melt.
14 I will bring back the captives of my people Israel,

And they shall build the desolate cities, and shall inhabit them;
And they shall plant vineyards, and drink the wine of them?
They shall also make gardens, and eat their fruit.
15 I will plant them in their land,
And they shall no more be rooted up from the land, which I have given them,
Saith Jehovah, thy God.

There are a few references to music in this book. The first occurs in chapter ii. 2.

Shouting—sound of the trumpet.—This refers to the destruction which was to fall upon wicked Moab. Fire and sword were to lay her desolate. The war trumpet was to be sounded for an attack upon her bulwarks. This is the *shophar* or crooked trumpet (vid. Rem. on Ex. xix. 16; Lev. xxv. 9). The word translated *shouting* is *teruah* in the original, signifying to sound an alarm (vid. Rem. on Num. x. 5; xxix. 1). In chapter iii. 6, *trumpet* (*shophar*) occurs again in a similar sense, as in Amos ii. 2. In chapter v. 23, *viols* and *songs* occur. For *songs* the usual term *shîr* is used. *Viol* is the *nebhel* or *psaltery* (vid. Rem. on I Sam. x. 5; II Sam. vi. 5).

Chant, viol, instruments of music (Amos vi. 5).—The Hebrew of *chant* is a derivative of the verb פָּרַט (*parat*), *to prate, to chatter.* It may be applied to music, and would signify the utterance of sound in a garrulous manner. *Nebhel* (*psaltery*) is here translated *viol.*

Instruments of music, literally, *instruments of song.*—The Hebrew is כְּלֵי־שִׁיר (*k*^{e}*ley-shîr*) (vid. Rem. on I Chron. xv. 16; I Sam. xviii. 6). In chapter viii. 3, 10, the word *songs* occurs. The plural of *shîr* is used in both cases.

THE BOOK OF HABAKKUK.

INTRODUCTORY REMARKS.

THIS book was written B. C. 612-598. Habakkuk is supposed to have been contemporary with Jeremiah. He dwells upon the sins of the Jewish people, graphically describes the destruction of Judah and Jerusalem by the Chaldæans in consequence of their wickedness, and finally comforts the Jews under their trying afflictions. The first part of this prophecy is in the form of a dialogue between the prophet and Deity. The remainder is an ode of great beauty and sublimity.

The inspired penman's description of the ferocity of the Chaldæans is exceedingly vivid and startling. The last part of the prophecy is regarded by Bishop Lowth as one of the most perfect specimens of the Hebrew ode extant. The imagery is grand almost beyond description. The writer describes the majestic movements of Jehovah through the Jewish economy. His march commences in the wilderness of Paran—he is clothed with light—the pestilence goes before him—the earth moves—the nations are scattered—the mountains bow—his arrows fly—his spear glitters—the sun and moon stand still! The description is in the highest degree sublime. Read the song as translated by Noyes.

HABAKKUK i. 1-17.

1 The prophecy which was revealed to the prophet Habakkuk.

2 How long, O Jehovah, do I cry, and thou dost not hear!
How long do I complain to thee of violence, and thou dost not save!

3 Why dost thou suffer me to see iniquity, and behold wickedness?
For spoiling and violence are before me;
There is contention, and strife exalteth itself!
4 Therefore the law faileth,
And judgment is not pronounced according to truth;
For the wicked encompasseth the righteous,
Therefore wrong judgment is pronounced.
5 Behold ye among the nations, and look!
Yea, wonder and be astonished!
For I do a work in your days,
Which ye will not believe, though it be told you.
6 For behold, I raise up the Chaldæans,
A fierce and swift people,
Which go over the breadth of the earth,
To take possession of dwelling-places that are not their own.
7 They are terrible and dreadful;
Their decisions and decrees go forth according to their pleasure.
8 Their horses are swifter than leopards,
And fiercer than evening wolves.
Their horsemen leap proudly;
Their horsemen come from far;
They fly like an eagle, hastening to devour.
9 All of them come for violence;
The multitude of their faces is directed forwards,
And they gather captives as the sand.
10 They also scoff at kings,
And princes are to them a laughing-stock;
They deride every strong-hold,
For they heap up earth, and take it.
11 Then their spirit is renewed, and they transgress, and become guilty;
This their strength is made their god.

12 Art thou not from everlasting, O Jehovah, my God,
my Holy One?
We shall not die!
Thou, O Jehovah, hast appointed them for judgment;
Thou, O Rock, hast ordained them for chastisement.
13 Thou that art of purer eyes than to behold evil,
And canst not look on wickedness!
Why then dost thou look on transgressors,
And art silent, when the wicked swalloweth up the
man that is more righteous than he?
14 And why makest thou men as the fishes of the sea,
As the reptiles that have no ruler over them?
15 They take up all of them with the hook,
They catch them in their net,
And gather them in their drag;
Therefore they rejoice and exult.
16 Therefore they sacrifice to their net,
And burn incense to their drag;
Because by them their portion is fat,
And their food plenteous.
17 Shall they therefore empty the net,
And slay the nations continually without mercy?

Ewald calls this song Dithyrambic verse. The recital of it was doubtless intended to be accompanied with instrumental music. There are allusions to music in chapter iii. 1, 3, 9, 13, 19. In the first verse or title the term *shigeonoth* occurs. It means an *ode* or *song*. A similar term is used in the title of the seventh psalm, where it probably means a *wandering, plaintive song* (vid. Rem. on Ps. vii. Title).

In verses 3, 9, and 13, *selah* occurs, probably in the sense of *silence*. In verse 19 we are informed that this song is dedicated to the *chief singer* (vid. Rem. on Ps. iv. Title). The term for *stringed instruments* is *negtnoth*, the usual term (vid. Rem. on Job xxx. 9; Ps. iv. Title).

THE BOOK OF ZEPHANIAH.

INTRODUCTORY REMARKS.

THIS book was written B. C. 640–609. Zephaniah is supposed to have been contemporary with Jeremiah, and his prophecies resemble those of that seer. Some critics maintain that this composition is an abridgment of that of Jeremiah; but it is evident from the contents that the prophecies of Zephaniah preceded those of Jeremiah (cf. Jer. ii. 5, 20, 22, with Zeph. i. 4, 5, 9).

The inhabitants of Judah had become contaminated with idolatry and other heinous sins, and Zephaniah was commissioned to charge upon them their revolting wickedness, to announce the destruction awaiting them, and urge them to repentance. He then foretells the final discomfiture of their enemies, and promises that the Jews shall be blessed of Heaven.

The style of this prophet is not characterized by the abruptness, impetuosity, and sublimity of some of his contemporaries. He seems to possess qualities which belong to all, though not strikingly developed. He is calm, grave, solemn, and sometimes vehement and furious. Zephaniah is poetical, but his writings do not exhibit the highest beauties of refined poetry.

There are three or four allusions to music in the book. Chapter i. 16, *trumpet.* This is the *shophür*, or war trumpet. The writer is speaking of the judgments which were to fall upon Judah and Jerusalem. The *trumpet* indicates *war.* Their enemies shall destroy them. Chapter ii. 14, *sing.* Here is a terrific idea. The prophet is speaking of the destruction of

Nineveh. After describing its utter desolation, he declares that the cormorant and bittern shall *sing* in the windows. The original is a derivative of *shīr*, usually translated *to sing*. Chapter iii. 14, *sing—shout*. A derivative of *ranan* is used for *sing* (vid. Rem. on Lev. ix. 24). This is the language of triumph. Israel was eventually to exult over her enemies, and *shout* for victory. Verse 17, *singing*. The original of this is also a derivative of *ranan*, indicating rejoicing under the blessings of God.

THE BOOK OF ZECHARIAH.

INTRODUCTORY REMARKS.

THE prophecies contained in this book were made B. C. 520–518. Zechariah was undoubtedly one of the captives who returned to Jerusalem on account of the decree of Cyrus. He prophesied concerning the restoration of the temple, the incarnation of the Messiah, the war of the Romans against the Jews, and the final coming of Christ. Some parts of the book are obscure, from the fact, doubtless, that its predictions are not yet all fulfilled. Zechariah is considered as next to Isaiah in the evangelical character of his prophecies. The book is quite prosaic, but the language is pure, and the style natural and adapted to the subjects discussed, being in the historical parts very simple, while in the prophetical portions it is elevated and often in the highest degree sublime (vid. Dr. Blayney's translation of Zech. Prel. Dis. pp. 15, 16). The writer, in some of his flights of inspiration, is exceedingly vivid, and inspires the reader with the most exalted emotions.

There are a few allusions to music in the book. Chap. ii. 10, *sing*. The original is a derivative of *ranan* (vid. Rem. on Lev.

ix, 24). Verse 10 in our translation is verse 14 in Hebrew. The prophet here calls upon Zion to sing and rejoice in view of the restoration of the temple. Chapter iv. 7, *shoutings.* This refers to the great joy which would occur at the completion of the temple. The original is not a musical term. It means noise, tumult, vociferations. Chap. ix. 9, 14. *Shout—blow the trumpet.*—The original of *shout* is a derivative of *rua* (רוּעַ), meaning to make *a noise, or tumult.* The prophet foresees the Saviour approaching Jerusalem, amid the acclamations of the people, as described in the Gospels. In v. 14, Jehovah is represented as defending his people. *He will blow the trumpet* (*crooked*, or *war trumpet*), and call out warriors to defend them from their foes. This is the last allusion to music in the Old Testament.

THE NEW TESTAMENT.

INTRODUCTORY REMARKS.

IN connection with our general remarks on Hebrew poetry, we have already shown that the poetic effusions of the New Testament have the same grand characteristics as those of the Old, the principal of which is different forms of parallelism (vid. p. 240, *supra*). It should be remarked that much of the poetry of the New Testament, with the exception of quotations from the Old, is of a prosaic character. Some of it, like the sermon on the mount, is didactic, and not highly poetic, if it can be considered as at all partaking of that character. The incarnation of Christ, his crucifixion, his resurrection from the dead, the final judgment, a heaven of blessedness, the pit of woe, and other exciting themes, elevate the imagination to the highest point, and are eminently poetical; but the subjects are not always described in that vivid and sententious style which is so prevalent in the Old Testament. The sermon on the mount has evidently characteristics of poetry, though not in the highest degree. The same is true of the parables, some of which exhibit great beauty, elegance, and sublimity. The writings of Paul are somewhat poetical; but it is the closing part of the New Testament—the Apocalypse—where we perceive the most splendid flights of imagination.

THE HISTORICAL BOOKS.

INTRODUCTORY REMARKS.

THESE are the Gospels—Matthew, Mark, Luke, and John, —and the Acts of the Apostles. The design of the former is to establish the truth that Jesus is the Messiah, and thus confirm the Christian's faith in the Son of God, and to refute the calumnies of opposers to piety. Matthew, Mark, and Luke describe the *works* and *doctrines* of Christ in *Galilee*, while John gives an account of his *actions* and *tenets* at *Jerusalem* and in *Judæa.*

The *music* of this part of the sacred volume is of a later age than that which we have been considering. When the New Testament was prepared, music, and the arts and sciences generally, had reached a high state of improvement.

THE GOSPEL BY MATTHEW.

INTRODUCTORY REMARKS.

THIS book was probably written about 37 or 38 years after Christ, though some eminent scholars place it at a much later date. It is maintained by some critics that it was originally written in Hebrew or Syro-Chaldaic, and by others that it was composed in Greek. The former opinion is sustained by the highest authority, and is probably the correct one. From numerous references to this Gospel by the Apostolic Fathers and their successors, its authenticity is fully established. Its style is simple, perspicuous, impressive, and energetic.

There are a few allusions to music in the book.

MATTHEW vi. 2.

Therefore when thou doest *thine* alms, do not sound a trumpet before thee as the hypocrites do, in the synagogues, and in the streets, that they may have glory of men. Verily, I say unto you, they have their reward.

Sound a trumpet.—The original of this is σαλπισης (*salpises*), from σαλπιζω (*salpidzo*), *to trumpet, to sound the trumpet. Salpinx* is employed in the Septuagint, for the Hebrew *shophar*, or *crooked trumpet*, for *qeren horn*, and for the *hătsotsĕra*, or *straight trumpet*, proving that it is the general term in the Greek language for *trumpet*. The idea in this passage is, that the Pharisees made themselves as conspicuous as possible in order to be seen of men, while the Saviour directed his disciples to take the opposite course. There is no evidence, as some suppose, that the Pharisees literally *blew a trumpet* before them.

MATTHEW ix. 23.

And when Jesus came into the ruler's house, and saw the minstrels and the people making a noise.

Minstrels.—The original of this is αυλητας (*auletas*), *flute-players*. There is here an allusion to the custom of wailing and howling for the dead. The custom was common among the Greeks and Romans. They rent their hair, hideously yelled, and played upon wind instruments of music. The Hebrew term for *flute*, is *halīl* (vid. Rem. on I Sam. x. 5; I Kings i. 40; II Kings iii. 15). The custom of mourning for the dead is very ancient. According to Townsend's chronological arrangement, the first instance on record is found in the patriarch Job (Job i. 20), when he heard that his children were no more. He arose, rent his mantle, shaved his head, fell upon the ground, and worshipped Jehovah. This was about 2130 years B. C., according to the usual computation. In verse 21 of the same chapter, also in Job ii. 8, and several other places in that book, there are allusions to the same custom. Abraham, B. C. 1871, came to mourn and weep for Sarah, as recorded in Gen xxiii. 2. There was mourning in respect to the anticipated death of Isaac, and on various other occasions (vid. Gen. xxvii. 41; cf. Num. xi. 10; I Sam. ii. 5; II Sam. iii. 31; xiii. 36; Ruth i. 9; Gen. xxxvii. 29, 30, 34, 35; xliv. 13, etc.)

Matthew xi. 17.

We have piped unto you, and ye have not danced; we have mourned unto you, and ye have not lamented.

Piped—danced.—The original of *piped* is a derivative of *αυλεω* (*auleo*), *to pipe*, *to flute* (vid. Rem. on Matt. ix. 23). There is an allusion here by our Saviour to the sports of children. The Pharisees are compared to children who refuse to engage in any play which they do not propose themselves.

Danced.—The original is a derivative of *ορχεω* (*orcheo*), *to jump*, *to hop by rule*, *to dance*. The same word is translated *danced*, in Matt. xiv. 6. Some commentators suppose that there is reference here to a *lascivious* dance; but it is hardly probable that Herod would be pleased with such a manner of dancing from his own daughter-in-law.

Matthew xxiv. 31.

And he shall send his angels with a great sound of a trumpet, and they shall gather together his elect from the four winds, from one end of heaven to the other.

Trumpet.—A derivative of *salpinx* is here used. There is reference in the chapter to the final judgment, and to the destruction of Jerusalem. The blowing of the *trumpet* probably represents the preaching of the Gospel and gathering the elect from all parts of the earth.

THE GOSPEL BY MARK.

INTRODUCTORY REMARKS.

MARK was the nephew of Barnabas, and son of Mary, who resided at Jerusalem. His Hebrew name was John, and he is supposed to have adopted the surname Mark when he visited foreign countries for the purpose of preaching the gospel. That he was the author of this composition is evident from the unanimous testimony of the ancient Fathers, and it is generally believed that it was written at Rome, probably between A. D. 60 and 63, though commentators do not agree in respect to it. The writer gives an account of the life of Christ, particularly from the time of his baptism till the occurrence of those tragical scenes which resulted in his death upon the cross. Some scholars have maintained that Mark abridged his Gospel from that of Matthew; but Michaelis and others have irrefragably proved that this was not the case.

His style is simple, graphic, and perspicuous. He discourses upon a great variety of subjects, describing some of the most stupendous events which ever transpired upon earth, yet the history is all condensed into a very small compass.

There seems to be no direct allusion to music in the book. In Chap. vi. 22. the term *danced* occurs. A derivative of *orcheo* is used in the original (vid. Rem. on Matt. ix. 23; xi. 17). Reference is made to the dancing of Herodias' daughter before Herod, described in Matt. xiv. 3–6.

THE GOSPEL BY LUKE.

INTRODUCTORY REMARKS.

LUKE was probably descended from Gentile parents, embraced Judaism while young, and was subsequently converted to Christianity. The unanimous testimony of ancient writers attests the genuineness and authenticity of this Gospel. Biblical scholars are generally agreed that it was composed A. D. 63 or 64, for the benefit of Gentile converts. The object of the writer was to furnish a genuine account of the life, works, and death of Jesus Christ, in opposition to many narratives of no authority, which were in circulation. According to the testimony of Paul, Luke was a physician and literary man. His style is pure, energetic, and flowing. The thought, in his writings, is original, like that of Paul; and the language simple, animated, and often pathetic as well as beautiful, much resembling that of some of the best classical writers of the age in which he lived.

The references to music are few.

LUKE ii. 13, 14.

13 And suddenly there was with the angel a multitude of the heavenly host praising God, and saying,

14 Glory to God in the highest,
And on earth peace, good will toward men.

This is a remarkable instance in which multitudes of angels descended from heaven and made the air resound with their exalted praises—with songs of unearthly sweetness in view of the incarnation of the Messiah. Their exclamations of praise to God were uttered in elevated strains of oriental poetry.

In the first chapter there are two instances of poetic effusions. One is from the lips of the Virgin Mary, as follows:

LUKE i. 46–55.

46 And Mary said,
My soul doth magnify the Lord,
47 And my spirit hath rejoiced in God my Saviour.
48 For he hath regarded the low estate of his hand-maiden:
For behold, from henceforth all generations shall call me blessed.
49 For he that is mighty hath done to me great things;
And holy *is* his name.
50 And his mercy *is* on them that fear him,
From generation to generation.
51 He hath showed strength with his arm;
He hath scattered the proud in the imagination of their hearts.
52 He hath put down the mighty from *their* seats,
And exalted them of low degree.
53 He hath filled the hungry with good things,
And the rich he hath sent empty away.
54 He hath holpen his servant Israel, in remembrance of *his* mercy,
55 (As he spake to our fathers), to Abraham, and to his seed, for ever.

The other instance is from Zacharias, the father of John the Baptist, as follows:

LUKE i. 68–79.

68 Blessed *be* the Lord God of Israel:
For he hath visited and redeemed his people,

69 And hath raised up a horn of salvation for us,
In the house of his servant David:
70 As he spake by the mouth of his holy prophets,
Which have been since the world began:
71 That we should be saved from our enemies,
And from the hand of all that hate us;
72 To perform the mercy *promised* to our fathers,
And to remember his holy covenant;
73 (The oath which he sware to our father Abraham),
74 That he would grant unto us,
That we, being delivered out of the hand of our enemies,
Might serve him without fear,
75 In holiness and righteousness before him,
All the days of our life.
76 And thou, child, shalt be called the Prophet of the Highest,
For thou shalt go before the face of the Lord to prepare his ways;
77 To give knowledge of salvation unto his people,
By the remission of their sins,
78 Through the tender mercy of our God;
Whereby the day-spring from on high hath visited us,
79 To give light to them that sit in darkness and *in* the shadow of death;
To guide our feet into the way of peace.

Luke vii. 32.

They are like unto children sitting in the market-place, and calling one to another, and saying, We have piped unto you, and ye have not danced; we have mourned to you, and ye have not wept.

Piped—danced.—This is the same expression as that which is found in Matt. xi. 17 (vid. Rem. on Matt. xi. 17, *supra*).

LUKE XV. 25.

And they began to be merry. Now his elder son was in the field: and as he came and drew nigh to the house, he heard music and dancing.

Music—dancing.—This refers to the remarkable parable of the prodigal son. After returning from his course of degradation and wickedness, to his father's house, he was received with affection and joy. When the older brother returned from the field, he heard *music* and *dancing*. The original for music is συμφωνιας (*sumphonias*) the plural of συμφωνια (*sumphonia*) *symphony*, a *concert of instruments of music*. There is here a reference to the ancient custom of holding musical concerts at feasts (vid. Hom. Od. xvii. 358). The original word for *dancing* is a derivative of *choreo* (vid. Rem. on Matt. xi. 17; xiv. 6; Mark vi. 22, *supra*).

ACTS OF THE APOSTLES.

INTRODUCTORY REMARKS.

THIS book connects the Gospels with the Epistles. It was composed by Luke, probably in the year 63, and is the first ecclesiastical history ever written. It is, however, a limited one, as the writer omitted the history of the Jews after the conversion of Paul, also the progress of the Christian religion in the East, and in Egypt. He says nothing about the church established at Rome, and presents but a small portion of Paul's history. His object seems to have been to confirm the truths of Christianity by a description of the manner in which the influences of the Holy Spirit were communicated on the day of Pentecost, and by a delineation of the miracles subsequently wrought by the Apostles. Another object of Luke was, to show that the Gentiles had a claim to admission into the church of Christ. In doing this he gives an account of the origin and progress of the church at Jerusalem from the time of Christ's ascension till the first Jewish persecution. He speaks of the dispersion of the disciples, the progress of Christianity among the Samaritans, the conversion of Paul, and finally, of the Gentiles who resided at a distance from Jerusalem. The style is similar to Luke's other writings,—pure, energetic, and elevated.

There seems to be but one reference to music in the book, and that is in chap. xvi. 25. Two prisoners, Paul and Silas, at midnight, in their cells, *sang* praises to God. The foundations of the prison were shaken, the doors flew open, and the fetters which bound the prisoners were broken in sunder.

THE EPISTLE OF PAUL TO THE ROMANS.

INTRODUCTORY REMARKS.

THIS Epistle was probably composed near the end of the year 57 or beginning of 58 A. D. Paul was at Corinth about that time, and the letter was obviously written at that city (cf. Rom. xv. 25–27; xvi. 23; II Tim. iv. 20). Its authenticity is attested by the Syriac and Latin versions, and by the ancient writers generally.

The *occasion* of this Epistle was the following. Paul had intended to visit the disciples at Rome in order to comfort them under their heavy afflictions and persecutions; but being prevented from going to that city on account of his journey to Spain, he addressed to them this masterly letter. That church was composed of Jewish and Gentile converts. The latter claimed equal privileges with the former, which fact the Jews vehemently opposed. To settle these differences was the object of the Apostle. He exhibits great power of thought, and his arguments are clear, strong, and irrefutable. The style is graphic, bold, elevated, and often sublime.

There is but one reference to music in the letter, and that is found in chap. xv. 9, where the word *sing* occurs. It is contained in a quotation by the Apostle from Psalm xviii. 49 (vid. Rem. on Psalm xviii. 49).

THE FIRST EPISTLE OF PAUL TO THE CORINTHIANS.

INTRODUCTORY REMARKS.

It appears that in the church at Corinth, as well as in that at Rome, there were important differences between the Jewish and Gentile converts. Some of them had become addicted to alarming vices. Paul, having heard of these disorders, and having been requested, in a letter from the Corinthian brethren themselves, to advise them in reference to marriage and other subjects, he penned this Epistle in reply. It was probably written at Ephesus about A. D. 56. Its authenticity is established from the fact that frequent citations are made from it by the Apostolic Fathers, and subsequent writers. The style of this letter is similar to that of Paul's other writings. The Apostle's characteristic, intellectual, and ratiocinative power is everywhere apparent.

There are a few allusions to music.

I Corinthians xiii. 1.

Though I speak with the tongues of men and of angels, and have not charity, I am become *as* sounding brass, or a tinkling cymbal.

Sounding brass and *tinkling cymbal.*—The original of the former is χαλκὸς ἠχῶν (*chalkos ēchōn*). *Chalkos* means *brass*, and *ēchōn*, *sounding*. The two united signify a *brazen wind instrument*—a modern *trumpet*. Some of the false teachers at Corinth were very eloquent, and the Apostle would intimate that, though they had the tongues of men or angels and had not love to God and man, their eloquence would be merely the sound of a wind instrument. The second expression—*tinkling cymbal*, is still more expressive (*κυμβαλον αλαλαζον kumbalon alalazon*) the vacant and clamorous sound of a cymbal. Instead of *tinkling* it should be, as Dr. Bloomfield justly observes, *clangerous cymbal.*

I Corinthians xiv. 7, 8.

7 And even things without life giving sound, whether pipe or harp, except they give a distinction in the sounds, how shall it be known what is piped or harped? 8 For if the trumpet give an uncertain sound, who shall prepare himself to the battle?

Sound—pipe—harp—sounds—piped—harped.—Here, again, Paul illustrates the manner in which false teachers exhorted the Corinthians, by reference to musical instruments, which were destitute of order or distinction of sounds. They merely exhort their hearers, and excite their feelings without any worthy object before them—they are vague and uncertain in their instructions, like numerous instruments of music playing without any tune or harmony, or rather perhaps uttering sounds different from those intended. Thus in war, if an advance is required and a retreat is sounded, no one knows what course to take. For *pipe* and *harp*, *αυλος* (*aulos*) *a flute*, and *κιθαρα* (*cithara*) a kind of *harp*, represented by the Hebrew *kinnor*, are employed (vid. Rem. on Gen. iv. 21).

In the latter part of the verse, the same terms are repeated, with the difference that they are participles instead of nouns.

Trumpet (I Cor. xiv. 8).—*σαλπιγξ salpinx* is the original term.

Sing (I Cor. xiv. 15).—The original is *ψαλω psalo.* Dr. Bloomfield supposes that it does not necessarily mean a *hymn sung*, but that it may signify a composition partly poetry and partly prose.

In verse 26, psalm (ψαλμος *psalmos*) is found. The passage refers to the fact that the value of the various talents bestowed upon us is to be estimated not by their *nature*, but by the manner and degree in which they are exercised.

I Corinthians xv. 52.

We shall not all sleep, but we shall all be changed, in a moment, in the twinkling of an eye, at the last trump, (for the trumpet shall sound, and the dead shall be raised incorruptible, and we shall be changed).

Trump (σαλπιγγι *salpingi*), *trumpet shall sound* (σαλπισει *salpisei*).—The Apostle here refers to a most solemn and awful event, the final judgment. Some suppose that trumpets will literally be sounded on that dreadful day. Dr. Bloomfield suggests that the earth, from some tremendous volcano, may utter a sound which will be heard throughout her borders. History informs us that the sound from the eruptions of Cotopaxi may be heard twelve hundred miles. It is probable, from the declarations of the scriptures, that there will be some external indication of the approach of that momentous event.

THE EPISTLE OF PAUL TO THE EPHESIANS.

INTRODUCTORY REMARKS.

MENTION is made of this epistle by some of the Apostolic Fathers, and by nearly all later ecclesiastical writers, as the composition of Paul. The letter is undoubtedly genuine, and was probably written during the Apostle's first imprisonment at Rome (vid. Eph. iii. 1; iv. 1; vi. 20). About A. D. 61, Paul was imprisoned by the Jews because he taught the people that an observance of the Mosaic law was not essential to secure the favor of God. He labored mostly among the Gentiles, and, fearing that the converts might be led away by false teachers during his confinement, he wrote this Epistle in order to confirm his brethren in the faith of the gospel. The style of this letter is exceedingly animated, as the writer had heard that the converts remained firm in the doctrines of Christ. He reasons powerfully upon the great plan of redemption, and on justification by faith. He exhibits a glowing eloquence, and rises sometimes to the grand and sublime.

There is but one allusion to music in the Epistle, and that is in chapter v. 19. *Psalms, hymns, spiritual songs, singing, making melody.*—These expressions indicate that when Christians feel cheerful, instead of singing dissolute songs as do the heathen, they should sing those which are spiritual. By the term *psalms* we understand not particularly the Psalms of David, but spiritual songs also of other composers. Dr. Bloomfield thinks that *psalms* (ψαλμοις *psalmois*), and *hymns* εμνοις *emnois*), have here nearly the same signification, and that in distinction from *spiritual songs* (ᾠδαῖς πνευματικαῖς *odais pneumatikais*), they indicate the celebration of the praises of God in strains suitable to be sung *in chorus*, while the ᾠδαι (*odai*) were religious poems designed probably to be *recited* or sung like our *solo-anthems*. The same expressions occur in Col. iii. 16, with a similar signification. That is the only allusion to music which we have noticed in Paul's letter to the Colossians.

FIRST EPISTLE OF PAUL TO THE THESSALONIANS.

INTRODUCTORY REMARKS

A Christian church composed of Jews and Gentiles was first formed at Thessalonica, under the ministry of Paul, about the middle of the first century after Christ. The unbelieving Jews raised such a persecution against the Apostle and his associates, that they were obliged to flee to Beræa, thence to Athens, and thence to Corinth. Thus Paul, being unable to visit the Thessalonians again as he expected to do, sent Silas and Timothy, and on their return, wrote this letter from Corinth, A. D. 52. The subscription to the epistle informs us that it was written from Athens; but that is considered as spurious. This is probably one of the earliest, if not the first letter which Paul addressed to any church. Its genuineness is undoubted. Timothy had brought a very favorable report from the Thessalonian church, and Paul's object in the letter was to confirm the brethren in the faith of the gospel, under the severe persecutions which they were enduring.

There are two references to music in the letter. The first is in chapter i. 8, *sounded*. This refers to the preaching of the gospel, and represents it as proclaimed by a *trumpet*.

I Thessalonians iv. 16.

For the Lord himself shall descend from heaven with a shout, with the voice of the archangel, and with the trump of God: and the dead in Christ shall rise first.

Shout—voice of the archangel—trump of God.—This is a remarkable passage, referring to the second advent of our Saviour—that terrible day when the *trumpet* shall arouse the dead from their slumbers and summon them to the final judgment. The imagery seems to be taken from the triumphal march of a sovereign to take possession of a kingdom by force of arms. The soldiers rush on with a *shout*, and the exciting sound of the *trumpet* is heard. What the sound of the last trumpet will be, or whether there will be any, we cannot tell; but that there will be some striking and terrific external indications is very probable. It is suggested by one, as we have already intimated, that it may be the voice of a volcano, extending perhaps to the centre of the earth, shaking its deepest foundations, and loud enough to be heard on every part of the globe (vid. Rem. on I Cor. xv. 52, *supra*).

THE EPISTLE OF PAUL TO THE HEBREWS.

INTRODUCTORY REMARKS.

THERE are different opinions in reference to the question who were the persons addressed in this Epistle; but the most probable supposition is, that they were Hebrews of Palestine residing at Cæsarea. The letter was probably written in Greek, though some maintain that it was first composed in Hebrew. Barnabas, Clement of Rome, Silvanus, Apollos, and Paul, have, each, by different critics, been considered as the author of this Epistle; but it is generally conceded that it was composed by Paul in Italy, and probably at Rome, A. D. 62, or in the early part of 63. The Jews had endeavored to draw away the disciples of Christ from the profession which they had made, by showing the latter that Judaism was superior to Christianity. The Apostle unanswerably refutes that idea, proving the divinity of Christ, and the great superiority of the Gospel over the institutions of Moses. He exhorts the Christians not to relapse into those vain ceremonies which they formerly observed, and shows that salvation by grace is the only ground of justification in the sight of God. He finally describes, with great eloquence, the nature and triumphs of the Christian faith. This letter is an admirable supplement to Paul's Epistles to the Romans and Galatians.

There are two allusions to music in this Epistle.

HEBREWS ii. 12.

Saying,
I will declare thy name unto my brethren,
In the midst of the church will I sing praise unto thee.

Sing.—This is a quotation from Psalm xxii. 22. The original is a derivative of ὑμνεω (*humneo*) *to hymn, to sing praises.*

HEBREWS xii. 19.

And the sound of a trumpet, and the voice of words; which *voice* they that heard, entreated that the word should not be spoken to them any more.

Sound of a trumpet.—Here is a reference to that majestic scene, when the Almighty descended upon Mount Sinai amid thunderings and lightnings, smoke, the shaking of the earth, and the blast of the trumpet, to deliver the ten commandments to Moses. It is described in Exodus xx. 18 (vid. Rem. on Ex. xx. 18; xix. 13, *supra*). It is the *crooked trumpet* (*shophar*) to which reference is made. The Apostle contrasts the fearful characteristics of the old dispensation with the mildness and mercy of the new.

In the Epistle of James, v. 13, there is an allusion to music. When Christians are persecuted or dejected, let them *sing psalms.* This is a general direction to the brethren, when they wish to be merry, not to use the sports of the heathen, but to be cheerful in a dignified and religious manner.

THE APOCALYPSE.

INTRODUCTORY REMARKS.

JOHN was the disciple whom Jesus loved, and doubtless he possessed something of that mildness and benignity of character which shone so brightly in the life of our Saviour. A remarkable sweetness of temper, and loveliness, pervade his writings. There is exhibited in his Gospel a tenderness and delicacy of expression which do not appear in the compositions of the other evangelists. In his Epistles, John is not imaginative, but grave, dignified, tender, and pathetic. He sits like a parent among his children, and imparts to them practical instruction, animated by the sympathies and feelings of a spiritual father.

In the *Apocalypse* he appears in a very different character, and some commentators have supposed that the "beloved disciple" could not have been the author of that wonderful book; but there is indubitable evidence that he composed it, and we can account for the marked difference in style from his other writings, only on the supposition that his feelings were more elevated than when composing his Gospel and Epistles.

In the *Apocalypse* the themes are grand, awful, and in the highest degree sublime.

The author was on a desolate island, and the "visions of God" poured upon him in overwhelming splendor and terror. He seems to be in the midst of scenes which human language cannot adequately describe. He witnesses the opening of the seals—the bursting of the vials of divine wrath—torrents of fire and blood—terrible conflicts—defeat—victory—exultation—agonies—hell yawning from beneath—heaven opening from above—chariots rushing to battle—blood flowing—the groans of the dying—doors opened in heaven and rejoicings there—wailings unutterable issuing from the bottomless pit—great multitudes speaking—trumpets sounding—lions roaring—dragons uttering their voices—earthquakes and thunderings reverberating—the sweet accents of the *new song* from the redeemed—the Eternal sitting upon his throne, too resplendent for mortal sight—and ten thousand times ten thousand angels chanting the symphonies of heaven!

Who could look upon scenes like these and not have his soul stirred and elevated far above its natural state?

The style of John, in the Apocalypse, admirably corresponds with the grandeur of the events which he describes. Many parts of the book are highly poetical, and some suppose the *whole* to be of the same character. It is certainly very symbolical. Eichhorn and others, on account of its changing actors and scenes, and its chorus, call it a drama. Some pronounce it a lyric poem. Stuart considers it an epopee. The object of the author is evidently to describe the incarnation of Jesus Christ, the establishment of Christianity, and its final triumph over all enemies, and the eternal happiness of the righteous in heaven. John, as we have intimated, was an exile on a desolate shore. The Saviour appeared before him and made known "*the things that are,*" i. e., the state of the Christian churches in Asia; and "*the things that are to be hereafter,*" i. e., the fate of the church from its commencement to its consummation in glory.

The authenticity of the Apocalypse was generally, if not universally, acknowledged during the first two centuries; but in the third, it began to be questioned by the opponents of a class of individuals who had absurd notions in respect to the Millennium. Its authenticity has been, however, well established, though Michaelis, Dr. Lell, and some other late critics, have endeavored to invalidate its authority; but without success. The book is a fit continuation of the prophecies of Daniel.

From the testimony of Epiphanius and Grotius, some suppose the book to have been composed during the reign of the Emperor Claudius. Others have thought, from its Syriac superscription (which is evidently spurious), that it was prepared by John in the island of Patmos during the reign of Nero. Others still maintain that it was composed before the time of Domitian and the Jewish war, but do not decide whether it was under Claudius or Nero. The more general opinion, however, and probably the correct one, is, that John was banished to Patmos near the close of Domitian's reign, and that the revelations contained in this book were made to him during his exile there. History informs us that the death of Domitian occurred in September, A. D. 96. John, with other exiles, was then released, and soon after, undoubtedly, the composition was made public. Basnage, Mill, Le Clerc, Tomline, Lardner, and other distinguished critics judiciously place its publication in the year 96 or 97.

Some parts of the Apocalypse are imperfectly understood, from the fact that its prophecies are not all fulfilled, but its general scope is obvious. Enough at least is evident, to convey to us important instruction. It is to us what the Old Testament prophecies were to the Jews.

A fine instance of elevated poetry is found in xviii. 2–20.

2 And he cried mightily with a strong voice, saying;
Babylon the great is fallen! is fallen!
And is become the habitation of devils,

And the hold of every foul spirit,
And a cage of every unclean and hateful bird:
3 For all nations have drunk of the wine of the wrath of her fornication,
And the kings of the earth have committed fornication with her,
And the merchants of the earth are waxed rich through the abundance of her delicacies.
4 And I heard another voice from heaven, saying,
Come out of her, my people,
That ye be not partakers of her sins,
And that ye receive not of her plagues.
5 For her sins have reached unto heaven,
And God hath remembered her iniquities.
6 Reward her even as she rewarded you,
And double unto her double according to her works:
In the cup which she hath filled, fill to her double.
7 How much she hath glorified herself, and lived deliciously,
So much torment and sorrow give her:
For she saith in her heart, I sit a queen,
And am no widow, and shall see no sorrow.
8 Therefore shall her plagues come in one day,
Death, and mourning, and famine;
And she shall be utterly burned with fire:
For strong is the Lord God who judgeth her.
9 And the kings of the earth, who have committed fornication and lived deliciously with her,
Shall bewail her, and lament for her,
When they shall see the smoke of her burning,
Standing afar off for the fear of her torment,
10 Saying, Alas, alas! that great City Babylon! that mighty City!

For in one hour is thy judgment come!
11 And the merchants of the earth shall weep and mourn over her;
For no man buyeth their merchandise any more:
12 The merchandise of gold, and silver, and precious stones,
And of pearls, and fine linen, and purple,
And silk, and scarlet, and all thyine wood,
And all manner vessels of ivory,
And all manner vessels of most precious wood,
And of brass, and iron, and marble,
13 And cinnamon, and odors, and ointments, and frankincense,
And wine, and oil, and fine flour, and wheat,
And beasts, and sheep, and horses,
And chariots, and slaves, and souls of men.
14 And the fruits that thy soul lusteth after are departed from thee,
And all things which were dainty and goodly are departed from thee,
And thou shalt find them no more at all.
15 The merchants of these things which were made rich by her,
Shall stand afar off for the fear of her torment, weeping and wailing,
16 And saying, Alas, alas! that great City,
That was clothed in fine linen, and purple, and scarlet,
And decked with gold, and precious stones, and pearls!
For in one hour so great riches is come to naught.
17 And every ship-master, and all the company in ships,
And sailors, and as many as trade by sea,
18 Stood afar off, and cried when they saw the smoke of her burning,
Saying, What *City is* like unto this great City!

19 And they cast dust on their heads, and cried,
Weeping and wailing, saying, Alas, alas! that great City,
Wherein were made rich all that had ships in the sea, by reason of her costliness!
For in one hour is she made desolate.
20 Rejoice over her, *thou* heaven,
And *ye* holy Apostles and Prophets;
For God hath avenged you on her.

In this remarkable passage, the destruction of Babylon, her inhabitants having filled up the measure of their iniquity, appears in all its horrors before the astonished view of the seer. He is in the highest degree excited, and describes the sad event in the most vivid manner.

There are, in the book, several references to music.

Revelations i. 10.

I was in the Spirit on the Lord's day, and heard behind me a great voice, as of a trumpet.

Voice—trumpet.—There is reference here to the wonderful vision of John in Patmos. He heard behind him a *great voice*, sounding like a *trumpet*. It is supposed to have proceeded from our Saviour in a glorified state. *Great* must here mean *loud*. The expression, *as a trumpet* (ὡς σαλπιγγος *hōs salpingos*) shows that the voice was not a common one in respect to *sound*, but that it was *loud* like a *trumpet*. It was a trumpet-like voice, *speaking*. There was evidently a *sound* which John heard; but what its character was farther than that it was *loud*, we have no means of ascertaining, unless the allusion to a trumpet might indicate a peculiar sweetness and richness of sound, as well as bold and terrific tones. It is probable that reference is really made to the *trumpet*, from the fact that it was so frequently used on important occasions (vid. Ex. xx. 18; Ps. xlvii. 5; Zech. ix. 14, etc). In the 15th verse the voice which John heard is said to be like the *sound of many waters*, beautifully referring to the roar of the ocean.

Revelations iv. 1.

After this I looked, and behold, a door *was* opened in heaven: and the first voice which I heard *was* as it were of a trumpet talking with me; which said, Come up hither, and I will show thee things which must be hereafter.

An overwhelming scene is here described. A door was opened in heaven, and the writer heard a celestial voice, as it were a *trumpet*, talking with him. This is the same manner of expression as that which we have just considered in Rev. i. 10. The *trumpet* is introduced, to give effect and importance to the event. John was in the Spirit, saw a throne, and Jehovah sitting upon it, clothed with glory and terror. From it thunders rolled, lightnings flashed, and many celestial voices were heard.

Revelations v. 8–12.

8 And when he had taken the book, the four
beasts, and four *and* twenty elders fell down before the Lamb, having every one of them harps,
and golden vials full of odors, which are the pray-
ers of saints. 9 And they sung a new song, saying,

Thou art worthy to take the book, and to open the seals thereof:

For thou wast slain, and hast redeemed us to God by thy blood
Out of every kindred, and tongue, and people, and nation;
10 And hast made us unto our God, kings and priests,
And we shall reign on the earth.

11 And I beheld, and I heard the voice of many Angels round about the throne, and the beasts, and the elders: and the number of them was ten thousand times ten thousand, and thousands of thousands; saying with a loud voice,

12 Worthy is the Lamb that was slain,
To receive power, and riches, and wisdom,
And strength, and honor, and glory, and blessing.

This passage contains a description of another wonderful scene. He who sat upon the throne had a sealed book, and no one was found in heaven or on earth who could open and read it. Finally the Lamb approaches the throne and opens the book. The living creatures and the four and twenty elders fall down before him, having *harps* (κιθαρας) *citharas*, the Hebrew *kinnor* (vid. Gen. iv. 21). *Harps* are mentioned as accompanying instruments in the anthems of praise which were to follow. *And they sung a new song* (v. 9). The Lamb had opened the seals of the book of life. It was a new and an unspeakably important occasion—an appropriate one to be celebrated by a *new song*. Then in the eleventh verse, the *voice of many angels* is heard around about the throne. Myriads—all heaven doubtless—joined in the solemn chorus. How entrancing and glorious! The Eternal sits upon his majestic throne—Jesus, the Lamb, approaches and takes the book—the elders seize their celestial harps, and ten thousand times ten thousand angels utter the praises of Immanuel. What can be conceived of as more exalted and sublime!

Revelations vi. 10.

And they cried with a loud voice, saying, 'How long, O Lord, holy and true, dost thou not judge and avenge our blood on them that dwell on the earth?'

Cried with a loud voice.—This sound, we are informed in the preceding verse, proceeded from the souls of those who had been slain for the sake of Jesus Christ and his cause. It is supposed that this remarkable language refers to those who had been persecuted on account of their attachment to the Saviour, and had sealed their testimony with their own blood. There may have been a special allusion to Christians in Palestine; but the writer doubtless intended also to include others, it may be, in all ages, who have fallen by the enemies of the cross. They cry for vengeance on those by whom they have been slain. From the sixth to the eleventh chapter, the Prophet seems to be in the midst of a tragical scene. The seals are opened by the *Lamb that was slain*, and this is the signal for fire and sword, famine and pestilence, death and hell, to pursue the enemies of God and of the church. These instruments of torture are personified, and cry out against the wicked. Every thing in heaven, earth, and hell seems to be combined to accomplish their destruction. As an army, before battle, is often exhorted, by a reference to the injuries received from the enemy about to be attacked, so, before this array of vengeance is put into execution, the souls of those who had been slain in persecutions are brought up to proclaim in the ears of Jehovah the dreadful tortures which they had received from their foes. The same expression occurs in chap. vii. 2, as in vi. 10. An angel is said to *cry with a loud voice* to four other angels, directing them not to hurt the earth till the servants of God should be sealed in their foreheads, so that they would not be harmed in the destruction of the wicked which was about to take place. A similar expression is employed in the 10th verse.

Revelations vii. 10–12.

10 And cried with a loud voice, saying,

Salvation to our God which sitteth upon the throne,
and unto the Lamb.

11 And all the Angels stood round about the throne, and *about* the elders and the four beasts, and fell before the throne on their faces, and worshipped God, saying,

12 Amen! Blessing, and glory, and wisdom,
And thanksgiving, and honor, and power, and might,
Be unto our God for ever and ever! Amen.

Here is the description of a halleluyah of praise to God from the innumerable multitude who had received the seal upon their foreheads. The language is clothed with splendid imagery, and was probably intended to indicate the sympathy of all the heavenly host in the conversion of souls on earth, and in the deliverance of the church from persecution and adversity of every kind.

Revelations viii. 1–13.

1 And when he had opened the seventh Seal,
there was silence in heaven about the space of half
an hour. 2 And I saw the seven Angels which
stood before God; and to them were given seven
trumpets. 3 And another Angel came and stood
at the altar, having a golden censer; and there was
given unto him much incense, that he should offer
it with the prayers of all saints upon the golden
altar which was before the throne. 4 And the

smoke of the incense, *which came* with the prayers
of the saints, ascended up before God out of the
Angel's hand. 5 And the Angel took the censer,
and filled it with fire of the altar, and cast *it* into
the earth: and there were voices, and thunderings,
and lightnings, and an earthquake. 6 And the
seven Angels which had the seven trumpets pre-
pared themselves to sound. 7 The first Angel
sounded, and there followed hail and fire mingled
with blood, and they were cast upon the earth:
and the third part of trees was burnt up, and all
green grass was burnt up. 8 And the second
Angel sounded, and as it were a great mountain
burning with fire was cast into the sea: and the
third part of the sea became blood; 9 And the
third part of the creatures which were in the sea,
and had life, died; and the third part of the ships
were destroyed. 10 And the third Angel sounded,
and there fell a great star from heaven, burning as
it were a lamp, and it fell upon the third part of
the rivers, and upon the fountains of waters. 11
And the name of the star is called Wormwood:
and the third part of the waters became worm-
wood; and many men died of the waters, because
they were made bitter. 12 And the fourth Angel
sounded, and the third part of the sun was smitten,
and the third part of the moon, and the third part
of the stars; so as the third part of them was
darkened, and the day shone not for a third part
of it, and the night likewise. 13 And I beheld,

and heard an Angel flying through the midst of heaven, saying with a loud voice, "Woe, woe, woe, to the inhabitants of the earth, by reason of the other voices of the trumpet of the three Angels, which are yet to sound!"

There is reference here to the last seal which was to be opened, and it would seem that this was to be the closing scene of disasters which were to fall upon the wicked; but the breaking of the seal is the premonitory signal of another series of catastrophes to the enemies of the cross. Seven angels sound as many *trumpets*, which are indications of war and bloodshed. This chapter includes a description of the sounding of the first four *trumpets*, intimating that judgments were to fall upon the earth, ocean, rivers, springs, and the heavens above. Before the trumpets are sounded, the supplication of the saints is made for the deliverance of the church, and the smoke of incense ascends before the throne. In answer to these entreaties, an angel is represented as casting down fire from heaven, causing thunderings, lightnings, and earthquakes, which are symbols of terrible judgments awaiting the ungodly.

In the first verse it is said, that *there was silence in heaven*, indicating the sympathy, suspense, and awe of the heavenly inhabitants before the opening of the series of calamities which were to fall upon the violators of God's law. The sublime anthems of Paradise are suspended for a short time, in view of such awful scenes. Some commentators suppose, without sufficient reason, we think, that *silence* here refers to the *Millennium.* In the second verse we are informed that *seven trumpets* (ἑπτὰ σάλπιγγες *hepta salpinges*) were given to the seven angels, as indications of the judgments which were to follow. When the angel had cast the fire of the altar upon the earth, there were *voices*, and *thunderings*, and *lightnings*, and an *earthquake* (v. 5), indicating the dreadful calamities which were to fall upon the human family. In verses 6, 7, 8, 10, and 12, four of the angels are said to have sounded and brought down judgments upon the wicked. In the 13th verse an angel is represented as flying through the midst of heaven, and pronouncing a woe upon the inhabitants of the earth by reason of the *trumpets* yet to sound. The imagery throughout the chapter is splendid and terrific.

REVELATIONS ix. 1, 9, 13, 14.

1 And the fifth Angel sounded, and I saw a star
fall from heaven unto the earth; and to him was
given the key of the bottomless pit. 9 And they
had breast-plates, as it were breast-plates of iron;
and the sound of their wings *was* as the sound of
chariots of many horses running to battle.
13 And the sixth Angel sounded, and I heard a
voice from the four horns of the golden altar which
is before God, saying to the sixth Angel which had
the trumpet, 14 Loose the four Angels which are
bound in the great river Euphrates.

REVELATIONS x. 3–8.

3 And cried with a loud voice, as *when* a lion
roareth: and when he had cried, seven thunders
uttered their voices. 4 And when the seven thun-
ders had uttered their voices, I was about to write:
and I heard a voice from heaven saying unto me,
Seal up those things which the seven thunders ut-
tered, and write them not. 5 And the Angel which
I saw stand upon the sea and upon the earth, lifted
up his hand to heaven, 6 And sware by him that
liveth for ever and ever, who created heaven, and

the things that therein are, and the earth, and the
things that therein are, and the sea, and the things
which are therein, that there should be time no
longer: 7 But in the days of the voice of the seventh
Angel, when he shall begin to sound, the mystery
of God should be finished, as he hath declared to
his servants the prophets.
8 And the voice which I heard from heaven spake
unto me again and said, 'Go, *and* take the little
book which is open in the hand of the Angel which
standeth upon the sea and upon the earth.

Revelations xi. 12–18.

12 And they heard a great voice from heaven,
saying unto them, 'Come up hither.' And they
ascended up to heaven in a cloud; and their ene-
mies beheld them. 13 And the same hour was
there a great earthquake, and the tenth part of the
city fell, and in the earthquake were slain of men
seven thousand: and the remnant were affrighted,
and gave glory to the God of heaven. 14 The
second woe is past; *and* behold, the third woe
cometh quickly.
15 And the seventh Angel sounded; and there
were great voices in heaven saying,

> The kingdoms of this world are become
> *The kingdoms* of our Lord, and of his Christ;
> And he shall reign for ever and ever.

16 And the four and twenty elders, which sat be-

fore God on their seats, fell upon their faces, and worshipped God, 17 Saying,

We give thee thanks, O Lord God Almighty,
Which art, and wast, and art to come;
Because thou hast taken to thee thy great power, and hast reigned.
18 And the nations were angry, and thy wrath is come,
And the time of the dead, that they should be judged,
And that thou shouldest give reward unto thy servants the prophets,
And to the saints, and them that fear thy name, small and great;
And shouldest destroy them which destroy the earth.

These passages include a continuation of the preceding imagery. The fifth angel sounded his *trumpet* (v. 1), and a *star* (meaning an angel) fell from heaven, and locusts were sent down to destroy those who had not the mark of the righteous in their foreheads, intimating that dire calamities, probably devastating wars, were to fall upn the earth. The sound of their wings is said (v. 9) to be as the sound of chariots of many horses running to battle. The sixth angel sounded (v. 13), and another woe was pronounced upon the wicked. Another angel cried with a loud voice (x. 3), and seven thunders uttered their voices. The angel declared that time should be no longer. Finally, (xi. 15) the seventh angel sounded, announcing the third woe upon the wicked, and the winding up of man's destiny. The salvation of the righteous is complete, and a halleluyah of praise ascends from the twenty-four elders and all of the heavenly host.

Revelations xii. 10.

And I heard a loud voice saying in heaven,
Now is come salvation, and strength,

And the kingdom of our God, and the power of his
Christ:
For the accuser of our brethren is cast down,
Which accused them before our God day and night.

Here is represented joy and exultation in heaven in view of the triumph of the church of Christ over her enemies.

REVELATIONS xiv. 2–18.

2 And I heard a voice from heaven, as the voice
of many waters, and as the voice of a great thun-
der: and I heard the voice of harpers harping with
their harps; 3 And they sung as it were a new song
before the throne, and before the four Beasts, and
the elders: and no man could learn that song but
the hundred *and* forty *and* four thousand, which
were redeemed from the earth. 4 These are they
which were not defiled with women; for they are
virgins: these are they which follow the Lamb
whithersoever he goeth: these were redeemed from
among men, *being* the first-fruits unto God and to
the Lamb: 5 And in their mouth was found no
guile: for they are without fault before the throne
of God.

6 And I saw another Angel fly in the midst of
heaven, having the everlasting gospel to preach
unto them that dwell on the earth, and to every
nation, and kindred, and tongue, and people, 7 Say-
ing with a loud voice, Fear God, and give glory
to him; for the hour of his judgment is come: and

worship him that made heaven, and earth, and the
sea, and the fountains of waters.

8 And there followed another Angel, saying, Baby-
lon is fallen! is fallen! that great city! because
she made all nations drink of the wine of the wrath
of her fornication. 9 And the third Angel followed
them, saying with a loud voice, 'If any man wor-
ship the Beast and his image, and receive *his* mark
in his forehead, or in his hand, 10 The same shall
drink of the wine of the wrath of God, which is
poured out without mixture into the cup of his
indignation; and he shall be tormented with fire
and brimstone in the presence of the holy Angels,
and in the presence of the Lamb. 11 And the
smoke of their torment ascendeth up for ever and
ever: and they have no rest day nor night, who
worship the Beast and his image, and whosoever
receiveth the mark of his name.' 12 Here is the pa-
tience of the saints: here *are* they that keep the
commandments of God, and the faith of Jesus. 13
And I heard a voice from heaven, saying unto me,
'Write, Blessed *are* the dead which die in the Lord
from henceforth, Yea,' saith the Spirit, 'that they
may rest from their labors; and their works do
follow them.'

14 And I looked, and behold, a white cloud, and
upon the cloud *one* sat like unto the Son of man,
having on his head a golden crown, and in his hand
a sharp sickle.

15 And another Angel came out of the temple,

crying with a loud voice to him that sat on the cloud, 'Thrust in thy sickle, and reap: for the time is come for thee to reap; for the harvest of the earth is ripe.' 16 And he that sat on the cloud thrust in his sickle on the earth; and the earth was reaped.

17 And another Angel came out of the temple
which is in heaven, he also having a sharp sickle. 18
And another Angel came out from the altar, which had power over fire; and cried with a loud cry to him that had the sharp sickle, saying, 'Thrust in thy sharp sickle and gather the clusters of the vine of the earth; for her grapes are fully ripe.'

This chapter consists of symbols of victory on the part of the saints over their enemies. John heard a *voice from heaven* like the *sound of many waters.* This probably refers to an innumerable number of the heavenly host, singing praises, individually and yet so harmoniously, that there appeared to be but one joyous sound, *As the voice of a great thunder.* This probably relates to the *power* of the mighty chorus. *Voice of harpers harping with their harps.* This expression shows particularly the *musical* character of that immense choir. The writer uses the term *citharais* (*harps*). The idea is that vocal and instrumental music were both employed. Each one who *sung* performed also with his *harp* at the same time. *They sung a new song.* This probably means simply a song having a new *theme*—a song which none could sing but those who had been redeemed by the blood of Christ. In the other verses quoted above, several angels are represented as uttering curses upon the wicked, or blessings upon the righteous.

REVELATIONS xv. 2, 3.

2 And the first went, and poured out his vial upon the earth: and there fell a noisome and grievous sore upon the men which had the mark of the Beast, and *upon* them which worshipped the image.
3 And the second Angel poured out his vial upon the sea; and it became as blood of a dead *man:* and every living soul died in the sea.

Here commences another thrilling scene. Seven angels pour out seven vials of the wrath of God. Before these judgments fall upon the wicked, the righteous exult as victors in anticipation. They had the *harps of God* (v. 2), *i. e.*, those used in the praises of Jehovah. They also *sung* the song of *Moses* and the *Lamb*, *i. e.*, they *sung* and *performed* upon their *harps*.

REVELATIONS xvi. 1, 17, 18.

1 And I heard a great voice out of the temple saying to the seven Angels, Go your ways, and pour out the vials of the wrath of God upon the earth.
17 And the seventh Angel poured out his vial into the air; and there came a great voice out of the temple of heaven, from the throne, saying, It is done.
18 And there were voices, and thunders, and lightnings; and there was a great earthquake, such as was not since men were upon the earth, so mighty an earthquake, *and* so great.

Now everything seems to be ready for the burst of vengeance from the Almighty upon the wicked. The seven vials were to be poured out by the seven angels upon the earth, ocean, rivers, fountains, and heavens above. *I heard a loud voice from the temple* (v. 1), *i. e.*, from the temple on high, or from Jesus who is in that temple. The Saviour is represented as calling with a loud voice upon seven angels to pour out their vials of wrath upon the wicked. The idea is terrific and sublime. *There went forth a loud voice from the temple, from the throne, saying, It is done* (v. 17). The fact that *throne* is mentioned would seem to indicate that Jehovah, the Father, is here represented as speaking. The last clause indicates that this is the close of the appalling woes which were to fall upon the sinner, and that the final consummation of all things was near at hand. The writer saw in prophetic vision its premonitory *lightnings*, heard its *thunders*, and felt the heaving of its *earthquakes*. The imagery is exceedingly beautiful and grand.

Revelations xviii. 2, 18–23.

2 And he cried mightily with a strong voice, saying, Babylon the great is fallen, is fallen, and is become the habitation of devils, and the hold of every foul spirit, and a cage of every unclean and hateful bird.

18 And cried, when they saw the smoke of her burning, saying, What city is like unto this great city!

19 And they cast dust on their heads, and cried, weeping and wailing, saying, Alas, alas, that great city, wherein were made rich all that had ships in the sea, by reason of her costliness! for in one hour is she made desolate.

20 Rejoice over her, *thou* heaven, and *ye* holy

Apostles and Prophets: for God hath avenged you on her.

21 And a mighty Angel took up a stone like a great millstone, and cast *it* into the sea, saying,

Thus with violence shall that great city Babylon be thrown down,
And shall be found no more at all.
22 And the voice of harpers, and musicians, and of pipers, and trumpeters,
Shall be heard no more at all in thee;
And no craftsman, of whatsoever craft *he be*,
Shall be found any more in thee;
And the sound of a millstone
Shall be heard no more at all in thee;
23 And the light of a candle
Shall shine no more at all in thee;
And the voice of the bridegroom and of the bride
Shall be heard no more at all in thee:
For thy merchants were the great men of the earth;
For by thy sorceries were all nations deceived.

In the fourteenth chapter the destruction of Babylon is proclaimed; in chapter sixteenth the shaking of its foundations is announced, and in chapter eighteenth the people of God are called upon to come out of the city, and her final and entire destruction declared. An angel of a superior order came down from heaven, illuminating the earth by his splendor, and *cried with a loud voice, Babylon the great is fallen* (verses 1 and 2). Sea-faring people cried out with the greatest surprise, when they saw the smoke of her torments ascend (verse 18). Then, in verse 21, a mighty angel cast a stone into the sea, as a token of her final and entire overthrow, and reiterates the awful announcement.

REVELATIONS xix. 1-7.

1 And after these things I heard a great voice of much people in heaven saying,

Alleluia! salvation, and glory, and honor, and power, unto the Lord our God:
2 For true and righteous are his judgments:
For he hath judged the great whore,
Which did corrupt the earth with her fornication,
And hath avenged the blood of his servants at her hand.

3 And again they said, Alleluia! And her
smoke rose up forever and ever!
4 And the four-and-twenty elders and the four
beasts, fell down and worshipped God that sat on
the throne, saying, Amen; Alleluia!
5 And a voice came out of the throne, saying,
Praise our God, all ye his servants, and ye that
fear him, both small and great.
6 And I heard as it were the voice of a great
multitude, and as the voice of many waters, and as
the voice of mighty thunderings, saying,

Alleluia! for the Lord God omnipotent reigneth.
7 Let us be glad and rejoice, and give honor to him.
For the marriage of the Lamb is come,
And his wife hath made herself ready.

Here seems to be the closing up of the mighty conflict, and

the halleluyahs of the heavenly world ascend in view of the glorious victory of the saints over their enemies. *I heard a great voice of much people in heaven* (verse 1). Then follows the hymn of thanksgiving by the heavenly host. In the sixth verse we perceive the immense *power* of that celestial chorus—*as the voice of many waters, the voice of mighty thunderings.* The united whole, with their voices and golden harps, sounding not only *melodiously*, but as *mighty thunderings.* Of the power, magnificence, and sublimity of such a scene, we can form but a faint conception in this life.

INDEX.

Gould and Lincoln's Publications.

(RELIGIOUS.)

LIMITS OF RELIGIOUS THOUGHT EXAMINED. By HENRY L. MANSEL, B D. Notes translated for American ed. 12mo, cl. $.100.

THE CRUCIBLE; or, Tests of a Regenerate State. By Rev. J. A. GOODHUE. Introduction by Dr. KIRK. 12mo, cloth. $1.00.

LEADERS OF THE REFORMATION. Luther — Calvin — Latimer — Knox. By JOHN TULLOCH, D. D. 12mo, cloth. $1.00.

BARON STOW. *CHRISTIAN BROTHERHOOD.* 16mo, cloth. 50 cents.

———— *FIRST THINGS:* or, the Development of Church Life. 16mo, cloth. 60 cents.

JOHN ANGELL JAMES. *CHURCH MEMBER'S GUIDE.* Cloth. 33 cts.

———— *CHURCH IN EARNEST.* 18mo, cloth. 40 cts.

———— *CHRISTIAN PROGRESS.* Sequel to the Anxious Inquirer. 18mo, cloth. 31 cents.

THE GREAT CONCERN. By N. ADAMS, D. D. 12mo, cloth. 85 cents.

JOHN HARRIS'S WORKS. *THE GREAT TEACHER.* With an Introductory Essay by H. HUMPHREY, D. D. 12mo, cloth. 85 cents.

———— *THE GREAT COMMISSION.* With an Introductory Essay by WILLIAM R. WILLIAMS, D. D. 12mo, cloth. $1.00.

———— *THE PRE-ADAMITE EARTH.* Contributions to Theological Science. 12mo, cloth. $1.00.

———— *MAN PRIMEVAL:* Constitution and Primitive Condition of the Human Being. Portrait of Author. 12mo, cloth. $1.25.

———— *PATRIARCHY:* or, The Family, its Constitution and Probation. 12mo, cloth. $1.25.

———— *SERMONS, CHARGES, ADDRESSES, &c.* Two volumes, octavo, cloth. $1.00 each.

WILLIAM R. WILLIAMS. *RELIGIOUS PROGRESS.* 12mo, cloth. 85 cts.

———— *LECTURES ON THE LORD'S PRAYER.* 12mo, cloth. 85 cents.

THE BETTER LAND. By Rev. A. C. THOMPSON. 12mo, cloth. 85 cents

EVENING OF LIFE; or, Light and Comfort amid the Shadows of Declining Years. By JEREMIAH CHAPLIN, D. D. 12mo, cloth. $1.00.

HEAVEN. By JAMES WILLIAM KIMBALL. 12mo, cloth. $1.00.

THE SAINT'S EVERLASTING REST. BAXTER. 16mo, cl. 50 cts.

Gould and Lincoln's Publications.

(LITERARY.)

THE PURITANS; or, the Court, Church, and Parliament of England. By SAMUEL HOPKINS. 3 vols., 8vo, cloth. $2.00 per volume.

HISTORICAL EVIDENCES OF THE TRUTH OF THE SCRIPTURE RECORDS, STATED ANEW, with Special Reference to the Doubts and Discoveries of Modern Times. Bampton Lecture for 1859. By GEORGE RAWLINSON. 12mo, cloth. $1.00.

CHRIST IN HISTORY. By ROBERT TURNBULL, D. D. A New and Enlarged Edition. 12mo, cloth. $1.25.

THE CHRISTIAN LIFE; Social and Individual. By PETER BAYNE. 12mo, cloth. $1.25.

ESSAYS IN BIOGRAPHY AND CRITICISM. By PETER BAYNE. Arranged in two series, or parts. 2 vols., 12mo, cloth. $1.25 each.

THE GREYSON LETTERS. By HENRY ROGERS, Author of the "Eclipse of Faith." 12mo, cloth. $1.25.

CHAMBERS' WORKS. *CYCLOPÆDIA OF ENGLISH LITERATURE.* Selections from English Authors, from the earliest to the present time. 2 vols., 8vo, cloth. $5.00.

——— *MISCELLANY OF USEFUL AND ENTERTAINING KNOWLEDGE.* 10 vols., 16mo, cloth. $7.50.

——— *HOME BOOK;* or, Pocket Miscellany. 6 vols., 16mo, cloth. $3.00

THE PREACHER AND THE KING; or, Bourdaloue in the Court of Louis XIV. By L. F. BUNGENER. 12mo, cloth. $1.25.

THE PRIEST AND THE HUGUENOT; or, Persecution in the age of Louis XV. By L. F. BUNGENER. 2 vols, 12mo, cloth. $2.25.

MISCELLANIES. By WILLIAM R. WILLIAMS, D. D. 12mo, cloth. $1.25.

ANCIENT LITERATURE AND ART. Essays and Letters from Eminent Philologists. By Profs. SEARS, EDWARDS, and FELTON. 12mo, cloth. $1.25.

MODERN FRENCH LITERATURE. By L. RAYMOND DE VERICOUR. Revised, with Notes by W. S. CHASE. 12mo, cloth. $1.25.

BRITISH NOVELISTS AND THEIR STYLES. By DAVID MASSON, M. A., Author of Life of Milton. 16mo, cloth. 75 cents.

REPUBLICAN CHRISTIANITY; or, True Liberty, exhibited in the Life, Precepts, and early Disciples of the Redeemer. By E. L. MAGOON. 12mo, cloth. $1.25.

THE HALLIG; or, the Sheepfold in the Waters. Translated from the German of BIERNATSKI, by Mrs. GEORGE P. MARSH. 12mo, cloth. $1.00.

MANSEL'S MISCELLANIES; including "Prolegomina Logica," "Metaphysics," "Limits of Demonstrative Evidence," "Philosophy of Kant," etc. 12mo. *In press.*

Gould and Lincoln's Publications.

(SABBATH SCHOOL.)

POPULAR CYCLOPÆDIA OF BIBLICAL LITERATURE. Condensed, by JOHN KITTO, D. D. Numerous Illustrations. 8vo. $3.00.

THE HISTORY OF PALESTINE; with Chapters on its Geography and Natural History, its Customs and Institutions. By JOHN KITTO, D. D. With Illustrations. 12mo. $1.25.

ANALYTICAL CONCORDANCE TO THE HOLY SCRIPTURES; or, The Bible under Distinct and Classified Topics. By JOHN EADIE, D. D. 8vo. $3.00.

CRUDEN'S CONDENSED CONCORDANCE. By ALEX. CRUDEN. 8vo. Half boards, $1.25. Sheep, $1.50.

COMMENTARY ON THE ORIGINAL TEXT OF THE ACTS OF THE APOSTLES. By H. B. HACKETT, D. D. 8vo. $2.25.

ILLUSTRATIONS OF SCRIPTURE. Suggested by a tour through the Holy Land. With Illustrations. New, Enlarged Edition. By H. B. HACKETT, D. D. 12mo, cloth. $1.00.

PROF. H. J. RIPLEY'S NOTES.

———————— *ON THE GOSPELS.* For Teachers in Sabbath Schools, and as an Aid to Family Instruction. With Map of Canaan. Cloth, embossed. $1.25.

———————— *ON THE ACTS OF THE APOSTLES.* With Map of the Travels of the Apostle PAUL. 12mo, cloth, embossed. 75 cents.

———————— *ON THE EPISTLE OF PAUL TO THE ROMANS.* 12mo, cloth, embossed. 67 cents.

COMMENTARY ON THE EPISTLE TO THE EPHESIANS. Explanatory, Doctrinal, and Practical. By R. E. PATTISON, D. D. 12mo. 85 cents.

MALCOM'S NEW BIBLE DICTIONARY of Names, Objects, and Terms, found in the Holy Scriptures. By HOWARD MALCOM, D. D. 16mo, cloth. 60 cents.

HARMONY QUESTIONS ON THE FOUR GOSPELS, for the use of Sabbath Schools. By Rev. S. B. SWAIM, D. D. Vol. I. 18mo, cloth backs. 13 cents.

SABBATH-SCHOOL CLASS-BOOK. By E. LINCOLN. 13 cents.

LINCOLN'S SCRIPTURE QUESTIONS; with Answers. 8 cents.

THE SABBATH-SCHOOL HARMONY; with appropriate Hymns and Music for Sabbath Schools. By N. D. GOULD. 13 cents.

EVIDENCES OF CHRISTIANITY, as exhibited in the writings of its apologists, down to Augustine. By Prof. W. J. BOLTON, Cambridge, England. 12mo, cloth. 80 cents.

Gould and Lincoln's Publications.

(RELIGIOUS.)

GOTTHOLD'S EMBLEMS; or, Invisible Things Understood by Things that are Made. By CHRISTIAN SCRIVER. Tr. from the 28th German Ed. by Rev. ROBERT MENZIES. 8vo, cloth, $1.00 Fine Edition, Tinted Paper, royal 8vo, cloth, $1.50.

THE STILL HOUR; or, Communion with God. By Prof. AUSTIN PHELPS, D. D., of Andover Theological Seminary. 16mo, cloth. 38 cents.

LESSONS AT THE CROSS; or, Spiritual Truths Familiarly Exhibited in their Relations to Christ. By SAMUEL HOPKINS, author of "The Puritans," etc. Introduction by GEORGE W. BLAGDEN, D. D. 16mo, cloth. 75 cents.

NEW ENGLAND THEOCRACY. From the German of Uhden's History of the Congregationalists of New England. Introduction by NEANDER. By Mrs. H. C. CONANT. 12mo, cloth. $1.00.

EVENINGS WITH THE DOCTRINES. By Rev. NEHEMIAH ADAMS, D. D. 12mo, cloth.

THE STATE OF THE IMPENITENT DEAD. By ALVAH HOVEY, D. D., Prof. of Christian Theology in Newton Theol. Inst. 16mo, cloth. 50 cents.

FOOTSTEPS OF OUR FOREFATHERS; what they Suffered and what they Sought. Describing Localities, Personages, and Events, in the Struggles for Religious Liberty. By JAMES G. MIALL. Illustrations. 12mo, cloth. $1.00.

MEMORIALS OF EARLY CHRISTIANITY. Presenting, in a graphic form, Memorable Events of Early Ecclesiastical History, etc. By Rev. J. G. MIALL. With Illustrations. 12mo, cloth. $1.00.

THE MISSIONARY ENTERPRISE. The most important Discourses in the language on Christian Missions, by distinguished American Authors. Edited by BARON STOW, D. D. 12mo, cloth. 85 cents.

THE RELIGIONS OF THE WORLD, and their Relations to Christianity. By FREDERICK DENISON MAURICE, Prof. of Divinity in King's Coll., London. 16mo, cloth. 60 cents.

THE CHRISTIAN WORLD UNMASKED. By JOHN BERRIDGE, A. M., Vicar of Everton, Bedfordshire. With a Life of the Author, by Rev. THOMAS GUTHRIE, D. D. 16mo, cloth. 50 cents.

THE EXCELLENT WOMAN, as described in the Book of Proverbs. With an Introduction by W. B. SPRAGUE, D. D. Twenty-four splendid Illustrations. 12mo, cloth. $1.00.

MOTHERS OF THE WISE AND GOOD. By JABEZ BURNS, D. D. 16mo, cloth. 75 cents.

THE SIGNET-RING, and its Heavenly Motto. From the German. Illustrated. 16mo, cloth, gilt. 31 cents.

THE MARRIAGE-RING; or, How to Make Home Happy. From the writings of JOHN ANGELL JAMES. Beautifully Illustrated edition. 16mo, cloth, gilt. 75 cents.

CPSIA information can be obtained
at www.ICGtesting.com
Printed in the USA
BVHW090103150120
569359BV00005B/137/P

9 781178 883367